MW01222722

Springer Education Innovation Book Series

Series Editors

Wing On LEE
David Wei Loong HUNG
Laik Woon TEH

Executive Editor

Siao See TENG

For further volumes:
http://www.springer.com/series/10092

Aims and Scope - Springer Education Innovation Book Series

Education holds the key to unlock human resources that a society needs to survive and flourish. This is particularly salient in a borderless knowledge economy. For the past decades, the sterling performance of economies such as Hong Kong, Finland, Japan, Singapore and Taiwan in international studies (e.g. TIMSS, PIRLS and PISA) has channeled much attention away from the traditional centers of education research in America and Western Europe. Researchers, policy makers and practitioners all over the world wish to understand how education innovations propel the emerging systems from good to great to excellent, and how different their trajectories were compared to the systems in America and Western Europe.

The *Education Innovation Book Series*, published by Springer, will delve into education innovations enacted by the Singapore education system and situate them in both the local and the boarder international contexts. Primary focus will be given to pedagogy and classroom practices; education policy formulation and implementation; school and instructional leadership; and the context and interface between education research, policy and practice. We believe that the latter is critical in making education innovations come to bear. Each volume will document insights and lessons learned based on empirical research (both quantitative and qualitative) and theoretical analyses. Implications to research, policy and professional practice will be surfaced through comparing and synthesizing Singapore's experience with those of successful systems around the world.

The audience of the edited volumes and monographs published in this series includes researchers, policy makers, practitioners, and students in the fields of education and teacher education, and public policies related to learning and human resources.

Series Editors

Wing On LEE
David Wei Loong HUNG
Laik Woon TEH
Office of Education Research
National Institute of Education
Nanyang Technological University
Singapore

Executive Editor

Siao See TENG
Office of Education Research
National Institute of Education
Nanyang Technological University
Singapore

Zongyi Deng • S. Gopinathan
Christine Kim-Eng Lee

Editors

Globalization and the Singapore Curriculum

From Policy to Classroom

 Springer

Editors
Zongyi Deng
National Institute of Education
Nanyang Technological University
Singapore

S. Gopinathan
National Institute of Education
Nanyang Technological University
Singapore

Christine Kim-Eng Lee
National Institute of Education
Nanyang Technological University
Singapore

ISBN 978-981-4451-56-7   ISBN 978-981-4451-57-4 (eBook)
DOI 10.1007/978-981-4451-57-4
Springer Singapore Heidelberg New York Dordrecht London

Library of Congress Control Number: 2013953579

Printed on acid-free paper

Springer is part of Springer Science+Business Media (www.springer.com)

Series Editors' Foreword

We are very pleased to present *Globalization and the Singapore Curriculum: From Policy to Classroom* coedited by Zongyi Deng, S. Gopinathan, and Christine Lee, as one of the first launching books of the Springer Series of Education and Innovation in Singapore. The Series has been designed to present to international readers the various aspects of education development in Singapore. In this volume, the editors have chosen a significant task, to look into how Singapore's curriculum development interacts with various levels of agenda including globalization and national policies and how curriculum implementation in the classroom is characterized by a myriad of these interactions. By choosing such a theme, the editors have taken a broad perspective towards curriculum, whereby curriculum can be investigated from the perspectives of policy curriculum, programmatic curriculum, and classroom curriculum. Indeed curriculum is more than teaching contents, and there are indeed pedagogical principles behind it. These pedagogical principles also reflect societal values and expectations and will illustrate the skills and values demanded of the younger generation that have to be elicited through curriculum design and its implementation.

As Michael Connelly points out, this is a distinguished book with a host of authorships coming from Singapore who "know the business." From our point of view, this book is especially valuable as it is a platform for academic dialogue between international and local authors through which "insider-outsider" perspectives are provided. The interwoven dialogue between authors is compelling to the degree that if each chapter were read anonymously, its international or local author representations would be hardly distinguishable. The valuable insight gained from the experience of organizing this book is that the Singapore authors are quite international in their approach as they all master the literature base comprehensively. Likewise, the international authors invited to participate in this project also demonstrate that they "know the business" through the ways they intricately and sophisticatedly analyze certain aspects of the Singapore curriculum.

In this book, readers can expect to read about how Singapore interacts with globalization, and it is quite clearly illustrated from the various chapters that although Singapore is physically a small island, its influence at the globalization arena goes far beyond its present size – Singapore is a key player in internationalization and interacts with the global world actively and proactively. Readers can also find out how several major initiatives have impacted the curriculum development agenda in Singapore, namely, "Thinking School, Learning Nation" (TSLN), "Teach Less Learn More" (TLLM), and twenty-first century competencies (21CC). The chapters discussing these initiatives illustrate Singapore's learning attitude toward the world, namely, how Singapore strives to encourage and develop higher-order thinking and critical thinking and how it continuously brings about efficiency and effectiveness in its curriculum targeting at TLLM. Moreover, the 21CC agenda has made the Singapore curriculum malleable, and this is evident in how it earnestly adapts itself to achieve the goals of nurturing the next generation as confident individuals, self-directed learners, concerned citizens, and active contributors to the society.

National Institute of Education,   Wing On Lee, David Hung,
Nanyang Technological University, Singapore   and Laik Woon Teh

Foreword

From Images of Controlled Perfection to Curricular Plausibility: Singapore Educational Reform

There is international fascination with Singapore and Singapore education partly because Singapore is so small and yet so well known and influential and partly because of its extraordinary success in international comparative student achievement tests. Potential readers will inevitably approach this book with questions asked in various ways, time and time again, by internationally known educators, comparative education policy and educational reform organizations, special interest national groups in various countries, and even by testing organizations such as OECD: "How has Singapore been able to do it?" "What is it about Singapore's educational system that makes it so successful?" Because these questions have been asked by so many people and by so many organizations, potential readers might be inclined to take a pass on the book. But this would be a mistake. The book is genuinely original and addresses the question of Singapore education in new ways with very different insights than one is accustomed to reading in the sometimes all agog literature on Singapore education.

A hint of what is at stake in the book is seen in an exchange I had with the editors when I was asked to undertake a publisher's review. One of my criticisms was that somewhat inconsistent Singapore educational histories appeared in various chapters. I wrote "It might be helpful to have an up-front chronology, probably no longer than a page, identifying major moments in Singapore's history and key policy dates. In this respect it might also be useful somewhere to sort out whether Singapore 'gained independence,' as Chapters 2, 13 and 14 suggest, or was 'jettisoned' out of Malaysia as suggested in Chap. 4."

Instead of the expected one-page chronology, one of the authors replied "As professor Gopinathan says, there has been but one party rule since the PAP (People's Action Party) took over the mantle of governance and the Singapore Chronicle will, in my view, be either too 1. hegemonic a narrative = there is no ONE Chronicle and I think it is okay/better if as scholars we even differ as to when we think globalization comes upon us, so it is okay if we differ about the narratives of our nation building, so therefore there is no need for (us) to cobble together THE narrative OR 2. Just as bad, it would be too simplistic a narrative."

This is a telling response. None of the book's authors convey a popularized "all agog" picture of Singapore education designed to satisfy those enamored by Singapore success and wanting to borrow and reproduce its features. Indeed, there is a tone of annoyance in the response indicative of the underlying sense of author autonomy, integrity, and legitimate academic description and critique that governs the book's account. Readers will learn a great deal from this book. But they will not learn answers to questions commonly asked of Singapore education. This book provides a nuanced picture of Singapore education both historically and in practice. There is description, critical bite, different perspectives among authors, and multiple interpretations of the state of Singapore education in a globalized world. I consider the underlying message in my exchange with the editors to be the central driving reason why this book should be read. Unlike the writings of education's equivalent of plastic surgeons, the book's authors expose Singapore's wrinkles revealing a weathered educational face.

This quality of the book conveys an image of Singapore education which markedly contrasts with the popularized unified visionary ideal of national harmony and success. The image is of an energetic successful system but one that is a grittier, more nuanced, educational system with difficulties, trials, and failures largely unseen in the comparative student achievement scores and worldwide response to them. Years ago Joseph Schwab (1978), one of North America's leading educators and most outstanding curriculum scholar, observed that educational thought had become overly abstract and theoretical with the result that discourse was about idea and theory at the expense of practice. Put another way, he argued that educators knew too little about what went on in schools and schooling and he argued for increased description of *what is* to complement theoretical discourse about *what should be*, precisely what is needed in the stylized international discourse on Singapore education. From a comparatively simplistic student achievement database, all manner of speculation exists on the purpose and workings of education in Singapore. In the middle of the last century when Schwab was prominent, comparative international educational discourse was driven by curriculum. Since then, Schwab and curriculum were mostly ignored as extreme forms of postmodern reconceptualism dominated the curriculum field (Connelly and Xu 2011). The impact was that curriculum mostly vanished from serious educational discussion. Even educational policy compendiums avoid discussion of curriculum policy (Connelly and Connelly 2010). Now, international comparative educational discourse is driven by testing and student achievement measures. This international discourse over educational reform might have been placed within a broader curriculum framework of the sort proposed by Schwab. Had this happened, we might have expected international discourse to display the more practical, descriptive, quality characterized by this book. But because of the fate of curriculum studies as a marginal theoretical discourse, that has not happened. I make these observations by way of pointing out that one of the reasons this book is profoundly important, and able to provide the nuanced picture that it does, is due to the editors' break with current approaches to imagining educational reform by adopting a curricular conception of their task.

In the opening paragraph of the introduction, the editors remark that the "globalized and networked world… (is) … leading us to fundamentally rethinking curriculum and pedagogy." But there is little rethinking of curriculum and pedagogy in the literature. One might say in response to the editors' comment, "Speak for yourselves," which they have, in fact, done. Curriculum, as Joe Schwab (1973) and countless others have noted, is a complex system involving teachers, students, curricular content, social settings, and all manner of impinging matters ranging from the local to the international. It is a system that needs to be understood systemically. The question is not which of the various factors explain high achievement, the current crime-solving model at work in the literature, but, rather, how it all works together. This book is remarkable in that it undertakes the task of making holistic curricular sense of the system. To provide some order, the editors organize the book into policy curriculum, programmatic curriculum, and classroom curriculum. Because their curricular task is complex, exceeding the search for best practices and achievement explanations, much could be written about the limitations of this structure, and what is not said in the book. I have a personal list of topics I would like to have seen addressed. But the fact is that this book takes on a difficult conception, a curricular one, which provides a believable account of Singapore education at odds with the popular conception.

Adopting a curriculum perspective creates certain risks. The benefit, of course, is immense in that the word "curriculum" for educational systems is something like the word "learner" for school purpose. There are no schools without learners and there are no educational purposes without learners. Learner is the "holistic center" of discourse in this area. Similarly, curriculum is a holistic center of discourse about system education. The word curriculum requires thought that reaches out to people, places, and things, to parents, communities, nations, and internationally, and it relates to what is taught – subject matter, character, and values – and it reaches out to interrelationships among teachers and students, administrators, parents, the community, and others. In short, educational discourse is simplified without the word curriculum, mightily complicated with it, yet more real, more vital and valid, with its use. Risks flow from this word as the holistic center of educational discourse. It is never possible to say enough, and whatever is said may be countered with alternate assumptions, starting points, and empirical facts. Joe Schwab (1962) understood this when he adopted the Aristotelian Topics for his purposes and wrote about curriculum "desiderata" later called commonplaces. Schwab's way out of the conundrum posed by having to say everything about everything when using the word curriculum was to argue that time, place, and circumstance dictated the appropriate shape of discussion. Times change and with them the arguments and the shape of the discourse. This book manages its task consistent with Aristotelian and Schwabian views.

Here is a book that deals with one of the best educationally known, yet one of the smallest, countries in the world setting out to discuss the history and character of educational reform since 1965 under the influence of changing national events and growing influence of globalization on national fortunes. One way to manage this panorama would be to pick one of the popular current international topics in educational reform, policy for instance or, perhaps, testing, subject matter content, best practices, implementation, program, teaching and instruction, citizenship, and more. Instead, the book takes them all on by choosing to analyze Singapore education in curricular terms.

I want to introduce one further marker for this book: The book is written by people who know what they are talking about. Almost all are Singaporeans. Some have lived through the entire period of national formation since 1965, and all either work in, or have worked in, Singapore education. Moreover, because of Singapore's size it is safe to assume that the authors have an experiential, working, knowledge of Singapore education at classroom, community, public, and government policy levels. It is common for Singapore policymakers, researchers, teacher educators, teachers, and administrators to meet together and to be present at the same conferences, speeches, and other relevant educational events. This book is not one of those "three weeks on-site and now a great book" ventures. This is a book written by people who know the history, the strengths, the weaknesses, and the warts of Singapore's ongoing educational practice from policy to program to classroom.

Three Interesting Themes

Because of the book's holistic curricular approach, different readers will have different entry points and thematic readings. Three themes stand out for me.

Practical Implementation of Policy and Program: Ever since curriculum implementation became an educational preoccupation, a preoccupation that came to the fore in the late 1950s and 1960s with the curriculum development approach to educational reform, the lack of congruence between school and classroom practices, and educational policies and programs, has been repeatedly documented. The relationship between practices and related policies and programs is likened by Larry Cuban (2010) to the furor of a storm on an ocean's surface (policy and program development) and the relatively calm seas several meters down (school and classroom practice). Academic careers and professional profiles have been built around local, national, and international efforts to bring the two sectors in line and create what the literature often calls "fidelity." But Singapore education, until this book, has seemed to be an outlier, a place where national vision ("the Singapore story") and educational practices were pretty much in line. If there was criticism of this imagined "fidelity," it was cast in terms of paternalism. This book disengages from the fidelity image. There are discontinuities between policy, program, and classroom practice. Singapore education, in this important sense, becomes familiar, something we all recognize, as the book's authors come to grips with the book's tripartite structure of policy, program, and practice. Readers will realize that the supposed paternalistic, visionary, control of practice is empirically in question. While it may break a global educational reformer's heart to recognize the evidence brought forward on this matter in the book, it is an important condition to notice by those in other countries looking to Singapore education for clues to homegrown reform.

Student achievement testing: Different chapters in the book offer different lines of inquiry on discrepancies among policy, program, and practice. One set of thoughts that stands out is testing which, it is argued, stifles innovation. This line of argument accepts the innovative quality of policy and program while claiming that Singapore's culture and practice of student testing and achievement emphasis prevents the adoption of new practices and innovative ideas at the practical classroom level. This line of thinking is not only interesting in itself but is also ironic in that worldwide interest in Singapore's educational system is driven by Singapore student performance on international comparative student achievement tests. I earlier remarked that because of the curricular conception at work in the book, readers might easily spot topics they wished were further developed. This is one of mine.

Vision and Citizenship Education: For North American readers such as me, the Singaporean sense of strong central government support for education, the continual reshaping of an educational vision and its policy and program content, and the role of citizenship education within policy, program, and practice is remarkable. The United States has a central office of education, but it is comparatively weak in the face of state education. Canada has no national office of education and education is a provincial matter. In the United States, much less so in Canada, there is public and political discussion of national educational purpose. But the context is so vastly different than that presented by Singapore that homologous practices and structures mostly do not exist. Nevertheless, US commentators, and no doubt others throughout the world, look to these qualities in Singapore as virtues as they search for practices to adopt.

Consistent with the book's curricular spirit of describing *what is* and saying *what should be* said, the Singapore focus on citizenship education is critiqued as being more political than educational. The critique of citizenship education as practiced in Singapore exhibits the descriptive, critical, attitude reflected in my opening exchange with the editors. It is often said families may critique themselves in ways that outsiders cannot. This book exhibits this family practice at its best.

Ontario Institute for Studies in Education   F. Michael Connelly
University of Toronto

References

Connelly, F. M., & Connelly, G. (2010). Curriculum policy: Formal, implicit and prudential curriculum policy. In C. Kridel (Ed.), *Sage encyclopedia of curriculum studies* (pp. 224–227). Thousand Oaks: Sage.

Connelly, F. M., & Xu, S. (2011). Curriculum and curriculum studies. In J. Arthur & A. Peterson (Eds.), *The Routledge companion to education* (pp. 115–124). New York: Routledge.

Cuban, L. (September 7, 2010). Larry Cuban on school reform and classroom practice. Are school reforms more like a pendulum or a hurricane? Retrieved February 28, 2013, from http://larrycuban. wordpress.com/2010/09/07/are-school-reforms-more-like-a-pendulum-or-a-hurricane/.

Schwab, J. J. (1962). The teaching of science: The teaching of science as enquiry (The Inglis Lecture). In J. J. Schwab & P. F. Brandwein (Eds.), *Elements in a strategy for teaching science in the elementary school*. Cambridge, MA: Harvard University Press.

Schwab, J. J. (1978). A language for curriculum. In I. Westbury & N. J. Wilkof (Eds.) (1982) *Joseph Schwab: Science, curriculum, and liberal education: Selected Essays*. Chicago: The University of Chicago Press.

Preface

This anthology provides a multifaceted and critical analysis of the Singapore curriculum in relation to globalization. It critically analyses how the government has responded in the curriculum and educational policy arena to the challenges of globalization as well as how curriculum reform initiatives have been translated into operational curricula and implemented in schools and classrooms. Further, it examines how reform initiatives, together with their curricular translation and classroom enactment, reflect on the one hand global features and tendencies and, on the other, distinct national traditions, concerns, and practices. Through this examination, the book reveals how curriculum reform policy, curriculum development, and classroom enactment in Singapore have responded to globalization in distinctive ways. Furthermore, it brings to light a set of issues, problems, and challenges that not only concern policymakers and reformers in Singapore but would be generally useful for policymakers, educators, and researchers in other countries.

The book is written by curriculum scholars, policy analysts, researchers, and teacher educators, mostly from the National Institute of Education in Nanyang Technological University, Singapore. It is intended to be an up-to-date reference book on the Singapore curriculum and curriculum reform for postgraduate students, scholars, and researchers in the areas of curriculum and instruction, comparative education, educational sociology, educational policy, and educational leadership in Singapore, the Asia Pacific region, and beyond. More specifically, the book is designed for two groups of readers. The first group includes researchers, policymakers, curriculum developers, and postgraduate students in Singapore who want to have a comprehensive and critical understanding of curriculum and curriculum reform in relation to globalization so as to consider ways to enhance the quality of Singapore schooling. In particular, the book is intended to be a must-have reference for postgraduate students in the areas of curriculum and instruction and educational leadership, policy, management, and sociology. The other group consists of international students, scholars, and researchers (particularly in the area of comparative and international education) who are interested in curriculum as part of the story of modern schooling around the globe, or the case of the curriculum in Singapore as an example of the curriculum in "another society" which may provide insights into a particular aspect of education they are studying. We expect the book to be widely adopted in comparative and international education courses in Asia and worldwide.

We are indebted to the authors for their willingness to collaborate with us through the process of book preparation and production and for their excellent contributions to the volume. We are also thankful for the support provided by the book series editors Lee Wing On, David Hung, and Teh Laik Woon. In particular, we are indebted to Michael Connelly for his extremely thoughtful and thorough review of the book, together with very meaningful and constructive comments and suggestions on revision. Our thanks also go to Ian Westbury and Allan Luke who have provided very useful and constructive comments on the book. We hope that through *Globalization and the Singapore Curriculum*, we can collectively continue to raise new questions and contribute to an enhanced understanding of curriculum and curriculum reform for the advancement of schooling in Singapore and beyond.

Singapore   Zongyi Deng, S. Gopinathan, and Christine Kim-Eng Lee

Contents

Part IV   Enacting Reform Initiatives in Classrooms

Part V   International, Comparative and Future Perspectives

Part VI   Conclusion

Abbreviations

21st CC	21st Century Competencies
C2015	Curriculum 2015
CDIS	Curriculum Development Institute of Singapore
CPDD	Curriculum Planning and Development Division
ITE	Institute for Technical Education
MOE	Ministry of Education
NA	Normal Academic
NE	National Education
NIE	National Institute of Education
NT	Normal Technical
OECD	Organisation for Economic Co-operation and Development
PAP	People's Action Party
PERI	Primary Education Review and Implementation
PSLE	Primary School Leaving Examination
SBCD	School-Based Curriculum Development
SEED	Strategies for Engaged and Effective Development
SERI	Secondary Education Review and Implementation
TLLM	Teach Less, Learn More
TSLN	Thinking School, Learning Nation

List of Figures

List of Tables

Part I
Introduction

Chapter 1
Introduction

Zongyi Deng, S. Gopinathan, and Christine Kim-Eng Lee

Our increasingly globalized and networked world is having a major impact on the nature and structure of education systems. We have moved from an era in which education systems were nation-centric in character to one of greater internationalism. Inward student mobility, new knowledges, advances in cognitive sciences, powerful technology platforms, and changes in economically – valuable competencies are leading us to fundamentally rethink curriculum and pedagogy. Further, international comparisons of student performance between countries and their education systems conducted by international organizations (e.g., IEA and OECD) have caused countries to reconsider their own forms of educational and curriculum policy against those which do differently or better. Many countries have embarked on curriculum reform to equip students with the understanding, skills and dispositions needed for participating in an increasingly competitive economic environment, via specifying competencies and outcomes across different school subjects in the curriculum (Yates and Young 2010). Across the globe many nations have been actively borrowing and adapting a common set of ideas about curriculum reform – promoted by international agencies like World Bank, UNESCO and OECD – into their particular contexts and situations (Anderson-Levitt 2008). The process of globalization has resulted in homogeneity on the one hand, and diversity and heterogeneity on the other – through hybridization "mediated and refracted by local variation and response" (Luke and Carrington 2002, p. 55).

Z. Deng (✉) • S. Gopinathan • C.K.-E. Lee
National Institute of Education, Nanyang Technological University, Singapore
e-mail: zongyi.deng@nie.edu.sg

Z. Deng et al. (eds.), *Globalization and the Singapore Curriculum: From Policy to Classroom*, Education Innovation Series, DOI 10.1007/978-981-4451-57-4_1,
© Springer Science+Business Media Singapore 2013

Singapore is a unique and fascinating place for the study of curriculum in the context of globalization. For the first half of the twentieth century it used, in English medium schools, a colonial curriculum, then a nation-centric curriculum, and is now beginning to address issues for twenty-first century competencies. At the "top of the class" on many of the international comparative measures on conventional educational achievement, Singaporean students have out-performed many of their counterparts in traditional educational centres in North America and Europe (Luke et al. 2005). This has created a widespread and growing international interest in Singapore's education system and, particularly, its curriculum (see Barber and Mourshed 2007; Darling-Hammond 2010).

Since the mid-1990s, Singapore has been at the forefront of reforming the curriculum in response to the perceived challenges of globalization.[1] Under the overarching framework of *Thinking Schools, Learning Nation* (1997) and the *Desired Outcomes of Education* (1998), a plethora of educational and curricular initiatives have been introduced to schools including: the critical thinking initiative (1997), the IT-Masterplans (1998–2002; 2003–2008; 2009–2014), National Education (a form of citizenship education) (1998), Innovation and Enterprise (2004), Teach Less Learn More (TLLM) (2004), and more recently, changes to primary and secondary schooling (MOE 2009, 2010). These initiatives represent prototypical attempts to address the new conditions of nationhood and globalization, calling for the cultivation of critical thinking, creativity, innovation, life-long learning, positive attitudes and values, and national identity. Most recently, the Ministry has developed a new vision for the national curriculum, *Curriculum 2015* (C2015), which enumerates a set of broad learning outcomes centred on twenty-first century competencies. Further, the locus of management has shifted from a directive Ministry of Education to the hands of school leaders and classroom teachers.

These reform efforts are, in many ways, unprecedented as many systems in the West still cling to industrial educational models, unwilling to take on substantive educational reform, and reasserting the value of a "back to basics," standard curriculum (Gopinathan 2007; Luke et al. 2005). While there is some research and an increasing number of articles discussing particular issues in curriculum planning and implementation in Singapore, what is missing is a comprehensive account that critically analyses the nature and character of the Singapore curriculum within the context of the system's current aspirations and curriculum reform initiatives as a response to the challenges of globalization.

Aims of the Book

This book critically analyses how the government has responded in the educational policy arena to the challenges of globalization as well as how curriculum reform initiatives have been translated into operational curricula and enacted in classrooms.

[1] It can be argued that the curriculum reform as a response to globalization had actually started in 1987 (see Chap. 2).

Further, it examines how reform initiatives, together with their curricular translation and classroom enactment, reflect on the one hand global features and tendencies and on the other, distinct national traditions, concerns and practices.

In other words, there are two related themes to be unpacked in the book. One concerns government-initiated curricular changes in response to globalization, together with their curricular (operational) translation and classroom realization/enactment. The other pertains to issues of convergence (due to influences and pressures associated with globalization) and of divergence (due to distinct national culture, tradition and practices) in relation to curriculum reform, curriculum development and implementation (Anderson-Levitt 2008). Through unpacking these two themes, the book relates what has been happening in Singapore to what has been happening in the world in terms of curriculum reform and globalization, and makes clear how curriculum reform initiatives, curriculum development, and classroom enactment in Singapore have responded to globalization in *distinctive* ways.

Conceptual Framework

The focus of the book is on curriculum reform in Singapore as a response to globalization rather than the impact of globalization on curriculum. We therefore build the conceptual framework of the book centred around the notion *curriculum* instead of *globalization*.

In dictionaries and common usage, the term "curriculum" is relatively simple, referring to a programme, a course of study, textbooks, and syllabuses, etc. In the academic literature the term is rather complex and highly contentious (see Jackson 1992; Connelly and Xu 2011). There is a multiplicity and proliferation of alternative definitions, *curriculum as experience, currere, selection of culture*, to name just a few. Furthermore, there are a variety of alternative and competing ways of conceptualizing curriculum, ranging from traditional conceptions such as *academic rationalism, social efficiency, self-actualization, and social reconstruction* (cf. Schiro 2008) to contemporary discourses that construe curriculum as *historical, political, racial, gender, phenomenological, poststructuralist, postmodern, autobiographic, aesthetic, theological, institutional text* (Pinar et al. 1995). The matter of defining and conceptualizing curriculum is in a state of "confusion" or "disarray" (Jackson 1992; also see Connelly and Xu 2011).

Our way out of this definitional and conceptual confusion is to place *curriculum* within the context of schooling as a public institution, with a close attention to the practice or the "inner work" of schooling (Westbury 2003a). Broadly construed, schooling is embedded in three layers of context, *societal* (international and national milieus, social structures and conditions, educational policies, discourses, social expectations on schooling, etc.), *institutional* (school types, streams or tracks, programmes, school subjects, grade-levels, assessment and examination policies, etc.), and *instructional* (teacher-student interactions, classroom activities, discourses, outside-classroom activities and events, etc.)

(Meyer 1980). Accordingly, we construe curriculum in terms of three domains, the *policy curriculum*, *programmatic curriculum*, and *classroom curriculum*.

The Policy Curriculum

This curriculum domain consists of educational policies and discourses at the inter-section between schooling, culture, and society, embodying a conception or paradigm of what schooling should be with respect to the society and culture. It "typifies" what is desirable in social and cultural orders, what is to be valued and sought after by members of a society or nation (Doyle 1992a, b).

Policy curriculum making involves the use of "images, metaphors, and nar-ratives as broad typifications of what can happen in a school" (Westbury 2000, p. 34). It frames what should go on in a school or school system in terms of broad goals and general approaches to education. In this way, the policy curricu-lum serves as a means of drawing attention to educational ideals and expecta-tions (presumably) shared within a society and putting forward the forms and procedures of schooling as responses to those ideals and expectations (Doyle 1992a, b). Because social and cultural contexts often change rapidly, in a cen-tralized education system like Singapore's, policy curriculum making has been always employed by the government as a "convenient instrument" to communi-cate responsiveness to outside communities and to provide directions for reform-ing the school curriculum (Doyle 1992b).

The making of the policy curriculum almost always involves soliciting options and suggestions from various representative groups, including policy advisory bod-ies, employers, industry representatives, education specialists, school leaders, and various civic and special interest groups (Deng 2010). The policy curriculum con-stitutes an arena where various alternative curriculum conceptions, ideologies, and discourses are put forward in debate and discussion. However, many of those afore-mentioned alternative conceptions and contemporary discourses are "ideas about the curriculum rather than the practices of schooling," and each of which "should be seen as a rhetorical form that seeks to stake out positions in the ideological space around the school" (Westbury 2003b, p. 534). They do not or cannot directly influ-ence the programmatic and classroom curricula.

The Programmatic Curriculum

The policy curriculum seeks to affect the classroom curriculum through the pro-grammatic curriculum – consisting of programmes, school subjects, and operational frameworks provided to schools or a system of schools (including school types and streams or tracks) (Doyle 1992a, b; Westbury 2000). The programmatic curriculum constitutes an organizational and operational structure within which classroom practice takes place, and which in turn shapes and influences practice. This is an arena where the dictionary or common definition of curriculum (as a programme or course of study) finds meaning and significance. The programmatic curriculum is expected to perform functions like credentialing for further education and work-place preparation, and thus "instantiate the public's understanding of 'education'" (Westbury 2002, p. 124).

Programmatic curriculum making is at the intermediate levels between policy curriculum making and classroom curriculum making; it translates the ideals and expectations embodied in the policy curriculum into programmes, school subjects, and curricular frameworks that constitute "the ultimate basis for a system of schools and their work" (Westbury 2000, p. 34; also see Doyle 1992a, b). The process of constructing a programme, subject or framework "is grounded in arguments that rationalize the selection and arrangement of subject matter content for schools of particular types and the transformation of that content into school subjects appropri-ate to those schools or school types" (Westbury 2000, p. 34). It involves a "theory of content" that connects content to the ideals/expectations at the policy level and the activities of teaching and learning in classroom (Doyle 1992a; Deng 2011).

The making of the programmatic curriculum is in many contexts a highly sophisti-cated endeavor, often undertaken by commissions or committees made up of repre-sentatives from governments, education ministries, schools, universities, business, industry, and civil society (Deng 2010). It occurs within "webs of societal and cultural ideologies and symbols, politics and organized interest groups, organizational and administrative structures and processes, and local understandings, beliefs and prac-tices" (Westbury 2008, p. 50). The programmatic curriculum is inexorably embroiled in socio-political questions of how content (i.e., educational knowledge) is selected, classified, framed, transmitted, and evaluated in a way that "reflects both the distribu-tion of power and the principles of social control"(Bernstein 1971, p. 47; also see Apple 1995, 2004). However, it cannot or does not affect the classroom curriculum or pedagogy in a direct, straightforward way (Westbury 2008).

The Classroom Curriculum

The classroom curriculum, also called the *enacted curriculum*, refers to what is taught and learned in classroom, represented by a cluster of events jointly devel-oped by a teacher and a group of students within a particular classroom (Doyle 1992a, b). In a classroom, we cannot disentangle what is taught from how it is taught. The enacted curriculum or *curriculum in use* (Decastell et al. 1989) is an evolving construction resulting from the interaction of the teacher and students over the programmatic curriculum (i.e., a school subject or course of study) within a specific instructional context.

Classroom curriculum making entails transforming the programmatic curricu-lum (embodied in curriculum materials) into "educative" experiences for students. It requires further elaboration of the content of a school subject or course of study, making it connect with the experience, interests, and the capacities of students in a particular classroom (Westbury 2000). The process is shaped in a powerful way by a range of factors, including the teacher's pedagogical beliefs, practice and expertise, students' interests and experience, school requirements, parental expectations, community and culture, high-stakes examinations, curriculum policies, and so forth (Deng 2010).

These three curriculum domains are "loosely-coupled" in a decentralized school system like the one in the US, where the federal or state-based curriculum making for change at the policy level is always seen as an instrument for steering curriculum discourse in the political and ideological arena; the discourse, however, often gets lost at the programmatic level and in schools and classrooms (Westbury 2008). However, in a centralized system like Singapore's where a greater alignment exists between the policy and programmatic curricula, state-based curriculum making in the policy arena is always expected to have a significant impact on the programmatic and enacted (classroom) curricula. How this actually turns out is an issue that is addressed in the book.

The policy, programmatic, and classroom curricula can also refer to the *abstract* or *ideal*, *analytic* or *technical*, and *enacted* curricula respectively (Doyle 2008). At the classroom level this system also includes the *achieved* curriculum, that which students actually have learned, but this is not the focus of the book. In addition, it is important to note that while this book focuses on the classroom curriculum, the enacted curriculum also takes place in school laboratories, libraries, canteens, assembly halls, and other informal settings.

These three domains of curriculum, together with the above mentioned notions of convergence and divergence, constitute the primary conceptual framework for organizing the contents of the book.

Overview of the Book

This book consists of 14 chapters written by curriculum scholars, policy analysts, researchers and teacher educators, mostly from the National Institute of Education (NIE) – the sole teacher education institute in Singapore. Framed largely according to the conceptual framework of the book, these 14 chapters bring various approaches and perspectives for analysing the different aspects of the Singapore curriculum in relation to globalization. Several chapters report empirical studies, some are historically-informed essays, some are philosophical or theoretically-oriented articles, while others contain comparative and international analyses. These 14 chapters also reflect the diverse curriculum perspectives – political, social, cultural, economic, practical and educational – taken by various contributors to analyse the complex nature of the Singapore curriculum.

The book is organized into four sections, apart from introduction and concluding chapters. Section One, *Globalization, Curriculum Reform, Vision and Discourses*, focuses on the policy curriculum. The key questions addressed include: How did the

Singapore curriculum originate and evolve into what it is today? How has the Singapore government responded in the educational policy arena to the perceived challenges of globalization? What discourses does the government employ to provide rationales and justifications for educational and curriculum reform initiatives?

This section consists of three chapters. In Chap. 2 Gopinathan and Mardiana provide a historical perspective on curriculum development and change (including streaming and examination policies) in Singapore between the period 1956 and 2010. They detail the Singapore state's efforts at responding to the local – global tensions brought about by nation-building efforts and the challenges of globalisation, and examine how the Singapore curriculum, which has been an effective instrument of wider political, social and economic purposes, will have to respond in an era of greater socio-economic challenges. To reveal the ideologies and discourses underpinning the policy curriculum, Tan (Chap. 3) examines the aims of schooling for the twenty-first century embedded in the Desired Outcomes of Education within the social and historical context of schooling. In Chap. 4 Koh analyses state narratives and conception of schooling for the twenty-first century in the TSLN reform to show how the government seeks to construct a new "educational imagining" which is essential for instituting curricular changes in a time of globalization. All these chapters unveil critical issues, problems and dilemmas pertaining to curricular and pedagogical reforms in a time of rapid social, economic and educational changes.

Part III, *Translating Reform Initiatives into Programmes, School Subjects and Operational Frameworks*, focuses on curriculum (making) at the programmatic level. In this section three chapters address the following major questions: In the context of a reform initiative what does curriculum making entail at the programmatic level? How have reform initiatives been *translated* into programmes, school subjects, and operational frameworks? How does curriculum making or translation reflect broader social, political, economic, and educational issues and concerns?

From a critical socio-political perspective, Sim (Chap. 5) examines what is entailed in curriculum making concerning National Education as a nation-building strategy in response to globalization. She asserts that the National Education curriculum is "more political than educational" and only promotes "a minimal interpretation of citizenship." Also, from a similar perspective, Chap. 6 (Lim) analyses how the critical thinking initiative is translated into the Thinking Programme and finds its way into various school subjects. The analysis is that the translation is inexorably linked with socio-political ideologies and interests. In contrast to these two chapters, Chap. 7 (Teo, Deng, Lee and Lim) takes a "practical" and "educational" perspective to critically analyse how TLLM is translated into various operational frameworks for implementation in schools. They contend that the considerations of the "what" (content) and "why" (purpose) of teaching – essential to TLLM – have largely faded away in the translation process, replaced by largely technical concerns about the "how" (method) of teaching.

Part IV, *Enacting Reform Initiatives in Classrooms,* focuses on the enacted or classroom curriculum. The key questions of discussion include: What is the intellectual quality of the classroom curriculum after the implementation of a major curriculum initiative (e.g., TLLM)? How have reform initiatives been enacted in schools and classrooms? What evidence do we have that the goals of curriculum reform initiatives are being met? What are the issues and challenges faced by classroom teachers and policy makers?

The section has four chapters reporting empirical studies at the school and classroom level. Based on the empirical data from a large classroom observation study and from surveys of classrooms, Hogan and colleagues (Chap. 8) examine the intellectual quality of the enacted curriculum in Secondary three Mathematics and English classes. They do so by analysing pedagogical practices via Hattie's framework of "visible learning." They argue that pedagogical practices in Singapore classrooms are far from consistent with our contemporary understandings of "good" pedagogy in the international literature. The focus of Chap. 9 is on how English language curriculum innovations are interpreted by teachers when implemented and enacted in multiple schools. Drawing on multiple sources of evidence, Silver, Christiansen, Wright and Stinson argue that there is virtually little evidence of curriculum innovation at the classroom level and explore the reasons for this. In Chap. 10 Ho provides two case studies examining how teachers and students understand national and global citizenship when enacting the current social studies curriculum in the classroom. Her analysis shows a strong commitment to national priorities and a rather week commitment to cosmopolitan values. Kapur and Lee (Chap. 11) analyse the complexity of enacting TLLM in mathematics classrooms through the lens of "productive failure," and in so doing, reveal the issues and challenges for policy makers who want to reform classroom teaching.

Part V, *International, Comparative and Future Perspectives*, presents three chapters concerning the international and comparative aspects and future direction of the Singapore curriculum. With a focus on the policy curriculum and (to some extent) the programmatic curriculum, this section addresses these key questions: To what extent are reform initiatives and discourses moving in the direction of more globally-recognized forms, and to what extent are they centred on distinct national issues and concerns? How are curriculum reforms in Singapore and Hong Kong similar and different? What might be the future direction of the Singapore curriculum and its implications for the international communities?

From the perspective of an "outsider," Kennedy (Chap. 12) discusses issues concerning the global and national (unique) features of the Singapore curriculum in relation to globalization, in view of trends and issues that are common across societies. In particular, he assesses the readiness of Singapore to take on a leadership role in the Asia-pacific region in terms of the curriculum as the key tool in the preparation of future citizens, and discusses the implications and challenges. In Chap. 13 Gopinathan and Lee compare and contrast curriculum reforms in Hong Kong and Singapore, identifying similarities and differences in policy responses to the challenges of globalization. Their analysis sheds further light on the global trends and unique (national) features embedded in the Singapore curriculum. With respect to citizenship education, Lee (Chap. 14) discusses how the social, political and economic contexts have impacted on the curriculum development in Singapore, and identifies the direction the curriculum is currently moving, the conception and forms which it is going to take in view of Curriculum 2015 (C2015).

It is worth noting that the book devotes three chapters on citizenship education (Chaps. 5, 10 and 14) given that it has long been an essential feature of the Singapore curriculum and has become an increasingly important topic of international concern in the age of globalization. Whereas Chap. 14 is largely concerned with the policy curriculum and its future direction, Chaps. 5 and 16 primarily deal with the programmatic and classroom curriculum respectively. These three chapters thus complement one another, providing a more sophisticated and multidimensional account of the citizenship curriculum in Singapore.

In the final chapter Deng, Gopinathan and Lee (Chap. 15) weave together the key insights of the contributors and discuss how policy, programmatic and classroom curricula reflect, on the one hand, global features and tendencies, and on the other, distinct national traditions and practices. Furthermore, they identify a set of issues, problems and challenges that not only concern policymakers and reformers in Singapore but (they believe) would be generally useful for policymakers, educators, and researchers in other countries.

References

Anderson-Levitt, K. M. (2008). Globalization and curriculum. In F. M. Connelly, M. F. He, & J. Phillion (Eds.), *The sage handbook of curriculum and instruction* (pp. 349–368). Thousand Oaks: Sage.

Apple, M. W. (1995). *Education and power* (2nd ed.). New York: Routledge.

Apple, M. W. (2004). *Ideology and curriculum* (3rd ed.). New York: Routledge.

Barber, M., & Mourshed, M. (2007). *How the world's best-performing school systems come out on top*. London: McKinsey & Company.

Bernstein, B. (1971). On the classification and framing of educational knowledge. In M. F. D. Young (Ed.), *Knowledge and control: New directions for the sociology of education* (pp. 47–69). London: Collier MacMillan.

Connelly, F. M., & Xu, S. (2011). Curriculum and curriculum studies. In J. Arthur & A. Peterson (Eds.), *The Routledge companion to education* (pp. 115–124). New York: Routledge.

Darling-Hammond, L. (2010). *The flat world and education: How America's commitment to equity will determine our future*. New York: Teachers College Press.

Decastell, S. C., Luke, A., & Luke, C. (Eds.). (1989). *Language, authority and criticism*. London: Falmer Press.

Deng, Z. (2010). Curriculum planning and systems change. In P. Peterson, E. Baker, & B. McGraw (Eds.), *International encyclopedia of education* (Vol. 1, pp. 384–389). Oxford: Elsevier.

Deng, Z. (2011). Revisiting curriculum potential. *Curriculum Inquiry, 41*(5), 538–559.

Doyle, W. (1992a). Constructing curriculum in the classroom. In F. K. Oser, A. Dick, & J. Patry (Eds.), *Effective and responsible teaching: The new syntheses* (pp. 66–79). San Francisco: Jossey-Bass.

Doyle, W. (1992b). Curriculum and pedagogy. In P. W. Jackson (Ed.), *Handbook of research on curriculum* (pp. 486–516). New York: Macmillan.

Doyle, W. (2008, August). *Competence as a blurred category in curriculum theory*. Paper presented at Research on vocational education and training for international comparison and as international comparison, Göttingen: Georg-August-Universität.

Gopinathan, S. (2007). Globalization, the Singapore developmental state & education policy: A thesis revisited. *Globalization, Societies and Education, 5*(1), 53–70.

Jackson, P. W. (1992). Conceptions of curriculum and curriculum specialists. In P. W. Jackson (Ed.), *Handbook of research on curriculum* (pp. 3–40). New York: Macmillan.

Luke, A., & Carrington, V. (2002). Globalisation, literacy, curriculum practice. In R. Fisher, G. Brooks, & M. Lewis (Eds.), *Raising standards in literacy* (pp. 231–250). London: Routledge Falmer.

Luke, A., Freebody, P., Lau, S., & Gopinathan, S. (2005). Towards research-based innovation and reform: Singapore schooling in transition. *Asia Pacific Journal of Education, 25*(1), 5–28.

Meyer, J. W. (1980). Levels of the educational system and schooling effects. In C. E. Bidwell & D. M. Windham (Eds.), *The analysis of educational productivity* (Issues in macroanalysis, Vol. 2, pp. 15–63). Cambridge: Ballinger.

Ministry of Education. (2009). *Report of the Primary Education Review and Implementation (PERI) Committee.* Singapore: Ministry of Education.

Ministry of Education. (2010). *Report of the Secondary Education Review and Implementation (SERI) Committee.* Singapore: Ministry of Education.

Pinar, W. F., Reynolds, W. M., Slattery, P., & Taubman, P. M. (1995). *Understanding curriculum: An introduction to the study of historical and contemporary curriculum discourses.* New York: Peter Lang.

Schiro, M. S. (2008). *Curriculum theory: Conflicting visions and enduring concerns.* Los Angeles: Sage.

Westbury, I. (2000). Teaching as a reflective practice: What might *Didaktik* teach curriculum. In I. Westbury, S. Hopmann, & K. Riquarts (Eds.), *Teaching as a reflective practice: The German Didaktik tradition* (pp. 15–39). Mahwah: Erlbaum.

Westbury, I. (2002). The educational situation as concerns the elementary school: Implications for our time. *Journal of Curriculum and Supervision, 17*(2), 120–129.

Westbury, I. (2003a). Evaluating a national curriculum reform. In P. Haug & T. A. Schwandt (Eds.), *Evaluating educational reforms: Scandinavian perspectives* (pp. 189–207). Greenwich: Information Age Press.

Westbury, I. (2003b). Curriculum, school: Overview. In J. W. Guthrie (Ed.), *The encyclopedia of education* (2nd ed., pp. 529–535). New York: Macmillan.

Westbury, I. (2008). The making of formal curricula: Why do states make curricula, and how? In F. M. Connelly, M. F. He, & J. Phillion (Eds.), *The Sage handbook of curriculum and instruction* (pp. 45–65). Thousand Oaks: Sage.

Yates, L., & Young, M. (2010). Globalisation, knowledge and the curriculum. *European Journal of Education, 45*(1), 4–10.

Part II
Globalization, Curriculum Reform, Vision and Discourses

Chapter 2
Globalization, the State and Curriculum Reform

S. Gopinathan and Abu Bakar Mardiana

Introduction

In this chapter we provide an overview of curriculum responses in Singapore between the period 1956 and 2010. We argue that in the first phase, between 1956 and 1987, the post-colonial state showed remarkable foresight and capacity in dealing with fundamental challenges in the political, economic and social domains. The post-colonial challenge, in the context of a multiethnic, divided and impoverished island, was to build political legitimacy, foster economic growth and strengthen social cohesion. Education was central to this effort. Out of weakness and division, a strong state emerged that, in three decades, was able to effectively address the challenges that confronted it.

The second phase, the globalisation phase between 1987[1] and 2010, produced its own set of challenges. In the wake of the 1985 recession, the Ministry of Trade and Industry convened an Economic Committee which reported that despite "great strides in raising our standard of education, our average education levels are still far behind developed nations" (Ministry of Trade and Industry 1986, para. 37),

---

[1]While many believe the year 1997 signifies the government response to globalization (e.g., Chaps. 3 and 4), we mark 1987 as the year globalisation became an important variable in the Singapore education landscape. It was mooted in the *Toward Excellence in Education Report* that the independent school initiative was mooted, and a shift towards decentralisation and devolution began to take root in response to the needs for education to become more responsive to international economic trends (MOE 1987). Beginning in 1988, several well-established schools were allowed to become largely independent of the Ministry of Education and designated as "independent schools". The independent school initiative sharpened the system's ability to prepare an academic elite and gave schools greater flexibility and independence to experiment with new ideas (Tan 2010). Flexibility was highlighted by the Singapore Economic Report of 1986 as a "fundamental" for Singapore to move forward as "trends in the world economy are beyond our control" (para. 67).

S. Gopinathan (✉) • A.B. Mardiana
National Institute of Education, Nanyang Technological University, Singapore
e-mail: s_gopinathan@ymail.com

Z. Deng et al. (eds.), *Globalization and the Singapore Curriculum: From Policy to Classroom*, Education Innovation Series, DOI 10.1007/978-981-4451-57-4_2,
© Springer Science+Business Media Singapore 2013

The report emphasised that the driving force of growth "lies in factors such as the education level of the population, and the maturity of the structure of firms in the economy. In terms of both of these factors, Singapore has a long way to go" (para. 36). The state now needs its economy to be simultaneously national and global, enhance creativity and productivity in its labour force to compete better in the global auction for talent, to manage new vistas of diversity and to seek to become even more cosmopolitan, a world city no less. It has to do this without ignoring its past and the particular histories of its ethnic groups, strengthen civic and national identity and continue efforts at strengthening social cohesion. Once again, education was made central to this effort.

Our starting position in this chapter is that the nascent Singapore state saw schooling as a means for social cohesion and economic reconstruction, a platform to shape a new identity, and build a nation out of disparate, often contending ethno-linguistic groups. The big divide, in educational terms, was that between the English and non-English educated. The roots of that divide were a tangle of competing nationalisms, anti-colonial sentiment, and frustration over meagre economic opportunities for the non-English educated. At the regional level, Singapore was a tiny, Chinese-dominant island state in a region where Chinese migrants were viewed with suspicion; and the immediate post-war global dimension it confronted was of decolonisation, and a need to construct a new national identity, while at the same time grasping an opportunity to build upon the infrastructure, links and markets inherited from its colonial master (Gopinathan 1974; Doraisamy 1969; Wilson 1978).

That opportunity was seized with vigour and determination. A hybrid, free market-state capitalism model was developed. Today, Singapore, in GDP per capita terms, is amongst the five richest countries in the world. The triumph of the state-led capitalism is admired by many nations; its innovative policies in public housing, transportation, and health services, among others, and its pragmatic welfare provision, are envied and emulated by many. Its infrastructure is world class. The state developed education as a key lever for modernization and economic growth; it expanded provision, modernised the curriculum and developed technical and vocational education. On international tests of student achievement such as Trends in International Mathematics and Science Study (TIMSS), Program for International Student Assessment (PISA), and Progress in International Reading Literacy Study (PIRLS), Singapore's students are amongst the top five (also see Chap. 12). Singapore's students are warmly welcomed into US Ivy League and Commonwealth leading institutions. Finally, in governance terms, Singapore is highly regarded for its commitment to efficiency, a corruption-free administration, multiculturalism and meritocracy.

The political framework that best describes why such an achievement was possible in four decades lies in the concept of the "developmental state" (Johnson 1995; The World Bank 1993). The developmental state theory postulates that new states gain legitimacy via economic growth which provides resources for public services (Gopinathan 1998, 2011). The newly-formed Singapore state had to secure legitimacy. The conventional wisdom was that as a small city state with no resources Singapore would not be able to survive on its own. A merger with Malaya, Sabah and Sarawak was agreed upon but was short-lived and lasted only from 1963 to 1965, floundering on irreconcilable political philosophies and ethnic issues. Ethnic tension had increased considerably and there was also Indonesian hostility to contend with. The newly sovereign Singapore state, which came into being on 9th August 1965, fashioned a "backs-to-the-wall-but-we-shall-succeed" narrative to mobilise its citizens with economic growth, security, rising living standards and widening opportunities as the goal of nation building. This period is known as the "survival" phase in Singapore's development. Singapore's political and administrative leadership, which has remained with the same political party since independence, eschewed ideology in favour of pragmatism and rational policy making, and recognised the need not just to make cost-effective policies, but to ensure efficient resource distribution and implementation. The modernization of education was crucial to the task of building an industrial economy, as was the need to use the socialisation opportunities afforded by schools to build social cohesion and a sense of common destiny (Goh and Gopinathan 2008; Wilson 1978).

Developing and Implementing the Post-Colonial Curriculum: 1956–1987

During British rule, there was a complex system of government schools, government-assisted schools, and private schools that were not brought under one common system until independence. There was a wide range of schools, varying in terms of the management structure, government control and supervision, medium of instruction, curricula and the quality of teaching staff (Doraisamy 1969; Hirschman 1972). Besides providing for a few years of free primary education in the Malay language for a small number of ethnic Malays, the colonial administration made no substantial provision for English-medium, Chinese-medium or Tamil-medium education. It was left to the Christian missionaries and philanthropists-merchants from various ethnic communities to establish and run English-medium schools. The segmented school system had multiple curriculums. For example, the English-medium schools adopted the British grammar school curriculum while Chinese-medium schools used curriculum and textbooks from China. Medium of instruction issues were contentious and politicised, and a linguistic, cultural and often economic divide existed between the English-educated and non-English educated. The state faced four educational-curricular challenges (Gopinathan 1974; Goh and Gopinathan 2008):

1. To achieve an acceptable settlement on the medium of instruction,
2. To provide school learners with the knowledge and skills needed in an industrialising economy,
3. Use schools to build and enhance social cohesion and citizenship values, and to seed an education culture of high quality founded on merit-based opportunities.

The All-Party Report on Chinese Education is crucial in directing policy to meeting these ends (see All-Party Committee on Chinese Education 1956). The commitment it made towards "equality of treatment" for all four official languages – a formula with English as the medium of instruction and with Malay as the national language and Malay, English, Mandarin and Tamil as the four official languages – was a politico-linguistic settlement that has stood the test of time. Its impact on education and cultural policy has been profound. The key to the success of this politico-linguistic settlement is that the commitment to equality was effectively implemented. Its recognition of the necessity and value of English as an international language, mastery of which would provide societal and individual advantages has undoubtedly helped Singapore's socio-economic modernization, and more recently, smoothed over some of the challenges of globalisation (also see Chaps. 5, 13 and 14).

While the study of languages, Mathematics and Science was central to the curriculum, one other major innovation from this period was the emphasis on the study of technical subjects. Successful industrialisation required a labour force skilled in the new industrial technologies and methodologies. This required technical-vocational curriculum development and enactment. There was considerable resistance, especially in English medium schools where the desired goal of education was university education and professional careers. Some subjects had to be made compulsory, and female students were also encouraged to participate. In 1960, a Commission of Inquiry into Vocational and Technical Education in Singapore was set up (Chan Chieu Kiat Commission 1961). It recommended establishing a 2 year secondary vocational education stream in schools for weaker students. Resources were committed towards establishing centralised workshops, vocational centres were established and polytechnic education modernized. This comprehensive approach and successful industrialization has done much to position technical and vocational education as both academically rigorous and occupationally valuable. Although the perceived status of technical education as a track for poorer performers remains to be completely dispelled, the Singapore state has successfully set up one of the best technical education system in the world, and the image of vocational training has changed significantly for the better (Gopinathan 1998; Lee et al. 2008).

The civics and citizenship education curriculum posed a different set of challenges. Several needs had to be met. Students had to be prepared for a democratic future, civic responsibility had to be spelled out and cultivated, and the rich resources of traditional culture tapped for values and moral education. Ethnic sensitivities had to be managed, and a plausible yet inspiring narrative of successful state building and distinctiveness created (Baildon and Sim 2010; Tan 2011; also see Chap. 14). This had to happen while the system was expanding and disparate elements in the system were being slowly integrated to form a national system. One example of an early civics education curriculum was the Education for Living syllabus introduced in 1974 to all Singapore primary schools. Its aim was to help students understand the purpose and importance of nation building, appreciate the desirable elements of both Eastern and Western traditions, and cope successfully with changing national and social conditions. It was replaced in 1981 with the Being and Becoming programme (Gopinathan 1988, 2011), which had values and moral education as its main focus (Sim and Print 2005).

A more radical departure in values education curriculum making was the introduction of the Religious Knowledge (RK) curriculum in 1984. While Singapore had a tradition of faith-based schooling, notably such church-founded schools as the Anglo-Chinese School, Convent of the Holy Infant Jesus, Saint Andrews, and the madrasahs set up by Muslim philanthropic families and bodies, state-founded schools were secular. What seems to have been the trigger for the RK curriculum was a desire to anchor values education more firmly amidst the pressures of modernisation and Westernisation, and religion was felt to provide a framework for this. There was a concern that the rapid transformation that Singapore was experiencing, with its impressive rise in living standards, had engendered a growing consumer culture that might undermine the ethic of hard work and lead to a neglect of traditional Asian values found in Hinduism, Confucianism, Islam, etc. The government made it clear that the curriculum was about imparting religious knowledge, not conversion to a particular faith. Local and foreign experts developed syllabi for Bible Knowledge, Buddhist Studies, Hindu Studies, Confucian Ethics and Islamic Religious Knowledge. However, the initiative was undone by internal and external factors. While the government had hoped that a large number of ethnic Chinese students would opt for Confucian Ethics, this turned out to be the least popular choice. Externally, Singapore was witnessing a phase of "aggressive and insensitive evangelisation" as a government sponsored survey of religion had termed it and the government was keen to shield the school system from this encroachment (Lai 2008). The RK curriculum came to an end in 1989, barely 5 years after its implementation (Gopinathan 1995; Lee and Gopinathan 2012; Tan 2007).

Even in an efficient, meritocratic system such a radical attempt to transform and modernize the curriculum was bound to pose difficulties. Often, in these circumstances well intentioned policies do not adequately take into account complexities at school and classroom level, teacher capacity, textbook availability etc. In Singapore, in the late 70s, a few years after the PAP government achieved its aim of providing universal free primary education, evidence surfaced of high attrition, semi-literate school leavers and the bilingual policy falling short of its aims. A government-appointed committee headed by then Deputy Prime Minister Goh Keng Swee reported on the issues in the Report on the Ministry of Education (Goh 1979). It argued for a two-tier curriculum on the grounds that ability differentials were the cause of the problem, not unreasonable curriculum expectations. It noted that a majority of students then came from dialect speaking homes and Chinese students faced instruction in two foreign languages: English and Mandarin. Early streaming, which the report recommended, continues to be a feature of the system, and remains an enduring variable in the Singapore students' experiences of schooling and patterns of academic achievement (Barr and Skrbis 2009; Gopinathan 2007; Mardiana 2012; Kang 2005).

Consequent to the Goh report, the New Education System (NES) was implemented in 1980, which created a two-tier curriculum and a three tracks system at the primary school level. Pupils are tracked into three streams based on the results of the end of the year Primary 3 examination carried out by the schools:

1. The Normal Bilingual, stream where pupils would learn English and Mother Tongue and take the Primary School Leaving Examination (PSLE) at the end of Primary 6.

2. The Extended Bilingual Stream where pupils take on the same curriculum as the Normal Bilingual Stream pupils but sit for their PSLE at the end of Primary 8.
3. The Monolingual Stream where pupils were taught to a curriculum which "focus on language and basic numeracy to prepare them for vocational training" (Tan et al. 2008, p. 114). Pupils in this stream sit for the Primary School Proficiency Exam (PSPE) at the end of Primary 8.

Three similar streams were also created at the secondary level with the implementation of the NES. They are:

1. The Special Bilingual stream where students would offer both English and Chinese at first language level and take their "O" level exams at the end of Secondary 4. In 1980, the Ministry of Education (MOE) designated nine Chinese-medium secondary schools as Special Assistance Plan (SAP) schools for the purpose of this stream.
2. The Express stream where students offer English at first language level and Mother tongue at second language level, and sit for their "O" level exams at the end of Secondary 4.
3. The Normal stream in which students are taught to a reduced curriculum and sit for the GCE 'N' at the end of secondary 4. Students who do well in this exam proceed to a 5th year and sit for the "O" level at the end of this year.

It has been more than 30 years since the Goh Report put streaming into place and reinforced the necessity of high stakes examinations at the end of the primary and secondary education. Primary school streaming has seen two forms since then. Tan (2010) summarised these thus:

> Following the publication of an Education Ministry report in 1991, the streaming exercise was delayed by a year and all students were to complete their primary schooling in six years. The recent attempt in 2008 to blur the previously rigid streaming policy was undertaken in response to repeated complaints from the public that streaming at such an early age was premature, overly divisive and had serious consequences for students' subsequent educational advancement and life-chances (p. 159)

Despite various reforms and reviews at both the primary and secondary school levels in the past three decades, the PSLE and the "O" levels remain purveyors of a nation-wide obsession with excelling in examinations given that "examination results are seen as the way into the top streams and the top schools in the country, and to that end, parents, students, and teachers are all drawn into the competition" (Cheah 1998, p. 196). Lee (1991) discussed the implications of "examination-orientated schooling" in East Asian societies, and argued that the hidden curriculum of such education systems is "education for earning, not learning" (p. 227). The enacted curriculum of schools continues to be dictated by these high-stakes examination. Hogan and Gopinathan (2008) pointed to "very tight coupling between the high stakes examination system and classroom instruction" (p. 370) while Curdt-Christiansen and Silver (2011) speak of the tensions when "existing structures" such as high-stakes examinations work counter to newer initiatives (p. 2). It should also be noted that with the introduction of the Integrative Programme initiative the stranglehold of the "O" levels has weakened as students in the programme have the option not to take the "O" levels. Finally, since mid-2012, there have been concerted calls from for the PSLE to be abolished. In September 2012, the Prime Minister responded by saying that Singapore's education system could not do away with the Primary School Leaving Examination (PSLE) that but Singapore should look at how it could reduce the pressure of a single examination and a single grade (Channelnewsasia 2012).

Another consequence of the meritocratic approach and early streaming was that even while the system expanded, failure to pass the grade 6 examination led to students having to leave school at a young age. Singapore did not then have compulsory education and today education is only compulsory at the elementary level. Fortunately, an expanding economy in the 70s and 80s created many low skill job opportunities. However, as the economy modernised and low skill-low wage industries relocated, many less educated Singaporeans found themselves unemployable, unable to master the new technologies and job related skills in newer industries. Thus while the economy grew and wealth was created, the link between education qualifications, work-ready skills and occupational opportunities was becoming more apparent.

Though the reforms introduced by Goh in 1979 left a strong imprint on the shape of Singapore's school system in curricular terms, they represented the beginnings of policy debate over how to best deal with ability and aptitude differences, curricular standardization and stratification, state-sponsored curriculum materials and textbook development via the establishment of the Curriculum Development Institute of Singapore (CDIS) in 1980 (Lee et al. 2008). The 80s is often labelled the "efficiency period" in recognition of the reduction in attrition and improved pass rates that were a consequence of streaming. This period could also be viewed as one in which a national system took shape, supplanting the segmented system inherited from its colonial days. A firm structure had been laid for a Singapore model of bilingual education based on an English-knowing bilingualism (Pakir 1991). Additional facilities for technical vocational education were created when the Institute for Technical Education (ITE) was established as a post-secondary education institution in 1992. A comprehensive system of polytechnics had been steadily built up earlier with the mission to train middle-level professionals to support the technological and economic development of Singapore since the late 1960s. There are now a total of five polytechnics which absorb about 40 % of each primary 1 cohort (Lee et al. 2008).

In spite of the difficulties noted above, it would be fair to say that overall, the Singapore state was able to set new goals of education, one more appropriate to a post-colonial situation, unify a fragmented system, win public support for often contentious policies e.g., bilingualism, technical and vocational education, and develop and implement major changes in the curriculum. Curriculum reform has resulted in the emergence of a Singapore-centred identity, deepened social cohesion and transformed and upgraded skills of school leavers and strengthened knowledge of and respect for difference. A system of high-stakes examinations, the Primary School Leaving Examination (PSLE), "O" and "A" levels, ensured effort on the part of students and a system-wide emphasis on performance.

Globalisation and Curriculum Reform 1987–2010

Globalisation is a complex phenomenon, with differential impacts in a number of sectors, and in Friedman's terms, "a flat world" (Friedman 2005) has emerged although in some contexts it is still a very uneven and lumpy world; most developing economies are simultaneously agricultural, industrial and post-industrial. The Giddens (1991) and Daun (2002) identify globalisation as a consequence of technological innovation, resulting in the compression of time and space, and transforming social and economic relations. This, combined with the rise of the neo-liberal market ideology, has led to the development of global markets, financial and human capital mobility on an unprecedented scale, an increased role for the World Bank and the International Monetary Fund (IMF). It has led to calls to reduce the power of the state, especially in economic matters, and in the emergence of private capital like Microsoft, Apple and Pearson in the development and delivery of services like education. The rise in private schooling, international academic achievement rankings like TIMSS, PISA and PIRLS, increased use of vouchers and charter schools in the US and of a culture of accountability and performance, are evidence of a trend towards a "marketization of education" (Tan 2011).

The power and pervasiveness of globalisation have led some to proclaim the death of the "nation state." This has proved to be a false prediction; while some state power has been trimmed, and in some contexts public-private partnerships are working well, the emergence of Brazil, Russia, India and China, collectively referred to as the BRIC nations, among others, shows the power and potential of state-led capitalism. What is pertinent for our purposes is that even though Singapore is a tiny island, the circumstances of its emergence as an independent country meant a big role for the state. The "developmental miracle" that is Singapore was due largely to an astute and development-focussed political and administrative elite. Human capital development and a consistent insistence on its relevance to socio-economic growth was a key driver of education policy and practice (Castells 1996, 1998; World Bank 2010; Gopinathan 2007; also see Chap. 12).

The Singapore state is well positioned to ride the "globalisation wave." Well before the 80s, the People's Action Party (PAP) had become the dominant party. Its commitment to raising living standards, and delivering on this, its successful economic policies manifested in improvements in housing, medical, educational and transport infrastructure, and increasing opportunities in education and training gave citizens hope for a prosperous future. Equally important was effective government policies that regulated social solidarity, and rewarded merit and effort; and a state that believed that the best response to globalisation was good governance not less governance.

An economic downturn in 1987 showed the need for Singapore to restructure its economy and to move into knowledge-intensive industries. There was mounting competition from other low wage economies; China was emerging as a major competitor for both investment and production. In economic terms, Singapore had to opt for value-added manufacturing to create niche manufacturing sectors, e.g., biotechnology and pharmaceuticals, stepped up its investment in research and development, and improve the financial and tourism sectors. An education system focused on efficiency and standardisation, with a premium on examination success was proving inappropriate. The need was for an education system that was flexible, varied, provided multiple pathways, and one which placed a greater emphasis on innovation and creativity, entrepreneurship and problem solving.

Although in the phase after efficiency, "ability-driven," is conventionally used as marking the era of significant curricular and pedagogic reform following then Prime Minister Goh's (1997) "Thinking Schools, Learning Nation" (TSLN) speech, we believe that the publication of Towards Excellence in Education (1987) was the initial marker in the beginnings of education reform in response to globalisation. It began the process of de-centralisation and the granting of greater autonomy at school level. While such a privilege was limited to nine leading schools beginning in 1988, it was soon followed by the creation of autonomous schools in 1994 which today number 29. This was followed up by the creation of school clusters in 1997, and later, in 2000 into zones. Such a move was essential in preparing schools for the greater pedagogic freedom, and local responsiveness that was required after 1997, especially after the launch of the Teach Less, Learn More (TLLM) initiative in 2004. The 1997 and 2004 speeches, both by Prime Ministers, indicate just how important and central education is to Singapore politics and society. What is also worth noting is the inclusion as an appendix of an article by American political scientists Chubb and Moe (1988) in the Towards Excellence in Education Report (1987), extolling the virtues of private sector involvement and praising vouchers. While certainly a nod to neo-liberal market ideology it would be wrong to assume that the Singapore independent schools are private and that admission to these schools is by anything other than demonstrated merit. Rather, the freedom given to these schools to modify and enrich their curriculum to extend and challenge high ability learners foreshadowed the directions of TSLN that Goh would lay down a decade later.

In his seminal TSLN speech, Goh (1997) called for Singapore's education institutions to respond to the knowledge economy by using, creating, critiquing and applying knowledge rather than showing off a mastery of content in examinations (see Chap. 4). He extolled the robustness of the Singapore education system and its many successes, but asserted that past successes were unlikely to prove sufficient for an unpredictable future in a rapidly changing and globalising world. Goh's TSLN speech led to a "veritable hurricane of reform initiatives in Singapore's schools" (Deng and Gopinathan 2003, p. 51). It heralded Singapore's Ministry of Education (MOE) commitment "to an ambitious program of pedagogical reform in Singaporean schools in anticipation of the kind of institutional challenges – particularly those in increasingly globalized labour markets – that young Singaporeans were likely to face in the coming decades" (Hogan and Gopinathan 2008, p. 369). Policy makers had realised in the mid-80s that the mandated curriculum and an examination-dominant pedagogy were too restrictive for the emergent knowledge-based economy. In 1986, the MOE launched Fostering Innovation and Creativity in Schools. This led to a number of school-based efforts to foster creative and critical thinking.

Goh's TSLN speech needs to be seen in the context of three other initiatives announced earlier in the year. The first, the IT MasterPlan, argued for the creative integration of information technology into the Singapore education system in order to produce more independent learners (Fu 2010). The second was the critical thinking initiative centred on the introduction of critical and creative thinking into the curriculum. The third initiative, National Education (NE), speaks to the concern for citizenship and values education (see Chaps. 5 and 14). It seeks to address the issue of how to develop Singaporean citizens in the fullest sense of the word. It aims to foster Singaporean identity, pride and self-respect, to teach about the rationale and success of Singapore's socio-economic development strategy and for students to appreciate Singapore's unique developmental challenges, constraints and vulnerabilities (Hawazi 2002).

Profound changes to the structure of Singapore education have been initiated since 2000 to provide flexibility, "pathways and bridges" (Ng 2009, p. 2) for students at the low end of the educational spectrum. The two-track streaming system put in place in the 80s has been altered by wider curricular options and by more and flexible pathways (Gopinathan 2007, 2011), with possible positive consequences for weaker students. The curriculum today is more diversified and offers greater choice for students in the lower tracks. At the primary school level, the introduction of the Subject-based Banding policy in 2008 is a move to dismantle the rigidity of the two-tiered curriculum structure by providing weaker learners with 17 choices of subject combinations across the two levels of the Standard and Foundation curriculums (Tan 2010; Mardiana 2012; MOE 2011).

At the secondary level, more pathways have been built into the lower and lowest tracks of the Normal Academic (NA) and the Normal Technical (NT).[2] The new NA curriculum planned for implementation in 2013 will provide two new "through-train" pathways for students who do well in their Singapore-Cambridge General Certificate Examination (GCE) N-level examinations via direct admission into the polytechnics, and to the higher diploma courses in ITE. NA students may also take a maximum of any two GCE "O" Level examination subjects at Secondary 4 from an expanded range of subjects (MOE n.d.). A similar revamp of the NT curriculum allows for a closer articulation of subject choices across the NA and the NT streams, thus enabling NT students to take on subjects of the NA curriculum.

The proliferation of bridges and pathways also now include access built into higher levels of schooling as well as into different trajectories of specialised schools and schools dedicated for different ability groups. The Direct Schools Admissions (DSA) program, introduced in 2004 for students who are in primary 6 and secondary 4, has allowed more and more schools and colleges to accept their preferred

---

[2] In current streaming practice secondary school students are placed into either of the following streams – Express, Normal Academic (NA) and Normal Technical (NT) – based on their performance on PSLE. Express is a 4 year programme leading to the Singapore-Cambridge General Certificate of Education "O" level exam. NA is also a 4 year programme leading to a Normal Level ("N" level) examination, with the possibility of a fifth year followed by an "O" level exam. NT is a 4 year programme in which students take subjects more technical in nature.

profile of pupils directly, bypassing the Ministry's central allocation. Secondary schools and junior colleges have not only gained more autonomy in choosing their students but the DSA initiative has led to a profileration of 'niche schools' at the secondary school level. Secondary schools have been competing to establish niches (Goh and Tan 2009) in everything from robotics to floorball and soccer to national education, environmental education, rock climbing and performing arts so that they may be allowed 5 % independent intake under this scheme. There are now about 50 such secondary schools. The other 40 secondary schools in the DSA program include the independent schools, the autonomous schools, those offering the Integrated Programme (IP)[3] and the three Specialised Independent Schools.[4] The percentages of direct admissions vary according to these categories, with more privileges given to schools with more elite and specialised curriculum: Independent Schools without IP are granted 20 %, Autonomous Schools without IP 10 %, while schools with IP and Specialised Independent Schools are granted up to 100 %. In 2013, a school dedicated for Normal Technical students opened with its first cohort. Six years earlier, in 2007, a school was established for students with difficulties handling the mainstream curriculum and at risk of dropping out of school.

As early as 2001, then Prime Minister Goh had spoken about the need to "invest more effort into developing assessments which do not have just one answer. This way, students will be encouraged to exercise their thinking skills and innovative spirit to come out with different solutions for the same problem" (Goh 2001). Coursework and new assessment items and methods have been developed at various levels of schooling, with more autonomy given to schools to set these assessments. These include the school-based interdisciplinary Project Work for pre-university students in 2003 as part of university admission criteria and the school-based Science Practical Assessment (SPA) as a coursework initiative for secondary and pre-university students since 2006. Tan (2011) however asserts that these assessment reforms are emphasizing and perpetuating structural efficiency rather than improving the quality of learning. A major research project undertaken to examine the quality of teacher assignments and associated student work in 59 Singapore primary and secondary schools by Koh and Luke (2009) found assessment tasks to be of low authentic and intellectual quality in all subject areas except for Primary 5 Social Studies, the only non-examinable subject. In an education system in which high-stakes examinations continue to dominate, assessment reform has been timid. The use of such examination results as a sorting mechanism continues to result in a strong focus on grades and content acquisition rather than learning and holistic development.

---

[3] Pioneered by independent and elite schools such as Raffles Institution, Raffles Girls School, Hwa Chong Institution (formerly The Chinese High School) and Nanyang Girls' High School in 2004, the IP allows students to skip the O-level at secondary four and be admitted directly to junior colleges.

[4] Specialised Independent Schools include Singapore Sports School which was opened in 2004, NUS High School of Math and Science which started in 2005, and Specialised School for the Arts, begun in 2007.

The Ministry had recognised that the goals of structural and curricular changes mandated from the centre can only be achieved if there are changes in pedagogy, and that meant both transforming attitudes and competencies at the school and classroom levels. Prime Minister Lee's (2004) TLLM speech is an attempt to encourage a loosening of a dominant pedagogic script, one focused not on examination performance but on inquiry, experimentation, exploration and application. Following this, a "TLLM Ignite!" package was provided to schools to catalyse School-based Curriculum Innovations (SCI). Further, "PETALS: The Teacher's Toolbox" was developed by the MOE to support teachers in this new initiative (See Chap. 7). The Ministry also encouraged the formation of professional learning communities at the school, cluster and zone levels within this TLLM vision.

The Report of the Primary Education Review and Implementation (PERI) Committee argued the need to change mindsets on curriculum and pedagogy as well as the building of teacher and school capacity to implement curricular change (also see Chap. 13). It recommended more active outside-the-classroom-learning experiences and a stronger emphasis on non-academic aspects of the curriculum. It supported changes in assessment practices at the lower primary level (MOE 2009). Similarly, the Secondary Education Review and Implementation (SERI) Committee's report emphasised a range of initiatives from strengthening the social-emotional support for secondary school students to strengthen the articulation of students to post-secondary education (MOE 2010; also Chap. 13).

The period 1997–2010 could be characterised as the "big bang" period of education-curricular reform in Singapore. But even as the Ministry was implementing the key thrusts of the IT Masterplans, National Education, TSLN, TLLM, it was already looking ahead. In 2008, a Committee made up of MOE staff and school personnel began work on a consultation document. The Curriculum 2015 (C2015) was formulated to guide thinking about future changes in three broad areas: new skills and competencies for the twenty-first century; people skills, working in teams and across cultures; and rootedness and values (Ng 2008; also see Chap. 14). C2015 proposed a framework founded on strong fundamentals and future learning, yet retaining the system's "core strengths in traditional curriculum" (Ng 2008, par. 29). Mathematics, Science, Languages, Humanities would remain therefore significant in the proposed curriculum, as would an emphasis to approach "problems with an inter-disciplinary lens and integrate the sciences and humanities to solve problems" (Ng 2008, par. 23). It also signalled the need for an integrated citizenship and character education programme.

New Directions in the Singapore Curriculum

Curriculum reform is, in a sense, an education policy response to new challenges and opportunities. In the earlier phase, the introduction of bilingualism, technical and vocational education, for example, were necessary responses to the need to acknowledge societal multilingualism and transform the skill base of the labour force.

The shift from an industrial economy to a globalising economy led to policies to strengthen citizenship (National Education), ride on the power of information technology (IT Masterplan), and transform attitudes to knowledge and pedagogy (TSLN, TLLM). System flexibility was achieved through such initiatives as the independent and autonomous schools, creation of clusters and zones and the creation of a more responsive and flexible school system. The School Excellence (SEM) Model facilitated autonomy, enhancing the school's capacity to respond better to specific school needs (see Chap. 3).

New socio-economic pressures now confront the Singapore state and nation, and the education system will once again be called upon to play a significant role in meeting these new challenges. In what follows we detail some of these society-wide issues, provide a preliminary check on how well the post-1987 reforms have worked and what future-coping policies are required. We examine the new political, economic and social contexts which will provide a frame for a critique of existing education-curriculum issues.

The 2011 general elections were a watershed. While the People's Action Party still dominates Parliament, it does so with a weakened mandate. Some saw its policies as being elitist, and increasingly out of touch with voter needs and aspirations. Major policies in housing, transportation, health, immigration and in education came in for wide-ranging criticisms. Many commentators noted the emergence of a more energised, active citizenry which wanted to be consulted more (Bhaskaran et al. 2012).

A major source of dissatisfaction was increased income inequality, the rising cost of living and the large number of immigrants competing with citizens for educational places and jobs. State legitimacy, previously built upon rapid economic growth, rising living standards, and thus a capacity to meet rising aspirations and expectations, was under stress. The Gini co-efficient, a measure of inequality, had risen from 0.444 in 2000 to 0.48 in 2010 (Todayonline May 9 2011; also see Chap. 12). A low-wage segment of the labour force was finding it difficult to make ends meet. Social mobility through education was seen to be at risk and there were demands, for instance, for increased opportunities in state-funded higher education; it was questioned if meritocratic criteria should be so applied that citizenship conferred no advantage. An increase in immigration, at both the low and high-skill labour markets since 2005, raised concerns about identity, integration and opportunities to access public goods, including education. Further, ethnic categorisation as a basis for identity formation, was seen as increasingly irrelevant, especially among the young and contradictory to aspirations to be a global city and enhanced cosmopolitanism. We believe that Singapore's prosperity-loyalty impact is currently under strain and will require new policy responses in education.

The structural and curriculum reform in the Singapore education system have been considerable since 1987, and especially since the TSLN reform. There is now a considerable body of research to examine how effective the reform initiatives have been at the point they matter most, the classroom. While some progress has been made in meeting the goals of TSLN and TLLM, we have at best a "hybrid pedagogy," with a teacher-dominated, transmissive model still dominant

(Hogan and Gopinathan 2008; also see Chap. 8). Wolf and Borkhorst-Heng (2008) provided evidence of how "policies of promise" are being held back by "practices of limit" at the school level (p. 151). While the TSLN initiative allowed teachers more freedom to innovate and implement curriculum, this led to less than optimal results as most teachers "saw pupil ability as a fixed, inherited, uni-dimensional quantum reliably assessed in high-stakes examinations" (Albright and Kramer-Dahl 2009, p. 214). Examination reform has been modest, acting as a brake on teacher pedagogic freedom. Albright and Kramer-Dahl (2009) concluded that the instrumental legacy of policy prior to 1997 has embedded within many teachers and administrators widespread, intractable, powerful and rarely examined systemic beliefs about teaching and learning (p. 214).

Teacher capacity building (Baildon and Sim 2010) curriculum leadership readiness and distributed leadership (Gopinathan and Deng 2006; Dimmock 2011) remain at best a work-in-progress (Mardiana 2012). With regard to efforts to build an active and responsible citizenry, Ho (2010) came to the conclusion that Singapore students from highly dissimilar socio-economic, academic and racial backgrounds shared a remarkably similar understanding of Singapore's historical narrative, especially with regard to citizenship and race. Sim and Print (2009, p. 396) concluded that "none of the teachers held a transforming position premised on confronting injustice and resisting oppressive government policy ... were reluctant to question the meaning of citizenship in ways that were critical of the system, reflecting an ideological consensus with governing power." Hogan (2011) contends that what we have in Singapore is a "lack of subjective nationhood." In his view, the social compact in which allegiance is given for benefits makes for qualified and contingent support and is a weak foundation for robust citizenship.

Finally, while a more flexible system has emerged and tracking made less rigid, thus increasing customisation, the system will need to guard against excessive diversity in school type. A preoccupation with employability for low achieving students must not lead to early vocationalisation; the goal must be for twenty-first century competencies for all students. C2015 has promised that there must be a reassertion of the fundamental approach "to develop every Singaporean child to his full potential, and across the spectrum of abilities and talents" (Ng 2008, par. 8)

Conclusion

This chapter has noted that Singapore's emergence as a modern nation state and the development of the school system and curriculum has been permeated from its earliest days by global processes such as colonialism, migration, the emergence of the postcolonial interstate system and capitalism (Gupta 1997; Amaidas 2009; Gopinathan 2007). The state has been a powerful semiotic and material force (Luke et al. 2005) and has, in comparison with many other post-colonial states been remarkably successful in using schooling as an instrument for economic growth, social cohesion, regulation and state legitimacy. As with the pre-globalisation period, the state has shown nimbleness and flexibility in meeting globalisation's challenges for the education system. But as we noted earlier, at the level of the enacted curriculum, more bold changes are required.

In an era of widening income disparity and anxieties over the education system's capacity to maintain social mobility for students from lower income backgrounds. The work of the Singapore curriculum now must be an even more focused and determined emphasis on new ways of encouraging learning, new ways of understanding and reorganising schooling and what the education system must seek to do to for all its citizens. The state must continue to open up access to a curriculum that embodies both "powerful knowledge" and "knowledge of the powerful" (Young 2008; Whitty 2010). The Singapore state has to tackle the core problem of inequality and this will require changes both at the societal level as well as at the school level. And as it does that, it cannot afford to become overly nation-centric but must provide a curriculum that is broad, diverse and global. As a former minister put it, a more inclusive, "more lively meritocracy", a more "authentic meritocracy" (Tharman 2007, para. 117) needs to be put in place. Only then can the Singapore curriculum be an effective instrument for negotiating social justice. It remains to be seen how well Singapore curriculum reform in the next decade will address these necessities so that the Singapore dream of equality and unity in diversity remains meaningful.

References

Albright, J., & Kramer-Dahl, A. (2009). The legacy of instrumentality in policy and pedagogy in the teaching of English: The case of Singapore. *Research Papers in Education, 24*(2), 201–222.

All-Party Committee on Chinese Education. (1956). *Report of the all-party report committee of the Singapore legislative committee on Chinese education.* Singapore: Government Printer.

Amaidas, M. (2009). The management of globalization in Singapore: Twentieth century lessons for the early decades of the new century. *Journal of Alternative Perspectives in the Social Science, 1*(3), 982–1002.

Baildon, M., & Sim, J. B.-Y. (2010). The dilemmas of Singapore's national education in the global society. In A. Reid, J. Gill, & A. Sears (Eds.), *Globalisation, the nation-state and the citizen: Dilemmas and directions for civics and citizenship education* (pp. 80–96). New York: Routledge.

Barr, M. D., & Skrbis, Z. (2009). *Constructing Singapore: Elitism, ethnicity and the nation-building project.* Copenhagen: Nias Press.

Bhaskaran, M., et al. (2012). *Singapore perspectives 2012 background paper: Singapore inclusive: Bridging divides.* Singapore: Institute of Policy Studies.

Castells, M. (1996). *The rise of the network society.* Oxford: Blackwell.

Castells, M. (1998). *End of millennium.* Oxford: Blackwell.

Chan Chieu Kiat Commission of Inquiry into Vocational and Technical Education in Singapore. (1961). *Report of the commission of inquiry into vocational and technical education in Singapore.* Singapore: Government Printer.

Channelnewsasia. (2012, September 27). *PM Lee explains need for PSLE.* Retrieved 19 Jan 2013, from http://www.channelnewsasia.com/stories/singaporelocalnews/view/1228167/1/.html

Cheah, Y. M. (1998). The examination culture and its impact on literacy innovations: The case of Singapore. *Language and Education, 12*(3), 192–209.

Chubb, J. E., & Moe, T. M. (1988). Politics, markets, and the organization of schools. *American Political Science Review, 82*(4), 1065–1087.

Curdt-Christiansen, X.-L., & Silver, R. E. (2011). Learning environments: The enactment of educational policies in Singapore. In C. Ward (Ed.), *Language education: An essential for a global economy (RELC Anthology #52)* (pp. 2–24). Singapore: SEAMEO, Regional English Language Centre.

Daun, H. (Ed.). (2002). *Educational restructuring in the context of globalisation and local demands*. New York: Routledge/Falmer.

Deng, Z., & Gopinathan, S. (2003). Continuity and change in conceptual orientations for teacher preparation in Singapore: Challenging teacher preparation as training. *Asia-Pacific Journal of Teacher Education, 31*(1), 51–65.

Dimmock, C. (2011, May/June). *Leadership and its relationship with teaching and learning*. SingTeach, 30. Retrieved 10 June 2011, from http://singteach.nie.edu.sg/issue-23-marapr-2010-/208-leadership-and-its-relationship-with-teaching-and-learning.html

Doraisamy, T. R. (Ed.). (1969). *150 years of education in Singapore*. Singapore: Stamford College Press.

Friedman, T. L. (2005). *The world is flat: A brief history of the twenty-first century*. New York: Farrar/Straus/Giroux.

Fu, G. (2010). Opening address by Ms Grace Fu, Senior Minister of State, Ministry of National Development and Ministry of Education at a COMPASS Convention.

Giddens, A. (1991). *Modernity and self-Identity: Self and society in the late modern age*. Stanford: Stanford University Press.

Goh, K. S. (1979). *Report on the ministry of education 1978*. Singapore: Ministry of Education.

Goh, C. T. (1997). *Shaping our future: Thinking schools, learning nation*. Speech by Prime Minister Goh Chok Tong at the Opening of the 7th International Conference on Thinking.

Goh, C. T. (2001). Shaping lives, moulding nation. Speech by Prime Minister Goh Chok Tong at the Teacher's Day Rally.

Goh, C. B., & Gopinathan, S. (2008). Education in Singapore: Development since 1965. In B. Fredriksen & J. P. Tan (Eds.), *An African exploration of the East Asian experience* (pp. 80–108). Washington, DC: The World Bank.

Goh, J. W. P., & Tan, C. H. P. (2009). Developing niche area in schools: Toward the marketization of education in Singapore. *The New Educational Review, 18*(2), 235–252.

Gopinathan, S. (1974). *Towards a national system of education in Singapore, 1945–1973*. Singapore: Oxford University Press.

Gopinathan, S. (1988). Being and becoming: Education for values in Singapore. In W. Cummings, S. Gopinathan, & Y. Tomoda (Eds.), *The revival of values education in Asia and the west* (pp. 131–145). Oxford: Pergamon.

Gopinathan, S. (1995). Singapore. In P. Morris & A. Sweeting (Eds.), *Educational and development in East Asia*. New York: Garland.

Gopinathan, S. (1998). Educational development in Singapore. *Commentary, 15*, 1–13.

Gopinathan, S. (2007). Globalisation, the Singapore developmental state and education policy: A thesis revisited. *Globalization, Societies and Education, 5*(1), 53–70.

Gopinathan, S. (2011). Educating the next generation. In B. Welsh, J. Chin, & T. H. Tan (Eds.), *Impressions of the Goh Chok Tong years in Singapore*. Singapore: National University of Singapore Press and co-published with the Institute of Public Policy.

Gopinathan, S., & Deng, Z. (2006). Fostering school-based curriculum development in the context of new educational initiatives in Singapore. *Planning and Changing: An Educational Leadership and Policy Journal, 37*(1 & 2), 93–110.

Gupta, A. F. (1997). When mother-tongue education is not preferred. *Journal of Multilingual and Multicultural Development, 18*(6), 496–506.

Hawazi, D. (2002). Globalisation and its impact on social cohesion and rootedness. Speech by Mr. Hawazi Daipi, Parliamentary Secretary (Education) at North Zone National Education Seminar.

Hirschman, C. (1972). Educational patterns in Colonial Malaya. *Comparative Education Review, 16*(3), 486–502.

Ho, L. C. (2010). "Don't worry, I'm not going to report you": Education for citizenship in Singapore. *Theory and Research in Social Education, 38*(2), 298–318.

Hogan, D. (2011). Yes Brian, at long last, there is pedagogy in England – and in Singapore too. A response to TLRP's ten principles for effective pedagogy. *Research Papers in Education, 26*(3), 367–379.

Hogan, D., & Gopinathan, S. (2008). Knowledge management, sustainable innovation, and pre-service teacher education in Singapore. *Teachers and Teaching: Theory and Practice, 14*(4), 369–384.

Johnson, C. (1995). *Japan, who governs? The rise of the developmental state*. New York: Norton.

Kang, T. (2005). *Creating educational dreams: The intersection of ethnicity, families and schools*. Singapore: Marshall-Cavendish.

Koh, K., & Luke, A. (2009). Authentic and conventional assessment in Singapore schools: An empirical study of teacher assignments and student work. *Assessment in Education: Principles, Policy and Practice, 16*(3), 291–318.

Lai, A. H. (Ed.). (2008). *Religious diversity in Singapore*. Singapore: Institute of Southeast Asian Studies & Institute of Policy Studies.

Lee, W. O. (1991). *Social change and educational problems in Japan, Singapore, and Hong Kong*. London: Macmillan.

Lee, H. L. (2004). Our future of opportunity and promise. Speech by Prime Minister Lee Hsien Loong at the National Day Rally.

Lee, S. K., Goh, C. B., Fredriksen, B., & Tan, J. P. (Eds.). (2008). *Toward a better future: Education and training for economic development in Singapore since 1965*. Washington, DC: The World Bank.

Lee, M., & Gopinathan, S. (2012). Global or glocal? Roadmaps for curriculum developments in Singapore and Hong Kong. *Curriculum and Teaching, 27*(1), 43–65.

Luke, A., Freebody, P., Lau, S., & Gopinathan, S. (2005). Towards research-based innovation and reform: Singapore schooling in transition. *Asia Pacific Journal of Education, 25*(1), 5–28.

Mardiana, A. B. (2012). *Of perspectives and policy: A case study of the implementation of the subject-based banding policy in one Singapore primary school*. Unpublished Ph.D. dissertation, National Institute of Education, Nanyang Technological University, Singapore.

Ministry of Education. (1987). *Towards excellence in education: A report to the ministry of education*. Singapore: Ministry of Education.

Ministry of Education. (2009). *Report of the Primary Education Review and Implementation (PERI) committee*. Singapore: Ministry of Education.

Ministry of Education. (2010). *Report of the Secondary Education Review and Implementation (SERI) committee*. Singapore: Ministry of Education.

Ministry of Education. (2011, January). *Subject-based banding: Catering to your child's abilities*. Retrieved 2 Jan 2011, from http://www.moe.gov.sg/education/primary/files/subject-based-banding.pdf

Ministry of Education (n.d.). *Changes affecting the normal course*. Retrieved 20 June 2012, from http://www.moe.gov.sg/education/secondary/normal/changes/

Ministry of Trade and Industry. (1986, February). *Report of the Economic Committee: The Singapore Economy: New Directions*. Singapore: Ministry of Trade and Industry.

Ng, E. H. (2008). Our journey in education – Taking stock, forging ahead. Speech by Dr Ng Eng Hen, Minister for Education and Second Minister for Defence, on 25 September at the MOE Work Plan Seminar 2008 t the Ngee Ann Polytechnic Convention Centre, Singapore.

Ng, E. H. (2009). Seizing opportunities to build a world class education system. Financial year 2009 Committee of Supply Debate: 1st Reply by Dr Ng Eng Hen, Minister for Education.

Pakir, A. (1991). The range and depth of English-knowing bilinguals in Singapore. *World Englishes, 10*, 167–179.

Sim, J. B.-Y., & Print, M. (2005). Citizenship education and social studies in Singapore: A national agenda. *International Journal of Citizenship and Teacher Education, 1*(1), 58–73.

Sim, J. B.-Y., & Print, M. (2009). The state, teachers and citizenship education in Singapore schools. *British Journal of Educational Studies, 57*(4), 380–399.

Singapore Economic Committee. (1986). *The Singapore economy, new directions.* Singapore: Ministry of Trade and Industry.

Tan, C. (2007). Islam and citizenship education in Singapore: Challenges and implications. *Education, Citizenship and Social Justice, 2*(1), 23–39.

Tan, J. (2010). Singapore: Schools for the future. In C. Brock & L. P. Symaco (Eds.), *Education in South-East Asia.* Oxford series in comparative education. UK: Symposium Books.

Tan, K. (2011). Assessment for learning in Singapore: Unpacking its meanings and identifying some areas for improvement. *Educational Research in Policy and Practice, 10,* 91–103.

Tan, Y. P., Chow, H. K., & Goh, C. (2008). *Examinations in Singapore: Change and continuity (1891–2007).* Singapore: World Scientific.

Tharman, S. (2007, October 2). Having every child succeed. Speech by Mr Tharman Shanmugaratnam, Minister for Education, at the MOE Work Plan Seminar 2007.

Todayonline. (2011, May 9). Stocks may rebound post-GE. Retrieved 13 May 2011, from http://www.todayonline.com/Business/EDC110509-0001043/Stocks-may-rebound-post-GE

Whitty, G. (2010). Revisiting school knowledge: Some sociological perspectives on new school curricula. *European Journal of Education, 45*(1), 28–45.

Wilson, H. E. (1978). *Social engineering in Singapore: Educational policies and social change 1819–1972.* Singapore: University of Singapore Press.

Wolf, J. M., & Bokhorst-Heng, W. (2008). Polices of promise and practices of limit: Singapore's literacy education policy landscape and its impact on one school programme. *Educational Research for Policy and Practice, 7,* 151–164.

World Bank. (1993). *The East Asian miracle: Economic growth and public policy.* New York: Oxford University Press.

World Bank. (2010). *The world bank annual report 2010.* Washington, DC: World Bank.

Young, M. F. D. (2008). *Bring knowledge back in: From social constructionism to social realism in the sociology of education.* London/New York: Routledge.

Chapter 3
Aims of Schooling for the Twenty-First Century: The Desired Outcomes of Education

Jason Tan

At the outset, I would like to state that in a fundamental way, many of the outcomes listed in the Desired Outcomes of Education document are in no way novel or surprising as they are fundamental human values that many societies attempt to inculcate in their young through the schooling system. The document, however, represented the first official attempt by the Ministry of Education (MOE) to categorise outcomes specifically according to the various stages of schooling. It also stated categorically that the document was a common blueprint to guide all education policies and programmes and was to serve as a basis for evaluating the success of these policies and programmes.

The chapter critically analyses the aims of schooling embedded in the 1998 and 2009 editions of the Desired Outcomes of Education document within the social and historical context of schooling in Singapore, in an attempt to reveal the ideologies and discourses that underpin the policy curriculum. It argues that the document represented the government's attempt to gear schools to meet the economic, social and cultural challenges posed by globalisation. At the same time, the chapter poses critical questions related to equality and equity, such as whether the outcomes are really meant to be attained by every student, whether the various stakeholders in education truly desire these outcomes, and whether the various stakeholders are in fact equally well-placed to attain these outcomes.

Early Pangs of Desire

Soon after the People's Action Party swept to power in the 1959 general elections, it sought progressively through the 1960s and 1970s to unify a school system that was previously segmented into four language streams – English, Chinese, Malay and

J. Tan (✉)
National Institute of Education, Nanyang Technological University, Singapore
e-mail: engthye.tan@nie.edu.sg

Z. Deng et al. (eds.), *Globalization and the Singapore Curriculum: From Policy to Classroom*, Education Innovation Series, DOI 10.1007/978-981-4451-57-4_3,
© Springer Science+Business Media Singapore 2013

Tamil – with differing curricula, examination systems and teacher qualifications. This push for a national education system was meant not only to foster social cohesion in a multilingual, multi-ethnic and multi-religious population but also to harness education as a key means of providing skilled manpower for industrialisation (People's Action Party 1959; State of Singapore 1959). By the early 1970s, students in the various language streams underwent the same number of years of schooling and sat for common national examinations (Doraisamy 1969; Wong 1974). In addition, the number of privately-run schools was progressively reduced as the number of government and government-aided schools increased, thus ensuring State domination over policy-making, regulation and funding. Soon after Singapore attained full political independence in 1965, the government attempted yet another means of instilling a sense of commonality among students by instituting daily rituals for all schools from 1966 onwards. These rituals included the raising and lowering of the national flag, accompanied by the singing of the national anthem and the reciting of the national pledge (also see Chap. 2).

As part of this unifying project in education, general statements were issued periodically about the common purposes of the education system. The following quote, taken from a Ministry of Education publication in 1970, is typical of the period:

> Education in Singapore seeks to develop to the fullest extent the potentialities of the individual as well as to ensure the collective welfare of the society. In particular, it aims to instil a love of freedom, truth, and justice with respect for fundamental human rights, an acceptance of the democratic way of life and an appreciation of racial and religious tolerance. It seeks to inculcate habits and attitudes leading to the development of adaptability, creativity, social responsibility and loyalty to the Republic. It endeavours to provide the knowledge and skills necessary for the economic development of the country. (Tan 1970, p. 6)

One can immediately make a few observations about this statement. First, it has echoes of a few of the key tenets – racial and religious tolerance, justice, democracy – embodied in the national pledge.[1] Second, it mentions crucial knowledge, skills and values that need to be inculcated in students. Third, it highlights the key objectives of the People's Action Party for the education system, namely, to support national economic development and to foster social cohesion. Another interesting quote from the same publication mentions the need to foster greater community participation in education:

> It is the policy of the Government to encourage community participation in the process of education. Government-aided schools are administered by committees of management comprising private individuals, while government schools have advisory committees. These committees, along with parent-teacher associations and old boys' associations, provide valuable links among the schools, the Ministry of Education and the community. (Tan 1970, p. 9)

---

[1] The National Pledge, which was written in 1966, a year after the attainment of political independence, reads as follows: "We, the citizens of Singapore, pledge ourselves as one united people, regardless of race, language or religion, to build a democratic society based on justice and equality, so as to achieve happiness, prosperity and progress for our nation."

This chapter will subsequently show that the ideas encapsulated in the Desired Outcomes of Education document in 1997 were in fact, for the most part, "desired" by officialdom right from the start of self-government and political independence. This point is especially crucial in Singapore, where there is often a tendency to lose sight of historical continuity in education policies and programmes and a corresponding tendency to over-state the novelty of newly announced policy initiatives.

A variety of key Ministry of Education reports in the 1970s and 1980s continued to mention desirable attributes that the schools were supposed to foster. In his response to the recommendations of the Goh Report of 1979, which led to the institutionalisation of streaming in primary and secondary schools, the then Prime Minister Lee Kuan Yew mentioned the need "to educate a child to bring out his [sic] greatest potential, so that he [sic] will grow up into a good man [sic] and a useful citizen" (Goh 1979, p. iii). Lee thought that

> the litmus test of a good education is whether it nurtures citizens who can live, work, contend and cooperate in a civilised way. Is he loyal and patriotic? Is he, when the need arises, a good soldier, ready to defend his country, and so protect his wife and children, and his fellow citizens? Is he filial, respectful to elders, law-abiding, humane, and responsible?...Is he a good neighbour and a trustworthy friend? Is he tolerant of Singaporeans of different races and religions? Is he clean, neat, punctual, and well-mannered? (Goh 1979, pp. iv–v)

In a similar vein, the Ong Report on moral education, which was published later that year, made reference to "desired moral values and concepts" such as "integrity, honesty, self-respect, honour, courage, perseverance, ...patience, spirit of inquiry,...self-discipline, temperance,...respect for elders, loyalty, tolerance,... civic consciousness, respect and care for others, care for public property, respect for law and order,...harmony, group-spirit,...co-operation, friendship,...understanding and appreciation of one's cultural heritage, understanding of and respect for others' cultures and beliefs,...sense of national identity and commitment, protection and upholding of the democratic system, defence of our country, patriotism, loyalty, justice and equality,...understanding the internal and external threats to Singapore's survival and prosperity" (Ong 1979, p. 9). The report was published by a committee consisting of Parliamentarians and chaired by a Cabinet member Ong Teng Cheong. The Committee had been directly commissioned by the then Education Minister Goh Keng Swee (author of the Goh report) in direct response to Lee's concern over moral education.

During the mid-1980s, there was a great deal of official rhetoric about the importance of creativity and innovation. For instance, the then Deputy Prime Minister Goh Chok Tong spoke of the need to allow top-performing schools the flexibility and independence to innovate and experiment with new ideas. Goh's sentiment was echoed the following year by the then Education Minister Tony Tan, who asserted the need for creativity and innovation in Singapore schools. Tan's talk of creativity and innovation echoed the findings of an Economic Committee set up by the Ministry of Trade and Industry in the wake of the 1985–1986 economic recession. The report had recommended the education of each individual to his or her maximum potential, and the development of creativity and flexible skills in order to maintain Singapore's economic competitiveness vis-a-vis countries such as Taiwan,

Japan and the United States (Ministry of Trade & Industry 1986). Creativity was mentioned once again in 1991 as a key goal of Singapore's education system, this time in a government coffee-table book, *The Next Lap*. This book also highlighted other goals such as the nurturing of leadership qualities and good work ethics, and the cultivation of civic and moral values (Government of Singapore 1991, p. 55; also see Chap. 2).

The drumbeat of securing Singapore's global competitive edge grew louder as the 1990s wore on. Yet another Ministry of Trade and Industry report in 1991 envisioned Singapore entering the league of developed nations and urged schools to develop creativity and innovation in students in the pursuit of this objective (Ministry of Trade & Industry 1991, p. 56). Two years later Goh, who was then the Prime Minister, warned of growing global competition for foreign investments and of multinational corporations moving low-skilled jobs away from Singapore to other countries like Indonesia and Thailand with lower wages. Part of his proposed solution to this crisis was for Singapore to improve educational and skill levels. He also warned of the prospect of growing income inequalities in Singapore and of the possible adverse consequences on the social compact ("Narrower income gap" 1993). Goh's rhetoric bore clear hallmarks of various renowned authors who at the time claimed that the survival of a nation within the global economy would depend increasingly on the ability of its citizens to enhance their skills and market them in the global market (Drucker 1993). Furthermore, having a highly skilled labour force was crucial for international capital investment (Marshall and Tucker 1992; Reich 1992).

Making the Desire Explicit

1997 was a momentous year in the annals of Singapore's education system. It marked the appointment of a new Education Minister charged with a dynamic mission: to launch a series of large-scale, systemic education reforms, the effects of which are still being felt nearly two decades later. The most major of these was launched by Goh in June. Labelled *Thinking Schools, Learning Nation* (or TSLN for short), this initiative focused on developing students into active learners with critical thinking skills, and on developing a creative and critical thinking culture within schools. Its key strategies included: (1) the explicit teaching of critical and creative thinking skills; (2) the reduction of subject syllabi content; (3) the revision of assessment modes; and (4) a greater emphasis on processes instead of on outcomes when appraising schools (MOE 1997b; also see Chap. 6).

Just a few weeks earlier, another key initiative had been launched by the then Deputy Prime Minister. Labelled *National Education*, or NE for short, it had grown out of publicly aired worries by Goh and Lee about the state of Singaporean youth (see Chap. 5). In 1996, Lee had commented on young people's alleged greater concern for their individual and family's welfare and success than for their community or society's well-being (Lee 1996). This was in fact a lament that he had made three decades earlier in 1966 (Lee 1966). Meanwhile, Goh had claimed in 1995 that students needed to be made aware of the strategic vulnerabilities that Singapore faced and to be taught the skills to survive amid these constraints ("Teach students" 1995). The following year, Goh had claimed that younger Singaporeans were woefully ignorant of recent national history and that their ignorance might lead to their taking peace and prosperity for granted (Goh 1996). In response to these politicians' concerns, NE was launched in order for students to:

- Develop a Singaporean identity, pride and self-respect;
- Understand Singapore's nation-building successes against the odds;
- Understand Singapore's unique developmental challenges, constraints and vulnerabilities; and
- Subscribe to key values such as meritocracy and multiracialism, as well as the will to prevail, in order to ensure Singapore's continued success. (MOE 1997a)

A third major initiative, the *Masterplan for Information Technology in Education* (or the IT Masterplan for short), was launched in 1997. It was an ambitious attempt to incorporate information technology in teaching and learning in all schools, and targeted up to 30 % of curriculum time to be devoted to the use of information technology for all subjects by the year 2002 (MOE 1997b). The Education Ministry subsequently categorised the IT Masterplan as part of the TSLN policy initiative (see Chap. 2).

With the launching of these three policy initiatives within the space of a few months, the stage was set for the publication of the Desired Outcomes of Education at the beginning of 1998. After having circulated a draft version among teachers and school principals in November 1997, the first edition of the document was published in early 1998. In a clear reference to the challenges posed to Singapore by globalisation, some of which had already been outlined a few years earlier by Goh and Lee, the Education Ministry claimed that

Singapore has joined the first league of developed nations and must compete therein. We are in transition to a knowledge-based economy, where creativity, technology and innovation are absolutely critical to growth....But in addition to skills and competencies, Singaporeans must also possess the values and instincts to face up to the non-economic challenges of progress: preserving social cohesion, maintaining rootedness to the nation and grounding sound moral values...

The Desired Outcomes of Education is a product of intensive studies into trends emerging in Singapore, the region and the world today. MOE [the Ministry of Education] undertook this study as part of the Thinking Schools, Learning Nation vision....As we contemplated various scenarios Singapore could find herself in [sic] the 21st century, we delineated a list of skills, values and instincts Singaporeans must have to survive and succeed in a bracing future. (MOE 1998, paras 2, 3)

One sees in this statement clear evidence of the Education Ministry trying to keep abreast of international trends. In this respect, the Ministry was by no means alone, as many other governments attempted to do the same as part of a growing worldwide convergence in policy rhetoric and direction (see for instance, Education Commission 2000). In addition, the Desired Outcomes of Education document was meant to "establish a common purpose for educators, drive our policies and

Table 3.1 Intermediate outcomes of primary education

1998 edition	2009 edition
Be able to distinguish right from wrong	Be able to distinguish right from wrong
Have learnt to share and put others first	*Know their strengths and areas for growth*
Be able to build friendships with others	*Be able to cooperate, share and care for others*
Have a lively curiosity about things	Have a lively curiosity about things
Be able to think for and express themselves	Be able to think for and express themselves *confidently*
Take pride in their work	Take pride in their work
Have cultivated healthy habits	Have healthy habits *and an awareness of the arts*
Love Singapore	*Know and* love Singapore

Sources: MOE (2004, 2010a)
Italics indicate differences between the 1998 and 2009 editions

Table 3.2 Intermediate outcomes of secondary education

1998 edition	2009 edition
Have moral integrity	Have moral integrity
Have care and concern for others	Believe in their abilities *and be able to adapt to change*
Be able to work in teams and value every contribution	Be able to work in teams and *show empathy for others*
Be enterprising and innovative	*Be creative and have an inquiring mind*
Possess a broad-based foundation for further education	*Be able to appreciate diverse views and communicate effectively*
Believe in their ability	*Take responsibility for own learning*
Have an appreciation for aesthetics	*Enjoy physical activities* and appreciate the arts
Know and believe in Singapore	Believe in Singapore *and understand what matters to Singapore*

Sources: MOE (2004, 2010a)
Italics indicate differences between the 1998 and 2009 editions

programs, and allow us to determine how well our education system is doing" (MOE 2010a, p. B-1). Another feature of the document was the segmentation of what were termed "intermediate learning outcomes" across the primary, secondary and junior college (2 or 3 years of pre-university) levels of schooling, along with outcomes for post-secondary students in technical institutes, polytechnics and universities. The idea was for the developmental outcomes to proceed sequentially as students progressed through the school system (MOE 2010a, p. B-1). A specific set of outcomes was listed as well for "potential leaders" (MOE 2004).

An examination of Tables 3.1, 3.2, 3.3 and 3.4 reveals a degree of continuity between earlier official statements (mentioned in the previous section of this chapter) about the objectives of education in Singapore and the outcomes listed in the 1998 document. Also, as mentioned earlier in this chapter, many of these values are unobjectionable and would find a place in practically every country's Ministry of Education policy objectives. At the same time, there are clear attempts to incorporate key elements of TSLN and NE within the document.

Table 3.3 Intermediate outcomes of junior college education

1998 edition	2009 edition
Be resilient and resolute	*No intermediate outcomes of junior college*
Have a sound sense of social responsibility	*education*
Understand what it takes to inspire and motivate others	
Have an entrepreneurial and creative spirit	
Be able to think independently and creatively	
Strive for excellence	
Have a zest for life	
Understand what it takes to lead Singapore	

Sources: MOE (2004, 2010a)
Italics indicate differences between the 1998 and 2009 editions

Table 3.4 Outcomes of post-secondary and tertiary students

1998 edition	2009 edition
Be morally upright, be culturally rooted yet understanding and respecting differences, be responsible to family, community and country	*Have moral courage to stand up for what is right*
Believe in our principles of multiracialism and meritocracy, appreciate the national constraints but see the opportunities	*Be able to collaborate across cultures and be socially responsible*
Be constituents of a gracious society	*Pursue a healthy lifestyle and have an appreciation for aesthetics*
Be willing to strive, take pride in work, value working with others	*Be purposeful in pursuit of excellence*
Be able to think, reason and deal confidently with the future, have courage and conviction in facing adversity	Be able to think *critically and communicate persuasively*
Be able to seek, process and apply knowledge	*Be resilient in the face of adversity*
Be innovative – have a spirit of continual improvement, a lifelong habit of learning and an enterprising spirit in undertakings	Be innovative and enterprising
Think global, but be rooted to Singapore	Be proud to be Singaporeans and understand Singapore in relation to the world

Sources: MOE (2004, 2010a)
Italics indicate differences between the 1998 and 2009 editions

Another point of historical continuity in the 1998 document occurred in the Ministry's statement that

> …it is what our teachers do in the classroom and what our principals do in the schools that will determine how far we can succeed with these outcomes. MOE is committed to giving every support to schools to enable them to achieve these outcomes.…parents and the public have their part to play as well. (MOE 1998, para 6)

This statement echoes the 1970 assertion (mentioned in the previous section of this chapter) that schools needed community participation in order better to

Table 3.5 Desired outcomes of pre-school education

Pre-school education 2000 edition	Primary education 1998 edition
Know what is right and what is wrong	Be able to distinguish right from wrong
Be willing to share and take turns with others	Have learnt to share and put others first
Be able to relate with others	Be able to build friendships with others
Be curious and able to explore	Have a lively curiosity about things
Be able to listen and speak with understanding	Be able to think for and express themselves
Be comfortable and happy with themselves	Take pride in their work
Have developed physical coordination and healthy habits	Have cultivated healthy habits
Love their family, friends, teachers and kindergarten	Love Singapore

Sources: MOE (2004, 2011)

accomplish their objectives. Accordingly, the Ministry set up an advisory council called COMPASS (short for Community and parents in support of schools) in December 1998. This council, which was chaired by a senior politician in the Ministry, was supposed to promote greater home-school-community collaborations in a common pursuit of the Desired Outcomes of Education (MOE 2000b). For the first time, the term "stakeholders" came into common use in Singapore education. The COMPASS secretariat assigned each of the stakeholder groups – students, parents/grandparents, teachers, principals, the MOE headquarters, wider community, business/industry and alumni associations – specific roles to play in partnership with other groups.

In a follow-up attempt to assure consistency of purpose across the whole spectrum of schooling, the Education Ministry published the Desired Outcomes of Pre-School Education 2 years later in 2000. These outcomes, listed in Table 3.5, were clearly meant to be closely aligned to the Intermediate Outcomes for Primary Education. However, in the case of pre-school education, the outcomes are perhaps less binding because the Ministry is much less interventionist in curriculum matters in a sector dominated by a wide variety of private operators.

A further attempt to entrench the status of the Desired Outcomes of Education and to ensure that all schools took them seriously came in the form of the School Excellence Model (SEM), which was a quality assurance model introduced to all schools in 2000. The model was meant to help schools appraise their own performance in various areas of school processes and student outcomes (MOE 2000a). A cursory glance at the various processes and outcomes reveals evidence of the Desired Outcomes of Education, such as aesthetic development, a healthy lifestyle, moral integrity and national identity. Each school is supposed to subject itself every 6 years or so to validation of its internal quality assurance exercise by an external team headed by staff from the Ministry's School Appraisal Branch. Part of the SEM involves the awarding of a panoply of awards, such as Achievement Awards, Development Awards, Sustained Achievement Awards, Best Practice Awards, that recognise achievement in areas such as aesthetics, sports, physical health and character development.

In retrospect, it is easy to see how the entire exercise of formalising the Desired Outcomes of Education as a common guide for all schools as well as for evaluating schools was part of a wider government exercise to revamp the public service. The exercise, known as Public Service for the twenty-first Century, or PS21 for short, had been launched in 1995, just 2 years before the Outcomes were. It was meant to "inculcate an attitude of continuous improvement in the Public Service" (Public Service Division 2007, para 2). Part of PS21 involved "having robust systems and processes within organizations to ensure efficiency, effectiveness and sustainability" (Public Service Division 2007, para 4). This meant the overnight mushrooming of mission and vision statements, as well as quality assurance mechanisms, across all departments in various Ministries and statutory boards. For its part, the Education Ministry issued an Education Service Mission Statement, *Moulding the future of the nation*, in October 1996. The Ministry claimed that this Mission Statement represented its "manifesto" or "corporate philosophy" (MOE 1996a, para 13). The Mission Statement included skills, knowledge and values – for instance, taking pride in work, flexibility, resolve and confidence to stand together as one people, to overcome threats and challenges – that would be included a year later in the Desired Outcomes of Education (MOE 1996b, paras 4, 5, 6). Before long, the advent of the Mission Statement and the Desired Outcomes of Education had spawned a proliferation of mission and vision statements, many of which revolved around a few of the Desired Outcomes of Education, in all schools.

Revisiting the Desired Outcomes of Education; Twenty-First Century Competencies

As the first decade of the twenty-first century wore on, the frenetic pace of education reform showed little signs of slowing down. For instance, in 2003 one of the Desired Outcomes of Education, innovation and enterprise, was a focus of attention by Ministry officials and the schools. Two years later, the Teach Less, Learn More (TLLM) movement was launched as part of the TSLN vision in a bid further to engage learners and to prepare them for life. During the decade, a variety of new specialised independent schools were established and a few pre-existing prestigious schools were allowed to experiment with curricula and assessment as part of what Education Ministry officials trumpeted as the beginnings of a more diverse education landscape (MOE 2010a; also see Chap. 1).

In 2008 yet another acronym, C2015, an abbreviated form of Curriculum 2015, came into being (Ministry of Education 2008) (also see Chaps. 2 and 14). C2015 represented a Ministry attempt to relook curriculum, pedagogy and assessment. This acronym was followed in 2009 by 21CC, short for twenty-first century competencies. In formulating 21CC, the Ministry stated that "[w]hile Singapore has strong academic standards in math, science and literacy, we could do better in developing soft skills and competencies such as critical thinking and creativity among our students" (MOE 2010a, p. 9). This statement was a tacit acknowledgement that a

Table 3.6 Outcomes for potential community, business or professional leaders

1998 edition	2009 edition
Be committed to improving society	*No outcomes for potential leaders*
Be proactive in surmounting our constraints	
Have compassion towards others	
Be able to inspire, motivate and draw out the best from others	
Be able to chart our destiny and lead	
Be able to forge breakthroughs in a knowledge-based economy	
Be creative and imaginative	
Have the tenacity to fight against the odds and not quit	

Sources: MOE (2004, 2010a)
Italics indicate differences between the 1998 and 2009 editions

decade of TSLN had yet to bear full fruit. With the advent of 21CC, the original Desired Outcomes were revised in several ways. First, the junior college intermediate outcomes were removed (see Table 3.3), as were the outcomes for potential community, business or professional leaders (see Table 3.6). Secondly, there was tweaking of the primary and secondary intermediate outcomes in part to strengthen aspects related to self-awareness and interpersonal relationships (see Tables 3.1 and 3.2). Thirdly, the various Desired Outcomes were categorised into four headings – a confident person, a self-directed learner, an active contributor and a concerned citizen. These four headings served as pillars for the development of a series of competencies deemed essential for survival in a globalised twenty-first century world characterised as being "fast-changing and highly-connected" (MOE 2010b, para 1). Among the competencies were:

- Civic literacy, global awareness and cross-cultural skills;
- Critical and inventive thinking;
- Information and communication skills;
- Social and emotional competencies: self-awareness, self-management, social awareness, relationship management and responsible decision-making;
- Core values: respect, responsibility, integrity, care, resilience and harmony. (MOE 2010b, Diagram 1)

As was the case with the earlier edition of the Desired Outcomes of Education, the 21CC rhetoric is remarkably similar to policy initiatives in other countries like the UK and Australia as various governments borrow ideas internationally in a seemingly endless quest for that one magical formula for reforming education (see for instance Department for Education 2011).

How Desirable Are the Desired Outcomes of Education?

The Desired Outcomes of Education documents of 1998 and 2009 represented impressive attempts by the Education Ministry to lay out a common approach for guiding education policies and programmes and for evaluating these policies and programmes. However, their introduction left several fundamental questions unanswered. The first of these concerns equality and equity issues. The documents offer the egalitarian promise of equal outcomes for all students. However, the reality is that this promise might prove rather elusive in an education system characterised by competitive high-stakes national examinations that serve as gatekeepers and sorting devices (see Chap. 2). The active implementation of various forms of tracking or streaming at both primary and secondary levels since 1979 and 1980 respectively has meant the segregation of students into different paths with different curricular offerings (also see Chap. 2). These offerings have implications for students' subsequent chances of educational advancement to higher levels of schooling (also see Chaps. 2 and 5). The practice of streaming or tracking is consistent with founding Prime Minister Lee's desire for the education system to produce a "pyramidal structure" consisting of three strata: "top leaders," "good executives" and a "well-disciplined and highly civic-conscious broad mass" (Lee 1966, pp. 10, 12, 13; also see Chap. 5).

After more than three decades of streaming, there is research evidence of prejudice on the part of students in faster-paced streams, and teachers as well, towards students in slower-paced streams (see for instance, Kang 2004; Tan and Ho 2001). Under this sort of regime, can it be reasonably possible for all students to leave schools with equal outcomes? Or are schools instead aiming for all students to leave schools with a common basic minimum level of all the Desired Outcomes, with different students emerging with differing quantities, as it were, of each of the Outcomes?

These questions have become more pressing as the Education Ministry provides what it terms a more diverse education landscape. As the school system grows ever more segmented, what extent of equality or equity of distribution is there for various students to attain the Desired Outcomes? Furthermore, the intensification of inter-school competition since the early 1990s as manifested for instance in the publication of annual league tables has been exacerbated somewhat by the introduction of the SEM in 2000. There is a substantial amount of anecdotal evidence of schools narrowing their curricular and co-curricular offerings in order to boost their chances of securing the various awards each year (Tan 2008). The competition has also fuelled intense inter-school rivalry in terms of attracting students who are deemed as potential 'assets' in terms of academic and non-academic achievement (see for instance, Tan 2010). Amid all the competition, there is anecdotal evidence of imbalances in ethnic and social class representation across schools (Tan 2010). These imbalances throw up their own set of questions, such as whether students will "be able to collaborate across cultures" if they have hardly any opportunities to mix with students from different ethnic backgrounds during their schooling years (see for instance, Ramani 2012).

The introduction of TSLN has shown little evidence of cooling down the feverish quest among many parents and students for examination success. If anything, the introduction of streaming has raised the stakes and contributed to the mushrooming of a private tutoring industry. Academics have reported that after a decade of TSLN, traditional classroom pedagogies still predominate in Singapore classrooms

(Curdt-Christiansen and Silver 2012; Hogan et al., as cited in Dimmock and Goh 2011; also see Chaps. 8 and 9). The persistence of these pedagogies points to the second question, namely, that of whether the various stakeholders in education, who are supposed to work in partnership to attain the Desired Outcomes of Education, do in fact, subscribe to the Outcomes. It might be conceivable for many parents, for instance, to voice their support for Desired Outcomes such as having a lively curiosity for things, but to be openly encouraging their child to engage in rote learning and repeated practice of sample examination papers in order to attain examination success. Likewise, many school principals might face dilemmas in balancing the need to ensure a balanced education for their students with the need to compete against other schools in academic and non-academic areas in order to secure their personal and schools' prestige.

A final question is related to whether different stakeholders are equally placed to support or to attain the Desired Outcomes of Education. It is easy to envisage middle-class parents, with superior financial and material resources, playing a more active role to secure the Outcomes, as well as educational success, for their children. Likewise, prestigious schools, with the advantages of superior student intakes, reputations and funding, are better placed than struggling schools could be to develop Desired Outcomes. However, at the other end of the spectrum, working class Malay[2] youths struggle within social structures that are inimical to high educational aspirations (Fadzli 2012).

Conclusion

This chapter has traced the evolution of the 1998 and 2009 editions of the Desired Outcomes of Education. It has shown how many of the Desired Outcomes are not exceptional to Singapore. At the same time, many of them had been enunciated over the past four decades by previous policymakers. The Desired Outcomes of Education documents represented a bold attempt by the Education Ministry to lay down clear guidelines for policies and school programmes and also for the evaluation of these policies and programmes. The guidelines were segmented according to different levels of schooling on the premise that the process of Desired Outcome development would be sequential as students progressed through their schooling years. The evaluation came in the form of the School Excellence Model that was introduced in 2000, 2 years after the publication of the first edition of the Desired Outcomes of Education. Overall, the documents showed evidence of the Ministry of Education's attempts to prepare for the political, social and economic challenges posed to Singapore by globalisation.

---

[2] The educational problems facing ethnic Malays, who constitute about 13.4 % of Singapore's population, have been well documented (see for instance, Tan 1997). They are over-represented in the slowest-paced streams or tracks at the primary and secondary levels and under-represented in local universities and the professional and managerial sectors of the workforce.

The publication of the Desired Outcomes of Education coincided with the launching of the vision of Thinking Schools, Learning Nation (TSLN) and the policy initiatives of National Education and the Masterplan for Information Technology in Education in 1997. In addition, the Desired Outcomes of Education document could also be viewed as part of the Singapore government's attempt in the mid-1990s to revamp the Public Service, in part by laying out clear vision and mission statements for each government department. The strength of the document was given a symbolic boost with the inauguration of the COMPASS Secretariat in 1998 in order to foster community partnerships in support of the Desired Outcomes. The pace of education reform then continued at a relentless pace in the first decade of the twenty-first century, with the eventual publication of the 2nd edition of the document.

The chapter has also discussed how the Desired Outcomes of Education document fails to answer fundamental questions. These questions relate, firstly, to whether it is desirable or even possible for all students to attain equal amounts of these Desired Outcomes. Secondly, there is the question of whether various stakeholders do in fact support the Desired Outcomes. Lastly, the official rhetoric leaves unanswered the question of whether various stakeholders are equally well-placed to support or to attain the Desired Outcomes. In short, the chapter suggests that certain structural features of the education system, as well as other education policy initiatives, form the backdrop against which the Desired Outcomes of Education need to be imbued in students. Far from being the egalitarian document that it appears to be at first glance, it instead raises crucial far-reaching issues of equality and equity in Singapore's education system.

This chapter illustrates how a government, accustomed to exercising tight centralised control of its education system, and perennially preoccupied with securing economic competitiveness and social cohesion, has attempted to concretise its aspirations in the form of a guiding document for all education policies and programmes. It has also tried to ensure schools' adherence to the ideals espoused in the document by incorporating these ideals within a school quality assurance framework. The chapter is instructive for the many other governments worldwide who are similarly concerned with how best to grapple with the challenges posed by globalisation. While it points out the admirable attempts to align policy with practice, it also highlights the need to address wider issues related to equality and equity.

References

Curdt-Christiansen, X. L., & Silver, R. E. (2012). Educational reforms, cultural clashes and classroom practices. *Cambridge Journal of Education, 42*, 141–161.

Department for Education. (2011). *The framework for the national curriculum: A report by the expert panel for the national curriculum review*. Retrieved 18 Jan 2012, from http://www.education.gov.uk/publications

Dimmock, C., & Goh, J. W. P. (2011). Transformative pedagogy, leadership and school organisation for the twenty-first-century knowledge-based economy: The case of Singapore. *School Leadership and Management, 31*(3), 215–234.

Doraisamy, T. (Ed.). (1969). *150 years of education in Singapore*. Singapore: Teachers' Training College.

Drucker, P. (1993). *Post-capitalist society*. New York: Harper Business.

Education Commission. (2000). *Review of education system reform proposals: Consultation document*. Hong Kong: Author.

Fadzli, B. A. (2012). Taking the gravel road: Educational aspirations of working class Malay youths. *Asian Journal of Social Science, 40*, 153–173.

Goh, K. S. (1979). *Report on the ministry of education*. Singapore: Ministry of Education.

Goh, C. T. (1996). Prepare our children for the new century: Teach them well. In J. Tan, S. Gopinathan, & W. K. Ho (Eds.), *Education in Singapore: A book of readings* (pp. 423–491). Singapore: Prentice Hall.

Government of Singapore. (1991). *The next lap*. Singapore: Times Editions.

Kang, T. (2004). Schools and post-secondary aspirations among female Chinese, Malay and Indian Normal Stream students. In A. E. Lai (Ed.), *Beyond rituals and riots: Ethnic pluralism and social cohesion in Singapore* (pp. 114–145). Singapore: Eastern Universities Press.

Lee, K. Y. (1966). *New bearings in our education system*. Singapore: Ministry of Culture.

Lee, K. Y. (1996). Picking up the gauntlet: Will Singapore survive Lee Kuan Yew? *Speeches, 20*(3), 23–33.

Marshall, R., & Tucker, M. (1992). *Thinking for a living: Education and the wealth of nations*. New York: Basic Books.

Ministry of Education. (1996a). *Speech by Mr Lee Yock Suan, Minister for Education, at the promotion ceremony and launch of the Education Service Mission Statement on 28 Oct 96 at Shangri-La Hotel, Island Ballroom at 9.30am*. Retrieved 11 June 2012, from http://www.moe.gov.sg/media/press/1996/st00396.htm

Ministry of Education. (1996b). The Singapore education service. Retrieved 11 June 2012, from http://www.moe.gov.sg/media/press/1996/st00296.htm

Ministry of Education. (1997a). *Launch of national education*. Singapore: Author.

Ministry of Education. (1997b). *Towards thinking schools*. Singapore: Author.

Ministry of Education. (1998). *Perspective: The desired outcomes of education*. Retrieved 29 June 2011, from http://www1.moe.edu.sg/contact/vol14/web/pers.htm

Ministry of Education. (2000a). *The school excellence model: A guide*. Singapore: Author.

Ministry of Education. (2000b). *Stakeholders in education*. Singapore: COMPASS Secretariat.

Ministry of Education. (2004). *Desired outcomes of education*. Retrieved 16 Aug 2011, from http://www3.moe.edu.sg/corporate/desired_outcomes4.htm

Ministry of Education. (2008). *Recent developments in Singapore's education system: Gearing up for 2015*. Retrieved 29 June 2011, from www.eduweb.vic.gov.au/edulibrary/public/commrel/events/ield/singaporecasestudy.pdf

Ministry of Education. (2010a). *Building a national education system for the 21st century: The Singapore experience*. Retrieved 29 June 2011, from http://www.edu.gov.on.ca/bb4e/Singapore_CaseStudy2010.pdf

Ministry of Education. (2010b). *MOE to enhance learning of 21st century competencies and strengthen art, music and physical education*. Retrieved 29 June2011, from http://www.moe.gov.sg/media/press/2010/03/moe-to-enhance-learning-of-21s.php

Ministry of Education. (2011). *Pre-school education*. Retrieved 29 June 2011, from http://www.moe.gov.sg/education/preschool

Ministry of Trade & Industry. (1986). *The Singapore economy: New directions*. Singapore: Author.

Ministry of Trade & Industry. (1991). *The strategic economic plan: Towards a developed nation*. Singapore: Author.

Narrower income gap but this may widen again. (1993, August 16). *The Straits Times*, p. 25.

Ong, T. C. (1979). *Report on moral education*. Singapore: Ministry of Education.

People's Action Party. (1959). *The tasks ahead: PAP's first five-year plan 1959–1964 part 2*. Singapore: Petir.

Public Service Division. (2007). PS21 movement. Retrieved 8 June 2012, from http://www.psd.gov.sg/PublicServiceRole/BuildCapacity/Movement/

Ramani, V. (2012, June 6). Xenophobia, or is it more? *Today*, p. 25.

Reich, R. B. (1992). *The work of nations: Preparing ourselves for 21st century capitalism*. New York: Vintage Books.

State of Singapore. (1959). *Ministry of education annual report 1959*. Singapore: Government Printer.

Tan, P. B. (1970). *Education in Singapore*. Singapore: Educational Publications Bureau, Ministry of Education Singapore.

Tan, J. (1997). Improving Malay educational achievement in Singapore: Problems and policies. *Asia Pacific Journal of Education, 17*, 41–57.

Tan, J. (2008). The marketisation of education in Singapore. In J. Tan & P. T. Ng (Eds.), *Thinking schools, learning nation: Contemporary issues and challenges* (pp. 19–38). Singapore: Prentice Hall.

Tan, J. (2010). Education in Singapore: Sorting them out? In T. Chong (Ed.), *Management of success: Singapore revisited* (pp. 288–308). Singapore: Institute of Southeast Asian Studies.

Tan, J., & Ho, B. T. (2001). 'A' levels or a polytechnic diploma? Malay students' choices of post-secondary options. In J. Tan, S. Gopinathan, & W. K. Ho (Eds.), *Challenges facing the Singapore education system today* (pp. 207–223). Singapore: Prentice Hall.

Teach students to live with S'pore's constraints: PM. (1995, March 5). *The Straits Times*, p. 1.

Wong, H. K. (1974). *Educational innovation in Singapore (Experiments and Innovations in Education No. 9)*. Paris: The Unesco Press.

Chapter 4
A Vision of Schooling for the Twenty-First Century: Thinking Schools and Learning Nation

Aaron Koh

Singapore is a city of imaginations. This 'imagination' does not refer to common notions of wishful thinking and fantasy in the everyday imagining. Instead, what I am alluding to is a purposeful driven *national* imagination orchestrated at the level of the state that explores possibilities that would "move beyond impasses and absences, even beyond inherited ways of thinking" (Kenway and Fahey 2009, p. 4).

Indeed, Singapore has definitely moved beyond its impasses in terms of nation building: from a fishing village it has flourished into a global city; from a failed venture with the Malaysian state, it had overcome inherited ways of thinking from critics that said Singapore wouldn't make it because the odds for nationhood were against it. But, Singapore's imagination coupled with its will to succeed as a nation has proven otherwise. Its imaginary, however, does not stop there; Singapore is in a continuous search for new narratives to fuel its imagination. Singapore is of course not alone in the enterprise of imaginings. All countries in fact create fictions, imaginings, and national narratives. Queensland, Australia, for example, imagines itself to be a "Smart State" to re-position itself for the knowledge economy (Hay and Kapitzke 2009) and most recently in the State of the Union Address in 2011, President Obama articulates his visions of education and economics with a larger vision of meeting the needs of global capitalism (Collins 2012).

This chapter is devoted to an analysis of another kind of imagination that takes place in the domain of "education" and "schooling" in Singapore. Yet the domain of what I call its "educational imagining" is symbiotically related to its national imaginaries as I will argue later. I draw on the work of the Canadian philosopher, Charles Taylor (2004) and his notion of "social imaginary" to frame Singapore's educational imagination with specific reference to the "Thinking School, Learning Nation" (hereafter TSLN) education policy that has been instrumental for a series of education reforms that took place since 1997. The TSLN policy did not emerge

A. Koh (✉)
National Institute of Education, Nanyang Technological University, Singapore
e-mail: aaron.koh@nie.edu.sg

Z. Deng et al. (eds.), *Globalization and the Singapore Curriculum: From Policy to Classroom*, Education Innovation Series, DOI 10.1007/978-981-4451-57-4_4,
© Springer Science+Business Media Singapore 2013

out of a clean slate; it had a precursor (in)text(uality) shaped from a new vision of schooling first articulated by Singapore's second Prime Minister Goh Chok Tong when he delivered the keynote speech, "Shaping our future: Thinking Schools, Learning Nation" at the opening of the 7th International Conference on Thinking (see Chaps. 2 and 3).

While the ideological function of education for nation building and subject formation is by now a familiar and undisputed thesis in the literature of Singapore's education (Hill and Lian 1995; Gopinathan 2009; Koh 2010), what is significant about the TSLN policy is that the discourse of globalization first entered "the social imaginary" of its educational imagining when the TSLN vision of schooling was articulated. This vision deploys specific discourses that construct new narratives that pave the way for educational change. While I am aware that policy texts are amenable to "interpretations of interpretations" (Rizvi and Kemmis 1987, cited in Ball 1994, p. 17), my aim in this chapter is to unpack the discourses in the TSLN policy that are deployed to construct a new educational imaginary for Singapore.

To achieve this, I work with two sets of toolkit in the chapter: one conceptual and the other analytical, which is how the chapter is also organized. The conceptual section draws on Taylor's notion of social imaginary to understand Singapore's national imaginary and its perpetual renovation due to the shifting sands of capitalism and vagaries of globalization (Chong 2010b). This contextual understanding is necessary to make way for the argument that the TSLN policy is the embodiment of Singapore's social imaginary used by the government to speak to its subjects about the need to usher in a new paradigm of educational imagining for Singapore at a time when "globalization" was an emerging discourse afloat in the global and local social imaginaries. Drawing on Norman Fairclough's (1989) model of critical discourse analysis, the second section proceeds to analyze the discourses used to construct preferred ways of schooling and subjectivities that speaks to its national imaginary.

Singapore's Social Imaginary and Its Emergent (National) Imaginaries

To develop my analysis of the nexus between Singapore's social imaginary and the utility of the ideological state apparatus of TSLN policy for subject construction and nation building, I turn to Charles Taylor's (2004) idea of social imaginary as a conceptual resource to understand Singapore's national imagination. I am using "national imagination" as opposed to Taylor's "social imaginary" to signal to the well scripted hegemonic social imaginaries propagated by the PAP government. I will take up this point later after providing a basic definition of "social imaginary".

Taylor (2004) defines "social imaginary" as "the way people imagine their social existence, how they fit together with others, how things go on between them and their fellows, the expectations that are normally met, and the deeper normative notions and images that underlies these expectations [p. 23]". A core conceptual element central to this definition is the power of *imagination* and how imagination, in all its embodiments, underpins people's "social imaginary".

He goes on to explain that his use of "imaginary" refers to the way ordinary people imagine their social surroundings aided by images, stories and legends. He dismisses any suggestion of a heavily theorized notion of "imaginary" that would exclude, but a "social imaginary" that will have a wider reach. Here Taylor seems to imply that the imaginary has the utility of reaching and *unifying* the masses when he says that "the social imaginary is …shared by large groups of people, if not the whole society" (p. 23). There is also the suggestion that the imaginary can be mobilized as a resource to promote "common practices and a widely shared sense of legitimacy [p. 23]".

For a social imaginary to have currency and developed into a hegemonic social practice, disparate imaginations won't do; instead, what is required is a *collective* imagination that is given coherence and identity so that people can relate to and identify with this imagination. In our contemporary world, this is made possible by the power of mass media, new social media (such as YouTube, facebook, blogs, twitter and etc.), popular culture and also the work of narratives, myths, parables, stories, images and legends (Rizvi and Lingard 2010). Taylor's idea of social imaginary conceptually strikes a familiarity to the seminal work of Benedict Anderson (1991) on imagined communities, where he argues that the media such as novel and newspaper were instrumental in disseminating the idea of the nation in medieval Europe. In similar ways, contemporary media and mediascapes are powerful conduits and platforms for manufacturing and circulating dominant social imaginaries.

Social imaginaries are therefore not free-floating; their legitimacy are perpetuated, amplified and reified to become common sense ideology because the media circulates and mystify them as regimes of truth. Fazal Rizvi (2011) gives the example of the popular appeal of "the clash of civilization" thesis which remains a powerful social imaginary circulating in our contemporary world. This imaginary is sustained because of the "continuing work on political myths that have long existed, myths to which Edward Said refers collectively as "Orientalism" [pp. 230–231]". The same can also be said of the way political myths are invoked to construct Singapore's national imaginaries.

The Singapore government mobilizes the fragile birth of Singapore's nationhood to construct an official narrative known as the Singapore story (see also Chaps. 5 and 10). The genesis of this story was first narrated by Lee Kuan Yew (1998) himself in his memoir, but it has since been narrated by others as an official narrative about Singapore's nation building. Terence Chong (2010a), for example, gives a crisp account of the story which begins with the "moment of anguish" when Singapore was jettisoned by the Malaysian state left to overcome the challenges of mass housing, high unemployment and an uncertain future. Like all stories with moral intent, the Singapore story ends with a triumphant account of how through sheer determination and good governance, the People's Action Party (PAP) led Singapore to overcome all the odds and challenges of nation building to become what it is today: from third world to first. And like all stories, the Singapore story is not without a theme. The theme, which is also strongly didactic, is about observing the fundamentals that have led to Singapore's success; that is, the national ethos and values of hard-work, social/self discipline, guided by a sense of pragmatic realism that places its national economy above everything else because Singapore's success is premised on how well its economy performs.

The Singapore story remains in circulation in its national imaginary and continues to be heard and told in political speeches, national campaigns, school textbooks and curriculum until most recently it took the life in the form of a memoir intertwining the story of the founding of Singapore with the life history of Lee Kuan Yew as the founding father. *The Singapore Story: Memoirs of Lee Kuan Yew* (1998) has truly become the embodiment of Singapore's social imaginary. It uses the literary form to construct a shared, 'legitimate' story about Singapore's tumultuous times as an emergent nation. Like all literary texts, a multiplicity of readings as well as oppositional readings can be constructed out of the Singapore story. On one hand, the Singapore story in Lee's memoir can be read as a purposeful attempt to fuel Singapore's national imagination with "the regime of authenticity", that is, "to install timeless values within the idea of the nation" – a necessary political project to anchor Singapore against the ferocious stream of capitalism and modernity (Chong 2010b, p. 504).

Yao Souchou (2007), on the other hand, offers an oppositional reading. He re/interprets the Singapore story as an ideological narrative served to evoke the sentiments of trauma to reveal "the psychological tenor of the State actions: its moralistic bend and anxious posturing, its heightened imagining of social and economic doom, and its 'over-responses' to crises" (p. 39). This is not all to the effect *and* affect of the story telling; I argue that it infects its national imaginary and its subjects with state generated anxiety designed also to discipline and shape their conduct. The social imaginary of Singapore can therefore be said to reach deep into the psychic and social discipline of the Singapore body politic with a view to reproduce and cultivate subjectivities that are bound by national ethos and values. More importantly, I argue that the work of national imaginations, for it to have wider reach and become hegemonic, requires the enlistment of state ideological apparatus such as education and schooling to experiment and reproduce specific subjectivities for Singapore and its economy. There are no better mechanisms to f(ill)uel Singapore's imagination than to turn to the *disciplinary site of schooling*.

In the next section, the TSLN policy is taken up as an example of Singapore's national imaginary embodied as an educational imagination – a vision of schooling for the twenty-first century. I begin with a descriptive account of the TSLN policy by drawing attention to the context (i.e. how the policy came about), the premises (i.e. why such a policy is needed) and its "illocutionary intent" (Luke and Wood 2009, p. 197) (i.e. what the policy sets out to do).

Singapore's Educational Imagination Through "Thinking Schools, Learning Nation"

Ostensibly, the term "educational imagination" suggests "an imagined future state of affairs" in the way an education system is envisioned (Rizvi and Lingard 2010, p. 5). Singapore's educational imagination is however much more than this. It is an ideological and teleological project motivated by the interest of its economy and for subject formation. As I have argued earlier, its educational imagination must be understood as an ideological state apparatus for materializing its national imagination. My analysis of the TSLN policy will show, the text draws on emergent discourses about a new social imaginary of economic realities and global conditions to argue for a specific trajectory of educational change.

There is a persuasive logic to its educational imagination, also evident in the conception of the TSLN policy. Taylor et al. (1997) have argued that "there is always a prior history of significant events, a particular ideological and political climate, a social and economic context (p. 16)". In other words, the form and content of educational change are invariably driven by a (global) desired outcome to address the (local) needs and/or problems of the larger society (Taylor et al. 1997). The articulation of the TSLN policy follows this similar logic. It is conceived because of a perceived "global future" that is questioning the relevance of the state of education in Singapore.

In this regard, the context for the TSLN policy making is primarily in response to a "global future" that is characterized by intense competition, where it is argued "knowledge and innovation" will be absolutely essential if countries want to keep up. Because of these reasons, the PM argues that "education and training are central to how nations will fare in this future" (Goh 1997, p. 1). Goh alludes to another context for the formulation of TSLN policy, which is gleaned from a global reassessment of other education systems, namely the United States, the U.K. and Japan. He admitted to the need for "policy borrowing" when he said that "as we prepare for the future, we will draw valuable lessons from how the US, Japan and other nations reform their educational systems to meet their needs" and "…learn and adapt from foreign experiments" (p. 2).

That, however, is the "global" context that motivated the articulation of the TSLN policy. There is an unspoken "local" context problematized as the culture of rote learning endemic in Singapore's education system. Although students in Singapore have achieved first place in public and international Mathematics and Science Olympiads, such achievements are attributed to the "spoon-feeding" culture and well trained "exam-smart" students of its education system. This myth of the passive learner, exam-smart students has, however, been challenged in educational research (See Watkins and Bigg (2001) and Chan and Rao (2009)). Classroom documented research has further revealed that Asian classrooms combines teacher-centered and student-centered learning that benefits the learner (Mok 2006). Yet in the TSLN reform, it is the rhetoric of preparing and training Singaporeans students for the new economy that holds sway. This is why under the TSLN policy, "creative and critical thinking" becomes a core curriculum initiative in Singapore schools. This "unspoken" context of exam-smart, passive Singapore students must be taken into account as the micro history of an education system that is attempting to undo things.

There are three curriculum priorities that constitute the TSLN policy. The TSLN policy prioritizes the inclusion of three core curriculum areas that includes Critical Thinking, using IT in the classroom for teaching and learning, and National Education. Critical Thinking is not taught as a stand-alone subject, but infused in all subject areas, whereas the use of IT in the classroom is mandatory (See Baildon and Sim (2009) and Lim (2007) for sampler accounts of the uptake and constraints of teaching Critical Thinking and the integration of ICT in Singapore classrooms). Teachers are expected to conduct 30 % of their lessons using IT. The use of IT in teaching and learning has been made possible under the IT Masterplan which saw the provision of "soft" and "hardware" in all schools. Lastly, National Education (NE) is citizenship education in a new name, which aims to cultivate a strong sense of belonging and national identity.

The underlying premise for the TSLN policy is that the old industrial model of schooling was for an old economy. It was time for change. As Kress (2000) has succinctly argued, "in periods of relative social and economic stability, it is possible to see the curriculum as a means for cultural reproduction" (p. 133), where education works to reproduce "the stabilities of well-defined citizenship or equally stable subjectivities as a participant in stable economies" (p. 139). A new globalized economy, however, demands that education systems explore new ways to cultivate dispositions such as creativity, innovativeness, adaptability, while at the same time, coping with these changes comfortably (Kress 2000). This explains the operative trope in the TSLN policy: "thinking" and "learning", which endeavors to promote a culture of thinking in schools and life-long learning to keep up with change.

It is therefore not difficult to see the "illocutionary intent" of the educational imagination of the TSLN policy. It steers the whole education system in a deterministic paradigm of educational change that aims to reproduce subject-citizens who have the "right" skills to go "global" yet with their hearts rooted to "local"/"national" identity, traditions and values. It should not go unnoticed that its deterministic pathway of educational change is however met with overt and tacit resistance. Research has documented the resistance felt by teachers and students who are at the receiving end of the TSLN reform (See for example Liew (2008) and Ng (2004)). But such resistance is treated as mere noise and gets buried by the busyness of the reform. Ultimately, it is the enduring pragmatic realism that guides its educational imagination for as I have argued at the heart of its national imagination is a deep-seated preoccupation of the state of its economy lodged in its social imaginaries.

The Educational Imagination in TSLN:
A Critical Discourse Analysis

Imaginations are symbolic representations that are constituted and packaged as words, images, speech, artifacts and all kinds of multimodal texts. And because imaginations are "symbolic" and "packaged", they are motivated, and therefore ideological. The TSLN policy is an example of an educational imagination packaged as a "speech" that articulates a vision of schooling for the twenty-first century. Normal Fairclough (2001) would name such a text as "discourse driven social change" because the utility of language and discourses is central to the TSLN educational imagining.

In this part of the chapter, I set out to unpack the discourses in the TSLN policy using Critical Discourse Analysis (thereafter, CDA) as an analytical toolkit. It is not within the scope of this chapter to detour into the theoretical origins and concepts of CDA as others have adequately covered these grounds (See for example Wodak and Meyer (2001) and Wodak (2008)) except to make the point that my analytic focus on "discourse/s" has bearing to Foucault's (1984 cited in Wodak 2008, p. 5) notion of discourse because his point that "the production of discourse is at once controlled, selected, organized and canalized in every society" (p. 10) speaks to the educational imagination embodied in the TSLN policy speech. My analysis of the TSLN text will make clear how specific discourses are canalized to construct preferred was of schooling subjectivities vital for Singapore's economy.

Also of relevance to the text analyzed here is the ideological work that discourses do: they represent educational imagination as well as produce particular kinds of subjectivities (Walshaw 2007). This resonates with Foucault's (1972) point that discourses are "practices that systematically form the objects of which they speak… Discourses are not about objects; they do not identify objects, they constitute them and the practice of doing so conceal their own invention" (p. 49).

I set the parameters of my analysis on a selection of analytical categories. This include the analysis of (1) "classification schemes" (Goatly 2000, p. 64) in the first six paragraphs of the text and (2) "discourses" used to construct the education systems in the US, UK and Japan (from paragraphs 7–13) and "representations" of schooling and schooling identities (from paragraphs 17–23). To make sense of the overall analysis presented here, the TSLN policy speech must be read in conjunction with it. However, because of copyright the TSLN policy cannot be reprinted here in its entirety. Instead, the text can be retrieved online from http://www.moe.gov.sg/speeches/1997/020697.htm.

1. Classification schemes: Wor(l)ding the future as "crisis"

The choice of vocabulary in a text classifies things, people and the abstract into categories and sub-groups to construct a representation of the world and its belief system (Goatly 2000). Fairclough (1989) refers to the patterning and wording in a text as "classification schemes" (Goatly 2000, pp. 64–65). These schemes are grouped for patterns of co-occurrence, semantically related lexical items,

Table 4.1 Lexical classification

The twenty-first century
An intensely global *future*
Diminishing barriers
Competition between cities…will be intense
No guarantee
Knowledge and innovation will be absolutely critical
Human innovation
Organised human mastery of technology
Companies and nations organised themselves to generate, show and apply new technologies and ideas…
It will be one of *change*
…increasingly *rapid change*
…*change* as a permanent state
Change will be unpredictable
A *future* of intense competition and shifting competitive advantages
A *future* where technologies and concepts are replaced at an increasing pace
A *future* of *changing* values
A *future* that we cannot really predict
The world today is very different from the world 10 or 20 years ago
Change will occur at even a faster rate
The world in 10 or 20 years times …radically different

denotations and connotative meanings, grammatical metaphors and other distinctive semantic patterns (Fairclough 1989, 2001). My analysis of Goh's speech is drawn to the representation of the "twenty-first century" or "the future" as the "text population" (Talbot 1992, cited in Goatly 2000, p. 64) points semantically to this classification scheme. The lexical items associated with this category are charted above (see Table 4.1).

The inherent "properties" of the "twenty-first century" or "the future" are outlined in this classification scheme. Here, the twenty-first century is presented as intricately related to a borderless world, a competitive economic environment, the use of new technologies, rapid change and innovation. In fact, the intrinsic properties of the future are itemised in the construction of the future. The discourse marker, "first", "second" and "third" discursively lists the twenty-first century as partly actual and partly potential. There is no attempt at exploring this representation of the twenty-first century through a systematic explanation of why, what and how the future is or could be (Fairclough 2000). For example, in the assertion that "no country or region will have permanent advantage" the cause and effect is omitted. The textual effect of such a representation presents the twenty-first century not as a mere conjecture but as 'truth', particularly as this claim to the 'truth' is authenticated by the authority of the Prime Minister himself. Correspondingly, the twenty-first century also demands specific skills and knowledge, and these are also itemised as "knowledge and innovation", the ability to "apply new technologies", to display a "mastery of technology" and to "generate ideas". Indeed, these lexical choices point to the language of new capitalism which Fairclough claims is a new discourse created to capture this new reality (Gee et al. 1996; Fairclough 2000).

Table 4.2 Relational processes

…*it* (referring to the future) (Carrier) will be an *intensely global future* (Attribute), with *diminishing barriers* (Attribute)…
Competition between *cities, countries, sub-regions and regions* (Carrier) will be *intense* (Attribute)
[] *country* or *region* (Carrier) will have *[no] permanent advantages* (Attribute)
There (Carrier) is *no guarantee* (Attribute) that…
…*it* (Carrier) will be one of *change* (Attribute), and *increasingly rapid change* (Attribute)

In the construction of "the future", there are no explicit agents. Instead of attributing the agency to managerial elites or transnational corporations, the agents are nominalized as abstract entities and things, identified as "human innovation", "increasingly rapid change", "mastery of technology" and "competition". Nominalization works to transform a process into a thing or noun (Fairclough 1989, 2000; Goatly 2000, p. 76). For example, instead of attributing "competition" to a specific multinational corporation, 'nouning' the clause "competition between cities, countries, sub-regions will be intense" leaves the agency unclear. There is no specification of who is doing the act of competing. Hence, "competition" becomes a real, material phenomenon of the future.

As well as constructing the future as a real, material phenomenon, what is striking about the construction of the future is the representation of the future as an era of "crisis." The transitivity pattern alludes to this negative construction. According to Halliday's (1994) systemic functional grammar, "transitivity" is a semantic concept that shows us how meaning is represented in a clause. Briefly, Halliday identifies three types of processes that are used to project the experience of the world. These processes are actions (i.e., material processes), states of mind (i.e., mental processes) or simply states of being (i.e., relational processes). In other words, the "wor(l)ding" of text conceptualises and represents the social world, as well as tells us who the participants are and what they are doing to each other. These processes can be further grouped into two broad categories belonging to actional and relational processes (Okta 2001). The former deals mainly with material, mental and verbal processes, whereas the latter establishes a relation between two entities or between an entity and a quality.

My analysis of the transitivity pattern in relation to the construction of "the future" shows predominantly relational processes. For example (Table 4.2).

Significantly, the representation of the future is underscored by the negative connotations of the attribute in the clauses. There is a sense of 'crisis' suggested, brought on by the unpredictability of the future and the vagaries of change. The "overwording" of the lexical item "change" (which occurs six times) and "the future" (used repeatedly five times) further shows a "preoccupation with some aspect of reality – which may indicate that it is a focus of ideological struggle" (Fairclough 1989, p. 115). The overwording foregrounds that change is an inevitable process which will be intrinsic of the future; however, constructing the future as a crisis works ideologically to legitimise the intervention of the government and its managerial role in managing crisis. Politically, generating narratives of national crisis has

Table 4.3 Identifying discourses

Paragraph 8   The Americans …produce highly *creative*, *entrepreneurial* individuals.
Their best schools produce *well-rounded*, *innovative* students…
Their academic institutions and research laboratories …infused with *entrepreneurial spirit*
They have developed *strong links between academia and industry*, society and government

been a form of "governmentality" (Foucault 1979) in the one-party dominated political hegemon of Singapore – a point I alluded to earlier that crisis construction is crucial to Singapore national imagination.

2. Discourses at work

Before articulating his vision of "Thinking Schools, Learning Nation", Goh builds up his case for education change by giving a snapshot of what the US, UK and Japan are doing to their education system. From paragraphs 7–13, there are specific discourses that are drawn upon in his global reassessment of education and later, the conceptualisation of TSLN policy.

First, in relation to the strengths of the American education system, we note that (Table 4.3).

Here, the American education system is infused with an economising discourse that valorises the inter-relations between educational priorities and economic concerns (Ozga 2000). In other words, education is concerned with producing attributes and dispositions that are of service to the economy. The economising agenda is clearly suggested by the tropes of "creative, entrepreneurial individuals", "well-rounded, innovative students", "entrepreneurial spirit", "academic and industry" linkage. These noun phrases, while patently identifying selective attributes and schooling dispositions, also reflect and constitute the language of new capitalism (Gee et al. 1996).

However, despite their strengths, the American education system is cast in a discourse of "crisis". The same can also be said of the UK and Japan. What is striking is that there are no explanations or logical accounts that detail how the crisis comes about. The crisis merely emerges out of nowhere and is treated as a factual occurrence. In the US, the crisis is the result of "the low average levels of literacy and numeracy among the young", the "watered-down curriculum" and "a tyranny of low expectations", whereas in the UK, they are faced with "a drift in standards" nation-wide. For the Japanese it is a case of a conjectural "worry" that its current education system is not keeping up with what is required of the new knowledge-driven industries.

These layering of discourses embody particular ideologies (Fairclough 1989). The crisis discourse on education works ideologically with the discourse of management to legitimatise state intervention and education reform. The overlapping of discourses foregrounds the relevance and efficacy of an education policy that is intertwined with economics and the state. Thus in the US, the agency of education reform is attributed to "President Clinton's Call to Action" for "a bold national plan" that "introduce(s) national standards and national tests" and the provision of the Internet in every classroom. In the UK, it is also "the new Government" that sets the education agenda of "levelling up" and "not levelling down". As for Japan, it is an education policy that looks into "strengthening post-graduate education" and a "revamp" of university education.

Foucault's (1972) insight that discourses are productive as they produce the objects spoken of as real is apparent in the TSLN text. A certain truth about the "crisis" of the economic realities of the world and the necessity to re-align education priorities to meet new economic imperatives is a dominant narrative constructed in the text. As well as constructing regimes of truth, discourses are also fused with power/knowledge which is re-worked to produce discursive effects in 'local' institutional settings and cultural fields. The build-up throughout Goh's speech, from the construction of "the future" as crisis to the global "crisis" of education, has discursive and material effects on the specific education trajectory for the imagination of Singapore's education.

In addition, the discourses have regulatory and disciplinary effects on the formation of specific subjectivities and social identities (Danaher et al. 2000; Foucault 1980). These preferred subjectivities and social identities can be easily mapped out according to classification schemes (as in the previous section) as Goh explains his conceptualization of "Thinking Schools" and "Learning Nation". I have identified these schemes as vision of schooling and schooling identities (Table 4.4).

Table 4.4 Vision of schooling and schooling identities

Vision of schooling	Schooling identities
Learning will not end in the school	The capacity of its people to learn
The task of education must provide core knowledge and skills, and habits of learning	Their imagination
Critical difference that education will make	Ability to seek out new technologies …and apply
Relook education system	Collective capacity to learn
Assessing their strengths and weaknesses	Education and training are central
Place reforms to better prepare for…the future	How people learn and adapt
Total learning environment	Learn continuously throughout their life
Develop future generations	Can think for themselves
Undertaking a fundamental review of its curriculum	Thinking and committed citizens
Develop the creative thinking skills and learning skills required for the future	Capable of making good decisions to keep Singapore vibrant
Cut back on the amount of content knowledge	Teachers and students to spend more time on projects that can develop (creative thinking and learning skills)
Use IT widely to develop communication skills	Retain mastery over the core knowledge and concepts
Strengthen national education	Retain high standards to stretch all our pupils and keep them striving for excellence

(continued)

Table 4.4 (continued)

Vision of schooling	Schooling identities
Develop stronger bonds between pupil and a desire to contribute to something larger than themselves	A passion for learning
Thinking schools must be the crucibles for questioning and searching...to forge this passion for learning among our young	Have the desire and aptitude to continue discovering new knowledge...
Thinking schools will also redefine the role of teachers	The capacity to learn will define excellence in future
Every school must be a model learning organisation	
Teachers and principals will constantly look out for new ideas and practices, and continuously refresh their own knowledge	
Teaching will itself be a learning profession	
Teachers must be given time to reflect, learn and keep up-to-date	
Give more autonomy to schools	
Teachers and principals can devise their own solutions to problems	
Thinking schools will be sites of learning for everyone	
Schools will provide lessons on how policies are working on the ground, and give feedback on whether policies need to be changed	
Knowledge spiralling up and down will be a defining feature of education for the future	

By charting out the lexical resources and classifying them into schemes, we can see the way in which discourses are institutionalised to produce and construct subject-positions within the disciplinary boundary of the school and education policy. From the analysis, not only the preferred schooling identities are projected in Singapore's educational imagining but also what constitutes schooling, and the professional identities of teachers are defined and imbricated in the global discourses on economic change and education reform.

Conclusion

Singapore never runs out of resources for its imagination. Its imagination is necessary for orienting the course of its nation-building project which is on-going. This is why it will always be in search of new narratives for its social imagination. While the Singapore story remains sedimented as a historical resource for its national imaginary, the format and content of crises construction will be in perpetual renovation contingent on the problem the political hegemon wants to address at a historical moment. However, what remains a preoccupation in its national imaginary is its economy, which is zealously guarded.

Not unrelated to Singapore's national imagination is the way the ideological state apparatus of schooling is also enlisted to materialize the course of its national imagination. In this chapter, I analyzed the TSLN policy with a view to make explicit how discourses are used to mobilize Singapore's educational imagination for subject formation and its economy. My analysis illuminates that the discourses used have productive and discursive effects, to use the insights of Foucault (1980). It produces knowledge on and about global education reform that is closely aligned to a global imaginary of economic realities. This knowledge then works through a national educational imagining that constructs a new paradigm of schooling that aims to reproduce preferred schooling identities and subjectivities for its economy.

Finally, I end this chapter with an anecdotal reflection. I make no attempt to critique the TSLN vision of schooling in this chapter because I have done it elsewhere (see Koh 2002, 2004). Yet after having taught in two different education systems with a somewhat different political and cultural context from Singapore, I am persuaded to believe that for a nation to thrive the power of "modern social imaginaries" (Taylor 2004) is *sine qua non*. If there isn't a coherent and collective imagination but the contrary, a stunted imaginary will hinder the progress of a nation. Relatedly, if educational systems lack imagination, they will remain stuck in the mud and put the nation at risk in the now competitive global knowledge economy. While I do not know what Singapore's imaginaries will be next, what I do know is that its imaginaries will be a permanent feature in its characteristic style of nation building.

Acknowledgments I thank Fazal Rizvi for drawing my attention to Charles Taylors work on social imaginary. His sharing has helped shaped the thinking that has gone into this chapter.

References

Anderson, B. (1991). *Imagined communities*. London: Verso.
Baildon, M. C., & Sim, J. B.-Y. (2009). Notions of criticality: Singaporean teachers' perspectives of critical thinking in social studies. *Cambridge Journal of Education, 39*(4), 407–422.
Ball, S. (1994). *Education reform: A critical and poststructuralist approach*. Buckingham: Open University Press.
Chan, C. K. K., & Rao, N. (Eds.). (2009). *Revisiting the Chinese learner: Changing contexts, changing education*. Hong Kong: Springer/Comparative Education Research Centre/University of Hong Kong.
Chong, T. (2010a). Introduction: The role of success in Singapore's national identity. In T. Chong (Ed.), *Management of success Singapore revisited* (pp. 1–18). Singapore: Institute of Southeast Asian Studies.
Chong, T. (2010b). Fluid nation: The perpetual "renovation" of nation and national identities in Singapore. In T. Chong (Ed.), *Management of success Singapore revisited* (pp. 504–519). Singapore: Institute of Southeast Asian Studies.
Collins, R. (2012). Mapping the future, mapping education: An analysis of the 2011 state of the union address. *Journal of Education Policy, 27*(2), 155–172.

Danaher, G., Schirato, T., & Webb, J. (2000). *Understanding Foucault*. Australia: Allen & Unwin.

Fairclough, N. (1989). *Language and power*. London: Longman.

Fairclough, N. (2000). Discourse, social theory, and social research: The discourse of welfare reform. *Journal of Sociolinguistics, 4*(2), 163–195.

Fairclough, N. (2001). The discourse of new labour: Critical discourse analysis. In M. Wetherell, S. Taylor, & S. J. Yates (Eds.), *Discourse as data: A guide for analysis* (pp. 229–266). London: Sage/Open University Press.

Foucault, M. (1972). *The archaeology of knowledge*. London: Routledge.

Foucault, M. (1979). Governmentality. *Ideology & Consciousness, 6*, 5–21.

Foucault, M. (1980). *Power/knowledge: Selected interviews and other writings, 1972–1977* (Gordon, Colin, Tans.) New York: Pantheon.

Gee, J. P., Hull, G., & Lankshear, C. (1996). *The new work order: Behind the language of the new capitalism*. St Leonards: Allen & Unwin.

Goatly, A. (2000). *Critical reading and writing: An introductory coursebook*. London: Routledge.

Goh, C. T. (1997). Shaping our future: Thinking schools, learning nation. Singapore: Ministry of Education. Available: http://www.moe.gov.sg/speeches/1997/020697.htm. Accessed 7 Jan 2012.

Gopinathan, S. (2009). Educating the next generation. In B. Welsh, J. Chin, A. Mahizhnan, & T. H. Tan (Eds.), *Impressions of the Goh Chok Tong years in Singapore* (pp. 240–251). Singapore: NUS.

Halliday, M. A. K. (1994). *An introduction to functional grammar* (2nd ed.). London: Arnold.

Hay, S., & Kapitzke, C. (2009). 'Smart state' for a knowledge economy: Reconstituting creativity through student subjectivity. *British Journal of Sociology of Education, 30*(2), 151–164.

Hill, M., & Lian, K. F. (1995). *The politics of nation building and citizenship in Singapore*. London: Routledge.

Kenway, J., & Fahey, J. (2009). Imagining research otherwise. In J. Kenway & J. Fahey (Eds.), *Globalizing the research imagination* (pp. 1–39). London: Routledge.

Koh, A. (2002). Towards a critical pedagogy: Creating "thinking schools" in Singapore. *Journal of Curriculum Studies, 34*(3), 255–264.

Koh, A. (2004). Singapore education in 'new times': Global/local imperative. *Discourse: Studies in the Cultural Politics of Education, 25*(2), 335–257.

Koh, A. (2010). *Tactical globalization: Learning from the Singapore experiment*. New York: Berg/Peter Lang.

Kress, G. (2000). A curriculum for the future. *Cambridge Journal of Education, 30*(1), 133–145.

Lee, K. Y. (1998). *The Singapore story: Memoirs of Lee Kuan Yew*. Singapore: Prentice Hall.

Liew, W. M. (2008). The realities of teaching amid the pressures of education reform. In J. Tan & P. T. Ng (Eds.), *Thinking schools, learning nation: Contemporary issues and challenges* (pp. 104–134). Singapore: Pearson.

Lim, C. P. (2007). Effective integration of ICT in Singapore schools: Pedagogical and policy implications. *Educational Technology Research Development, 55*, 83–116.

Luke, A., & Wood, A. (2009). Policy and adolescent literacy. In L. Christenbury, R. Bomber, & P. Smagorinsky (Eds.), *Handbook of adolescent literacy research* (pp. 197–219). New York: Guildford Press.

Mok, T. A. C. (2006). Shedding light on the East Asian learner paradox: Reconstructing student-centredness in a Shanghai classroom. *Asia Pacific Journal of Education, 26*(2), 131–142.

Ng, P. T. (2004). Students' perception of change in the Singapore education system. *Educational Research for Policy and Practice, 3*, 77–92.

Okta, L. (2001). The ideological organization of representational process in the presentation of us and them. *Discourse & Society, 12*(3), 313–346.

Ozga, J. (2000). *Policy research in education settings: Contested terrain*. Buckingham: Open University Press.

Rizvi, F. (2011). Beyond the social imaginary of 'clash of civilisations'? *Educational Philosophy & Theory, 43*(3), 225–235.

Rizvi, F., & Kemmis, S. (1987). *Dilemmas of Reform – An overview of issues and achievements of the participation and equity program in Victorian Schools 1984–1986*. Geelong: Deakin University Press.

Rizvi, F., & Lingard, B. (2010). *Globalizing education policy*. London: Routledge.

Talbot, M. (1992). The construction of gender in a teenage magazine. In N. Fairclough (Ed.), *Critical language awareness* (pp. 174–199). London: Longman.

Taylor, C. (2004). *Modern social imaginaries*. Durham and London: Duke University Press.

Taylor, S., Rizvi, F., Lingard, B., & Henry, M. (1997). *Education policy and the politics of change*. London: Routledge.

Walshaw, M. (2007). *Working with Foucault in education*. Rotterdam: Sense Publishers.

Watkins, D. A. & Biggs, J. B. (Eds.). (2001). *Teaching the Chinese learner: Psychological and pedagogical perspectives*. Hong Kong: Centre for Education Research/University of Hong Kong.

Wodak, R. (2008). Introduction: Discourse studies: Important concepts and terms. In R. Wodak & M. Krzyzanowski (Eds.), *Qualitative discourse analysis in the social sciences* (pp. 1–29). Basingstoke: Palgrave Macmillan.

Wodak, R., & Meyer, M. (Eds.). (2001). *Methods of critical discourse analysis*. London: Sage.

Yao, S. C. (2007). *Singapore: The state and the culture of excess*. London: Routledge.

Part III
Translating Reform Initiatives into Programmes, School Subjects and Operational Frameworks

Chapter 5
National Education: Framing the Citizenship Curriculum for Singapore Schools

Jasmine B.-Y. Sim

Citizenship education has historically been an overarching goal of public schooling in every society. Formal schooling, Apple (2003) points out, "by and large is organized and controlled by the government" (p. 1). It is an important ideological state apparatus to mould subjects with the right kind of dispositions and sensibilities. Curriculum is the very substance of schooling; it defines what schools purposefully do in making decisions concerning the knowledge, skills, and dispositions that constitute the experience and outcome of schooling (Westbury 2003, 2008; Deng 2010). Curriculum is often configured so that schools create the types of citizens governments believe are appropriate to that country.

Traditional citizenship is predominantly a nationalist one (Law 2011). Globalization is resulting in shifting scales of belonging, creating stresses in identity formation, citizenship behaviour and sense of belonging at societal level. This calls for new arrangements between nation-states, markets and citizens. In particular, nation-states are developing new strategies to manage transnational flows of people, ideas, goods, media, and technologies, and to remain competitive in the global economy requires responsive populations able to flexibly and quickly adapt to ever changing circumstances.

The Singapore government is constantly strategizing how to work with globalization to reposition Singapore in the larger scheme of capital flows. As a nation, Singapore is simply too small to function economically on its own. While the government works with globalization, it also tries to reinforce national citizenship and citizen loyalty. Tharman Shanmugaratnam (2007), then Minister of Education, explained:

> Our response has to rest on both economic and social strategies. As Singaporeans leave our shores to work and live overseas, as new immigrants join our Singapore family; as incomes widen; and as Singaporeans get exposed to and even bombarded with alternative views, ideologies, lifestyles, we have to work harder to keep a sense of shared identity amongst all our citizens and keep our society cohesive. (n.p.)

J.B.-Y. Sim (✉)
National Institute of Education, Nanyang Technological University, Singapore
e-mail: jasmine.sim@nie.edu.sg

Z. Deng et al. (eds.), *Globalization and the Singapore Curriculum: From Policy to Classroom*, Education Innovation Series, DOI 10.1007/978-981-4451-57-4_5,
© Springer Science+Business Media Singapore 2013

Against the challenges globalization poses for national allegiance and identity, the Ministry of Education (MOE) introduced National Education (NE) into all Singapore schools in 1997, aimed at shaping positive knowledge, values and attitudes of the younger citizenry towards the nation (MOE 2012). This chapter critically analyzes National Education by examining what National Education programmatic curriculum-making entails; and the issues and tensions surrounding it. I use Goodlad's (1979) conception of curriculum-making to inform my analysis, emphasizing the substantive and the political-social aspects. The former deals with the goals, subject matter, materials, and the like; while the latter deals with the political-social that focuses on the connections between educational institutions and differential cultural, political, and economic power. The third aspect is the technical-professional, though important, is not a direct focus of this chapter.

The Formation of National Education

"[T]here is always a prior history of significant events, a particular ideological and political climate, a social and economic context" that drives the form of curriculum change (Taylor et al. 1997, p. 16). Singapore's expulsion from Malaysia in 1965 is arguably the most traumatic moment for its political leaders. That Singapore was, and remains vulnerable, has developed into a political discourse used to rationalize policies, including shaping the school curriculum. I begin this section by situating National Education in its context, tracing its development in terms of the ideology that underlies it, and the catalyst that launches it.

Ideology of Survival

A former British colony, Singapore is a multiracial society built by immigrants from China, Malaysia, and Southern India. It became independent when it separated from Malaysia in 1965. As a tiny island with few natural resources, it faced multiple challenges to its existence from the very beginning. The threat of communism and racial riots in the early years of independence emphasized to the People's Action Party (PAP) government, which has been consistently returned to power, that for Singapore to survive, nation-building and modernizing the economy were urgent priorities (Chua 1995).

The PAP consolidated the country's independence through the politics of survival and economic pragmatism (Chan 1971). Economic survival was seen as the basic premise without which there would be no nation. It is one of the few goals that a diverse society can agree on. The government pursued a strategy of infrastructure modernization to attract multinational corporations and foreign investments, resulting in Singapore becoming the prototypical developmental state, able to gain legitimacy by promoting and sustaining economic development (Castells 1992). The PAP government turned to schools as allies in the nation-building cause. The education system was centralized and brought under strong direction of the state. The aims of education in Singapore are inextricably linked with the political aims of the government.

In two decades or so, the PAP government propelled Singapore out of the material difficulties of a Third World ex-colony to a First World economy, with its citizens enjoying one of the highest standards of living in the world (Lee 2000). The ability to promote and sustain high rates of economic growth, leading to the betterment of people's standard of living, is arguably the source of the PAP's political legitimacy (Castells 1992). The PAP capitalizes on its economic management and success to promote a sense of pride and patriotism among Singaporeans (Han 2009; also see Chaps. 2, 4 and 14).

However, the PAP government feels a profound sense of vulnerability, recognizing that its achievements are always transient. This has shaped the worldviews of the political leaders, as they adopt a garrison mentality, which views Singapore as under constant threat. Policies are designed "to organize the population into a tautly-controlled, efficient and achievement-oriented society" (Bedlington 1978, p. 211). They develop a tight system of political control that allows few opportunities for dissent to maintain the social order necessary for economic development. An official narrative of the government providing what matters most to people – safety, security, and prosperity – in exchange for economic discipline and social conformity provided the common shared national history education that helped forge the young nation.

"Serious Gap in Knowledge": A Catalyst

In 1996 Lee Kuan Yew suggested that Singapore could rejoin Malaysia, if the latter adopted meritocracy, and pursued as successfully the same goals of bringing maximum economic benefits to its people. Lee's statement met with lukewarm reactions in Singapore, as the issue did not grip young Singaporeans (Serious gap in the education of Singaporeans 1996, n.p.). The political leaders saw this as a lack of consensus among young Singaporeans in the definition of threats to the nation, a "problem" that needed to be addressed. A poll conducted by the local newspaper showed a lack of knowledge and interest in Singapore's recent history among young Singaporeans. This was confirmed by an MOE survey on Singapore's recent history that involved 2,500 students.

That the "gap in knowledge" was a serious problem must be seen against a post-Independence generation that now constitutes 47 % of the population. They have not lived through the events surrounding Singapore's independence, and are "ignorant of the basic facts of how we became a nation, and the principles of meritocracy and multi-racialism which underpin our entire society and political culture" (Goh 1996, n.p.). They may not understand Singapore's vulnerabilities and constraints – important messages that may be gleaned from Singapore's recent history. These events constituting "our shared past," "should bind our communities together" and provide a common bond for nation-building. Young Singaporeans might take peace and prosperity for granted. National Education was conceived in this context.

Consistent with the ideology of survival, the knowledge deficit was cast in a narrative of crisis. Then Deputy Prime Minister Lee Hsien Loong claimed,

> This ignorance will hinder our effort to develop a shared sense of nationhood. We will not acquire the right instincts to bond as one nation, or maintain the will to survive and prosper in an uncertain world. For Singapore to thrive beyond the founder generation, we must systematically transmit these instincts and attitudes to succeeding cohorts. (Lee 1997, n.p.)

Globalization has problematized the PAP government's promotion of economic development as a nation-building strategy. The PAP government realizes it can no longer guarantee sustained prosperity, and the betterment of people's living standard. This challenges its single most powerful ideological tool, and its legitimacy.

What marks National Education is the explicit recognition that globalization "will strain the loyalties and attachments of young Singaporeans" (Gopinathan 2007, p. 61). Growing up amidst economic wealth and political stability, young Singaporeans today are well-educated, widely-travelled, and technologically savvy. They have diverse needs and aspirations, with many wanting more control in personal spheres and more say in the collective decision-making. The PAP government worries that many of them "will pack their bags and take flight when our country runs into a little storm" (Goh 2001). The local newspaper revealed as many as 53 % of Singaporean teens indicated they would consider emigrating (Lim 2006, p. H4). The issue is how to deepen national consciousness among a new generation of Singaporeans; the tension is between societal change and the government's penchant for control.

Launch of National Education

In Singapore, a political speech is often read as if it were a policy document. National Education "was literally spoken into existence" (Koh 2010, p. 69). At the Teachers' Day Rally in 1996, then Prime Minister Goh lamented the lack of knowledge of Singapore's recent past among young Singaporeans. He explained that the gap in knowledge was the result of a deliberate policy not to teach students about the events leading up to political independence, because it had been thought that this was still "fresh" and "raw". Goh explained that National Education was the remedy for the "knowledge gap", and must become "a vital component of our education process". It was meant to develop "instincts" in every child, such as "a shared sense of nationhood" and "an understanding of how our past is relevant to our present and future" (Goh 1996).

The MOE quickly translated Goh's speech into a programme. In 1997, National Education was launched. It is the form that citizenship education takes in Singapore (Sim and Print 2005, 2009; Chap. 2). Citizenship is nationalist and emphasizes the social collectivity. When globalization is unleashing individualizing tendencies, and pulling young Singaporeans into allegiances that challenge the hold on the nation-state, calling the progamme *National* rather than *citizenship* education downplays individual agency and refocuses attention on the nation (also see Chap. 4).

National Education Curriculum-Making

The Substantive Aspect: Aims, Messages, Outcomes and Curricula Forms

The focus of National Education is with events related to the development of nation-hood, encapsulated in the 'Singapore Story'(see Chaps. 4, 10 and 13). National Education aims to develop national cohesion, the instinct for survival and confidence in Singapore's future by:

- Fostering a sense of identity, pride and self-respect as Singaporeans;
- Knowing the Singapore story – how Singapore succeeded against the odds to become a nation;
- Understanding Singapore's unique challenges, constraints and vulnerabilities, which make us different from other countries; and
- Instilling the core values of our way of life, and the will to prevail, that ensures our continued success and well-being. (MOE 2012, n.p.)

The aims were translated into six key messages to facilitate implementation in the schools. They are:

- Singapore is our homeland; this is where we belong. *We treasure our heritage and take pride in shaping our own unique way of life.*
- We must preserve racial and religious harmony. *We value our diversity and are determined to stay a united people.*
- We must uphold meritocracy and incorruptibility. *We provide opportunities for all, according to their ability and effort.*
- No one owes Singapore a living. *We find our own way to survive and prosper, turning challenge into opportunity.*
- We must ourselves defend Singapore. *We are proud to defend Singapore ourselves, no one else is responsible for our security and well-being.*
- We have confidence in our future. *United, determined and well-prepared, we have what it takes to build a bright future for ourselves, and to progress together as one nation.* (MOE 2012, n.p.)

The MOE specifies the different outcomes that teachers should seek to achieve in students at different levels. At the primary level, National Education is structured around the outcome of "Love Singapore." Primary students should be inculcated with correct values and attitudes; they should develop a sense of pride in Singapore, as well as children of different races and abilities. At the secondary level, the outcome is "Know Singapore." Secondary students should "develop instincts based on what they know and feel", which means that they need to acquire knowledge of how Singapore has arrived where it has, its constraints and vulnerabilities, as well as its challenges for the future. Finally, at the pre-university level, the outcome is "Lead Singapore." The NE outcomes are further differentiated for students of the Institutes of Technical Education, the polytechnics, junior colleges and universities (MoE 1997, n.p.), and more will be said about this later.

Unlike past citizenship education programmes which were subject driven, National Education was conceived as "part of Total Education" to be infused across the formal and informal curricula. It must involve every teacher; appeal to the heart and mind, and develop thinking; and be reinforced by society. Every subject in the formal curriculum would be used to infuse National Education. Certain subjects such as social studies, civic and moral education, history, geography, mother tongue language, the General Paper, lend better in this regard (MOE 2012, n.p.).

Primary social studies would be started earlier at Primary One instead of Primary Four. Upper secondary history syllabus would be extended to include the immediate post-Independence years up until 1971. In 2001, a new subject, social studies was introduced at the upper secondary level as the major vehicle for National Education. Social studies is a compulsory subject for 15–17 years old students that culminates in the national examinations. I have written about social studies elsewhere (Sim and Print 2005; Sim and Ho 2010; Sim 2011). Suffice it to mention here that social studies emphasizes understanding of national issues, organized around the National Education messages. Social studies frequently utilizes national myths to promote "a deep sense of shared destiny and national identity" (MOE 2008, p. 3). For example, the syllabus regularly highlights certain key traumatic episodes such as the racial riots of the 1950s and 1960s between the Chinese and the Malays. Stories of national achievement, such as the rapid development of the Singapore economy, are also given prominence.

In the informal curriculum, all schools were to observe four core events, identified as defining moments in Singapore's history. They are: Total Defence Day, to commemorate Singapore's fall to the Japanese in 1942, and serves to remind students they have a role in defending Singapore; Racial Harmony Day, to mark the outbreak of racial riots in 1964, which serves to remind students not to take racial harmony for granted but to work on maintaining it; International Friendship Day, to remind students of the importance of maintaining cordial relations with neighbouring countries; and National Day, to commemorate Singapore's Independence in 1965.

Students also embark on Learning Journeys to historical sites and national organization to appreciate the nation's heritage and vulnerabilities, and to develop a sense of pride and confidence about how Singapore had overcome its developmental constraints. To instill social responsibility and commitment to the community and the nation, all students must also perform a mandatory 6 h of volunteer work as part of the Community Involvement Programme each year. Finally, all Primary Six and Secondary Four or equivalent students have to participate in and pass the National Education Quiz.

The Political-Social Aspect: Top-Down, State-Driven Curriculum-Making

Who Makes the Decision?

A famous question, long posed in curriculum development asks, "What knowledge is of most worth?" Before we can ask that question, we must pose, as Apple (1992) suggests, an even more contentious question, "Whose knowledge is of most worth?" Such a question raises significant questions about the move to establish National Education. Why National Education? Who makes the curricula decisions? Why now? How defensible is the curriculum?

National Education exemplifies a top-down, state-driven curriculum-making. What is striking is the scale and pervasive nature of National Education, which underscores the conscious attempt to discipline the prescribed identity. Ironically, this makes it less authentic and undermines its own intentions. The speed at which NE was implemented in all schools marked the urgency and perceived high-stake nature of the task. From then Deputy Prime Minister's speech to the launch of National Education took less than a year. In the same way, upper secondary social studies, was introduced in 2001, taking barely 4 years from conceptualization to implementation in all schools. National Education was given the highest priority with then Prime Minister Goh and then Deputy Prime Minister Lee wielding direct influence over it. Goh appointed top civil servant, Lim Siong Guan, then Permanent Secretary in the Prime Minister Office (PMO) concurrently as Permanent Secretary for Education to oversee the development of National Education. An executive committee was set up, chaired by Lim, comprising senior representatives from the MOE, Ministry of Information and the Arts, Ministry of Defence and PMO to translate the political imperatives and develop the strategic approaches and measures for implementation of National Education (MOE 1997).

All National Education curricula that addressed citizenship such as social studies, history and civics and moral education, and their respective textbooks were developed by officers at the Curriculum Planning and Development Division (CPDD) in the MOE, under the directive of the National Education Committee. This was to ensure that the curricula objectives and content were congruent with national goals. Apple and Christian-Smith (1991) argue that curricula materials signify "particular constructions of reality" (p. 4), and are often used as "ideological tools to promote a certain belief system and legitimize an established political and social order" (p. 10). A National Education Branch was set up to co-ordinate the development and implementation of National Education in schools. Within the educational system, co-ordinated and sustained effort was made to transmit the official knowledge and values to shape the Singaporean subjectivity.

Notably, the alignment of National Education and the military, reflected in the composition of the MOE's National Education Committee, which includes a key military officer of at least Colonel rank. The National Education messages were originally taken from the Singapore Armed Forces. Two new messages on racial and religious harmony, and meritocracy and incorruptibility were added based on the political leaders' assessment of the nation's current challenges. Suffice it to say that Singapore is an "educational security state", coupling educational plans for economic growth and development with the military demands of the nation-state (Spring 1998). The structure of the committee and the process of curriculum-making were such that they were designed to produce a curriculum outcome consistent with the instituted policy.

Why Now?

National Education was initiated in the absence of any war or "real" crisis. From time to time, states engender crisis in the citizenry so that the political leaders can present themselves as possessing means to solve people's crises. This is a strategy used openly and consciously to enhance a sense of dependence on the state. The purpose is to reinforce the ideological consensus so as to maintain the nation (Hill and Lian 1995). This is not new in the history of education in Singapore. As with the "crisis" of deculturalization and westernization in the 1980s that led to experimentation with various forms of moral education (Gopinathan 1988; Chew 1998; Tan 1997), so it is with National Education. The launch of National Education coincided with an intense worldwide interest in citizenship education against the destabilizing effects of globalization. A critical reading suggests that National Education is an attempt by the political leaders to maintain power in contexts in which that power is increasingly challenged.

How Defensible?

Therefore National Education is not primarily concerned with curriculum defensibility in terms of making the most justifiable decisions deliberatively (Schwab 1969; Walker 2003). Schwab (1973) theorized that there are four commonplaces to be considered, comprising the subject matter, learner, teacher and milieu, around which decisions about curricula should be made. Deliberation about problems deals with the mutual influences among them, although for particular problems all commonplaces may not be equally relevant. National Education curriculum-making however considered a particular milieu at the expense of others. Deep-seated fears of vulnerability and survival undergird the top-down, state-driven curriculum-making. The purpose of National Education is to transmit "instincts and attitudes to succeeding cohorts" of students, and make them "part of the cultural DNA which makes us Singaporeans" (Lee 1997, n.p.). The representation of these in National Education present a particular view of events, actions and relations, in which scholars have claimed, is closely intertwined with the fate of the ruling party (Tan and Chew 2004; Selvaraj 2007; Han 2009; Koh 2010).

This creates an inherent tension; the common aims and purpose, which supposedly encapsulate the shared aspirations of the people were formulated with minimal consultation with the people. Given that citizenship is contested, the absence of negotiation between state and citizens reflects a clear disconnect that problematizes National Education. One should realize that curriculum-making is essentially a manipulative strategy, in which "some interests come to prevail over others so that these ends and means rather than others emerge" (Goodlad 1979, p. 17). What students learn in schools, when, how and under what conditions, is the result of what certain people want them to learn, constructed in a way to meet predetermined needs and further their interests.

The curriculum is not neutral, but "a reality creating agency serving the interests of those in power in any society or country" (Smith and Lovat 2003, p. 34). Hence National Education needs to be understood as some group's construction of reality though such construction may not always be explicit or apparent. Westbury (2003) highlights that programmatic curriculum-making frames the character of schools and classrooms organizationally, and the ways schools might be seen. If NE is statecraft, then schools are political tools (Han 2009). Curriculum-making becomes an ideological act with NE signalling priorities, and setting agendas for schools.

Issues and Tensions

This section examines the issues and tensions surrounding a top-down state-driven National Education curriculum-making. I highlight the issues and tensions related to the substantives aspects of the curriculum, such as the curricula conception and definition, and learning outcomes.

A Prescribed Solution

National Education is prescriptive with an expedient and practical purpose of what appears to be solving the problem of students' knowledge deficit of Singapore's recent past. Prescriptive curriculum provides us with what 'ought' to happen. It takes the form of a plan, or some kind of expert opinion about what needs to take place in the course of study in order to solve the problem (Ellis 2004). In prescriptive curriculum however, the problem is often simplified and stripped of its complexities to facilitate the prescribed solution. Learning outcomes are pre-determined, and specify exactly what is to be achieved as a result of the learning.

Take for instance, ethnic pluralism and social cohesion. Ethnicity is equated with race in an unproblematic manner, and this reduces the challenge of creating a sense of nationhood among an ethnically diverse population to one of preserving harmony, in accordance to the state's Chinese, Malay, India and Others (CMIO) model of multiracialism (Lai 2004). Stripped of its complexities, social cohesion can then be simplified into an National Education message: "We must preserve racial and religious harmony. *We value our diversity and are determined to stay a united people,"* where schools are required to adopt the clearly defined and commonly identified norms and goals. This makes it convenient to prescribe solutions such as Racial Harmony Day and National Day, platforms in which the ethnic cultures and identities are ritualized and symbolized in celebratory forms. The sheer spectacle of a solution orchestrated as a celebration serves powerfully to shape students' perceptions that multiracialism is necessary for social cohesion, and the role good governance plays in achieving harmony. Ideologically, this serves the interest of those in power.

Set against the uncertainties and sometimes, destructive elements of globalization, state-driven curriculum-making of National Education in contrast demonstrated the responsiveness of the government in presenting "solutions" and "plans that work" to the "problem" identified (Koh 2010). While the prescribed solution may not always produce the unambiguous results anticipated by the state, the appeal of specified goals and outcomes lies in its promise of a semblance of order, control, and certainty compared with the uncertainly and unpredictability" wrought by globalization (Smyth and Dow 1998). It depicted positively a particular ideological and managerial skill of the government in the eyes of the public. This in turn enhanced its legitimacy to intervene and rule. Hence control was exercised symbolically by way of state-driven decisions (Westbury 2008).

Adopting an "identification stance", a particular view of the past is used to justify current social arrangements, "and a story of development that avoids considering alternatives is an effective way of legitimating the status quo" (Levstik and Barton 2001, p. 135). National Education centres on the 'Singapore Story' – a straightforward tale adopted by the political leaders that charts how an independent Singapore overcame the odds to become a peaceful and prosperous country, highly regarded by the international community (also Chaps. 4 and 10). It is a means to rally the people in a nation when globalization challenges their allegiances. Implicit is the central role of the PAP government leading Singapore from a Third World to a First World nation. With National Education, knowledge and forms of learning are justified on utilitarian grounds, so that the basis for the selection of curriculum content is a consideration of nothing more than its instrumental value. For instance, on the theme of 'Understanding Governance' in the upper secondary social studies curriculum, the capable and forward-looking political leadership is emphasized by contrasting with a deliberate selection of Sri Lanka and Northern Ireland, countries presented as besieged by civil wars and strife.

Privileging Intentions Over Experiences

Consistent with a prescriptive nature, National Education can be defined as curriculum as intention (Eisner 2002; Ellis 2004). The state possesses the ideal conception of citizenship embodied in National Education, and transmits it to students through planned activities, such as the Learning Journeys. National Education outlines what is *intended* to happen, and assumes what should happen actually does happen. However, it is well known that the existence of even a well-planned body of curricula materials is no guarantee that they will be used effectively in the classroom. Such a definition is narrow and restrictive with primarily technical interests of control (Smith and Lovat 2003).

In top-down, state-driven curriculum-making, the National Education intentions are developed by someone other than the person who is supposed to implement them. The plan or intention is therefore separated from its implementation. Haft and Hopmann (1990) argue that with this separation, the state and policy-makers can evade responsibility for their decisions. The claim that the problem is not with the policy or programme, but with those charged with its implementation – that is, the teachers, students and schools – is always available. Consequently, National Education "teaching is necessarily imaged as a passive agency implementing or realizing both an organizationally sanctioned programme and its legitimating ideology" (Westbury 2003, p. 531). The availability of a curriculum well planned in advance also presents the state as forward-looking, and this serves to breed confidence that what will be offered will be worth the students' time and effort.

Central to curriculum is experience (Dewey 1902). However, experience is not given much emphasis in National Education, though the reality of a curriculum for a student is largely determined by the quality of the experience in the school and not simply a piece of paper on which an activity is planned. Characteristically, experience is personal, individual and existential (Smith and Lovat 2003). The question is can one plan the experience of another. The state might plan an activity in which certain assumptions are made about what it might like the students to experience, but each individual will experience the activity differently, and some not experiencing anything of what the state has intended.

Intentions are privileged in National Education because it promotes the view that National Education and its values can be explicitly taught. Conversely, the notion of experience is downplayed, pushing the view that National Education and its values are caught, and sometimes serendipitously, to the background. By suggesting that national values and sense of belonging are cultivated by chance makes light of the PAP government that believes in being practical and forward-looking. How best can a conducive environment be created for citizens to "catch" this elusive emotion in a milieu of competing allegiances? Ideologically, adopting a restrictive definition of National Education as intention has to do with control. Given the high-stake nature of National Education, the state is accountable for what students learn. With experience, there is the issue of the unintended, in which students develop attitudes and gain knowledge perceived to be harmful or undesirable. The state might not wish to accept that each individual student learns different things. Its interests are best served if it appears to be "in-charge", and controlling what it is that students are learning, and showing that all students are generally learning the same and what is intended.

Differentiated Tracks for Different Students

The metaphor of a running track for curriculum is a useful one for understanding National Education. Eisner (2002, p. 25) explains, "This notion implies a track, a set of obstacles or tasks that an individual is to overcome, something that has a beginning and an end," through which all students are to complete. Successful completion of the course warrants a certification of competency, indicated by a pass in the National Education quiz. If we think about the characteristics that different running tracks might have, we should be able to identify different types of curriculum or factors, which are important in providing an effective curriculum for learners. NE provided different curricula for learners from different ages and abilities, such as "Love Singapore," "Know Singapore," and "Lead Singapore" (MOE 2012). There is an evident hierarchical pedagogical outcomes that take into consideration the emotional and intellectual development of children, which focus on the affect at the primary level, moving on to knowledge at the secondary level, and then action for the pre-university section.

It seems that students of different academic abilities will perform different social and political roles. This explains why they are to be regarded differently where National Education is concerned. Students in the vocational track Institutes of Technical Education (ITE) are expected to "understand that they would be helping themselves, their families and Singapore by working hard, continually upgrading themselves and helping to ensure a stable social order." Polytechnic students, who are higher up the academic level are to be convinced that "the country's continued survival and prosperity will depend on the quality of their efforts". Junior College university-bound students should have the sense that "they can shape their own future in Singapore." As potential future leaders, they should "appreciate the demands and complexities of leadership" and "be instilled with a desire to serve the community." They must be educated so that they are not "ignorant or naïve about the way countries, societies and humankind behave," and be prepared to overcome challenges responsibly and ingeniously (MOE 1997).

Access to a citizenship curriculum that develops the knowledge, skills, and values to "Lead Singapore" is only available to the academically able. There appears to be a policy to encourage a relatively small elite comprising the academically most able, to think independently about national issues and to arrive at their own conclusions about these issues (Sim 2012). It is troubling that National Education problematizes the notion that citizens of most democratic states should, at least in theory, be political equals regardless of their social, economic and ethnic backgrounds (Marshall 1950; Faulks 2000). While there have been disputes over the purposes of education and the necessity of differentiated curricula, few question that all young citizens should have equal access to the same knowledge, attitudes, values, and skills required for active citizenry, because schools are morally obliged to give all children an education that allows them to take advantage of their political status as citizens (Gutmann 1999).

That National Education does not provide equitable access to civic learning opportunities militates against the Singapore national pledge of allegiance that affirms a national goal of building "a democratic society based on justice and equality" (Singapore National Heritage Board 2004). The challenge of creating a sense of nationhood has been the basis of National Education, particularly when globalization is widening income inequalities and class stratification. Singapore's Gini score of 42.5 was ranked second highest among the world's most advanced economies (Businessweek 2009). National Education is meant to pull young Singaporeans together through common experiences and shared aspirations. Instead its outcomes set students apart according to their academic abilities.

The differentiated National Education curriculum conditions students' opportunities and outlook, and situates them in different social and economic positions. This reproduces the stratified view of society espoused by Lee Kuan Yew in 1966, in which he envisioned a "pyramidal structure" consisting of "top leaders," "good executives" and a "well-disciplined and highly civic conscious broad mass" (Lee 1966, p. 13) (also see Chap. 4). Barr (2006) calls this "a culture of elite governance." Elitism conjures a class divide. Dye and Zeigler (2009, p. 1) wrote, "Elites are the few who have power; the masses are the many who do not." Because Singapore is a small country, the impact of class divide could exacerbate to the extent it threatens social stability. Clearly, National Education is challenged with the social inequalities and social cohesion that permeates its underlying framework. The tension can become a potentially divisive force in the nation-building project (Tan 2007).

Concluding Remarks

There is no single answer to the question of how globalization is affecting educational policy and practice worldwide (Burbules and Torres 2000). In Singapore, the leadership has decided that within the education system, a National Education agenda should be promoted around a revitalized conception of nationalism and citizen loyalty. Such a focus is not new the source of which can be traced to the circumstances surrounding Singapore's independence. Similarly, the development of National Education must be seen within the chronology of a single-minded pursuit of citizenship education for the purpose of nation-building (Sim and Print 2005; Baildon and Sim 2010).

National Education promotes a minimal interpretation of citizenship (McLaughlin 1992; Kerr 2003), and generates a particular way of thinking that is nation-centric and statist. Citizenship in National Education is particular and exclusive, with elitist interests in society being promoted. The agenda is built upon a fixed and unproblematic notion of national identity; the belief that there either is, or can only be, one identity. Consequently, a prescribed scripted national narrative is imposed, where National Education is organized around messages to be learnt rather than broad questions that require young Singaporeans to learn to deliberate together. The attempt to create a sense of belonging by focusing on consolidating a unified national identity is increasingly at odds with realities on the ground. It ignores the reality of alternative locus where young Singaporeans can participate in alternative forms of citizenship and belonging. National identity, like other forms of individual or collective identities, is not immutable. It is a social construct that is constantly in the process of construction, deconstruction and reconstruction (Biersteker and Weber 1996; Reicher and Hopkins 2001). Consequently, the attributes of the nation are in flux and have to be constantly negotiated among the people who make up the "imagined community" and not simply imposed top-down (Anderson 1991).

As it stands, National Education speaks to a curriculum oriented towards cultural reproduction, one that is more political than educational (Kelly 2009). The state decides on the particular set of knowledge and values, and neatly packages them into sanitized messages to be imbued in young Singaporeans. Durkheim (1956, p. 71) described this as "methodical socialization of the younger generation" Children are taught to fit into the existing social order, and to fulfill their role as citizens in an appropriate manner (Ochoa-Becker 2007). Notably, the National Education goals are explicitly specified rather than the process. This suggests that the state's motivation in introducing National Education is far clearer than the concern about the motivation of students to engage with the programme.

Surely, students must not lose sight of the many things that have allowed Singapore to be successful, for instance, rewards for effort based on merit, a commitment to hard work, a strong defence and civic pride. But imposing a scripted national narrative, stripped of the critical nuances that underscore the tough decisions that were made at the many crossroads of nation-building is not the way forward. It "creates a blind spot for Singaporeans to contemplate the new challenges that lie ahead" (Chin 2007, p. 93), because National Education messages saturate them with acceptance of national institutions and values, and belief in the status quo. This renders National Education counter-productive and fans speculations of propaganda.

Every society inducts the young into its customs, values and behaviours to continue its existing practices and strengthen social cohesiveness. But we cannot be unconscious citizens, living by the unexamined assumptions that structure our activities. An ever-changing global society requires responsive populations and continuing negotiation by thoughtful citizens. To this end, we need to reconceptualize National Education. Socialization needs to be balanced by fostering independent thinking and responsible social criticism, active and vigorous reasoning. This requires an appraisal of what has been learned through socialization. It does not mean a rejection of the former, but calls for individuals to reach their own conclusion through a thoughtful and critical analysis of beliefs (Ochoa-Becker 2007).

Where emphasis is given to this aspect of citizenship education, the primary target group is the academically able students. However, if all Singaporeans have the right to vote, then surely they should all be given equal access to civic learning opportunities. There needs to be a rethinking about our society from one based on a hierarchical division of societal roles to one where each citizen is given equal opportunity to shape the values of the nation. This will provide the population with a larger stake and hence strengthen their commitment to their fellow Singaporeans and country (Chin 2007). Precisely because the future is so uncertain that there is a need for a citizenship education that empowers all Singaporeans to navigate confidently into the unknown together.

This chapter is by no means a comprehensive analysis of National Education. The focus has been on selective aspects of what National Education curriculum-making at the programmatic level entails, and the issues and tensions surrounding it. Tan and Gopinathan (2000, p. 10) have pointed out, "The larger problem for Singapore's educational reform initiative is that Singapore's nation-building history resulted in an omnipresent state that cherishes stability and order." If the desired outcome is to have Singaporeans stand by the nation in times of crisis, a logical step would be a more balanced approach in presenting National Education to allow for criticism of the enshrined values (Chin 2007). This may open the PAP government to critique, but it can help overcome the blind spots, as young Singaporeans learn to identify together with the state and with fellow citizens what needs to be improved, and the role they can play in making it a reality. In this way, young Singaporeans learn to negotiate their personal aspirations with that of the nation and their fellow citizens. This, I believe will have a better potential for developing genuine bonds of trust among Singaporeans, and in strengthening their emotional attachment to the country.

References

Anderson, B. (1991). *Imagined communities: Reflections on the origin and spread of nationalism* (Rev. ed.). London: Verso.

Apple, M. (1992). The text and cultural politics. *Educational Researcher, 21*(7), 4–11.

Apple, M. (2003). *The state and the politics of knowledge*. London: Routledge Falmer.

Apple, M. W., & Christian-Smith, L. K. (1991). The politics of the textbook. In M. W. Apple & L. K. Christian-Smith (Eds.), *The politics of the textbook* (pp. 1–21). New York: Routledge.

Baildon, M., & Sim, J. B.-Y. (2010). The dilemmas of Singapore's National Education in the global society. In A. Reid, A. Sears, & J. Gill (Eds.), *Globalization, the nation-state and the citizen: Dilemmas and directions for civics and citizenship education* (pp. 80–96). New York: Routledge.

Barr, M. D. (2006). Beyond technocracy: The culture of elite governance in Lee Hsien Loong's Singapore. *Asian Studies Review, 30*, 1–17.

Bedlington, S. (1978). *Malaysia and Singapore: The building of new states*. Ithaca/New York: Cornell University Press.

Biersteker, T. J., & Weber, C. (1996). The social construction of state sovereignty. In T. J. Biersteker & C. Weber (Eds.), *State sovereignty as social construct* (pp. 1–21). Cambridge: Cambridge University Press.

Burbules, N. C., & Torres, C. A. (2000). Globalization and education: An introduction. In N. C. Burbules & C. A. Torres (Eds.), *Globalization and education: Critical perspectives* (pp. 1–26). London: Routledge.

Businessweek. (2009, October 16). *Countries with the biggest gaps between rich and poor.* Available at: http://finance.yahoo.com/banking-budgeting/article/107980/countries-with-the-biggest-gaps-between-rich-and-poor. Accessed 15 May 2015.

Castells, M. (1992). Four Asian tigers with a dragon head. In R. P. Appelbaum & J. Henderson (Eds.), *States and development in the Asian Pacific Rim* (pp. 33–70). Los Angeles: Sage.

Chan, H. C. (1971). *Singapore: The politics of survival, 1965–67*. Singapore: University Press.

Chew, J. O. A. (1998). Civics and moral education in Singapore: Lessons for citizenship education. *Journal of Moral Education, 27*(4), 505–524.

Chin, Y. (2007). Reviewing National Education: Can the heart be taught where the home is? In N. Vasu (Ed.), *Social resilience in Singapore* (pp. 81–96). Singapore: Select Publishing.

Chua, B.-H. (1995). *Communitarian ideology and democracy in Singapore*. London: Routledge.

Deng, Z. (2010). Curriculum planning and systems change. In P. Peterson, E. Baker, & B. McGaw (Eds.), *International encyclopedia of education* (Vol. 1, pp. 384–389). Oxford: Elsevier.

Dewey, J. (1902). *The child and the curriculum*. Chicago: University of Chicago Press.

Durkheim, E. (1956). *Education and sociology*. Glencoe: Free Press.

Dye, T. R., & Zeigler, H. (2009). *The irony of democracy: An uncommon introduction to American politics* (14th ed.). Boston: Wadsworth Cengage Learning.

Eisner, E. W. (2002). *The educational imagination* (3rd ed.). Ohio: Merrill Prentice Hall.

Ellis, A. K. (2004). *Exemplars of curriculum theory*. New York: Eye on Education.

Faulks, K. (2000). *Citizenship*. London: Routledge.

Goh, C. T. (1996). *Prepare our children for the new century: Teach them well*. Speech at the Teachers' Day Rally. Available at: http://www.gov.sg/mita/speech/v20n5001.htm. Accessed 15 May 2012.

Goh, C. T. (2001). *Remaking Singapore – Changing Mindsets*. Available at: http://www.gov.sg/nd/ND02.htm. Accessed 15 May 2012.

Goodlad, J., & Associates. (1979). *Curriculum inquiry: The study of curriculum practice*. New York: MacGraw-Hill.

Gopinathan, S. (2007). Globalisation, the Singapore developmental state and education policy: A thesis revisited. *Globalisation, Societies and Education, 5*(1), 53–70.

Gopinathan, S. (1988). Being and becoming: Education for values in Singapore. In W. K. Cummings, S. Gopinathan, & Y. Tomoda (Eds.), *The revival of values education in Asia and the West* (pp. 131–145). Oxford: Pergamon.

Gutmann, A. (1999). *Democratic education*. Princeton: Princeton University Press.

Haft, H., & Hopmann, S. (1990). Curriculum administration as symbolic action. In H. Haft & S. Hopmann (Eds.), *Case studies in curriculum administration history* (pp. 143–158). London: Falmer.

Han, C. (2009). Creating good citizens, or a competitive workforce, or just plain political socialization? Tensions in the aims of education in Singapore. In M. Lall & E. Vickers (Eds.), *Education as a political tool in Asia* (pp. 102–119). London: Routledge.

Hill, M., & Lian, K. F. (1995). *The politics of nation building and citizenship in Singapore*. New York: Routledge.

Kelly, A. V. (2009). *The curriculum: Theory and practice* (6th ed.). Los Angeles: Sage.

Kerr, D. (2003). Citizenship: Local, national and international. In L. Gearon (Ed.), *Learning to teach citizenship in the secondary school* (pp. 5–27). London: Routledge Falmer.

Koh, A. (2010). *Tactical globalization: Learning from the Singapore experiment*. Bern: Peter Lang.

Lai, A. E. (2004). Introduction: Beyond rituals and riots. In A. E. Lai (Ed.), *Beyond rituals and riots: Ethnic pluralism and social cohesion in Singapore* (p. 140). Singapore: Marshall Cavendish.

Law, W.-W. (2011). *Citizenship and citizenship education in a global age: Politics, policies, and practices in China*. New York: Peter Lang.

Lee, K. Y. (1966). *New bearings in our education system*. Singapore: Ministry of Education.

Lee, H. L. (1997). *Developing a shared sense of nationhood*. Speech at the launch of National Education. Available at: http://www.moe.gov.sg/speeches/1997/170597.htm. Accessed 15 May 2012.

Lee, K. Y. (2000). *From third world to first: The Singapore story: 1965–2000* (Vol. 2). Singapore: Times Edition.

Levstik, L. S., & Barton, K. C. (2001). Committing acts of history: Mediated action, humanistic education, and participatory democracy. In W. B. Stanley (Ed.), *Critical issues in social studies research for the 21st century* (pp. 119–147). Greenwich: Information Age Publishing.

Lim, J. (2006, July 27). Youth seeking to uproot an 'urgent' concern. *The Straits Times*, p. H4.

Marshall, T. H. (1950). *Citizenship and social class and other essays*. Cambridge: Cambridge University Press.

McLaughlin, T. H. (1992). Citizenship, diversity and education: A philosophical perspective. *Journal of Moral Education, 21*(3), 235–246.

Ministry of Education. (1997). *Launch of National Education*. Available at: http://www.moe.gov.sg/media/press/1997/pr01797.htm. Accessed 15 May 2012.

Ministry of Education. (2008). *Combined humanities GCE Ordinary Level (Syllabus 2192)*. Singapore: Ministry of Education.

Ministry of Education. (2012). *National Education*. Available at: http://www.ne.edu.sg/. Accessed 15 May 2012.

Ochoa-Becker, A. S. (2007). *Democratic education for social studies: An issue-centred decision making curriculum*. Greenwich: Information Age Publishing.

Reicher, S., & Hopkins, N. (2001). *Self and nation*. London: Sage.

Schwab, J. (1969). The practical: A language for curriculum. *The School Review, 78*(1), 1–23.

Schwab, J. (1973). The practical: Translation into curriculum. *The School Review, 81*(4), 501–522.

Selvaraj, V. (2007). *Responding to globalization: Nation, culture and identity in Singapore*. Singapore: Institute of Southeast Asian Studies Press.

Serious gap in the education of Singaporeans. (1996, July 18). We are ignorant of our own history. *The Straits Times*, p. 41.

Sim, J. B.-Y. (2011). Social studies and citizenship for participation in Singapore: How one state seeks to influence its citizens. *Oxford Review of Education, 37*(6), 743–761.

Sim, J. B.-Y. (2012). The burden of responsibility: Elite students' understandings of civic participation in Singapore. *Educational Review, 64*(2), 195–210.

Sim, J. B.-Y., & Ho, L.-C. (2010). Transmitting national values through social studies: A Singapore case study. In T. Lovat, R. Toomey, & C. Neville (Eds.), *International handbook on values education and student well-being* (pp. 897–917). Dordrecht: Springer.

Sim, J. B.-Y., & Print, M. (2005). Citizenship education and social studies in Singapore: A national agenda. *International Journal of Citizenship and Teacher Education, 1*(1), 58–73.

Sim, J. B.-Y., & Print, M. (2009). The state, teachers and citizenship education in Singapore schools. *British Journal of Educational Studies, 57*(4), 380–399.

Singapore National Heritage Board. (2004). *National symbols: The pledge*. Available at: http://www.nhb.gov.sg/PE/resources/national_symbols/pledge.html. Accessed 15 May 2012.

Smith, D. L., & Lovat, T. J. (2003). *Curriculum: Action on reflection*. New South Wales: Social Science Press.

Smyth, J., & Dow, A. (1998). What's wrong with outcomes? Spotter planes, action plans, and steerage of the educational workplace. *British Journal of Sociology of Education, 19*(3), 291–303.

Spring, J. (1998). *Education and the rise of the global economy*. Mahwah: Lawrence Erlbaum.

Tan, J. (1997). The rise and fall of religious knowledge in Singapore secondary schools. *Journal of Curriculum Studies, 29*(5), 603–624.

Tan, T. W., & Chew, L. C. (2004). Moral and citizenship education as statecraft in Singapore: A curriculum critique. *Journal of Moral Education, 33*(4), 597–606.

Tan, J., & Gopinathan, S. (2000). Education reform in Singapore: Towards greater creativity and innovation? *NIRA Review, 7*(3), 5–10.

Tan, J. (2007). Pulling together amid globalisation: National education in Singapore schools. In P. D. Hershock, M. Mason, & J. H. Hawkins (Eds.), *Changing education: Leadership, innovation and development in a globalizing Asia Pacific* (pp. 183–198). Hong Kong: Comparative Education Research Centre (CERC), The University of Hong Kong, and Springer.

Taylor, S., Rizvi, F., Lingard, B., & Henry, M. (1997). *Education policy and the politics of change*. London: Routledge.

Tharman, S. (2007). Speech at the Network Conference. Available at: http://www.moe.gov.sg/media/speeches/2007/sp20070814.htm. Accessed 15 May 2012.

Walker, D. F. (2003). *Fundamentals of curriculum: Passion and professionalism*. New Jersey: Lawrence Erlbaum.

Westbury, I. (2003). Curriculum, school: Overview. In J. W. Guthrie (Ed.), *The encyclopedia of education* (2nd ed., pp. 529–535). New York: Macmillan.

Westbury, I. (2008). Making curricula: Why so states make curricula, and how? In F. M. Connelly, F. H. Ming, & J. Phillion (Eds.), *The SAGE handbook of curriculum and instruction* (pp. 45–65). Los Angeles: Sage.

Chapter 6
Recontextualizing Critical Thinking in the Singapore Classroom: Political Ideology and the Formation of School Subjects

Leonel Lim

Since the 1990s, education systems in developed countries around the world have begun to focus their attention on the inclusion of critical thinking instruction in the school curriculum (Lipman 2003; Paul 1992; Siegel 1997; Swartz et al. 2010). Many international measures of student achievement have also highlighted the development of higher-order thinking skills as the linchpin of nations' educational success (OECD 2007, 2010). As Singapore, with its first-world economy and highly educated citizenry, becomes increasingly interconnected with the international marketplace of careers and ideas, its schools have not remained impervious to these global educational influences (Luke et al. 2005). In 1997, with the launch of *Thinking Schools, Learning Nation*, a plethora of educational and curricular initiatives that sought to respond to the perceived challenges of a globalized and knowledge-driven world, the Ministry of Education (MOE) signaled an unequivocal emphasis on developing in students a crucial set of critical thinking skills. More recently, curricular and pedagogical innovations such as *Teach Less, Learn More* (TLLM) (2005), through the substitution of more thoughtful and engaging pedagogies for sheer quantity of knowledge transmitted, demonstrate the MOE's continued commitment to these emphases (see Chaps. 2 and 7).

Discernible in these recent initiatives is a subtle shift in curricular focus, one underpinned by what Yates and Collins (2010, p. 98) refer to as a conception of the "curriculum as preparing the person in the world rather than developing or conveying the world in the person." Instead of having the curriculum specifying and students mastering bodies of knowledge and facts, the curricular emphases now turn upon transmitting select competencies and skills. In many ways, this shift is not unique to the Singapore education system but increasingly prevalent amongst developed countries. There is an emerging recognition that, at least amongst these countries, such shifts constitute the education system's response to both a common

L. Lim (✉)
National Institute of Education, Nanyang Technological University, Singapore
e-mail: leonel.lim@nie.edu.sg

Z. Deng et al. (eds.), *Globalization and the Singapore Curriculum: From Policy to Classroom*, Education Innovation Series, DOI 10.1007/978-981-4451-57-4_6,
© Springer Science+Business Media Singapore 2013

set of external pressures rooted in the global economy and the related issue of how best to prepare students for employment in an increasingly competitive and interdependent global economic environment (Yates and Young 2010; also Chap. 1). Yet as we note these overarching global concerns, it is also important – perhaps even more so – to pay attention to the ways in which, at the national level, meeting these pressures necessarily involves responding to distinct local exigencies.

This chapter suggests that, insofar as the MOE's critical thinking initiative partakes in global pressures to equip students with "knowledge skills" for the "knowledge economy," its translation into concrete curricular programmes simultaneously involves a crucial recontextualization that takes into account the ideologies of neoliberalism and anti-liberalism. The first section of the chapter develops the notion of curriculum translation in terms of Bernstein's concept of pedagogic recontextualization. This, as I will show, is essential in unmasking the centrality of socio-political ideologies as these mediate the process of translating curriculum policy into curricular programmes. The second section turns to analyze how the critical thinking initiative is translated into the school curriculum, elaborating on its emphases, goals, and frameworks, as well as the pedagogical strategies employed in its transmission. In the final section, to demonstrate the significance and necessity of recontextualizing critical thinking in Singapore, dominant Western conceptualizations of the subject are considered. There it is argued that the latter both connect to and presuppose a set of liberal democratic social ideals that can potentially run counter to the ideological framework consistently leveraged upon by the Singapore government. To be sure, the ideologies of neoliberalism and anti-liberalism have for long been integral to the nation-state's official consciousness, expressing commitments to both a particular vision of social order, hierarchy, and authority, as well as the preservation and consecration of a distinct relationship between schooling, state, and society.

Curriculum Translation and Recontextualization

A crucial task involved in understanding how broad social ideas and institutional policies find their way into the operational frameworks and programmes in a school or system of schools – i.e. from the policy curriculum to the programmatic curriculum (see Chap. 2) – lies in unpacking the notion of curriculum translation. The latter, Doyle (1992) tells us, refers to the process of translating a curricular ideal or aim into curriculum programmes and school subjects provided to schools or a system of schools. What is presupposed in this process, Doyle (1992) identifies, is really a "theory of content," a set of implicit assumptions and interpretations to do with the fundamental nature of the content and how it may be represented to students at various grade levels. This translation process "is grounded in arguments that rationalize the selection and arrangement of subject matter content for schools of particular types and the transformation of that content into school subjects appropriate to those schools or school types" (Westbury 2000, p. 34). But perhaps of most importance, such a theory of content raises the intrinsically political question of how that content can be interpreted *and* taught in ways that contribute to the reification and aggrandizement of certain social ideals and ideologies – and, it is instructive to note, not others (Apple 1995, 2004).

In this connection, Basil Bernstein's development of a theory of the curriculum that remains fundamentally attuned to both the structure of power relations in society and the ideologies of social and political institutions lends itself as a valuable way to think through the politics of curriculum translation intimated in the preceding paragraph. Specifically, his (Bernstein 1990, p. 192; see also 2000) illuminative work on pedagogic recontextualization, the process through which any curriculum is necessarily a recontextualized text that, being "modified by selection, simplification, condensation, and elaboration […] has been repositioned and refocused", is worth rehearsing at the outset.

For Bernstein, pedagogic recontextualization – which is largely undertaken by the state through its departments of education[1] – selects and creates school subjects and curricular knowledge (what he calls specialized forms of pedagogic communication) by embedding two discourses: an instructional discourse of skills of various kinds and their relations to each other, and a regulative discourse of social order, relations, and identity. Bernstein (2000) points out that oftentimes, people in schools and classrooms distinguish between the transmission of skills and the transmission of values, as if education is about values on the one hand, and about competencies on the other, the two always kept apart. By introducing the notion of pedagogic recontextualization, however, he argues that there is in fact only one discourse: "the instructional discourse is embedded in the regulative discourse, and the regulative discourse is the dominant discourse" (Bernstein 2000, p. 33). In this way, pedagogic recontextualization works to create a single text, one that is always fundamentally shaped by the regulative order. Depending on the given "content" and the particular social and moral "context", this recontextualized text is always historically and culturally specific. Bernstein's insistence on these matters means that any piece of (programmatic) curriculum that professes to teach supposedly instrumental/technical skills is always and already emblematic of particular social and moral ideologies.

Pedagogic recontextualization thus involves delocating a discourse, relocating it, and refocusing it, in order to advance a curricular text that perpetuates a given set of ideologies and therefore a given distribution of power relations and social order. What is important to recognize in the process, Bernstein emphasizes, is that "as this discourse moves, it is ideologically transformed; it is not the same discourse any longer" (Bernstein 2000, p. 33). The centrality of ideology here connects to other traditions in social theory and should not be glossed over. As Barthes (1972) notes, ideological work is required in transforming the ideas of dominant groups (such as the state and religious institutions) into so-called "natural" laws or "natural" ways of social practice (see also Althusser 1971; Apple 2004). This gives the ideas their

---

[1] See Dale (1989) for a very careful treatment of the relationship between the state and its apparatuses.

sense of public authority and objectivity so that they constitute the only rational, universally valid beliefs for members of the society (Gramsci 1971). For Bernstein, because the pedagogic communication laid out in the recontextualized text necessarily adheres to a particular ideological schema and so acts on the potential knowledge that is available to be transmitted and acquired, pedagogic recontextualization is integral to the functioning of the curriculum as the "symbolic regulator of consciousness" (Bernstein 2000, p. 37). These deep (almost structuralist) relations between the specialized forms of pedagogic communication, recontextualization, and social and ideological control thus form the basis of Bernstein's theory of the curriculum. Drawing upon this brief exposition of Bernstein's analytic framework, the next section turns to detail Singapore's critical thinking curriculum.

Translating Critical Thinking into School Subjects

The vision of "thinking schools" in the MOE's *Thinking Schools, Learning Nation* slogan represents one of the major initiatives for dealing with the challenges of the twenty-first century and the information age. The basic idea animating this vision consists in preparing younger Singaporeans to become better thinkers by inculcating in them the ability to think critically and reflectively. In unveiling the initiative, the then Prime Minister Goh Chock Tong challenged schools to be the "crucibles for questioning and searching, within and outside the classroom", stating that only by doing so could schools "develop future generations of thinking and committed citizens, capable of making good decisions to keep Singapore vibrant and successful in future" (Goh 1997; also see Chap. 4).

To translate these institutional ideas into the programmatic curriculum, the curriculum specialists at the MOE developed a thinking programme that has drawn heavily on Marzano et al.'s (1988) *Dimensions of Thinking* – namely focusing, information-gathering, remembering, organizing, analyzing, generating, integrating, and evaluating. These eight skills, deemed to be essential for critical thinking, investigation, problem solving, and decision making, were then later incorporated into Marzano's (1992) *Dimensions of Learning* framework which revolved around: (1) positive attitudes and perception about learning; (2) thinking involving acquiring and integrating knowledge; (3) thinking involving extending and refining knowledge; (4) thinking involving using knowledge meaningfully; and (5) productive habits of mind (Chua and Leong 1998). It was expected that through such a core thinking skills framework, students would be able to acquire and integrate knowledge, to extend and refine it for subsequent meaningful use, and, above all, to develop as critical thinkers.

This programme, piloted in 1996 and by 2000 covering all secondary schools, was delivered primarily through the explicit teaching of the above thinking skills/ attributes, and additionally through infusion into subject areas. The explicit teaching of thinking, for instance, usually involved a framework of metacognitive questions that asked students to describe what kind of thinking they were engaged in and how they did it, as well as to evaluate and plan their thinking. As reported by Chua and Leong (1998), some of the more popular strategies used here included questioning, cooperative learning, active learning (e.g. K-W-L, reciprocal teaching, 3-min pause), language of thinking (Tishman et al. 1995), and the promotion of productive habits of mind (Marzano 1992). In particular, the productive habits of mind framework was highlighted as essential to the development of critical thinking through its emphasis on particular cognitive qualities such as being accurate and seeking accuracy; being clear and seeking clarity; being open-minded; and being aware of your own thinking.

In the infusion approach, select critical thinking skills such as organizing, analyzing, generating, focusing, information gathering, integrating, and evaluating were infused into the content of core school subjects (science, English language, mathematics, etc.). Even though these skills were taught explicitly in the context of a content subject area, where the latter provides some background information for acquiring and exercising the thinking skills, the utilitarian purport of the skills nevertheless remain evident. Through such an approach, it was hoped that students would be able to "extend and refine the knowledge that they have acquired and integrated... so that it could be put into some meaningful use, like in making a decision or solving a problem" (Chua and Leong 1998, p. 81).

As pointed out by Deng (2001) however, undergirding the programme was a highly instrumental conception of critical thinking; thinking was understood as comprising discrete and generic skills which were to be mastered and later applied universally to a range of situations. As he notes, such a conceptualization pays scant attention to the construction of knowledge in particular subject areas. In identifying the specific critical thinking skills to be taught, then, such a conceptualization pays scant attention to the construction of knowledge in particular subject areas. As Deng (2001, p. 197) notes, "whether skills are taught in a non-curricular context or within the context of a particular subject matter, they nevertheless retain their individual identity, independent of the subject matter". Not only did such a conception preclude any approach to the teaching of thinking through substantive content (for example, subject immersion or a philosophies-of approach[2]), it also made possible the valuation of thinking solely in terms of its uses and the specific outcomes it produces, and not its intrinsic worth. Put equivalently, the concept of critical thinking became narrowly tied to the possession of a set of generic skills, rather than to unique ways of exploring and being in the world, as these are intimated by the various disciplines (McPeck 1990). Indeed, such an understanding of critical thinking was recently underscored by the then Minister for Education in his reiteration of the importance of these skills for all levels of education. He stressed that

> our children will need to learn better ways to handle information. The struggle now is not with having insufficient information – but the converse, having too much and having to make sense of voluminous inputs. [...] The premium is therefore no longer on collecting facts but on critical analysis - knowing what questions to ask, what information you need and the value of different sources of information. (Ng 2008)

---

[2] See, for example, Scheffler (1973).

Understanding critical thinking, or critical analysis in this way makes explicit the instrumentalist assumptions of the critical thinking curriculum founded upon Marzano's framework. Cast as a key thinking skill, critical thinking is here identified as a set of subject independent information processing skills that schools need to inculcate through the curriculum.

While Deng is undoubtedly justified in his critique of the instrumental nature of the MOE's critical thinking framework, for our purposes it is precisely such a formulation that represents what Bernstein refers to as pedagogic recontextualization. In employing Marzano's framework to translate the policy curriculum into concrete school programmes, the MOE recontextualized the notion of critical thinking into a set of discrete and generic information processing skills; critical thinking became simplified, condensed, and modified for certain purposes and towards certain aims. It was delocated, relocated, and refocused. In the process, a specialized pedagogic discourse was created that functioned to set boundaries on and legitimate which forms of thought constituted critical thinking and which were to be excluded.

At this juncture, two sets of questions inevitably arise. Firstly, what was the MOE recontextualizing critical thinking *from*? What were the alternative conceptions? Why was the MOE delocating its concept of critical thinking from these alternatives? Secondly, why did the MOE espouse such a concept of critical thinking (i.e. one founded upon Marzano's framework)? Which ideologies and commitments are served by such an understanding of critical thinking? The final section undertakes a scrutiny of these issues.

A Critical Scrutiny

In this section, Singapore's understanding of critical thinking as a set of individualized and instrumental information processing skills is contrasted against the dominant understanding of the subject in Western scholarship and literature. What is significant is the fact that for many of the proponents of critical thinking in the US and the UK, mastery of the modes of argumentation and argument analysis is of vital importance *precisely* because it equips individuals with the skills needed to understand, analyze, and resolve the various everyday problems in a liberal democratic state (see, for example, Giroux 1994; Hooks 2010; Lipman 2003; Nussbaum 1997, 2004; Paul and Elder 2005; and Siegel 1988, 1997). Critical thinking, on this account, functions as fundamentally constitutive of the process of democratic deliberation.[3]

This engendering of critical thinking and liberal democracy – as well as their inextricable relationship – constitutes a growing global discourse. However, it should be pointed out that such a discourse is also one that grows from intellectual roots in Western (Greek) philosophical traditions. Plato's (1968) Socrates, it will be remembered, defended himself against the charge of "corrupting the young" on the grounds that democracy needs citizens who can think for themselves rather than

[3] I have argued at length for this position elsewhere. See Lim (2011).

simply deferring to authority, who can reason together about their choices rather than just trading claims and counter-claims. Closer to our times, Israel Scheffler – one of the most influential contemporary educational philosophers – makes plain the importance of critical thinking and education to the healthy functioning of democracy. For democracy, he tells us,

aims so to structure the arrangements of society as to rest them ultimately upon the freely given consent of its members. Such an aim requires the institutionalization of reasoned procedures for the critical and public review of policy; it demands that judgments of policy be viewed not as the fixed privilege of any class or elite but as the common task of all, and it requires the supplanting of arbitrary and violent alteration of policy with institutionally channeled change ordered by reasoned persuasion and informed consent. (Scheffler 1973, p. 137)

Scheffler's account of democracy foregrounds the participatory role of the citizen in critiquing and having an active interest in the betterment of society. To be sure, the democratic citizen needs to be able to examine public policy concerns; to grasp fully the nature of democratic institutions so as to embrace fully their responsibilities; to judge intelligently the multiple issues facing his/her society; to seek reasons for and challenge proposed changes (and continuations) of policy; to assess these reasons fairly and impartially; to treat his/her fellow citizens as equal partners in political life; and so on. Indeed, so widely has the societal function of critical thinking been acknowledged that it has become largely synonymous with the subject's stated purpose. Siegel (1988, p. 61), for example, points out that "[a]n education which takes as its central task the fostering of critical thinking is the education most suited for democratic life."

But there is another dimension to understanding the significance of critical thinking in these formulations of the subject, one that needs to be appreciated intertextually as well as historically. This involves restoring to our collective memories that, in many ways, the inclusion of thinking as an explicit educational goal – at least in the developed Western world – contains progressive elements and represents a partial victory by educators lobbying for schools to go beyond a "banking" model of education (Kliebard 2004; see also Freire 1970). Thus, in the U.S. the 1983 report, *A Nation at Risk*, that voiced an at least decade-long concern that instruction in thinking should be emphasized across all levels of the formal curriculum was in part constituted by the demand that schools recognize and cater to the moral and intellectual growth of *all* students, not just those that prove academically "gifted" (Walters 1994). An education emphasizing autonomy, self-actualization, and the creation and pursuit of individual aspirations was thus in fact a sustained critique of and a counter-discourse to popular, instrumentalist views of schooling that sought merely to (re-)produce a "skilled" and docile workforce (Brown 1998). For many of the philosophers in the critical thinking movement, the development of critical thinking was seen as the crucial bulwark against both an authoritarian mentality and the pervasive (and perversive) influence of that mentality on social and political institutions (Kaplan 1991; Siegel 1988; Winch 2005).

I want to sum up the discussion here by suggesting that latent in the global discourse on the subject is an "emancipatory thesis." To be sure, the above allusions to both democratic engagement and individual autonomy carry strong overtones of personal freedom, social justice and transformation, the common good, and liberation from established forms of domination. An education in critical thinking, so understood, reflects the capacity of schools to nurture a citizenry that is empowered with the necessary faculties to address social problems and redress social wrongs, ultimately serving as the critical consciousness of, and the voice against, systems of class, race, ethnicity, and gender oppression. On this reading – which is not mine alone (see, for example, McLaren 1994; Paul 1994) – the "critical" of critical thinking is not unaligned to that of critical theory and critical pedagogy, fields of inquiry that take up an explicit focus on exposing the ways existing social relations and institutions such as schools simultaneously structure and mask issues of inequality and discrimination (see also Apple 1995, 2004; Freire 1970; Giroux 1981, 1994; McLaren 2006). For, despite important differences in their historical trajectories (Burbules and Berk 1999), all assume a general population in society who are to some extent lacking in the abilities that would allow them to discern certain kinds of falsehoods, inaccuracies, and distortions. All share a concern with how these falsehoods, inaccuracies, and distortions limit their engagement with society. And all believe that the well-being of individual citizens and democracy itself lies in the (self-) clarification of these ideas (Hooks 2010).

Such discourses, however, are non-existent in the Singapore curriculum. To be sure, while the latent emancipatory thesis that underpins the Western discourse on critical thinking conveys ideals of liberal democracy, autonomy, and enlarged citizenship responsibilities, and while such a social ideal is cherished in many Western liberal societies, it is also potentially threatening to the status quo, opening up the space for a radical consciousness outside that constituted by official knowledge (Apple 2000). The sense of this conflict is especially heightened in non-liberal – even anti-liberal – societies in East and South-East Asia, and especially Singapore (Bauer and Bell 1999; Bell 2006; Chua 1995; Tan 2004).[4]

In the latter, a dominant one-party state with a deliberately weak and underdeveloped language of individual rights, such Western liberal ideals as open dissension, political conflict, freedoms of speech, press, and assembly have been portrayed as not essential and even threatening to the stability and growth of the polity. Indeed, liberalism has very shallow roots in Asia, many parts of which have only in recent decades emerged as independent nations and are still struggling with developing distinct national identities and culturally and historically sensitive forms of governance. Still remembered as ex-colonizers, any outright attempt by members of Western nations to promote liberal democracy in these regions as the only legitimate embodiment of a higher social and moral ideal is often ignored, if not altogether resisted (Chua 2010). Instead, and as most powerfully witnessed in the case of Singapore, the pursuit and achievement of economic prosperity spearheaded by an elite, technocratic government is often foregrounded as the purveyor of an increase in material standards of living across the population, which in turn generates peace and harmony in civil

---

[4] Here, the distinctions between liberal and communitarian democracies (the latter of which the Singapore state identifies itself) are especially pertinent (Bell 2000; Chua 2010).

society (Lim 2013a; Mauzy and Milne 2002). For many commentators, to the extent that since its independence the political leadership has largely succeeded in gaining huge advances in poverty alleviation, expanding educational and career opportunities, and fostering strong bonds of social cohesion, the Singapore story (see Chaps. 4, 5, 10, and 13) has contributed immensely towards both debunking the very necessity of these Western freedoms to the creation of a peaceful and prosperous polity and legitimizing a new set of relationships between state and society (Friedman 2011; Mahbubani 2008; Zakaria 2004). In this latter set of relationships, founded upon a strong state presence in the management of citizens' lives and a collectivist mindset that prioritizes the interests of the social over the individual, it is hardly surprising that the radical emancipatory thesis of critical thinking, insofar as it is evocative of liberal assumptions and potentially challenging to the state's definitions of the common good, is one that finds little affinity with its educational discourse, and therefore needs to be distilled from the curriculum.

The teaching of critical thinking skills thus cannot be considered a neutral commodity abstracted from the ideological context of its transmission (Lim 2012). Again, Bernstein's ideas on pedagogic recontextualization are worth revisiting. As he notes, given that "the manner of [its] transmission and acquisition socializes the [individual] into [its] contextual usages," we need to consider "the structure of social relationships which produces these specialized competencies" (Bernstein 1977, p. 147; see also Bourdieu and Passeron 1977). Forms of rationality, reasoning, and thinking, to be sure, are culturally specific formations established upon an extensive hierarchy of power relations and principles of social control. For example, as has been discussed above, in many Western liberal societies the professed aims of education have always emphasized the "liberation" of the individual through the cultivation of rational autonomy. To facilitate this, critical social capacities are often epitomized as social and educational ideals, accompanied by a state-society relationship that tends towards the idealization of a small state presence and an enlarged and garrisoned set of essential individual rights. However, as has been variously noted, left unchecked this sense of individualism can also result in (some say *has resulted in*) the growth of entitlement cultures and a diminishing attention to collective social needs and responsibilities (Eztioni 1998).

In contrast – or more accurately, in response to the perception of a socially decadent West and the prospect of its being ungovernable – in many Asian societies such as Singapore, the sense of a social collectivity (as well as the need to maintain and reinforce it) is in political discourse often foregrounded and given exigence, and in policy formulations elected to outweigh the priorities of individuals. In addition, given their relatively young status as nations, and the necessary insecurities as objects-in-the-making, many Asian countries have shown a tendency to tightly embrace their citizens, incorporating them within a bounded "national" space and inscribing upon them a "national" identity (Chua 2010). For example, it will be remembered that in 1991 the Singapore government instituted a national ideology of "Shared Values," consecrating, among others, the tenets of "nation before community," and "community before self" (White Paper 1991). Several years later, these were given concrete expression in the new National Education curriculum that sought to develop "instincts" in every child of a "shared sense of nationhood" and a "sense of history and shared destiny" (Goh 1997, pp. 425–426). It is not uncommon in these societies, then, that education is often and explicitly accorded the crucial task of socializing the individual into a prevailing sense of social order, hierarchy, and authority. Given that the programmatic curriculum in fact forms the cornerstone of this larger social and moral order, fundamental shifts in forms of rationality, thinking, and questioning can potentially challenge and threaten the established authority structure of both the school and the society.[5]

But there is another ideology at play in understanding how critical thinking is recontextualized in the Singapore curriculum. As mentioned earlier, the *Thinking Schools, Learning Nation* initiative was promulgated by the MOE as a response to the perceived threats of globalization. Given the neoliberal ideologies that have characterized the policies and directions of the Singapore state (Harvey 2005; Teo 2011; Yeung 2000), it is of little surprise that both these "threats" and the corresponding official discourse on critical thinking have been interpreted in a narrowly economistic sense. To be sure, neoliberalism, with initiatives that encourage private enterprise, consumer choice, and an "ethic" of efficiency and cost-benefit-analysis, calls into order certain forms of thinking essential for the continued expansion and advancement of the economy, and ipso facto, the nation's well-being (Apple 2006; Harvey 2005). Thus, in response to the changing terrain of careers and prospects brought about by the globalized marketplace, the MOE has affirmed that the focus of education "must shift from efficiency to diversity, from knowing to thinking, and from fitting people to specific jobs to equipping them for lifelong learning and creating their own opportunities" (Ministry of Education 2002, p. i). The instrumental connections here between the economy (jobs) and education (thinking skills) are unmistakable. In such a context, the skills of critical thinking and argument analysis are far from redundant. Just months into office the current Minister for Education, in renewing his ministry's commitment to the teaching of critical thinking, proclaimed that

> Students will need to be discerning, to be able to judge the reliability and accuracy of the information they access. They will need to be able to make sense of the information, to synthesise it and to communicate purposefully and meaningfully. [...] As mechanistic jobs will be increasingly offshored or relegated to machines, the knowledge worker of the future will have to compete on higher levels — of critical thinking, synthesis and creativity. (Heng 2011)

Bernstein's insights into pedagogic recontextualisation are once again highly pertinent in understanding how broad curricular policies and initiatives are translated into curricular programmes for schools. As highlighted earlier, through recontextualisation, a discourse is delocated from its original site of production and relocated

---

[5] It should not be assumed that the distinction between liberal and collectivist societies is a binary one, and that consequently societies fall neatly into one category or the other. This cannot be further from the truth. In framing the above discussion in terms of ideological discourses, it should be apparent that all ideological discourses (liberalism included) really function as moralising statements rather than descriptions of extant conditions.

to another site, where it is altered as it is related to other discourses. Not only are prior ideological affiliations broken down, the recontextualized discourse becomes embedded in a new set of ideological/power relations. In the Singapore curriculum, the recontextualisation of critical thinking proceeds by altering the ways in which the subject is related to other discourses – i.e., by delocating it from the discourse of liberal democracy and by relocating it to discourses of economic growth, careers, material wealth, etc. In all this, the conception of "skill" is always embedded in the regulative discourse of the social order, effectively specifying the raison d'être of the subject. Indeed, and as this section has demonstrated, in thus translating critical thinking into the programmatic curriculum the subject is framed as an assemblage of cognitive skills that the knowledge economy requires of its workers; stripped of its "critical," emancipatory dimensions, it instead functions paradoxically to maintain if not advance the status quo.

Concluding Remarks

By employing Bernstein's notion of pedagogic recontextualization to understand the process of curriculum translation, this chapter has discussed how one integral component of the Singapore curriculum – the teaching of critical thinking skills – has been transformed from the global discourse and adapted into curricular programmes for schools. Particularly, the chapter demonstrated how the Singapore state continues to promote and preserve through its curricular framework and guidelines on the subject a set of ideologies rooted in neoliberalism and anti-liberalism. As a result, it is suggested, critical thinking has been delocated from its liberal underpinnings and relocated as a set of information processing skills closely tied to the discourse of economic imperatives.

All this, however, says very little about how these prescribed curricula are, as a matter of fact, enacted in real classrooms, and the ways in which teachers and students interpret, negotiate, and even contest them. Indeed, far from assuming the passivity of teachers' work and students' submissiveness (see, for example, Apple 1986; Willis 1977), it should not be surprising – and we should even expect – to find instances where teachers and/or students are more than a little creative, enacting the curriculum in genuinely transformative/empowering ways that elide officially sanctioned discourses. It may be noted, for example, that the premium placed on reason and rationality has already signaled the privileging of a new model of classroom discourse and interaction. By focusing more on questioning, inquiry, reasoning processes, and their related dispositions, rather than solely on, say, accumulated bodies of knowledge and traditional models of seniority and hierarchy, more students are now more able to challenge the teacher's voice in the classroom, effectively requiring the latter to enter into new forms of pedagogic relations with the former in order to maintain the legitimacy of his/her position. Indeed, it may be that to preserve the authority structure in the classroom – itself significant as the foundation of the larger social order – the basis of the pedagogic relationship needs to be reconsidered and reestablished.

Given the constraints of space and the focus of this chapter on documenting how global educational discourses are translated into curricular programmes in Singapore, it can do little more than point to these very real and important issues. To understand the complexities inherent in them, the analysis provided by Bernstein on pedagogic recontextualization, while immensely illuminative of the ways in which the state (and other powerful groups in society) exercises its influence on shaping the curriculum, nevertheless needs to be complemented by research that is founded upon close analyses of classroom instructional activities and interactions.[6]

References

Althusser, L. (1971). *Lenin and philosophy and other essays*. London: New Left Books.
Apple, M. W. (1986). *Teachers and texts*. New York: Routledge & Kegan Paul.
Apple, M. W. (1995). *Education and power* (2nd ed.). New York: Routledge.
Apple, M. W. (2000). *Official knowledge* (2nd ed.). New York: Routledge.
Apple, M. W. (2004). *Ideology and curriculum* (3rd ed.). New York: Routledge.
Apple, M. W. (2006). *Educating the "Right" way: Markets, standards, God and inequality* (2nd ed.). New York: Routledge.
Barthes, R. (1972). *Mythologies*. New York: Hill & Wang.
Bauer, J. R., & Bell, D. A. (Eds.). (1999). *The East Asian challenge for human rights*. Cambridge: Cambridge University Press.
Bell, D. A. (2000). *East meets West: Human rights and democracy in East Asia*. Princeton: Princeton University Press.
Bell, D. A. (2006). *Beyond liberal democracy: Political thinking for an East Asian context*. Princeton: Princeton University Press.
Bernstein, B. (1977). *Class, codes and control: Towards a theory of educational transmission* (Revth ed.). New York: Routledge.
Bernstein, B. (1990). *Class, codes and control: The structuring of pedagogic discourse* (2nd ed.). New York: Routledge.
Bernstein, B. (2000). *Pedagogy, symbolic control and identity: Theory, research, critique* (Revth ed.). Lanham: Rowman & Littlefield.
Bourdieu, P., & Passeron, J. C. (1977). *Reproduction in education, society and culture*. London: Sage.
Brown, K. (1998). *Education, culture and critical thinking*. Aldershot: Ashgate.
Burbules, N. C., & Berk, R. (1999). Critical thinking and critical pedagogy: Relations, differences, and limits. In T. S. Popkewitz & L. Fendler (Eds.), *Critical theories in education* (pp. 45–66). New York: Routledge.
Chua, B. H. (1995). *Communitarian ideology and democracy in Singapore*. London: Routledge.
Chua, B. H. (2010). Disrupting hegemonic liberalism in East Asia. *Boundary 2: An International Journal of Literature and Culture, 37*(2), 199–216.
Chua, M. H. P., & Leong, H. (1998). An overview of the thinking program in Singapore. In M. L. Quah & W. K. Ho (Eds.), *Thinking processes: Going beyond the surface curriculum* (pp. 79–83). Singapore: Prentice Hall.
Dale, R. (1989). *The state and education policy*. Milton Keynes: Open University Press.
Deng, Z. (2001). The centrality of subject matter in teaching thinking: John Dewey's idea of psychologizing the subject matter revisited. *Educational Research Journal, 16*(2), 193–212.

---

[6] These issues are taken up in my doctoral dissertation (Lim 2013b).

Doyle, W. (1992). Constructing curriculum in the classroom. In F. K. Oser, A. Dick, & J.-L. Patry (Eds.), *Effective and responsible teaching: The new synthesis* (pp. 66–79). San Francisco: Jossey-Bass.

Etzioni, A. (1998). *The essential communitarian reader*. Lanham: Rowman & Littlefield.

Freire, P. (1970). *Pedagogy of the oppressed*. New York: Continuum.

Friedman, T.L. (2011). Serious in Singapore. Accessed 17 June 2012, from http://www.nytimes.com/2011/01/30/opinion/30friedman.html?_r=2&ref=opinion

Giroux, H. (1981). *Ideology, culture and the process of schooling*. London: Falmer Press.

Giroux, H. A. (1994). Towards a pedagogy of critical thinking. In K. S. Walters (Ed.), *Re-thinking reason: New perspectives in critical thinking* (pp. 199–204). Albany: State University of New York Press.

Goh, C.T. (1997). *Shaping our future: Thinking schools, learning nation*. Speech presented by Prime Minister Goh Chok Tong at the opening of the 7th international conference on thinking. Suntec City Convention Centre Ballroom, Singapore.

Gramsci, A. (1971). *Selections from the prison notebooks*. New York: Lawrence & Wishart.

Harvey, D. (2005). *A brief history of neoliberalism*. New York: Oxford University Press.

Heng, S.K. (2011). Keynote speech by Mr. Heng Swee Keat, Minister for Education, at the IBM Centennial Dinner. Accessed 17 June 2012, from http://www.moe.gov.sg/media/speeches/2011/11/02/keynote-speech-by-mr-heng-swee-keat-at-ibm-centennial-dinner.php

Hooks, B. (2010). *Teaching critical thinking: Practical wisdom*. New York: Routledge.

Kaplan, L. D. (1991). Teaching intellectual autonomy: The failure of the critical thinking movement. *Educational Theory, 41*(4), 361–370.

Kliebard, H. (2004). *The struggle for the American curriculum: 1893–1958* (3rd ed.). New York: Routledge/Falmer.

Lim, L. (2011). Beyond logic and argument analysis: Critical thinking, everyday problems and democratic deliberation in Cambridge International Examinations' thinking skills curriculum. *Journal of Curriculum Studies, 43*(6), 783–807.

Lim, L. (2012). Ideology, class and rationality: A critique of Cambridge international examinations' thinking skills curriculum. *Cambridge Journal of Education, 42*, 4,481–495.

Lim, L. (2013a). Meritocracy, elitism and egalitarianism: A preliminary and provisional assessment of Singapore's primary education review. *Asia-Pacific Journal of Education, 33*(1), 1–14.

Lim, L. (2013b). *Knowledges sacred and profane: Power and politics in recontextualizing critical thinking*. Unpublished PhD dissertation, University of Wisconsin-Madison.

Lipman, M. (2003). *Thinking in education*. Cambridge: Cambridge University Press.

Luke, A., Freebody, P., Shun, L., & Gopinathan, S. (2005). Towards research-based innovation and reform: Singapore schooling in transition. *Asia Pacific Journal of Education, 25*(1), 5–28.

Mahbubani, K. (2008). *The new Asian hemisphere*. New York: Public Affairs.

Marzano, R. J. (1992). *A different kind of classroom: Teaching with dimensions of learning*. Alexandria: Association for Supervision and Curriculum Development.

Marzano, R. J., Brandt, R. S., Hughes, C. S., Jones, B. F., Presseisen, B. Z., Rankin, S. C., & Suhor, C. (1988). *Dimensions of thinking: A framework for curriculum and instruction*. Alexandria: Association for Supervision and Curriculum Development.

Mauzy, D. K., & Milne, R. S. (2002). *Singapore politics under the people's action party*. New York: Routledge.

McLaren, P. L. (1994). Foreword: Critical thinking as a political project. In K. S. Walters (Ed.), *Re-thinking reason: New perspectives in critical thinking* (pp. IX–XV). Albany: State University of New York Press.

McLaren, P. L. (2006). *Life in schools: An introduction to critical pedagogy in the foundations of education*. Boston: Allyn & Bacon.

McPeck, J. E. (1990). *Teaching critical thinking: Dialogue and dialectic*. New York: Routledge.

Ministry of Education. (2002). Report of the Junior College/Upper Secondary Education Review Committee, 2002. Accessed 17 June 2012, from http://www.moe.gov.sg/jcreview/JC_Upp_Sec_Review_Report.pdf

Ng, E.H. (2008). Speech by Dr. Ng Eng Hen, Minister for Education and Second Minister for Defence, at the MOE Work Plan Seminar 2008. Accessed 17 June 2012, from http://www.moe. gov.sg/media/speeches/2008/09/25/speech-by-dr-ng-eng-hen-at-the-moe-work-plan-seminar-2008.php

Nussbaum, M. C. (1997). *Cultivating humanity: A classical defense of reform in liberal education.* Cambridge: Harvard University Press.

Nussbaum, M.C. (2004). Liberal education and global community. *Liberal Education, winter, 90*(winter), 42–47.

Organisation for Economic Cooperation and Development. (2007). *Assessing higher education learning outcomes.* Accessed 17 June 2012, from http://www.oecd.org/dataoecd/15/5/39117243.pdf

Organisation for Economic Cooperation and Development. (2010). *PISA 2009 assessment framework.* Paris: OECD Publishing.

Paul, R. (1992). *Critical thinking: What every person needs to survive in a rapidly changing world.* Tomales: Foundation for Critical Thinking.

Paul, R. (1994). Teaching critical thinking in the strong sense: A focus on self-deception, world views, and a dialectical mode of analysis. In K. S. Walters (Ed.), *Re-thinking reason: New perspectives in critical thinking* (pp. 181–198). Albany: State University of New York Press.

Paul, R., & Elder, L. (2005). *Critical thinking competency standards.* Tomales: Foundation for Critical Thinking.

Plato. (1968). *The Republic* (trans: Bloom, A.). New York: Basic Books.

Scheffler, I. (1973). *Reason and teaching.* New York: Bobbs-Merrill.

Siegel, H. (1988). *Educating reason.* New York: Routledge/Chapman & Hall.

Siegel, H. (1997). *Rationality redeemed? Further dialogues on an educational ideal.* London: Routledge.

Swartz, R., Costa, A. L., & Beyer, B. K. (2010). *Thinking-based learning: Promoting quality student achievement in the 21st century.* New York: Teachers College Press.

Tan, S. (2004). *Confucian democracy: A Deweyan reconstruction.* Albany: State University of New York Press.

Teo, Y. Y. (2011). *Neoliberal morality in Singapore: How family policies make state and society.* London: Routledge.

Tishman, S., Perkins, D., & Jay, E. (1995). *The thinking classroom: Learning and teaching in a culture of thinking.* Boston: Ally & Bacon.

Walters, K. S. (1994). *Re-thinking reason: New perspectives in critical thinking.* Albany: State University of New York Press.

Westbury, I. (2000). Teaching as a reflective practice: What might Didaktik teach curriculum? In I. Westbury, S. Hopmann, & K. Riquarts (Eds.), *Teaching as a reflective practice: The German Didaktik tradition* (pp. 15–40). Mahwah: Erlbaum.

White Paper. (1991). *Shared values.* Singapore: Singapore National Printers.

Willis, P. (1977). *Learning to labor: How working class kids get working class jobs.* New York: Columbia University Press.

Winch, C. (2005). *Education, autonomy and critical thinking.* London: Routledge.

Yates, L., & Collins, C. (2010). The absence of knowledge in Australian curriculum reforms. *European Journal of Education, 45*(1), 89–102.

Yates, L., & Young, M. (2010). Globalisation, knowledge and the curriculum. *European Journal of Education, 45*(1), 4–10.

Yeung, H. W. C. (2000). State intervention and neoliberalism in the globalising world economy: Lessons from Singapore's regionalisation programme. *The Pacific Review, 13*(1), 133–162.

Zakaria, F. (2004). *The future of freedom: Illiberal democracy at home and abroad.* New York: Norton.

Chapter 7
Teach Less, Learn More: Lost in Translation

**Juin Ee Teo, Zongyi Deng, Christine Kim-Eng Lee,
and Christina Lim-Ratnam**

Introduction

This chapter analyses how the Teach Less, Learn More (TLLM) initiative was *translated* into operational frameworks for implementation in schools and classrooms. TLLM was first introduced by Prime Minister Lee Hsien Loong in 2004 and was subsequently launched by then Minister for Education Mr Tharman Shanmugaratnam in 2005. TLLM was developed to address the gap between instructional practices and various educational initiatives introduced since 1997 under the Thinking Schools Learning Nation (TSLN) vision. Between 2004 and 2007, the TLLM initiative was translated into three operational frameworks: (1) the TLLM framework, (2) the TLLM *Ignite!* package, and, (3) the PETALS™ framework.

We start with clarifying the notion of *curriculum translation* in view of the policy, programmatic and classroom curricula introduced in Chap. 1. Next we discuss what TLLM entails in the policy arena, and analyse the translation of TLLM into the three operational frameworks with a focus on the key interpretive moves involved. We argue that substantive considerations of the "what" (content) and "why" (purpose) of teaching fundamental to TLLM have faded away in the translation process, overshadowed by largely technical concerns about the "how" of teaching driven by the imperative of meeting the needs of learners. Invoking the German *Didaktik* tradition, we argue that TLLM is a quintessential *curricular* idea which has to do with the "what" and "why" of teaching, and is inexorably associated with historically-rich curricular and educational thinking and discourses. We conclude by discussing the reasons for the loss of the "what" and "why" questions in the translation of TLLM and surface key insights about curriculum translation.

J.E. Teo (✉) • Z. Deng • C.K.-E. Lee • C. Lim-Ratnam
National Institute of Education, Nanyang Technological University, Singapore
e-mail: teo.juin.ee@gmail.com

Z. Deng et al. (eds.), *Globalization and the Singapore Curriculum: From Policy
to Classroom*, Education Innovation Series, DOI 10.1007/978-981-4451-57-4_7,
© Springer Science+Business Media Singapore 2013

Curriculum Translation

The notion of curriculum translation can be discussed with reference to the policy, programmatic and classroom curricula articulated by scholars such as Doyle, Westbury, and Deng (see Chap. 1). Each of these curriculum domains entails a particular kind of "curriculum making." In this chapter we are concerned with curriculum translation at the programmatic level, that is, with the process of translating a curriculum initiative into models or operational frameworks for the implementation of that policy or initiative in schools and classrooms. In the words of Westbury (2000), curriculum translation involves "the procedure through which one or another curricular vision is translated into an operational framework for systems of schools, and for understanding what social, cultural, and educational images mean for the character of work in classrooms" (p. 34).

Curriculum translation is in essence an interpretive and deliberative activity (Schwab 1973), which involves collaborative sense-making of what a curricular ideal or initiative entails in the policy arena and how that ideal or initiative can be put into practice in schools and classrooms. Because there are many ways to interpret an educational ideal or vision, translation of the ideal or vision into operational frameworks for school implementation always involves selective judgments and decision making. It entails bringing various discourses or models to bear on the process of decision making to develop workable and justifiable operational frameworks.

Therefore, it is reasonable to think that some interpretations and decisions are more sound or valid and workable than others depending on the *consistency between* the curriculum ideal or intent of the initiative, *and*, the way of enabling teachers to put the ideal or initiative into practice. Hence, making visible the interpretations and decisions made in the process of translating an abstract curricular idea into implementation frameworks allows us to interrogate the assumptions shaping particular translations. Such analytical work opens up discursive space for reconsidering interpretations and their consistency with curriculum ideals or intents, ultimately for the purpose of clarifying how translation work can be improved.

In the ensuing section we clarify what TLLM entails in the policy arena, before proceeding to examine how the initiative of TLLM has been translated into the three operational frameworks.

What TLLM Entails

As noted earlier, TLLM was initially introduced by Prime Minister Lee Hsien Loong in 2004, and was subsequently elaborated by then Minister for Education Mr Tharman Shanmugaratnam in 2005. Several articles have been written to discuss the meanings and implications of this concept (e.g. Deng 2012; Ng 2008; Tan and

Abbas 2009). The interpretations of TLLM discussed in these articles have informed our clarification of what TLLM entails in the context of Singapore's changing educational landscape.

At his inaugural National Day Rally Speech in 2004, the Prime Minister sketched out the need for Singapore to "develop new strengths and strategies to thrive in a different world" and consequently, the need for "a qualitative change, a quantum leap" in education where "new ways" of teaching engage students in experiential learning to prepare them for the exigencies of life in a globalised and rapidly changing world. His exhortations reiterate educational reform intents set in motion by the overarching Thinking Schools, Learning Nation (TSLN) vision launched in 1997. The various reform initiatives introduced since 1997 to achieve the TSLN vision "together call for the cultivation of critical thinking, creativity, innovation, life-long learning, positive attitudes and values, and national identity" to prepare students with the capabilities and dispositions needed for thriving in fluid, complex and socially diverse milieus (Deng 2012, p. 18).

Even as various initiatives sought to change classroom pedagogy from a focus on content and skill mastery for examinations towards a focus on helping students develop capabilities and attributes deemed imperative for the twenty-first century, extensive baseline research conducted in Singapore classrooms revealed that teaching practices remained mostly examination-driven, premised on knowledge and skills transmission (Hogan 2009; also see Chap. 8). For many teachers, parents and students caught in these winds of change, education in Singapore seemed to involve more and more new imperatives layered on top of an unchanging systemic, social and cultural demand for good grades in examinations.

The TLLM initiative was designed to address these concerns and the challenges of changing classroom practices. The Prime Minister stated:

> In fact, I think we should cut down on some of this syllabus. It would mean less pressure on the kids, a bit less rote learning, more space for them to explore and discover their talents and also more space for the teachers to think, to reflect, to find ways to bring out the best in their students and to deliver quality results. We've got **to teach less to our students so that they will learn more** [emphasis added]. Grades are important – don't forget to pass your exams – but grades are not the only thing in life and there are other things in life which we want to learn in school. (Lee 2004)

Thereafter, the Ministry of Education (MOE) endeavoured to further elaborate what TLLM entails. According to Mr. Tharman (2005), TLLM aims to shift the focus of classroom teaching from "quantity" (driven by content delivery and preparation for high-stakes examinations like the Primary School Leaving Examination (PSLE), the "O" and "A" levels, etc.) to "quality" (centred on preparing students for life and work in a changing world). This basic intent is further elaborated in the MOE's (2004) "What is Teach Less, Learn More?" website:

> It is about shifting the focus from "quantity" to "quality" in education. "More quality" in terms of classroom interaction, opportunities for expression, the learning of life-long skills and the building of character through innovative and effective teaching approaches and strategies. "Less quantity" in terms of rote-learning, repetitive tests, and following prescribed answers and set formulae.

In addition, two aspects of TLLM are discernible, outlining what teachers need to do in order to "teach less" and what it means for students to "learn more" (MOE 2004):

(1) TLLM calls on teachers to rethink the "why," "what," and "how" of teaching in order to teach "less" for content coverage and "more" for developing students holistically.

(2) TLLM envisions students as "engaged learners" actively involved in the process of learning "more" to be prepared for life and "less" for the sake of examinations.

Evidently, there are two essential aspects to TLLM. First, there is a notion of "engaged learners" and second, there is a call for school leaders and teachers to engage with the "core of education" or the purpose (why), content (what), and pedagogy (how) of teaching in view of the need to prepare students for the twenty-first century (MOE 2007a, p. 7). From the perspective of the Ministry, such engagement is essential for bringing about innovative pedagogical practices which can create ample opportunities for students to develop life-long learning abilities. "Teaching less" requires refraining from mere content delivery or overloading students with sheer bodies of information, concepts and procedures, so as to open up space and opportunities for transformative teaching (in terms of fostering critical thinking, creativity, innovation, and higher-order skills or competencies), that is, for "learning more."

In other words, TLLM is not only a psychological and pedagogical concept (concerning "engaged learners" and the "how" of teaching), but a *curricular* concept having to do with the "what" and "why" of teaching and learning. However, these curricular connotations have faded to the background, if not disappeared altogether, after TLLM was translated into operational frameworks.

TLLM: Lost in Translation

Following the Prime Minister's speech in 2004, the Ministry set up a TLLM Steering Committee "to explore how MOE and schools' efforts to realise TLLM could be coordinated and supported. The team consulted numerous teachers, school leaders, and teacher educators at National Institute of Education (NIE), and sent study missions out to several countries" (Tharman 2005). Between 2004 and 2007, the extensive consultations conducted by this steering committee resulted in the translation of TLLM into three operational frameworks: (1) the TLLM framework, (2) the TLLM *Ignite!* package, and, (3) the PETALS™ framework, each of which is a programmatic or curricular form.

These frameworks translate the general intent of TLLM (outlined in the above section) into specific operational guidelines for implementation in schools. Each translation involves making interpretive judgments about what TLLM entails and how it should be put into practice. According to Schön (1987), the weaving of such interpretive judgments into an overarching frame of reference involves "an ontological process" of "worldmaking" (a word coined by Goodman (1978)), which is accomplished through the interpretive moves of "naming and framing" of selected elements in a problematic situation to organise and direct problem solving in particular ways (p. 4). Biesta (2005) highlights the "worldmaking" or ontological nature of such interpretive moves: "linguistic or discursive practices **delineate** – and perhaps we can even say: **constitute** – what can be seen, what can be said, what can be known, what can be thought and, ultimately, what can be done [emphases added]" (p. 54). The interpretive moves of "naming and framing" selectively foreground and background particular elements and relationships, to "delineate" and "constitute" what TLLM entails for school leaders and teachers, ultimately influencing "what can be done" to realise TLLM.

The interpretive moves embodied in each framework were analysed with reference to what TLLM entails in the policy arena to discern how well these programmatic or curricular forms translate the meaning of TLLM.

The TLLM Framework: Curriculum Customisation for Diverse Learners

The TLLM framework (Fig. 7.1) shows how MOE would work with school leaders and teachers to meet the needs of learners who "are at the centre of everything we do as educators" (MOE 2007a, p. 8).

Fig. 7.1 The TLLM framework (MOE 2006a)

Central notions of this framework include: "top-down support for ground-up initiatives," "curriculum customisation," and "diverse learners." This framework translates "teach less to our students so that they will learn more" to mean students will learn more if their "diverse needs, abilities, aspirations and backgrounds" are catered to. Furthermore, according to this framework the "diverse needs" of learners are best catered to through finer-grained "curriculum customisation" by teachers as compared to what is called "mass customisation" by the MOE at the national planning level.

Mr. Tharman (2005) explained that this approach was influenced by his visit to Japan with MOE officials to plan strategies for implementing TLLM. They observed that changes in Japan's education system "were top-down, and implemented across the system" in a "uniform fashion" but "there appears to have been little buy-in on the ground" because people saw these reforms as "one-size changes for a very diverse student population." Hence, elements of the TLLM framework were defined to contrast directly with the situation observed in Japan: the MOE would provide "top-down support" while schools and teachers initiate "curriculum customisation" to meet the "diverse needs" of their learners.

As the first framework for TLLM implementation, the TLLM framework set the parameters and defined key concepts for subsequent implementation frameworks developed by the Ministry. The key interpretive move entailed in this framework is the redefinition of the "core of education" as constituted by "learners" in contrast to prevailing references to the core as constituted by consideration of "why we teach," "what we teach," and "how we teach." The explanation is: "Learners are at the centre of everything we do as educators. They have different learning needs and interests. The core of education lies in touching the hearts and engaging the minds of students" (MOE 2007a, p. 8).

This reinterpretation of what constitutes "the core of education" is represented visually in the TLLM framework in the form of "learners" and their "diverse needs" taking centre-stage, with all other elements directed towards "who we teach." As such the framework subsumes the consideration of "why we teach," "what we teach," and "how we teach" into the consideration of "who we teach," and particularly, their "diverse needs." By implication, "content" (what we teach) and "purpose" (why we teach) derive their substance and significance primarily from considerations about "learners" (who we teach). Hence, the need to rethink subject matter (what) and the broader purposes of education (why) are rendered invisible or unnoticeable. In contrast, "effective pedagogies" (how we teach) is emphasised in this framework. This foregrounding of "how we teach" while obscuring its necessary relationship with "what we teach" and "why we teach" is another key interpretive move carried through subsequent operational frameworks.

One might argue that the need to rethink education content (what we teach) is implied by the concept of "curriculum customisation" in the framework. However, this concept directs curriculum design towards the primary task of developing a curriculum that is "custom-made" or "tailored" to suit the particular needs and profile of learners. Rather than stressing the need to rethink education content as an important educational resource in its own right (and more will be said about this later in the chapter), the notion of curriculum customisation foregrounds the learner and tends to undermine or obscure other curriculum "commonplaces" – subject matter, teachers and milieus – which, according to Schwab (1973), are equally vital to "defensible" curriculum development, "[n]one of these can be omitted without omitting a vital factor in educational thought and practice" (pp. 508–509). In other words, the notion of curriculum customisation entails a partial and reductive approach to curriculum development.

The TLLM Ignite! Package: School-Based Curriculum Innovation

To oversee the implementation of curriculum customisation in schools under the TLLM framework, a new unit was set up within the Curriculum Planning and Development Division (CPDD) in the MOE: the Curriculum Policy and Pedagogy Unit (CPPU). The foregrounding of "Pedagogy" in the naming of this unit reflects the key interpretive move of focusing on "how we teach" as noted earlier. In 2006, the CPPU worked with 29 schools to "prototype their school-based curriculum innovations" (MOE 2007a, p. 2). Building on this prototype phase, the CPPU developed the TLLM *Ignite!* package, to be provided to about 100 schools each year from 2008 to 2010 (MOE 2008a).

The TLLM *Ignite!* package is a framework of "top-down support" provided over one school year to "catalyse School-based Curriculum Innovations (SCI)" which involve teachers in "designing, implementing and studying different approaches for engaged learning," approaches to SCI suggested by the MOE include "curriculum customisation, curriculum integration, differentiated instruction, inquiry-based learning and problem-based learning" (MOE 2008a, b). The central features of this framework which reflect key interpretive moves are:

(1) The SCI as the focal point for schools "to put their TLLM ideas into action" guided by a clear focus on "student engagement" (MOE 2008a, b); and,
(2) The Research Activist (RA) Scheme for one teacher per school to be attached to MOE Headquarters 2 days a week over 20 weeks, during which the "RAs embarked on action research training, and worked concurrently on carrying out research on their school-based innovation" (MOE 2006b; Tan et al. 2007, p. 2).

Other features of the TLLM *Ignite!* package come under an "integrated framework of support" (MOE 2006b) comprising "networks" and "sharing platforms", funding of "about \$15,000 per SCI per school," and, professional development workshops "relevant to the school's specific area of SCI" (MOE 2008a). The Ministry operationalised the notion of "top-down support" in terms of what is called the "One MOE Approach" (MOE 2006b) where the MOE Headquarters SCI "project facilitator" served as a "one-stop point of contact" coordinating "top-down support" for schools (MOE 2008a).

Evidently, the SCI was conceived as the *unit of activity* for implementing TLLM in schools to operationalise the notion of "ground-up initiatives". This key interpretive move of delineating the SCI as the unit of activity for implementing TLLM foregrounds the SCI project space as a site for experimentation, constituting change in classroom practices in terms of undertaking "innovation projects". When participating in these projects, teachers are expected to take "bold steps in pioneering **new strategies** and adopting or adapting **novel approaches** to meet the needs of their students [emphases added]" (MOE 2008a). This emphasis on "innovation" in the form of "new strategies" and "novel approaches" to "meet the needs of learners" reinforces preceding interpretive moves made by the TLLM framework to foreground the "how" of teaching and the "diverse needs of learners" while leaving in the background substantive considerations about the "what" (content) and "why" (purpose) of teaching. Similarly, the delineation of an action research project conducted by the RA to monitor and evaluate the SCI project advanced the foregrounding of technical concerns about the "how" of teaching to bring about increased "student engagement outcomes" (MOE 2007a, p. 47).

The PETALS™ Framework: Engaged Learning and Student-Centredness

The CPPU first developed the PETALS™ framework and disseminated it to schools in 2005. The framework was rearticulated in 2007 in a more elaborate form as "PETALS™: The Teacher's Toolbox" featuring selected SCI projects as exemplars of how the framework can be used to "influence the level of student engagement in learning" (MOE 2007a, p. 10). The PETALS™ framework sought to provide "a common language and professional vocabulary across all schools" to guide the planning of SCI projects and everyday classroom practices, its key interpretive moves were made with a view towards influencing what teachers should do to realise TLLM in classrooms (MOE 2007a, p. 8).

Consistent with the learner-centric view adopted in the TLLM framework, the PETALS™ framework (Fig. 7.2) positioned "student-centredness" in the middle of the framework surrounded by "five dimensions of engaged learning" believed to be useful for realising student-centredness (MOE 2007a, p. 10).

The five dimensions constitute a generic guide which can be used by all teachers to "plan student-centred and engaging lessons," the assumption is that "students are engaged when teachers:

- Select **Pedagogy** that considers students' readiness to learn and their learning styles;
- Design an **Experience of Learning** that stretches thinking, promotes interconnectedness and develops independent learning;
- Create a **Tone of Environment** that is safe, stimulating and which engenders trust;
- Adopt **Assessment** practices that provide information on how well students have performed and provide timely feedback to improve learning; and
- Select relevant and meaningful **Learning Content** that makes learning authentic for students" (MOE 2007a, pp. 10–11).

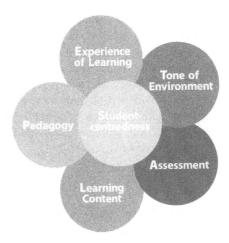

Fig. 7.2 The PETALS™ framework (MOE 2007b)

The key interpretive move of delineating a descriptive teaching guide foregrounds the technical aspects of teaching ("how-to" strategies and approaches), consistent with the emphasis of the other frameworks. Although "learning content" is a visible element in PETALS™, what teachers should do with learning content is delineated in terms of "customising" prescribed content in the MOE syllabuses through the use of "authentic real-world examples" to make content "meaningful and relevant to students" (MOE 2007a, pp. 38–39). This delineation of what teachers should do with learning content reiterates the foregrounding of "learners" and the "how" of teaching, yet again the content or the "what" of teaching is treated as something merely for *delivery* "to students" rather than as something with educational potential (see Deng 2011).

It is worth noting that the MOE's (2004) "What is Teach Less, Learn More?" website elaborates the "why," "what," and "how" of teaching. Teachers are *exhorted* to "remember why we teach," to "reflect on what we teach," and, to "reconsider how we teach." Descriptive statements and contrasting notions are outlined to help teachers operationalise the "why," "what," and "how," such as "We should keep in mind that we do what we do in education for the learner, his needs, interests and aspirations, and not simply to cover the content," "More for the Learner," and "Less to Rush through the Syllabus." However, the rich educational meanings and curricular significance of the call for sustained rethinking of the "why," "what," and "how" of teaching and their *interrelationship* becomes difficult to discern in the lists of discrete statements and pointers. The PETALS™ framework reiterates this pattern of interpretive moves in the delineation of the five dimensions to describe what teachers should do instead of engaging teachers in sustained and generative analyses of the "why," "what," and "how" of teaching.

Lastly, another key interpretive move evident in the PETALS™ framework is the delineation of "engagement in learning" and "student engagement" as "an end in itself as well as a means to an end" (MOE 2007a, p. 42). This interpretive move is justified by the rationale: "Engaged learning is important as research has shown that

it correlates positively with academic achievement [emphasis added]." (MOE 2008a). This justification confounds the basic intent of TLLM to shift the focus of teaching and learning away from narrow and quantitative understandings of education centred on academic achievement. Furthermore, this interpretive move deepens the eclipse of the "what," "why," and "how" of teaching through the extensive foregrounding of "learners," evident in all three frameworks. *Engaged learners* overshadows other curriculum "commonplaces" (Schwab 1973) to become *both* the means and end of education. The rich *curricular* meanings fundamental to TLLM have faded away in the translation process.

TLLM and "What" and "Why" of Teaching: The German *Didaktik* Tradition

In this section we argue that the "what" and "why" questions, which have become almost "invisible" in the three implementation frameworks, are fundamental to the idea of TLLM. To develop this argument, we look beyond the current discourse on TLLM in Singapore to the German *Didaktik* tradition where a similar idea has been solidly-articulated and richly-theorized.

The core of the tradition is encapsulated by the concept of *restrained teaching* (Hopmann 2007). Teaching is viewed *less* as a process of transmitting a body of knowledge and skills to learners, and *more* as a process of inducing a transformative impact on learners – in terms of attitudes, perspectives, ways of thinking, capabilities, and dispositions of mind. To achieve this, the teacher necessarily *restrains* himself or herself from an attempt to "overwhelm" learners with an excessive body of knowledge and skills by way of telling or direct instruction. Instead, the teacher "instigates" quality learning in a way that can bring about fundamental change in learners. This bears seeming resemblance to the intent of TLLM at the policy level in Singapore.

The German *Didaktik* tradition can be traced back to Johann Amos Comenius (1592–1670) and Johann Friedrich Herbart (1776–1814), both of whom had been instrumental for developing Didaktik into an established tradition of thinking about education and teaching in Germany and Northern Europe. The term *Didaktik* was first used by Johann Amos Comenius (1592–1670) in his classic *Didactica Magna*. In this book we can clearly see the notion of TLLM in a passage concerning the beginning and end of Didaktik.

> To seek and find a method by which the **teachers teach less and the learners learn more** [emphasis added], by which the schools have less noise, obstinacy, and frustrated endeavour, but more leisure, pleasantness, and definite progress, and by which the Christian State will suffer less under obscurity, confusion, and conflict, and will enjoy a greater amount of light, order, peace, and quiet. (Comenius 1627, in Ulich 1947/1954, p. 340)

According to Comenius, Didaktik in essence entails "teaching everything to everyone." Teaching means helping students to relate the "microcosmos" of instruction to the "macrocosmos" of the world (Gundem 2000, p. 239). To achieve this, the teacher sees the central task of teaching as creating a "meaningful encounter" between students and content – an interaction that can broaden students' horizons and bring about fundamental change in their attitudes, understanding, ways of thinking, and capabilities. To facilitate such an encounter, he or she necessarily examines the "what" question in view of the ultimate purpose of teaching or the "why" question. He or she needs to address "what the content of instruction should be like, where it came from, and how it was used," so the content can open up manifold meanings and significance. In addition, the teacher needs to take account of who the learners are, including their interests, motivations, experiences, learning progress and development (Gundem 2000).

Herbart defined the central purpose of education in terms of the moral and intellectual development of the individual. Teaching is construed as the central activity of education, entailing more than imparting a body of knowledge and skills to learners. The act of teaching in essence is "education by content." Like Comenius, Herbart believed that to teach is "to promote learning person's involvement with his or her world" through a meaningful encounter with cultural content (Krüger 2008, p. 227). This requires "an inviting unlocking of contents which stimulates understanding, and consequently elevates a child's *dialogue* with his or her world" (p. 227). To do this, the teacher necessarily attends to the "what" question in view of the central aim of education, or the "why" question. He or she seeks to create a lasting impact of teaching by way of reflection on the worth of content, through addressing questions of what the content can or should signify for the student and how the student can experience this significance.

The notion of restrained teaching, together with the need to unpack the "educative" meaning and significance of content in view of the central purpose of education, is further articulated in the *Didaktik* tradition. The tradition provides a meaningful way of translating the idea of restrained teaching (i.e., TLLM) into curriculum frameworks and into classroom practice. There are three basic tenets or commonplaces of the tradition: (1) the notion of *Bildung*, (2) the distinction between content and meaning, and (3) the autonomy of classroom teaching (Hopmann 2007).

Bildung encapsulates what it means to be educated in Germany and Continental Europe. It consists of a set of educational aims and values centred upon the formation of mind, the development of powers or capabilities and sensitivity, and the cultivation of liberty, dignity and freedom of the learner (cf. Hopmann 2007; Humboldt 2000). To achieve *Bildung*, a person needs to "grasp as much [of the] world [culture] as possible" and make contributions to humankind through developing one's own powers and faculties (Humboldt 2000).

With regard to the second tenet, all German states have a well-articulated state curriculum framework, the *Lehrplan*, which lays out school subjects and their contents to be taught in schools, resulting from special selection and organization of the wealth of the conceivable knowledge, experiences, and wisdom for *Bildung*. However, the curriculum framework does not prescribe (educational) meanings associated with the contents, which are to emerge from the interaction of students with content in a classroom, under the support and guidance of a teacher.

To facilitate such an encounter, in instructional planning the teacher necessarily interprets and unpacks content for educative meaning and significance in the light of *Bildung.*

In the German tradition teachers have a high level of professional autonomy; they are viewed as reflective professionals "working within, but not directed by" the state curriculum framework, informed by the idea of *Bildung* and the Didaktik way of thinking (Westbury 2000). Teaching is viewed as enabling a "fruitful encounter" between content and the learner (Klafki 2000). Through teaching, the teacher "opens up a world for the student, thus opening the student for the world" (Hopmann 2007, p. 115; also see Klafki 2000). Here we see the manifestation of Comenius' and Herbart's notions of classroom teaching.

In instructional planning the teacher is centrally concerned with interpreting and analysing content for educational meaning and significance, that is, for educational potential (Deng 2011). The interpretation and analysis needs to be conducted with reference to a learner or a particular group of learners within a particular historical context (present and future), from the perspective of *Bildung.* Klafki formulated a five-step set of questions that allow teachers to explore the educational potential of content which can be characterised in terms of (1) *exemplary value,* (2) *contemporary meaning,* (3) *future meaning,* (4) *content structure,* and (5) *pedagogical representations* (see Gudmundsdottir et al. 2000).

1. Exemplary value: What wider or general sense or reality does this content exemplify and open up to the learner? What basic phenomena or fundamental principle, what law, criterion, problem, method, technique, or attitude can be grasped by dealing with this content as an "example"?
2. Contemporary meaning: What significance does the content in question, or the experience, knowledge, ability, or skill, to be acquired through this topic, already possess in the minds of the children in my class? What significance should it have from a pedagogical point of view?
3. Future meaning: What constitutes the topic's significance for the children's future?
4. Content structure: How is the content structured (which has been placed in a specifically pedagogical perspective by questions 1, 2, and 3)?
5. Pedagogical representations: What are the special cases, phenomena, situations, experiments, persons, elements of aesthetic experience, and so forth, in terms of which the structure of the content in question can become interesting, stimulating, approachable, conceivable, or vivid for children of the stage of development of this class? (Klafki 2000)

Questions 1–3 explore the essential ingredients, features and significances that constitute the educational potential of the content. We can see an attempt to link content or school knowledge to the external world of students. Questions 4 and 5 deal with the means of actualising the potential – in terms of content structure and pedagogical representations – which is an outgrowth of analysing the content in terms of educational potential. It is important to note that the search for methods (the "how" of teaching) is the final step, the "crowning" moment in instructional preparation (Klafki 2000), which has to follow and is predicated on a careful analysis of the "what" in view of the "why" of teaching.

From the perspective of the German *Didaktik* tradition, "teach less" in the notion of TLLM entails an effort of the teacher to "restrain" himself or herself from "overwhelming" students with content (a sheer body of information, knowledge and skills), and instead to anchor the instruction on (a few) carefully and deliberately-identified essential ingredients, features and significances of the content. He or she plans and conducts teaching in a way that allows content to open up manifold "educative" opportunities in view of the central purpose of teaching (i.e., *Bildung*). This enables students to "learn more," by broadening perspectives, transforming ways of thinking, and cultivating capabilities and dispositions of minds. A sustained engagement with the "what" and "why" of teaching is crucial to restrained teaching, i.e., to TLLM.

One might question the relevance of the German tradition for the current context of curriculum and educational reforms in Singapore and elsewhere. How might the German tradition (which foregrounds the crucial role of academic content of school subjects in the cultivation of intellectual and moral capabilities) – have something to do with the development of the capabilities needed for the twenty-first century – such as critical thinking, creativity, innovation, and twenty-first century competencies? In this chapter the point of looking at the German *Didaktik* tradition is to call attention to a very different way of thinking about the role of content in teaching and learning with respect to the development of students' intellectual and moral capabilities – a way of thinking that cannot be found in the Anglo-Saxon tradition of curriculum and instruction (Westbury 2000). The German way of thinking challenges us to rethink the role of curriculum content (the "what" question) in our current context of teaching and learning for the development of higher-order thinking, desirable values and dispositions, and twenty-first century competencies (the "why" question). As Deng has argued elsewhere, content is as an important resource for widening students' horizons and developing critical thinking, attitudes and values *rather than* merely as a body of facts and concepts for transmission or delivery. When selected, framed and transformed by a teacher in a certain way, content can render manifold "educative" opportunities in terms of broadening perspectives, enhancing social awareness, and developing generic skills and capabilities (Deng 2009, 2010). How should teachers restrain themselves from the tendency of "overwhelming" students with the content of curriculum syllabuses (i.e., "teach less") so as to create space for the cultivation of critical thinking, positive values and attributes, and twenty-first century competencies (i.e. "learn more") – using content as an indispensable resource? This is a challenging question facing policymakers, reformers, educators and teachers in Singapore and worldwide. We have to pay serious attention to the "what" and "why" of teaching – in addition to the "how."

Concluding Discussion

In closing, we discuss two related questions, what might account for the loss of focus on the "what" and "why" of teaching in the translation of TLLM, and, what can we learn about curriculum translation from the TLLM case. Three interrelated factors contribute to the loss of focus: (1) the displacement of a language of *curriculum* or *education* by a language of *learning* in contemporary policy making (Biesta 2005), (2) the consequent translation of TLLM in ahistorical and technical terms (Deng 2012), and (3) a tendency for translation work to focus more on scaling up implementation and less on clarifying meaning and implications.

As noted earlier, curriculum translation is in essence interpretive and deliberative, it involves putting linguistic or discursive resources to work, to delineate and constitute elements in initiatives to direct implementation in *particular* ways. In short, *language* is vital to curriculum translation because it "makes some ways of saying and doing possible" while rendering other ways "difficult or even impossible" (Biesta 2005, p. 54). Many scholars involved in education research and practice in various fields and in different parts of the world have noted with deep concern the rise of *a language of learning and accountability* in place of *a language of and for education* in contemporary discourse and policy making (e.g. Biesta 2005; Connelly 2011; Contu et al. 2003; Hopmann 2008; Kemmis 2010). These scholars are deeply concerned about the increasingly reductive, individualistic, utilitarian and transactional understandings of education advanced by the rise of *learning* and *accountability* as key concepts in policy making.

Although Biesta (2005) notes the re-balancing value of an emphasis on learners and learning in the historical context of "provider-led and inflexible" approaches to education (p. 58), he nonetheless argues "against" the "new language of learning" on the basis of how it:

> allows for an understanding of education as an economic exchange between a provider and consumer. Such an understanding, exemplified in the idea of 'meeting the needs of the learner', not only makes it difficult to represent the contributions educators and teachers make to the educational process; it also makes it very difficult to have an informed, democratic discussion about the content and purpose of education. (p. 54)

We have shown how the dominance of the idea of "meeting the needs of the learner" has shaped the translation of TLLM into implementation frameworks which foreground the "how-to" questions about "engaging learners" while neglecting the "what" and the "why" of teaching. Biesta (2005) further explains these tendencies:

> The idea that education should be about meeting the needs of the learner is also problematic because it suggests a framework in which the only questions that can meaningfully be asked about education are technical questions, that is questions about the efficiency and the effectiveness of the educational process. The more important questions about the content and purpose of education become virtually impossible to ask, other, that is, than in response to the needs of the learner. (p. 59)

This is exactly what has happened in the case of the TLLM implementation frameworks, exemplified by the collapse of rich curricular deliberations into the notion of "curriculum customisation". Biesta (2005) and Kemmis (2010) argue that broader substantive discussions about the content and purposes of education have been "colonised" by discourses which are not in themselves *educational*, for example, *managerial, technical* and *psychological* discourses which construe *learning outcomes* and *engaged learners* as the *product* of education and notions of *accountability, diversity* and *choice* as the means for *delivery* of quality in education. The growing influence of such discourses can be accounted for by the marketisation of education and the increasing popularity of constructivist and socio-cultural theories of learning which foreground the learner's active construction of knowledge (among other trends and developments) (Biesta 2005). The marketisation of education in particular has greatly influenced education policy in Singapore as discussed by Tan (2008a): "Terms such as choice, competition, diversity, pleasing one's customers, stretch goals, accountability have now become commonplace in the Singapore education system over the past two decades." (p. 34).

Collectively, these trends in "the language or languages we have available to speak about education" (Biesta 2005, p. 54), construe educational practice in primarily technical and transactional terms "and thus erode the opportunities to use properly educational discourses to understand and interpret education under changing historical conditions and in different locations" (Kemmis 2010, p. 23). According to Kemmis (2010), "properly educational discourses" or ways of thinking and speaking about education which are oriented to the "practice-traditions of education" can "decline and disappear like one of the indigenous languages around the world today that suddenly loses the last of its speakers, taking with it not just the language but also the knowledge it articulated" (p. 24). Hence, Biesta (2005) argues for the pressing need to "reclaim" a "language of and for education" to resist the pervasiveness of reductive, individualistic and economic interpretations of the educational process in contemporary society (p. 54).

The need to "reclaim" a language of and for education in the Singapore context is clearly evident in the largely "ahistorical" and "under-theorized" discourse on the TLLM initiative (Deng 2012, p. 21). We have argued that sustained engagement with the "what" (content) and "why" (purpose) of education is fundamental to TLLM and have discussed how TLLM has been richly developed in the history of educational thought, drawing on the German *Didaktik* tradition (see Deng 2012 for a discussion of TLLM in the North American context). The atrophy of a language for education and the ahistorical disconnection of contemporary education practice from educational "practice-traditions" (Kemmis 2010) "prevents educators from engaging in a better informed, more thoughtful, and more responsible discussion" of ideas like TLLM (Deng 2012, p. 21). The focus on sustained engagement with the "what" and "why" of teaching to develop deeper understandings of the "how" can be reclaimed through "revisiting" and reinterpreting the "richness" of meanings associated with TLLM in the history of educational thought (Deng 2012, p. 28).

The loss of focus on the "what" and "why" of teaching in the translation of TLLM can also be accounted for by the tendency for translation work to focus more on scaling up implementation and less on clarifying meaning and implications through sustained deliberation. In the case of TLLM for example, the need for the CPPU to "ignite", facilitate and coordinate hundreds of SCI projects involving almost all schools in Singapore skewed the emphasis of frameworks like PETALS™ towards addressing pragmatic and technical concerns about "how" to develop, implement and evaluate the SCI projects. Against the backdrop of dominant operating discourses discussed above, the *slower* nature of interpretive and deliberative work in curriculum translation about the "what" and "why" of teaching is easily overtaken by the pressing technical concerns of planning for system-wide TLLM implementation.

The skewing of translation work towards designing implementation strategies can also be explained by the lack of awareness about *curriculum translation* as an important and substantive phase in curriculum making. A cursory scan of introductory curriculum texts surfaces the visibility of *curriculum implementation* as a well-researched and substantive chapter (e.g., Hewitt 2006; Marsh and Willis 2009; Morris 1996). By contrast, the complex nature of *translation* work in programmatic curriculum making tends to be discussed in terms of *curriculum development, design* and *decision making*. Given the dominance of technical concerns in education practice discussed earlier, the foregrounding of terms like *development, design* and *decision making* can collude with reader expectation for procedural guidelines and principles to obscure discussions about the deliberative nature of curriculum translation. Curriculum translation lies at the heart of curriculum making in terms of developing programmes, operational frameworks, and courses of study. It is not merely a technical task; rather, it entails interpretation, deliberation and action that "seeks to precipitate social, cultural, and educational symbols into a workable and working organizational interpretation and framework" (Westbury 2000, p. 531). The translation process, Deng (2010) argues, requires a careful rethinking, re-conceptualising, or reframing of content in view of a vision, idea or initiative, and with respect to school and classroom practices.

The importance of engaging with the realities of school and classroom practices is underscored by Hogan (2011) in a recent paper discussing the "fate" of the TLLM policy initiative. He observed that very little has changed in Singapore's "regime" of instructional practices since the launch of TLLM. The limited impact of TLLM can be traced to the "design of implementation strategies" which encouraged a proliferation of innovations but "many were not strategically valuable, rigorous, evidence-based, effective or sustainable" (Hogan 2011, p. 20). Hence, it is important for the Ministry to exercise clear and strong curriculum leadership through a translation process that "identif[ies] and drive[s] evidence-based, strategic priorities" for schools and teachers (Hogan 2011, p. 20). We argue that developing a culture of educational practice centred on unpacking the educative meanings of content (what) in a way that nurtures students for broadly construed educational purposes (why) constitutes a strategic priority for curriculum leadership in Singapore. Ironically, the hitherto prioritising of pedagogies (how) has had limited impact on classroom practices. We argue on the basis of historically-rich curricular ideas and established wisdom about the "content-specific character" of sophisticated "pedagogical reasoning" (Shulman 1987, pp. 10–13) that the "what" and the "why" of teaching constitute substantive bases for generating rich and meaningful understandings of "how" to teach. To realise the intent of TLLM, redirecting educational practice towards sustained engagement with the content and purposes of education is imperative for curriculum leaders in Singapore.

Furthermore, Hogan (2011) explained that the design of TLLM implementation strategies underestimated the resistance of the "tight coupling" between instructional practice and the national high stakes examination system (p. 20). Our findings from an analysis of the TLLM prototype schools' action research reports (Tan et al. 2007) are consistent with Hogan's (2011) observation. The majority of the 29 SCI projects involved lower primary or lower secondary students, reflecting the pragmatic approach taken by most schools to locate the TLLM SCI project away from graduating classes or higher grade levels, to minimise disruption to the very practice TLLM sought to change – the orientation of teaching and learning toward preparation for examinations. As such, the realisation of TLLM in Singapore requires significantly deeper engagement with the meaning and implications of TLLM at all levels of curriculum making. This includes serious rethinking about how the "authority" of the high stakes assessment system can be harnessed to "lift" the capacity of schools and teachers for pedagogical reform (Hogan 2011, p. 19; see also Tan 2008b for a discussion of TLLM and assessment practices). This represents another strategic priority for curriculum translation which policy makers and educators in Singapore must not overlook.

In closing, Schwab (1973) observed that "terminal formulation[s]" (i.e. curricular "embodiments" that merely state intentions and implementation guidelines) inevitably fail to translate the "values," "full meanings and real intentions of the parties to the curricular deliberation" (p. 506). He argued that such values, meanings and intentions can only surface through a "maturation process" where the "stated curricular intentions and curricular materials – are more realistically seen as elements in a maturation process by which values are realized reflexively." (p. 507). These material elements are subject to revision and "may even be discarded or replaced" as underlying values "come closer to the surface" through the "maturation process" of sustained deliberation and curriculum making (p. 507). In other words, a key question we should ask about translated programmatic curricular forms is to what extent these programmes, operational frameworks, and courses of study enable or support such a "maturation process" among educators or are they mainly "terminal formulations"?

The set of questions developed by Klafki (2000) under the German *Didaktik* tradition constitutes a generative analytical framework, which can engage educators in sustained and reflexive deliberation about the educative meanings of content integral to instructional planning. On the other hand, descriptive frameworks like PETALS™ invite teachers to change their teaching techniques through answering largely "how-to" questions in a mode of interaction akin to a Q&A (question and answer) forum where FAQs (frequently asked questions) are anticipated and foreclosed with helpful tips. Such descriptive frameworks have very limited capability for *instigating* sustained reflexive deliberation among educators for the deep process of maturation vital to curriculum realisation (Schwab 1973, p. 506).

Like a set of Russian dolls containing regressively smaller versions of the outermost shell, increasingly technical operational frameworks can reduce broad and rich educational meanings into empty slogans and shallow teaching principles. Given Singapore's long history of efficiency-driven centralised curriculum planning and entrenched culture of compliance to authority, operational frameworks can generate fervent activity in schools. However, such activity can be misguided as noted by Hogan (2011) if significant educational meanings are lost in translation as observed by Deng (2012). Following Schwab (1973), the challenge for educators engaged in curriculum translation lies in the development of reflexive and generative analytical frameworks to instigate sustained maturation processes among educators, which involve deliberation to unpack content in view of educational purposes, to form the basis for developing deeply meaningful pedagogies for the contexts and challenges of educational practice in the twenty-first century.

References

Biesta, G. (2005). Against learning: Reclaiming a language for education in an age of learning. *Nordisk Pedagogik, 25*(1), 54–66.

Connelly, M.F. (2011). *Joseph Schwab, curriculum, curriculum studies and educational reform*. Paper presented at the National Institute of Education, Nanyang Technological University, Singapore.

Contu, A., Grey, C., & Örtenblad, A. (2003). Against learning. *Human Relations, 56*(8), 931–952.

Deng, Z. (2009). The formation of a school subject and the nature of curriculum content: An analysis of liberal studies in Hong Kong. *Journal of Curriculum Studies, 41*(5), 585–604.

Deng, Z. (2010). Curriculum transformation in the era of reform initiatives: The need to rethink and re-conceptualize content. *Journal of Textbook Research, 3*(2), 93–113.

Deng, Z. (2011). Revisiting curriculum potential. *Curriculum Inquiry, 41*(5), 538–559.

Deng, Z. (2012). Teach less, learn more: Reclaiming a curricular idea. In J. Tan (Ed.), *Education in Singapore: Taking stock, looking forward* (pp. 17–31). Singapore: Pearson.

Goodman, N. (1978). *Ways of world making*. Indianapolis: Hackett.

Gudmundsdottir, S., Reinertsen, A., & Nordtømme, N.P. (2000). Klafki's *Didaktik* analysis as a conceptual framework for research on teaching. In I. Westbury, S. Hopmann, & K. Riquarts (Eds.), *Teaching as a reflective practice: The German Didaktik tradition* (pp. 319–334). Mahwah: Lawrence Erlbaum Associates.

Gundem, B. B. (2000). Understanding European didactics. In B. Moon, M. Ben-Peretz, & S. Brown (Eds.), *Routledge international companion to education* (pp. 235–262). London: Routledge.

Hewitt, T. W. (2006). *Understanding and shaping curriculum: What we teach and why*. Thousand Oaks: Sage.

Hogan, D. (2009). *Toward a 21st century pedagogy for Singapore*. A presentation to the Principals' Curriculum Forum on Assessment-Pedagogy Nexus, Ministry of Education, Singapore.

Hogan, D. (2011). *Culture and pedagogy in Singapore: An institutionalist account of the fate of the teach less learn more policy initiative*. Paper presented at the 4th Redesigning Pedagogy: Transforming Teaching, Inspiring Learning International Conference, National Institute of Education, Nanyang Technological University, Singapore.

Hopmann, S. (2007). Restrained teaching: The common cores of Didaktik. *European Educational Research Journal, 6*(2), 109–124.

Hopmann, S. (2008). No child, no school, no state left behind: Schooling in the age of accountability. *Journal of Curriculum Studies, 40*(4), 417–456.

Humboldt, W. V. (2000). Theory of Bildung. In I. Westbury, S. Hopmann, & K. Riquarts (Eds.), *Teaching as a reflective practice: The German Didaktik tradition* (pp. 57–61). Mahwah: Lawrence Erlbaum Associates.

Kemmis, S. (2010). Research for praxis: Knowing doing. *Pedagogy, Culture & Society, 18*(1), 9–27.

Klafki, W. (2000). Didaktik analysis as the core of preparation. In I. Westbury, S. Hopmann, & K. Riquarts (Eds.), *Teaching as a reflective practice: The German Didaktik tradition* (pp. 139–159). Mahwah: Lawrence Erlbaum Associates.

Krüger, R. A. (2008). The significance of the concepts "elemental" and "fundamental" in didactic theory and practice. *Journal of Curriculum Studies, 40*(2), 215–250.

Lee, H.L. (2004). *Our future of opportunity and promise.* Address by Prime Minister Lee Hsien Loong on 22 August at the 2004 National Day Rally at the University Cultural Centre, National University of Singapore. Singapore Government Press Release.

Marsh, C. J., & Willis, G. (2009). *Curriculum: Alternative approaches, ongoing issues.* New Jersey: Merrill Prentice Hall.

Ministry of Education. (2004). *What is teach less, learn more?* Retrieved 13 June 2012, from http://www3.moe.edu.sg/bluesky/tllm.htm/

Ministry of Education. (2006a). *The teach less, learn more framework* [Image]. Retrieved 13 June 2012, from http://www.challenge.gov.sg/magazines/archive/2006_09/creative/creative.html

Ministry of Education. (2006b). *Together, reaching 'TLLM heaven': Recommendations for TLLM.* Retrieved 13 June 2012, from http://www.challenge.gov.sg/magazines/archive/2006_09/creative/creative.html

Ministry of Education. (2007a). *The PETALS™ primer.* Singapore: Ministry of Education and Association for Supervision and Curriculum Development (Singapore).

Ministry of Education. (2007b). *The PETALS™ framework* [Image]. Retrieved 13 June 2012, from http://officialtllm.files.wordpress.com/2008/11/petals-framework.pdf

Ministry of Education. (2008a). *More support for school's "Teach less, learn more" initiatives,* [Press Release]. Singapore: Ministry of Education.

Ministry of Education. (2008b). *Features of the TLLM ignite! package* [Brochure]. Singapore: Ministry of Education.

Morris, P. (1996). *The Hong Kong school curriculum: Development, issues and policies.* Hong Kong: Hong Kong University Press.

Ng, P. T. (2008). Educational reform in Singapore: From quantity to quality. *Educational Research for Policy and Practice, 7*(1), 5–15.

Schön, D. A. (1987). *Educating the reflective practitioner.* San Francisco: Jossey-Bass.

Schwab, J. J. (1973). The practical 3: Translation into curriculum. *The School Review, 81*(4), 501–522.

Shulman, L. S. (1987). Knowledge and teaching: Foundations of the new reform. *Harvard Educational Review, 57*(1), 1–22.

Tan, J. (2008a). The marketisation of education in Singapore. In J. Tan & P. T. Ng (Eds.), *Thinking schools, learning nation: Contemporary issues and challenges* (pp. 19–38). Singapore: Prentice Hall.

Tan, K. (2008b). Rethinking TLLM and its consequential effects on assessment. In J. Tan & P. T. Ng (Eds.), *Thinking schools, learning nation: Contemporary issues and challenges* (pp. 246–257). Singapore: Prentice Hall.

Tan, C., & Abbas, D. B. (2009). The 'Teach Less, Learn More' initiative in Singapore: New pedagogies for Islamic religious schools? *KEDI Journal of Educational Policy, 6*(1), 25–39.

Tan, O. S., Ee, J., Lee, Y. P., & Lam, K. (Eds.). (2007). *Teach less, learn more (TLLM) school-based curriculum innovation: Research reports.* Singapore: Ministry of Education and Educational Research Association of Singapore.

Tharman, S. (2005). *Achieving quality: Bottom up initiative, top down support.* Speech by Mr. Tharman Shanmugaratnam, Minister for Education, on 22 September at the MOE Work Plan Seminar 2005 at the Ngee Ann Polytechnic Convention Centre, Singapore.

Ulich, R. (1947/1954). *Three thousand years of educational wisdom.* Cambridge: Harvard University Press.

Westbury, I. (2000). Teaching as a reflective practice: What might Didaktik teach curriculum. In I. Westbury, S. Hopmann, & K. Riquarts (Eds.), *Teaching as a reflective practice: The German Didaktik tradition* (pp. 15–39). Mahwah: Lawrence Erlbaum Associates.

Part IV
Enacting Reform Initiatives in Classrooms

Chapter 8
Visible Learning and the Enacted Curriculum in Singapore

David Hogan, Dennis Kwek, Phillip Towndrow, Ridzuan Abdul Rahim, Teck Kiang Tan, Han Jing Yang, and Melvin Chan

Introduction

In August 2004, the Singaporean Prime Minister announced the launch of the *Teach Less Learn More* (*TLLM*) initiative to improve the quality of teaching and learning in Singapore. The following year the Minister of Education in his annual address to school staff outlined the details of the plan, including its key implementation strategies (Shanmugaratnam 2005). Since then, the Ministry has progressively implemented the TLLM initiative across Singapore's school system, emphasizing, in particular the importance of a focus on the "quality" rather than the "quantity" of instruction, a greater focus on "quality of interaction" between teachers and students, advocating less "telling" and more "talking" and less drill and practice and more inquiry based learning strategies, and a greater emphasis on formative assessment and differentiated instruction (see Chap. 7).

In a series of papers and reports drawing on survey data from students and teachers, the first author has reported on the impact of TLLM on classroom practice in Singaporean schools some 6 years after the launch of the TLLM initiative (Hogan 2011, 2012; Hogan et al. 2011). In brief, he found that the impact of TLLM on instructional practice was very limited despite evidence here and there of some imaginative pedagogical innovation. He also judged that this occurred for a variety of reasons, including neglect of the tight coupling of the national assessment system and classroom instruction, a pervasive folk culture of teaching and learning across the system that impeded sustainable and effective instructional innovation, an implementation strategy unable to support substantial and sustainable pedagogical improvement, and the weak professional authority of teachers. But rather than dwell on these matters again here, what we want to focus on in this

---

D. Hogan • D. Kwek (✉) • P. Towndrow • R.A. Rahim • T.K. Tan • H.J. Yang • M. Chan
National Institute of Education, Nanyang Technological University, Singapore
e-mail: dennis.kwek@nie.edu.sg

Z. Deng et al. (eds.), *Globalization and the Singapore Curriculum: From Policy to Classroom*, Education Innovation Series, DOI 10.1007/978-981-4451-57-4_8,
© Springer Science+Business Media Singapore 2013

analysis is a quite different question: *not* did TLLM make a difference, *but* is current instructional practice in Singapore consistent with our most considered and evidence-based judgments about effective and productive pedagogy. In short, we want to ask how well current instructional practices stand up against contemporary understandings of good pedagogy. In answering this question we plan to draw upon a conception of good pedagogy developed by Professor John Hattie – a standard he terms as "visible learning."

Hattie has been publishing meta-analytic studies of the relationship between instruction and learning since 1987 (Hattie 1987, p. 187), culminating in a comprehensive meta-analytic study of "influences on student learning" encompassing some 52,637 individual studies (Hattie 2009, p. 22). A 2012 publication updated his meta-analytical inventory to almost 1,000 meta-analyses and an additional 7,518 additional studies. For Hattie, visible learning involves making the process of teaching and learning as transparent (or "visible") to *both* teachers and students as possible:

> Visible teaching and learning occurs when learning is the explicit goal, when it is appropriately challenging, when the teacher and the student both (in their various ways) seek to ascertain whether and to what degree the challenging goal is attained, when there is deliberate practice aimed at attaining mastery of the goal, when there is feedback given and sought, and when there are active, passionate and engaging people (teacher, student, peers, and so on) participating in the act of teaching. It is teachers seeing learning through the eyes of students, and students seeing teaching as the key to their ongoing learning. *The remarkable feature of the evidence is that the biggest effects on student learning occur when teachers become learners of their own teaching, and when students become their own teachers.* When students become their own teachers they exhibit their self-regulatory attributes that seem most desirable for learners (self-monitoring, self-evaluation, self-assessment, self-teaching). That is, it is visible teaching and learning by students that makes the difference (Hattie 2009, p. 22).

And again, in his 2012 publication, he insists that visible learning

> …refers first to making student learning visible to teachers, ensuring clear identification of the attributes that make a visible difference to student learning, and *all* in the school visibly knowing the impact that they have on the learning in the school (of the student, teacher and school leaders). The *visible* aspect also refers to making teaching visible to the student, such that they learn to become their own teachers, which is the core attribute of lifelong learning or self-regulation, and the love of learning that we so want students to value. The *learning* aspect refers to how we go about knowing and understanding, and then doing something about student learning (Hattie 2012, p. 1).

More broadly, Hattie is careful to point out that visible learning and visible teaching constitute a set of instructional *principles*, not a prescriptive algorithm or menu of instructional practices. What is critical about his approach is that he insists that the evidence very clearly indicates that effective teaching does not depend on sectarian fidelity to a singular instructional regime (whether it be traditional instruction, direct instruction, active teaching, authentic instruction, social constructivist teaching, or teaching for understanding) but rather *making visible to both teacher and learner what teaching and what learning is happening in the classroom.* So long as this maxim is honoured, the selection of particular instructional methods should depend on their demonstrable efficacy rather than their fealty to a particular instructional framework.

Broadly speaking, we consider Hattie is right to insist on the importance of the principle of visible learning, although we are not convinced that it is the *only* principle of good instruction that we need to attend to (Hogan et al. 2011). But it is clear that the evidence for visible learning is substantial and the notion conceptually elegant, theoretically sensible and especially useful in identifying instructional principles and practices that, on the international research evidence we currently have, are strongly linked with substantial student learning gains. Indeed, in this chapter our primary objective is to assess the degree to which teachers in Secondary 3 Mathematics and English classes in Singapore employ or exhibit instructional strategies consistent with the principle of visible learning. We will not, however, attempt here to report the relationship between instructional practices and student outcomes; consequently we cannot say how effective particular instructional strategies are in enhancing valued student outcomes. Here our task is simply to report some descriptive statistics that examine how likely teachers are to employ instructional practices associated with substantial learning gain scores in international research as reported by Hattie.

We can express our task here in the grammar of curriculum theory. What we propose to do in this chapter is to assess the quality of the *enacted curriculum* in Secondary 3 Mathematics and English in a large representative sample of schools in Singapore using criteria and standards identified by Hattie in *Visible Learning*. Strong educational systems are invariably characterized by high levels of articulation or "alignment" between assessment, instruction and curriculum. This maxim is certainly true of Singapore, by any measure one of the highest performing system of education across the globe. However, our broader research program has raised important questions about the degree to which the enacted curriculum – how and what teachers *actually* teach – is consistent, not so much with Singapore's prescribed curriculum or national syllabus (a task which we will address on another occasion), but with the normative standards established by a well-established evidence-based pedagogical framework – namely, the visible learning framework. Consequently, what we propose in this chapter is to assess the enacted curriculum not against the prescribed national curriculum but against the standards specified in the visible learning framework. Towards the end of the chapter, however, we will briefly place our findings and Hattie's standards of visible learning in a local policy context, particularly the government's *Teach Less, Learn More* initiative launched in 2004/2005.

But before we proceed to report our findings, we want to emphasize that we harbour some reservations about Hattie's framework. In particular, we believe that the visible learning framework could be improved substantially with a far more explicit and well conceptualized model of instructional tasks (and the instructional activities that support them) that foregrounds the epistemic and cognitive dimensions of the knowledge work associated with instructional tasks. In particular, we think that if teachers are clear and explicit about the nature of a range of instructional practices associated with *doing knowledge work* in the classroom – the epistemic focus of instructional tasks, the nature of the knowledge practices (including the generation, representation, communication and justification of knowledge claims), the epistemic *talk* in the classroom that helps makes these knowledge claims explicit, transparent and visible to students, the cognitive complexity of the knowledge work undertaken in instructional tasks, recognizing the contested nature of knowledge claims, engaging in principled epistemic talk, and so on – then this is likely to enhance the visibility of learning and improve student outcomes in the classroom. We term this kind of visibility, in the aggregate, *epistemic clarity,* and argue that without it, students work more or less in the dark about the nature, purpose and value of the knowledge work they engage in instructional tasks (Ball 2003; Bereiter and Scardamalia 2006; Boaler 2002a, b; Cohen 2011; Doyle 1983; Ford and Forman 2006, 2008; Hogan et al. 2012a; McConachie and Petrosky 2010; Rahim et al. 2012; Perkins 1998; Schraw 2006; Stein et al. 1996, 2009; Rittle-Johnson and Alibali 1999; Schoenfeld 1992).

While we by no means think that epistemic clarity is all that matters in enhancing visible learning in the classroom, we think it is pivotal to *disciplinary* forms of knowledge building at the student level, and will therefore pay substantial attention to it in the analysis that follows. It is true that Hattie at several points approaches such a perspective, particularly in his discussion of active teaching (Hattie 2009, pp. 37–38). But what Hattie fails to recognize is that active teaching by itself is not enough to develop the "deep-level, connected knowledge structures" that he values or that constructivist accounts of cognition and learning help explain the development of knowledge in students' minds. What is also necessary is that teachers also need to be mindful of, and attend to, the epistemic *nature* of the knowledge work that students engage in class. In short, along with active teaching and a constructivist account of learning, we also need, as the English sociologist Michael Young (2008) might put it, "to bring knowledge back in." It is this process of making explicit the nature of the knowledge work embedded in tasks and talk that facilitates epistemic clarity and, in so doing, visible learning. We are not in a position to test this argument directly – that is, we did not collect evidence from students that asked them directly whether they found particular kinds of knowledge work more accessible, engaging and meaningful if its underlying epistemic nature was made explicit – but we think it a reasonable assumption that we will test in subsequent research. Moreover, we are in a position to test whether the degree of epistemic clarity varies across the two subjects we report on here: Secondary 3 Mathematics and English. Our assumption here is that Mathematics is likely to exhibit greater epistemic clarity than English, but not differ substantially from English on other indicators of visible learning.

Data and Method

In the course of this chapter we principally report the findings from a large class-room observation study (the Core 2 Panel 3 Classroom Observation Study) on instructional practices in Secondary 3 Mathematics and English classrooms. In addition, we will also report a limited number of findings from a survey of a nationally representative stratified sample of Secondary 3 classes in 32 secondary schools.

The Panel 3 project is focused on detailed classroom observations of some 625 lessons nested in 115 units of work in Primary 5 and Secondary 3 Mathematics and English drawn from a nationally representative sample of 16 secondary schools and 15 primary schools. The Panel 3 classroom observations occurred between April through November, 2010.

In the Panel 3 study, teachers selected for observation were asked to nominate a unit of work – a full sequence of lessons around a particular topic, theme or content area. Rather than discrete, random lessons for observation, the stipulation of a unit of work facilitated subsequent analyses that charts, models and examines the developmental ebb and flow of knowledge building over the course of the entire unit. All lessons were video and audio recorded using two to three high definition video cameras and up to four digital audio recorders. Video recordings were coded by subject and level specialist researchers trained over 8 months in the use of a coding scheme developed specifically for Panel 3 over 12 months. Coders coded each lesson in 3-min intervals ('phases'), as well as larger events such as language activities or problem-solving activities; doing so allowed for a temporal examination of classroom practices from the start to the end of a lesson, and across the unit of lessons. Accordingly, a 30 min lesson would have 10 phases, a 45 min lesson 25 phases and an hour long lesson 20 phases. We used a binary coding scheme for almost all of the 30 separate scales (most with multiple subscales and indicators) to record whether or not an instructional event happened during the 3 min phase (No = 0, Yes = 1, with the default set at 0). We used a Likert Scale (typically 0–3) for a small number of scales where we particularly wanted to capture more details about the instructional event. Within scales, subscales and indicators were, in nearly all cases, not mutually exclusive: coders could code 1 for multiple categories within a scale or subscale, thereby permitting multiple responses per scale or subscale. Our binary coding scheme has the advantage of reducing measurement error and increasing interrater reliability, and the potential disadvantage of underreporting the frequency of instructional events. However, after months of trialling both Likert and binary coding schemes, we concluded that for the majority of scales, the level of underreporting was minimal and that the binary metric gave reliable and valid results. The coding for Secondary 3 English and Mathematics took almost a year to complete on top of the 8 months of training time.

In the tables reported below, we generally report the data at two levels: whether a particular instructional event occurred at least once during the 3 min phase, and the average (or mean) number of phases that the instructional event occurred during the lesson. We could in principle also report the same descriptive statistics at the unit rather than the lesson level, but since the mean score at the unit level is typically very close to the mean score at the lesson level, there is little advantage in doing so for the purposes of this chapter. Almost without exception, the statistics we report are descriptive in nature, although we report effect sizes (Cohen's h) as a standardized measure of statistical significance: values >0.4 are theoretically significant, while effect sizes >0.8 are considered large, statistically speaking. In later publications, we will systematically explore relationships at the bivariate and multivariate levels.

The full inventory of instructional practices that we have investigated in the Panel 3 research project and believe capable of significantly enhancing the visibility of teaching and learning in the Singapore classroom is reported in Appendix. Many of these instructional practices are explicitly indicated in Hattie's account of visible learning, particularly those associated with communicating learning objectives and assessment standards, monitoring, feedback, metacognitive self-regulation, clarity and structure, review, practice, direct instruction. Others, including those associated with epistemic clarity, are not mentioned at all.

Whither Visible Learning in Singapore?

Identifying and Communicating Learning Goals and Assessment Standards

The consensus view among researchers is that the clear and timely communication of learning goals and performance standards appears to significantly enhance student learning. Indeed, across some 604 studies and 11 meta-studies of the relationship between goal setting and student learning, Hattie estimated an effect size of 0.56, ranking it 34 out of the 138 influences on student outcomes that he measured (Hattie 2009, pp. 162, 201, 2012, pp. 47–54).

We report the results from Panel 3 of the frequency of teacher statements of the lesson topic and learning goals for the lesson in Table 8.1. Overall, 56 % of Mathematics and 42 % of English teachers declare their lesson topic *at least once* during the lesson (Over the course of an entire unit of work, teachers stated the lesson topic at least once 97 % and 91 % of the time respectively, although this statistic is not especially meaningful at a unit level). But teachers are far less likely to mention, even at least once, what their learning goals for the lesson are. In Mathematics, only 14 % of teachers communicate their learning goals at least once during the lesson; In English, only 12 % of teachers mention their learning objectives at least once. In both subjects, teachers that do communicate their learning goals are for far more likely to mention them with minimal or no detail. In light of Hattie's arguments concerning the importance of visible learning, this is hardly adequate. Indeed, what these figures suggest is that students operate in a learning environment in which the learning objectives of the lesson are, for all intents and purposes, *invisible*.

In addition, against a closely related criteria – the frequency with which teachers recapitulate or summarize the lesson – teachers only do marginally better. Overall, in 28 % of Mathematics lessons but only 17 % of English lessons, teachers recapitulate or summarize at least once during the course of the lesson.

The data reported in Table 8.1 also indicates that teachers in Mathematics communicate explicit performance standards at least once in 42 % of their lessons, while

Table 8.1 % occurrences and mean scores at lesson level and effect sizes
Secondary 3 Mathematics and English, 2010
Panel 3 observational data

N = 351 (lessons) N = 6,238 (phases)	Sec 3 Mathematics 2010 (N = 171/2,991)		Sec 3 English 2010 (N = 180/3,247)		Effect size: *Cohen's h*
	% lessons with at least one occurrence	% phases per lesson	% lessons with at least one occurrence	% phases per lesson	*% phases per lesson*
Communicating lesson topics					
Communicating lesson topics	0.56	**0.05**	0.42	**0.03**	*0.10*
Communicating learning objectives	0.14	**0.02**	0.12	**0.01**	*0.08*
Mention without detail	0.09	**0.01**	0.07	**0.00**	*0.20*
Mention with minimal detail	0.11	**0.01**	0.11	**0.01**	*0.00*
Mention with some detail	0.04	**0.00**	0.01	**0.00**	*0.00*
Mention with substantial detail	0.00	**0.00**	0.01	**0.00**	*0.00*
Recapitulation of learning goals	0.28	**0.04**	0.17	**0.01**	*0.20*
Mention without detail	0.10	**0.01**	0.02	**0.00**	*0.20*
Mention with minimal detail	0.13	**0.01**	0.08	**0.00**	*0.20*
Mention with some detail	0.15	**0.02**	0.08	**0.01**	*0.08*
Mention with substantial detail	0.06	**0.01**	0.02	**0.00**	*0.20*
Communicating performance standards					
Explicit performance standards	0.42	**0.08**	0.16	**0.03**	*0.23*
Exemplars of successful performance (with degree of explanation)	0.76	**0.28**	0.17	**0.02**	*0.83*
Whole class performances of understanding	0.03	**0.00**	0.01	**0.00**	*0.00*

English teachers only do so in 16 % of their lessons. Arguably, the percentage for Mathematics is reasonable enough, depending on the nature of the tasks students were asked to engage in, but the percentage for English looks very low by comparison. In addition, teachers in Mathematics were far more likely to provide exemplars of successful performances to students. However, they were no more likely than English teachers to demonstrate performances of understanding to their students in class, although this is hardly to say very much, given the extremely low (almost invisible) percentages reported.

Table 8.2 % occurrences and mean scores at lesson level and effect sizes: domain-specific activities/tasks
Secondary 3 Mathematics and English, 2010
Panel 3 observational data

N = 351 (lessons) N = 6,238 (phases)	Mathematics 2010 (N = 171/2,991)		English 2010 (N = 180/3,247)		Effect size: *Cohen's h*
	% lessons with at least one occurrence	% phases per lesson	% lessons with at least one occurrence	% phases per lesson	*% phases per lesson*
1. Activities/tasks: Mathematics	**0.42**	**0.15**			
Remembering activities	0.75	**0.19**	–	–	–
Routine procedural practice activities	0.80	**0.36**	–	–	–
Repetition activities	0.16	**0.03**	–	–	–
Review activities	0.84	**0.34**	–	–	–
Revision activities	0.04	**0.01**	–	–	–
Comprehension/knowledge manipulation activities	0.67	**0.20**	–	–	–
Procedural activities with connections	0.33	**0.08**	–	–	–
Doing mathematics	0.03	**0.01**	–	–	–
Activities/tasks: English			**0.10**	**0.05**	–
Coding/decoding activity	–	–	0.51	**0.19**	–
Comprehension activity	–	–	0.20	**0.08**	–
Interpretation and meaning making activity	–	–	0.27	**0.10**	–
Creative writing activity	–	–	0.06	**0.02**	–
Description activity	–	–	0.08	**0.04**	–
Explanation activity	–	–	0.09	**0.05**	–
Conveying activity	–	–	0.28	**0.13**	–
Expression activity	–	–	0.06	**0.03**	–
Persuasion activity	–	–	0.06	**0.03**	–

Epistemic Clarity: Instructional Tasks

We indicated earlier that Hattie overlooks the contribution that a focus on *epistemic clarity* might make to visible teaching and learning. Tables 8.2, 8.3, 8.4, 8.5, and 8.6 report the results from our observation study of six sets of indicators of epistemic clarity.

The first indicator focuses on the nature of the *domain-specific activities or tasks* that teachers set for students (Table 8.2). In the case of Mathematics, our taxonomy is derived from the Stein et al. (1996) taxonomy of mathematical tasks. In the case of English, we developed from a taxonomy developed by the Core 2 research program. The mathematics taxonomy is strongly hierarchical (or vertical) in nature, while the English one is only weakly hierarchical. While the activities/tasks differ across the two domains, teachers are more likely to ask students to engage in the

Table 8.3 % occurrences and mean scores at lesson level and effect sizes: epistemic focus
Secondary 3 Mathematics and English, 2010
Panel 3 observational data

N = 351 (lessons) N = 6,238 (phases)	Mathematics 2010 (N = 171/2,991)		English 2010 (N = 180/3,247)		Effect size: Cohen's h
	% lessons with at least one occurrence	% phases per lesson	% lessons with at least one occurrence	% phases per lesson	% phases per lesson
2. Epistemic (knowledge) focus					
Factual knowledge	0.95	**0.41**	0.88	**0.63**	*0.44*
Procedural knowledge	0.99	**0.80**	0.87	**0.57**	*0.50*
Conceptual knowledge	0.85	**0.27**	0.26	**0.06**	*0.60*
Epistemic knowledge	0.27	**0.05**	0.09	**0.02**	*0.17*
Rhetorical knowledge	0.35	**0.04**	0.30	**0.12**	*0.30*
Hermeneutical knowledge	–	–	0.14	**0.08**	*0.57*
Metacognitive knowledge	0.19	**0.03**	0.10	**0.02**	*0.06*
Moral and civic knowledge	–	–	0.06	**0.01**	*0.20*
Aesthetic knowledge	–	–	0.03	**0.00**	*0.00*

Table 8.4 % occurrences and mean scores at lesson level and effect sizes: knowledge practices
Secondary 3 Mathematics, 2010
Panel 3 observational data

N = 351 (lessons) N = 6,238 (phases)	Mathematics 2010 (N = 171/2,991)		English 2010 (N = 180/3,247)		Effect size: Cohen's h
	% lessons with at least one occurrence	% phases per lesson	% lessons with at least one occurrence	% phases per lesson	% phases per lesson
3. Disciplinary knowledge practices (Mathematics only)	**0.63**	**0.32**	–	–	–
Knowledge communication (syntax)	0.85	0.42	–	–	–
Knowledge representation	0.94	0.66	–	–	–
Knowledge generation	0.58	0.14	–	–	–
Knowledge deliberation	0.10	0.01	–	–	–
Knowledge justification	0.39	0.06	–	–	–
Knowledge communication (presentation)	0.96	0.65	–	–	–

specified domain-specific activities in Mathematics compared to English. In Mathematics, on average, teachers engage students in a domain-specific activity or task in 15 % of the phases in a lesson. In English, teachers engage students in

Table 8.5 % occurrences and mean scores at lesson level and effect sizes: cognitive demand
Secondary 3 Mathematics and English, 2010
Panel 3 observational data

N = 351 (lessons) N = 6,238 (phases)	Mathematics 2010 (N = 171/2,991)		English 2010 (N = 180/3,247)		Effect size: Cohen's h
	% lessons with at least one occurrence	% phases per lesson	% lessons with at least one occurrence	% phases per lesson	% phases per lesson
4. Cognitive demands of tasks					
Cognitive demand: functional or complex					
Functional cognition only	0.98	**0.59**	0.65	**0.06**	*1.26*
Complex cognition only	0.77	**0.20**	0.68	**0.08**	*0.35*
Both functional and complex cognition	0.75	**0.11**	0.44	**0.03**	*0.33*
Cognitive operations (English only)					
Remember	–	–	0.64	**0.06**	
Understand	–	–	0.49	**0.04**	
Apply	–	–	0.14	**0.01**	
Analyze	–	–	0.10	**0.01**	
Evaluate	–	–	0.12	**0.01**	
Create	–	–	0.38	**0.03**	

domain specific activities/tasks even less in just 5 % of the phases in a lesson. While we do not know of any benchmarks against which we might evaluate these findings, the percentages appear to us very low, especially in English.

We also lack benchmarks with respect to our second criteria, *epistemic focus*, but the findings are suggestive in both absolute and relative terms (Table 8.3). Teachers in Mathematics, for example, are far more likely to focus on procedural knowledge than in English (80 % versus 57 % respectively). Teachers in English are slightly more likely to focus on factual knowledge than procedural knowledge (63 % versus 57 %) and substantially more likely to focus on factual knowledge than their colleagues in Mathematics. But when it comes to conceptual knowledge – the form of knowledge that is most central to the development of understanding, meaning making and knowledge transfer – Mathematics teachers are far more likely to focus on it compared to English teachers (27 % versus 6 % respectively) although we suspect that the level for Mathematics is still low in absolute terms.[1] Teacher attention to epistemic knowledge (knowledge of the standards by which knowledge claims are judged, evaluated or justified) is very low in both subjects, but somewhat stronger in Mathematics than in English.

Our third key indicator of epistemic clarity focuses on the nature of the domain-specific *knowledge practices* that teachers ask students to engage in as part of the tasks teachers set for students (Table 8.4). In Mathematics, our

---

[1] We are currently testing this proposition using multi-level SEM modeling of the Core 2 Panel 2 survey data.

Table 8.6 % occurrences and mean scores at lesson level and effect sizes: epistemic authority, pluralism and deliberation
Secondary 3 Mathematics and English, 2010
Panel 3 observational data

N = 351 (lessons) N = 6,238 *(phases)*	Mathematics 2010 (N = 171/2,991)		English 2010 (N = 180/3,247)		Effect size: *Cohen's h*
	% lessons with at least one occurrence	% phases per lesson	% lessons with at least one occurrence	% phases per lesson	*% phases per lesson*
5. Epistemic authority					
Teacher appeal to evidence	0.01	**0.00**	0.04	**0.01**	*0.20*
Explicit teacher appeal to domain-specific knowledge	0.30	**0.08**	0.06	**0.01**	*0.37*
6. Epistemic pluralism and deliberation					
Knowledge as truth	0.98	**0.88**	0.98	**0.89**	*0.03*
Knowledge as a contestable claim					
Knowledge claim supported by reasons	0.17	**0.03**	0.04	**0.01**	*0.15*
Knowledge critique	0.04	**0.00**	0.03	**0.01**	*0.20*
Comparing and contrasting information/knowledge	0.01	**0.00**	0.01	**0.01**	*0.20*
Collective deliberation	0.01	**0.00**	0.01	**0.00**	*0.00*

taxonomy of knowledge practices – knowledge communication (syntax), knowledge representation, knowledge generation, knowledge deliberation, knowledge justification, knowledge communication (presentation) – is derived from a broader model of disciplinarity developed in the Core 2 research program (Hogan et al. 2011). We did not develop a similar taxonomy for English. However, in Mathematics, students engage in a domain-specific knowledge practice in about one third of the phases of a typical lesson. Of these, knowledge representation is the strongest (66 % of phases in a lesson) followed by knowledge communication (presentation) (65 %) and knowledge communication (syntax) (42 %). While all three of these are important, especially the first and the third, the weakness of the others suggests limited attention to key aspects of the disciplinarity of mathematics (Hogan et al. 2012a; Rahim et al. 2012).

Our fourth indicator of epistemic clarity focuses on the *cognitive complexity* of the instructional activities or tasks set by teachers. Again, we find a significant difference between Mathematics and English: in Mathematics, students have a much stronger chance to engage in cognitive activities that facilitate achievement of procedural proficiency and automaticity than students in English (59 % and 6 % respectively) as well as engage in more complex forms of cognition that facilitate conceptual understanding, meaning making and knowledge transfer and application (20 % and 8 % respectively) (Table 8.5). Again, we suspect that the absolute levels for complex forms of cognition are worryingly low.

On the two final measures that we believe can contribute to epistemic clarity – the location of epistemic authority and a recognition of the contested nature of knowledge claims – both Mathematics and English do very poorly (Table 8.6). In these two matters, as in others, instruction in Singapore is far from visible in either subject.

In sum, while we lack at this point in time benchmarks to establish standards of relatively good and relatively poor performance on these indicators, our general impression is that in the matter of epistemic clarity, Singapore pedagogy indicates a stubborn commitment to opacity rather than transparency, although less so in Mathematics than in English. We will have a better sense of what these standards might be after we complete our multi-level structural equation modelling (SEM) of the impact of variations in levels of epistemic clarity on student outcomes. We will report the results of this analysis in due course.

Epistemic Clarity: Epistemic Talk

In a classic essay, Douglas Barnes (1992, 2008) pleaded for a discursive regime in classrooms focused on "exploratory" talk that "worked on understanding" rather than testing to see whether students knew the right answer or not in performative "presentations." Contemporary educational researchers, however, have found precious little evidence of "exploratory talk" that "works on understanding" (Alexander 2000, 2004, 2008; Hodgkinson and Mercer 2008; Lemke 1989, 1990; Sinclair and Coulthard 1975; Mercer 1992; Mercer and Littleton 2007; Mehan 1979; Cazden 1988; Nystrand et al. 1991, 1999, 2001; Michaels et al. 2002, 2004, 2008; Lefstein and Snell 2010). Instead, in most classrooms they looked in, whatever the country, the typical lesson was likely to be dominated by the recitation script or Initiate-Response-Evaluate (IRE) sequences. But not only did they find the IRE pervasive in classrooms – they also found it less than benign in its educational consequences. In particular, they generally concluded that IRE sequences have very limited capacity to promote student understanding or cognitive depth. Indeed, the primary function of IRE is evaluative or performative rather than exploratory and constructive. Meanwhile, the conventional wisdom is that "dialogue" is by far and away the most effective means of promoting deep student learning. As Wells and Arauz put the conventional wisdom, "learning is likely to be more effective when students are actively engaged in the dialogic co-construction of meaning about topics that are of significance to them…[C]oming to know involves much more active participation by learners in which they construct and progressively improve their understanding through exploratory transactions with the cultural world around them" (2006, p. 379).

When we began the Core 2 project we assumed that dialogue was the royal road to meaning-making and understanding – indeed, that dialogue *was* understanding talk and that understanding talk *was* dialogue and nothing else. While we remain convinced that dialogue optimises opportunities for the development of student understanding and that all too often IRE sequences are essentially performative

Table 8.7   % occurrences and mean scores at lesson level and effect sizes
Secondary 3 Mathematics and English, 2010
Panel 3 observational data

	Mathematics 2010 (N = 171/2,991)		English 2010 (N = 180/3,247)		Effect size: *Cohen's h*
N = 351 *(lessons)* N = 6,238 *(phases)*	% lessons with at least one occurrence	% phases per lesson	% lessons with at least one occurrence	% phases per lesson	*% phases per lesson*
Epistemic talk					
Factual talk	0.96	**0.35**	0.87	**0.55**	*0.40*
Procedural talk	0.99	**0.72**	0.86	**0.51**	*0.44*
Clarifying talk	0.38	**0.05**	0.31	**0.04**	*0.05*
Connecting talk (scale mean)	0.61	**0.16**	0.51	**0.11**	*0.15*
Temporal connections	0.43	**0.08**	0.31	**0.03**	*0.23*
Conceptual connections	0.47	**0.07**	0.34	**0.07**	*0.00*
Framing talk	0.17	**0.02**	0.13	**0.01**	*0.08*
Reframing talk	0.12	**0.01**	0.06	**0.01**	*0.00*
Explanatory talk	0.52	**0.11**	0.27	**0.07**	*0.14*
Justification talk	0.24	**0.04**	0.03	**0.00**	*0.40*
Reflexive talk	0.26	**0.03**	0.09	**0.01**	*0.15*

rather than developmental in nature, we are no longer convinced that understanding talk *is* dialogue and nothing else or that IRE sequences are necessarily unable to help students "work on understanding" (Hogan et al. 2012b). But we remain convinced that epistemic talk – systematic talk about knowledge – is critical to visible teaching and learning and to enhanced student understanding and skill formation. Indeed, we might think of epistemic talk as a discursive mechanism that facilitates epistemic clarity. However, not all epistemic talk is, epistemically or cognitively speaking, of equal value. Classroom talk that focuses on conceptual connections and relationships in particular is critical to "working on understanding." Procedural talk too can prompt students to work on understanding, particularly if it is linked iteratively to conceptual talk. Indeed, we have some evidence, that this does happen in Singaporean classrooms, although it is more likely to happen in Mathematics classrooms than English classrooms (Hogan et al. 2012b).

In the Panel 3 study we coded for seven categories of epistemic talk: factual talk, procedural talk, clarifying talk, connecting talk, explanatory talk, justification talk, and reflexive talk. One of these – connecting talk – is especially generative in that it incorporates four categories of talk critical to "understanding talk": talk that makes temporal connections, talk that makes conceptual connections, framing talk, and reframing talk (See Table 8.7). Our findings from the Panel 3 observational study indicate that classroom talk in Singapore is overwhelmingly factual (especially in English) and procedural (especially in Mathematics) and characterized by short, performative orientated IRE rather than dialogical exchanges (Table 8.8).

Table 8.8 Mean scores/SD: structure of teacher talk and student talk
Secondary 3 Mathematics and English
Panel 3 observational data

N = 351 (lessons) N = 6,238 (phases)	Secondary 3 Mathematics (N = 171/2,991)		Secondary 3 English (N = 180/3,247)		*Effect size (Cohen's h)*
	% lessons with at least one occurrence	Mean score (phases per lesson)	% lessons with at least one occurrence	Mean score (phases per lesson)	*Lesson level*
Structure of classroom interaction					
Teacher talk					
Teacher questions: whole class					
Frequency of teacher **closed** question: whole class	0.96	**0.68**	0.91	**0.58**	*0.21*
Frequency of teacher **open** question: whole class	0.30	**0.04**	0.62	**0.14**	*0.36*
Teacher responses: whole class					
Teacher **short** response: whole class	0.48	**0.07**	0.41	**0.06**	*0.04*
Teacher **medium** response: whole class	0.35	**0.05**	0.35	**0.04**	*0.05*
Teacher **extended** response: whole class	0.27	**0.03**	0.22	**0.04**	*0.05*
Teacher questions: individual or group					
Frequency of teacher **closed** question: individual or group	0.67	**0.20**	0.58	**0.15**	*0.13*
Frequency of teacher **open** question: individual or group	0.19	**0.03**	0.27	**0.04**	*0.05*
Teacher responses: individual or group					
Teacher **short** response: individual or group	0.54	**0.11**	0.59	**0.09**	*0.07*
Teacher **medium** response: individual or group	0.44	**0.07**	0.53	**0.08**	*0.04*
Teacher **extended** response: individual or group	0.36	**0.06**	0.30	**0.05**	*0.04*
Student talk					
Student responses: whole class, individual or group					
Student **short** response to teacher: whole class, individual or group	0.98	**0.55**	0.96	**0.47**	*0.16*
Student **medium** response to teacher: whole class, individual or group	0.48	**0.07**	0.77	**0.12**	*0.17*
Student **extended** response to teacher: whole class, individual or group	0.25	**0.06**	0.22	**0.02**	*0.21*

(continued)

Table 8.8 (continued)

N = 351 (lessons) N = 6,238 (phases)	Secondary 3 Mathematics (N = 171/2,991)		Secondary 3 English (N = 180/3,247)		Effect size (Cohen's h)
	% lessons with at least one occurrence	Mean score (phases per lesson)	% lessons with at least one occurrence	Mean score (phases per lesson)	Lesson level
Student questions: whole class					
Frequency of student **closed** question to teacher: whole class	0.78	**0.13**	0.49	**0.10**	0.09
Frequency of student **open** question to teacher: whole class	0.11	**0.01**	0.11	**0.01**	0.00

Comparatively little talk in either subject has a strongly conceptual element to it, whether it be connecting talk, explanatory talk, epistemic justification talk or reflexive talk. While 35 % of Mathematics phases and 55 % of all English phases were characterized by factual talk, and 72 % of all phases in Mathematics and 51 % in English were characterized by procedural talk, the percentage of phases characterized by connecting talk in Mathematics and English lessons were much lower (16 % and 11 % respectively). The percentages for explanatory and other forms of talk were even lower in both subjects. Indeed, in a correlation analysis at the lesson level, the correlations between three of the four forms of connecting talk and factual talk are not significant in Mathematics, while the correlations between all four forms of connecting talk and procedural talk are not significant. For English, the correlations between three of the four forms of connecting talk and factual talk are not significant, while the correlations between three of the four forms of connecting talk and procedural talk are not significant.

In short, in our judgement, the low proportion of conceptual talk and the weak levels of association between factual and procedural talk, on the one hand, and conceptual talk, on the other, are highly unlikely to help make transparent and visible the underlying structure and logic of knowledge and knowledge building in the Singaporean classroom. And if this is the case, our findings indicate substantial room for instructional improvement going forward, and the need for a revamped pre-service training and a lot of demanding professional development to help make it happen.

The data reported in Table 8.8 focus on the nature of teacher questioning (closed or open), student responses (short, medium, extended) and teacher responses (short, medium, extended) to student responses or to student questions in whole class or group contexts. We report these findings here on the assumption that open questions and extended responses are more likely, all things considered, to constitute or approach a form of "exploratory talk," "dialogical exchange," "accountable talk" or "dialogical spell" or, in our terms, rich (or at least extended) epistemic talk, promote epistemic clarity and enhance student understanding as a consequence. In a very recent paper Alexander, for instance, reports that at a recent AERA sponsored conference held in Pittsburgh in September 2011, the conference concluded "that we now possess a critical mass of robust evidence demonstrating that classroom talk that is well-structured, reciprocal and cognitively challenging, and which immerses the student in a subject's distinctive conceptual and linguistic architecture and modes of enquiry, reasoning and argument, has a clear and positive impact on student attainment in English, mathematics and science as assessed by conventional tests" (Alexander 2012, p. 16; see also Resnick et al. 2012).

In light of this research consensus, our Panel 3 evidence from Singapore is not encouraging. The overwhelmingly dominant form of talk in Singaporean classrooms takes the form of short, restricted IRE exchanges with shallow cognitive content that are highly unlikely to provide substantial opportunity for the development of epistemic clarity about the curriculum content in question, have limited cognitive impact and fail to provide appropriate levels of scaffolding for students to "work on understanding." In Mathematics, teachers are far more likely to ask closed questions than open questions in whole class contexts (68 % of phases versus 4 %) over the course of a lesson; English has a slightly better ratio between open and closed questions but not by much (58 % versus 14 %). Extended student responses (whether in whole class, small group or one-on-one situations) are likewise extremely rare (6 % and 2 % respectively). Equally discouragingly, the percentage of extended teacher responses to student responses in whole class contexts over the course of a lesson in both subjects is very low (3 % and 4 % respectively). There is little evidence then of "exploratory talk," "dialogical exchanges" or "dialogical spells" that would enhance the epistemic clarity and cognitive impact of classroom talk in either Mathematics or English whole class lessons. The story is no better for small group contexts or individual one-on-one contexts.

Instructional Methods: Monitoring, Feedback and Learning Support

In his analysis of visible learning, Hattie rightfully makes much of the critical role that monitoring, feedback and self-regulated learning play in making learning visible both to teachers and students. Indeed, in both the 2009 volume and in the 2012 volume he makes a compelling case both for the strength of the association between monitoring (or, as Hattie would have it, feedback from students to teachers) and feedback (from teachers to students), on the one hand, and student achievement, on the other, and as leading expressions of visible learning. He has also emphasized the value of a focus on understanding, review, practice, teacher flexibility and differentiated instruction, direct instruction, active teaching, and self-regulated learning. We have no theoretical quibbles with him on any of these issues. What we do have some concern about though is a number of conceptual and specification issues with him at the measurement level. Specifically, in our Panel 3 study, we have developed differentiated notions of monitoring and feedback by type and audience/target and included multidimensional measures of checking for prior learning, learning support (scaffolding) and self-regulated learning.

The data reported in Table 8.9 indicates that that teachers did check for prior learning at least once in both subjects (although more so in Mathematics than in English), but rarely more than that. Mathematics teachers are also more likely to do formative monitoring (formative monitoring happens when teachers seek to establish or determine the level of student understanding or skill in a learning task), limiting the visibility of student learning to individual students. While there is quite substantial (and almost identical) levels of evaluative feedback in both subjects, the averages for the most efficacious and powerful form of feedback (formative) are extremely low in both subjects. This is highly unsatisfactory given the depth of the research supporting the value of formative feedback (see Hogan et al. 2011 for a review) and its contribution to visible learning (Hattie 2009). Values for detailed corrective feedback are stronger, but while this enhances the visibility of learning, the research of Black and Wiliam (1998) and others indicates that it is much less efficacious than formative feedback. Similarly, in the case of learning support, the most powerful form (strategic learning support, whether planned and fixed, or contextual and flexible), is essentially invisible in the teaching repertoire of Singapore's Mathematics and English teachers. Evidence of procedural learning support (whether planned and fixed, or contextual and flexible) is somewhat more obvious in both subjects, although slightly more in Mathematics classrooms than in English classrooms. Panel 3 coders found almost no evidence of instructional strategies focused on promoting self-regulated learning in the lessons they observed. Again, the broad impression we get from the classroom observation data is that apart from one or two indicators, the general picture is one of opacity rather than transparency or visibility.

Purposefulness and Knowledge Building at the Lesson Level

Our final set of indicators of the opacity or transparency of classroom pedagogy is also derived from the Panel 3 observational study. However, in this case the data reported are summative scores that the coders gave each lesson as a whole rather than at the phasal level (Table 8.10). All scales are ordinal and scaled on a four point metric (0–3). We have grouped our measures into two groups: those associated in one way or another with purposeful teaching, the second with knowledge building.

As we can see, Mathematics teachers are generally more likely than their English colleagues to communicate their learning goals or to provide exemplars of high quality performance – but even for Mathematics teachers, the absolute level is

Table 8.9 % occurrences and mean scores at lesson level and effect sizes: instructional practices *Secondary 3 Mathematics and English, 2010 Panel 3 observational data*

N = 351 (lessons) N = 6,238 (phases)	Mathematics 201 (N = 171/2,991)		English 2010 (N = 180/3,247)		Effect size: *Cohen's h*
	% lessons with at least one occurrence	% phases per lesson	% lessons with at least one occurrence	% phases per lesson	*% phases per lesson*
Instructional methods					
Checking for prior learning					
Prior activities	0.58	**0.06**	0.57	**0.06**	*0.00*
Prior specific content knowledge	0.67	**0.13**	0.52	**0.06**	*0.24*
Prior relevant knowledge	0.12	**0.01**	0.24	**0.03**	*0.15*
Monitoring					
Supervisory	0.73	**0.22**	0.82	**0.26**	*0.09*
Formative	0.78	**0.25**	0.65	**0.20**	*0.12*
Individual	0.85	**0.30**	0.71	**0.22**	*0.18*
Group	0.09	**0.02**	0.32	**0.12**	0.42
Feedback					
Type					
Evaluative	0.98	**0.54**	0.96	**0.50**	*0.08*
Prescriptive reformulation	0.27	**0.04**	0.19	**0.02**	*0.12*
Detailed corrective	0.69	**0.14**	0.69	**0.17**	*0.08*
Formative	0.06	**0.00**	0.02	**0.00**	*0.00*
Audience					
Individual students	0.87	**0.26**	**0.67**	**0.16**	*0.25*
Groups of students	0.07	**0.01**	**0.24**	**0.05**	*0.25*
Whole class	0.88	**0.41**	**0.88**	**0.38**	*0.06*
Student to student	0.17	**0.02**	**0.16**	**0.02**	*0.00*
Learning support					
Planned and fixed					
Logistical	0.08	**0.01**	**0.07**	**0.01**	*0.00*
Procedural	0.50	**0.10**	**0.64**	0.14	*0.12*
Strategic	0.13	**0.01**	**0.07**	**0.01**	*0.00*
Contextual and flexible					
Logistical	0.09	**0.01**	**0.09**	**0.02**	*0.08*
Procedural	0.84	**0.27**	**0.71**	**0.21**	*0.14*
Strategic	0.18	**0.02**	**0.14**	**0.03**	*0.06*
Self-directed learning					
Student agency/ co-regulation (scale mean)	**0.04**	0.00	**0.07**	0.01	*0.20*
Self-assessment	**0.01**	0.00	**0.02**	0.00	*0.00*

Table 8.10 Mean scores, SDs and effect sizes lesson summative scales
Secondary 3 Mathematics and English, 2010
Panel 3 observational data

N = 351 (lessons) N = 6,238 (phases)	Mathematics 2010 (N = 171/2,991)		English 2010 (N = 180/3,247)		Effect size
	Mean	SD	Mean	SD	Cohen's d
Purposefulness					
Communicating purposefulness: (0–3)	**0.82**	0.546	**0.49**	0.641	*0.565*
Learning goals (0–3)	**0.89**	1.124	**0.55**	0.814	*0.347*
Performance criteria and standards (0–3)	**0.35**	0.617	**0.58**	0.832	*0.317*
Exemplars of high quality performance (0–3)	**1.23**	1.076	**0.33**	0.746	*0.983*
Direction/progression (0–3)	**1.91**	1.005	**0.98**	0.875	*0.988*
Clarity of task/activity structure (0–3)	**1.67**	1.079	**1.04**	0.924	*0.626*
Backward mapping/framing/integration/closure (0–3)	**1.06**	1.067	**0.69**	0.786	*0.396*
Time (0–3)	**1.96**	0.972	**1.49**	0.977	*0.477*
Instructional flexibility/pedagogical judgment (0–3)	**1.09**	0.922	**0.62**	0.778	*0.554*
Dialogical exchanges: (0–3)	**0.04**	0.258	**0.52**	0.678	*0.922*
Reciprocity (0–3)	**0.04**	0.285	**0.52**	0.736	*0.865*
Purposefulness (0–3)	**0.05**	0.312	**0.62**	0.821	*0.900*
Cumulation (0–3)	**0.05**	0.262	**0.43**	0.733	*0.686*
Knowledge building					
Focus on knowledge building (0–3)	**1.89**	1.035	**0.72**	0.846	*1.244*
Metacognitive self-regulation (0–3)	**0.19**	0.489	**0.21**	0.604	*0.023*

quite low, indicating low visibility. Mean scores for lesson direction and progression are much better, but Mathematics teachers are almost twice as likely to show evidence of coherent development, progression, execution and closure in terms of the objectives set for the lesson. Mean scores for the summative measure of clarity of task or activity structure are slightly lower, but moderately respectable, although again Mathematics outshines English substantially. Mean scores for backward mapping/framing/integration/closure are substantially lower, and no longer respectable, with Mathematics again leading English substantially. As to whether there is evidence that the teacher gave the students sufficient time to complete the task and keep the students occupied for the period of the task, scores for both Mathematics and English are considerably better, but as always, Mathematics leading English. On our measure of instructional flexibility and pedagogical judgment, the scores drop back to the highly unrespectable again, although more so for English than Mathematics. However, when it comes to dialogical exchanges, Mathematics and English change places quite dramatically with English teachers easily outperforming their Mathematical colleagues, although again, the absolute levels are still very low. English teachers also do slightly better when it comes to metacognitive self-regulation, but the mean scores for both subjects are very, very low. Finally, mean scores for knowledge building improve substantially for both English and Mathematics, but the mean score for Mathematics is more than twice the size of the mean score for English.

In sum, our summative scales that measure purposefulness and knowledge building at the lesson level strongly indicate opaqueness rather than transparency and visibility, with English instruction scoring very highly on the opaqueness scale. Instructionally speaking, it's not a very pretty picture, and certainly not one that indicates a strong commitment to visible learning in Secondary 3 Mathematics and English classes across the system.

Conclusion

In the course of this chapter we have assessed the intellectual quality of key instructional practises as an expression of the enacted curriculum in Secondary 3 Mathematics and English classes using a framework derived from John Hattie's "visible learning" model of effective teaching and learning. In doing so, however, we have expanded Hattie's particular model of visible learning to include a range of instructional practices that we believe are critical to enhancing instructional transparency and student learning: greater epistemic clarity with respect to the nature and cognitive demands of the knowledge work involved in the design and implementation of instructional (and assessment) tasks; greater attention to variations in, and relationships between, different forms of epistemic talk in the classroom; greater attention to the quality of teacher questioning and their responses to student responses; more differentiated constructions of checking for prior learning, monitoring and feedback; the provision of learning support to students, especially strategic learning support, in ways that encourages challenging (but productive) learning and avoids unproductive success; a strong focus on understanding rather than memorization; and considered attention to the purposeful progression of the lesson and the process of knowledge building by students. Although we are not aware of studies that would allow us to benchmark all of these measures, we believe that extending the model of visible learning in these ways will significantly enhance the transparency and visibility of teaching and learning in Singaporean classrooms. Meanwhile, while we have no doubt of the commitment of Singaporean teachers to active teaching, their commitment to visible learning is much less evident. By any measure, this is a critical challenge to both pre-service and in-service teacher education programs going forward, particularly in light of the demands of the *Teach Less Learn More* policy initiative to improve the quality of teaching and learning in Singaporean classrooms. But it is also a challenge for the Ministry of Education as well, because it is far from clear to us that current curriculum and instructional frameworks supported by the Ministry support visible learning.

Appendix: Core 2 Research Program: Indicators of Visible Learning Panels 2 and 3 Data

Scale	Specification
Communicating lesson goals and assessment standards	
Communicating lesson topics	Teacher's announcement of the lesson topic, the mode of articulation and the stated rationale for learning the topic
Communicating learning objectives	Teacher's announcement of the learning objectives for the lesson, the mode of articulation, the level of detail provided for the objectives and the stated rationale for these objectives
Recapitulation of learning goals	Teacher's recapitulation of learning objectives, the mode of articulation and the level of detail when recapitulating
Communicating performance standards	Teacher's explicit mention of performance standards and criteria for the task, activity, student work or goals
Exemplars of performances of understanding	Teacher's explicit reference and explication of exemplars of performance, which can be successful, unsuccessful or incorrect exemplars. Important is the degree of explanation that follows the exemplar so that students know what to achieve, or avoid, when performing that task, activity or goal
Whole class performances of understanding	Teacher's demonstration and performance of particular goals, criteria, standards
Epistemic clarity: task structure	
Epistemic (knowledge) focus	Epistemic focus of the knowledge work that teachers are engaged in, or teachers ask students to engage in: factual, procedural, conceptual (a focus on meaning and making connections), epistemic (denoting the criteria and standards for establishing the epistemic warrant of knowledge claims), metacognitive, rhetorical (a focus on knowledge of grammar and syntax in EL), hermeneutical (a focus on principles of textual interpretation), aesthetic and moral and civic
Domain specific activities, tasks and practices	Focus on the instructional activities that teachers ask students to engage in. Domain specific in nature, the scales are hierarchical and assume increasing disciplinary and cognitive complexity

(continued)

(continued)

Scale	Specification
Mathematics tasks	Remembering tasks, routine procedural tasks, review tasks, revision tasks, comprehension/knowledge manipulation tasks, procedural tasks with connections, and "Doing Mathematics"
Domain-specific knowledge practices: mathematics	Knowledge communication (Syntax), knowledge representation, knowledge generation, knowledge deliberation, knowledge justification, knowledge communication (Presentation)
English language activities/tasks	Coding, comprehension, interpretation and meaning making, analysis, description, conveying, expressing, explaining, persuading
Cognitive demand/complexity/operations	Focus on the cognitive demands of instructional activities that teachers ask students to engage in. Activities are coded according to the cognitive operations required by students to achieve the activity goal
Locus of epistemic authority	Focus on the source of epistemic authority and the nature of epistemic authority (positional, procedural or artifactual). Scale is also coded when teacher explicitly appeals to domain-specific knowledge
Epistemic pluralism and deliberation	Focus on the openness of knowledge work which draws on multiple perspectives. Epistemic claims are deliberated, compared, debated, justified and accountable to specific epistemic authorities
Epistemic clarity: classroom talk	
Factual talk	Talk that focuses on propositional or factual knowledge (dates, events, facts, names, equations, definitions, algorithms, and etc.). It often involves descriptive talk – descriptions of a state of affairs
Procedural talk	Talk that focuses on how students complete a process or task specific to a discipline, subject or area of study. This is talk around genres, rules, procedures, resources, tools involved in solving a problem or doing knowledge work
Clarifying talk	Talk that focuses on clarifying questions or elaborations that invites the teacher or students to clarify what is meant in an earlier exchange or statement

(continued)

(continued)

Scale	Specification
Connecting talk	Talk that focuses on helping students to make meaning by establishing connections between prior knowledge or personal experiences to related concepts or topics, from previous to current lessons, between examples, between forms of disciplinary knowledge and language. Such connections aim to deepen conceptual understanding and build knowledge
Temporal connections	Talk that focuses on helping students make explicit, relevant, connections to earlier discussions in the current lesson, or to previous lessons or units, or to lessons or units that will come after the current lesson
Conceptual connections	Talk that focuses on explicit conceptual connections where the teacher asks students to make, or students initiate making, connections between concepts, representations, examples, analogies, out-of-school matter and curriculum content
Framing talk	Talk that focuses on taking a step back from an ongoing exchange to frame, interpret, situate the talk to a broader, conceptual, procedural or epistemic context. The connection is therefore between talk and context
Reframing talk	Talk that focuses on moving between vernacular talk and more abstract, technical, domain-specific disciplinary talk. The focus is between two distinct types of talk or grammars (vernacular and technical)
Explanatory talk	Talk that focuses on teacher or students giving reasons or explanation in response to initial statements made
Epistemic justification talk	Talk that focuses on teacher or students identifying and discussing domain specific epistemic norms (criteria and standards) to be used to establish the truth value, rigor, validity, reliability, authenticity, or reasonableness of a knowledge claim
Reflexive talk	Talk that focuses on meta-cognition and self-regulation – how students learn, or can learn, to manage their own learning more effectively

(continued)

(continued)

Scale	Specification
Structure of classroom interaction	
Teacher talk	Focus on the nature of teacher questions (open-ended or closed) directed at the whole class, individuals or groups, as well as the length of the teacher responses when addressing the class, individuals or groups. Short responses are typically a few words, medium responses are one or two sentences, extended responses are three sentences or more
Student talk	Focus on the nature of student questions (open-ended or closed) directed to the teacher in a whole class context, as well as the length of the student responses to the teacher. The responses can be made in a whole class setting, when the student is in a group, or when the student is interacting with the teacher individually. Short responses are typically a few words, medium responses are one or two sentences, extended responses are three sentences or more
Instructional strategies	
Checking on prior learning	Focus on the teacher checking on student's prior activities, concepts, topics, content knowledge, and specific knowledge from previous lessons
Monitoring	Focus on how the teacher monitors student learning. Monitoring may be supervisory where the teacher monitors whether students are complying with instructions provided or it may be formative where the teacher seeks to establish the level of understanding or skill that a student has for a given task. Monitoring may be directed at individuals or groups
Feedback	Focuses on the nature of feedback provided by the teacher *to* the student. Feedback may be evaluative or formative, or it may be a prescriptive reformulation of a student's incorrect response or a detailed correction of a student's response. The scale also captures the audience of the teacher's feedback – individuals, students, whole class, and in some cases when students provide feedback to other students

(continued)

(continued)

Scale	Specification
Learning support	Focus on the nature of support provided to students to complete an activity or to achieve understanding. Learning support may be planned and fixed whereby the teacher has decided in advance the kind of support needed by the students, or it may be contextual and flexible whereby the teacher provides timely support to enable their content mastery or task completion. The nature of the learning support may be logistical when guidance is provided on the use of tools or resources, procedural when guidance is provided on steps or procedures to complete a task, or strategic when explicit guidance on alternative strategies or options are provided to aid students to complete a task or achieve understanding
Self-directed learning	Focus on the extent to which the teacher offers opportunities for students to exercise autonomy over their own learning. The scale checks if students are able to establish, negotiate or modify classroom norms, learning goals, learning activities, topics, lesson structure, task design, assessment criteria and standards, or resources. It also checks if students are able to perform self-assessment or have opportunities to discuss alternative viewpoints or explanations that may contradict the teacher's
Structure and clarity scale (P2)	Asks if the teacher states the lesson objectives, gives clear directions and explanations for student tasks, organises information and explains difficult ideas
Flexible teaching (P2)	Asks if the teacher tries different teaching methods or allows students to get help from peers
Focus on understanding (P2)	Asks if the teacher's explanations, course materials, or homework tasks help students understand the topic
Quality of questioning (P2)	Asks if the teacher provides time to answer questions, asks quality questions, and rephrases the questions if students are unable to respond correctly

(continued)

(continued)

Scale	Specification
Teacher review (P2)	Asks if the teacher checks that students understand the lesson, and reviews the lesson before starting a new topic
Focus on practice	Asks if the teacher ensures that students focus on the lesson, pays attention, concentrates during class work and that they complete their work
Traditional instruction (P2)	Teaching that focuses on spending a significant amount of time on drill and practice using textbooks
Direct instruction (P2)	Teaching that focuses on structure and clarity of the lesson content and objectives, provides students with reviews of the content, and ensures that students are focused and are able to complete their work
Teaching for understanding (P2)	Flexible teaching that focuses on depth of understanding, engages in quality questions, engages students' curiosity and interest, provides scaffolding during group work, monitors student learning, provides personal and collective feedback
Co-regulated learning (P2)	Teaching that encourages students to practice self-directed learning through setting their own goals, identifying strategies to achieve them, and to conduct frequent checks on their own work
Knowledge building	
Lesson purposefulness	The lesson exhibited evidence that the teacher had planned thoughtfully, designed or selected learning tasks, selected instructional activities and steered classroom talk with specific educational goals in view
Direction/Progression over the course of the lesson	The lesson shows evidence of coherent development, execution and closure in terms of the objectives set for the lesson
Clarity of task/Activity structure	The lesson showed evidence of a clear sequence of tasks/activities that built on each other in an effective and appropriate manner
Backward mapping/Framing/Integration/Closure	The lesson showed evidence that the teacher recapitulated learning goals and summarized the learning from the unit of work

(continued)

(continued)

Scale	Specification
Time	There is evidence that the teacher gave the students sufficient time to complete the task
Instructional flexibility/Pedagogical judgment	Teacher showed evidence of flexibility and 'pedagogical agility' to take advantage of 'teachable moments'
Focus on knowledge building	There is evidence of 'knowledge building' through developing active engagement in knowledge practices that permitted them to develop conceptual and procedural understanding and skills
Focus on metacognitive self-regulation	There is evidence that the teacher tried to help students develop metacognitive knowledge and skills

References

Alexander, R. (2000). *Culture and pedagogy: International comparisons in primary education.* Oxford: Blackwell.

Alexander, R. (2004). *Towards dialogic teaching: Rethinking classroom talk.* York: Dialogos.

Alexander, R. (2008). *Essays on pedagogy.* London: Routledge.

Alexander, R. (2012). Moral panic, miracle cures and educational policy: What can we really learn from international comparison? *Scottish Educational Review, 44*(1), 4–21.

Ball, D. (2003). *Mathematical proficiency for all students: Towards a strategic research and development program in mathematics education.* Santa Monica: RAND.

Barnes, D. (1992). *From communication to curriculum* (2nd ed.). Portsmouth: Boynton/Cook-Heinemann.

Barnes, D. (2008). Exploratory talk for learning. In N. Mercer & S. Hodgkinson (Eds.), *Exploring talk in school* (pp. 1–16). London: Sage.

Bereiter, C., & Scardamalia, M. (2006). Education for the knowledge age: Design-centred models of teaching and instruction. In P. Alexander & P. Winne (Eds.), *Handbook of educational psychology* (2nd ed., pp. 695–714). New Jersey: Lawrence Erlbaum.

Black, P., & Wiliam, D. (1998). *Inside the black box: Raising standards through classroom assessment.* London: Assessment Reform Group, University of Cambridge, School of Education.

Boaler, J. (2002a) The development of disciplinary relationships: Knowledge, practice and identity in mathematics classrooms. *For The Learning of Mathematics, 22*(1), 42–47.

Boaler, J. (2002b). Exploring the nature of mathematical activity: Using theory, research and working hypotheses to broaden conceptions of mathematics knowing. *Educational Studies in Mathematics, 51*(1/2), 3.

Cazden, C. B. (1988). *Classroom discourse: The language of teaching and learning.* Portsmouth: Heinemann.

Cohen, D. (2011). *Teaching and its predicaments.* Cambridge: Harvard University Press.

Doyle, W. (1983). Academic work. *Review of Educational Research, 53*, 159–199.

Ford, M. J., & Forman, E. A. (2006). Redefining disciplinary learning in classroom contexts. In J. Green & A. Luke (Eds.), *Review of research in education* (Vol. 30, pp. 1–32). Washington, DC: American Educational Research Association.

Ford, M. J., & Forman, E. A. (2008). Redefining disciplinary learning in classroom contexts. In J. Green, A. Luke, & G. Kelly (Eds.), *Review of educational research* (Vol. 30, pp. 1–32). Washington, DC: American Education Research Association.

Hattie, J. (1987). Identifying the salient facets of a model of student learning: A synthesis of meta-analyses. *International Journal of Educational Research, 11*, 187–212.

Hattie, J. (2009). *Visible learning. A synthesis of over 800 meta-analyses relating to achievement.* London: Routledge.

Hattie, J. (2012). *Visible learning for teachers: Maximizing impact on learning.* London: Routledge.

Hodgkinson, S., & Mercer, N. (2008). *Exploring talk in school.* London: Sage.

Hogan, D. (2011). Evidence-based policy in education in Singapore. In T. Schuler & T. Burns (Eds.), *Evidence-based policy making in education.* Paris: CERI/OECD.

Hogan, D. (2012). Culture and pedagogy in Singapore: The fate of the Teach Less Learn More policy initiative, 2004–1010. In S. Paris, & K. Lee (Eds.), *Redesigning pedagogy.* Singapore: Springer.

Hogan, D., Towndrow, P., Rahim, R., Chan, M., Luo, S., Sheng, Y., et al. (2011). *Interim report on pedagogical practices in Singapore in Secondary 3 mathematics and English, 2004 and 2010.* Singapore: National Institute of Education.

Hogan, D., Rahim, R., Chan, M., Kaur, B., & Towndrow, P. (2012). Disciplinarity and the logic of mathematical tasks in Secondary 3 mathematics lessons in Singapore. In R. Gillies, (Ed.), *New developments in cognition and instruction research.* New York: Nova Science Publishers, Forthcoming.

Hogan, D., Chan, M., Rahim, R., Towndrow, P., & Kwek, D. (2012). Understanding classroom talk in Secondary 3 mathematics classes in Singapore. In B. Kaur (Ed.), *Connections, reasoning and communication: New directions in mathematics education.* Singapore: World Scientific.

Lefstein, A., & Snell, J. (2010). Classroom discourse: The promise and complexity of dialogic practice. In S. Ellis, E. McCartney, & J. Bourne (Eds.), *Insight and impact: Applied linguistics and the primary school.* Cambridge: Cambridge University Press.

Lemke, J. (1989). *Using language in the classroom.* Oxford: Oxford University Press.

Lemke, J. (1990). *Talking science: Language, learning and values.* Norwood: Ablex.

McConachie, S., & Petrosky, A. (Eds.). (2010). *Content matters: A disciplinary literacy approach to improved student learning.* San Francisco: Jossey Bass.

Mehan, H. (1979). *Learning lessons: Social organization in the classroom* (illustrated, Reprint edn.). The University of Michigan/Harvard University Press.

Mercer, N. (1992). Talk for teaching and learning. In: *Thinking voices: The work of the National Oracy Project* (pp. 215–223). London: Hodder & Stoughton (for the National Curriculum Council).

Mercer, N., & Littleton, K. (2007). *Dialogue and the development of children's thinking: A sociocultural approach.* London/New York: Routledge.

Michaels, S., O'Connor, C., Hall, M., & Resnick, L. (2002). *Accountable talk: Classroom conversation that works (CD-ROM set).* Pittsburgh: University of Pittsburgh.

Michaels, S., Sohmer, R. E., & O'Connor, M. C. (2004). Classroom discourse. In H. Ammon, N. Dittmar, K. Mattheier, & P. Trudgill (Eds.), *Sociolinguistics: An international handbook of the science of language and society* (2nd ed., pp. 2351–2366). New York: Walter de Gruyter.

Michaels, S., O'Conner, C., & Resnick, L. (2008). Deliberative discourse idealized and realized: Accountable talk in the classroom and civic life. *Studies in the Philosophy of Education, 27*, 283–297.

Nystrand, M., & Gamoran, A. (1991). Instructional discourse, student engagement, and literature achievement. *Research in the Teaching of English, 25*, 261–290.

Nystrand, M., Gamoran, A., Kachur, R., & Prendergast, C. D. (1999). *Opening dialogue: Understanding the language and learning in the english classroom.* New York: Teachers College Press.

Nystrand, M., Wu, L., Gamoran, A., Zeiser, S., & Long, D. (2001). *Questions in time: Investigating the structure and dynamics of unfolding classroom discourse.* Albany: The National Research

Center on English Learning & Achievement. Report Series 14005, University of New York (Albany).

Perkins, D. (1998). What is understanding? In M. S. Wiske (Ed.), *Teaching for understanding* (pp. 39–57). San Francisco: Jossey Bass.

Rahim, R., Hogan, D., & Chan, M. (2012). The epistemic framing of mathematical tasks in Secondary 3 mathematics lessons in Singapore. In B. Kaur (Ed.), *Reasoning, connections and communications in Singapore mathematics lessons*. Singapore: World Scientific.

Resnick, L.B., Asterhan, C., Clarke, C., & Hofkens, T. (Eds.) (2012, forthcoming) *Socializing intelligence* [papers from the September 2011 AERA conference 'Socializing intelligence through academic talk and dialogue' held at the University of Pittsburgh], Washington, DC: AERA.

Rittle-Johnson, B., & Alibali, M. W. (1999). Conceptual and procedural knowledge of mathematics: Does one lead to the other? *Journal of Educational Psychology, 91*(1), 175–189.

Schoenfeld, A. H. (1992). Learning to think mathematically: Problem solving, metacognition, and sense-making in mathematics. In D. Grouws (Ed.), *Handbook for research on mathematics teaching and learning* (pp. 334–370). New York: MacMillan.

Schraw, G. (2006). Knowledge: Structures and processes. In P. Alexander & P. Winne (Eds.), *Handbook of educational psychology* (2nd ed., pp. 245–264). Mahwah: Lawrence Erlbaum.

Shanmugaratnam, T. (2005). *Speech at the MOE work plan seminar 2005,* 22 Sept. Singapore: Ngee Ann Polytechnic Convention Centre.

Sinclair, J., & Coulthard, M. (1975). *Towards an analysis of discourse: The English used by teachers and pupils* (illustrated, Reprint edn.). Oxford University Press.

Stein, M., Grover, B., & Henningsen, M. (1996). Building student capacity for mathematical thinking and reasoning: An analysis of mathematical tasks used in reform classrooms. *American Educational Research Journal, 33*(2), 455–488.

Stein, M., Smith, M., Henningsen, M., & Silver, E. (2009). *Implementing standards-based mathematics instruction: A casebook for professional development* (2nd ed.). New York: Teachers College Press.

Wells, G., & Arauz, R. (2006). Dialogue in the classroom. *The Journal of the Learning Sciences, 15*(3), 379–428.

Young, M. (2008). *Bringing knowledge back in: From social constructivism to social realism in the sociology of education*. London: Routledge.

Chapter 9
Working Through the Layers: Curriculum Implementation in Language Education

Rita Elaine Silver, Xiaolan Curdt-Christiansen, Susan Wright, and Madonna Stinson

Introduction

Singapore is well-known for its global economic outlook coupled with locally oriented political and social policies. From the early days in Singapore's history, economic goals were grounded in international trade due to Singapore's limited material resources to turn into manufacturing strength. The intention was to build a cohesive social structure out of the post-colonial multicultural, multilingual citizenry which could then be leveraged for economic development (see, e.g. Silver 2005; Chap. 2). This led Singapore to take a global view of development before 'globalisation' became the buzz word of the moment in that Singapore made a concerted effort to build capacity internally by capitalizing on international trade networks. The idea of leveraging the skills of the citizenry led naturally to concern for educational policy. Three important policy goals from the early days of Singapore's nationhood and continuing into the present were:

- To design and maintain a national school system with a common syllabus and national examinations;
- To emphasise broad-based education at the primary school level, then progressively develop and strengthen education through levels of higher education which offer different pathways for students of different abilities and interests;
- To implement an English-knowing bilingual education policy with provision for a role for one official language for each ethnic group (Chinese, Malay, Tamil) plus English for all students as part of the core curriculum.

R.E. Silver (✉) • X. Curdt-Christiansen • S. Wright
National Institute of Education, Nanyang Technological University, Singapore
e-mail: rita.silver@nie.edu.sg

M. Stinson
School of Education and Professional Studies, Griffith University, Australia

Z. Deng et al. (eds.), *Globalization and the Singapore Curriculum: From Policy to Classroom*, Education Innovation Series, DOI 10.1007/978-981-4451-57-4_9,
© Springer Science+Business Media Singapore 2013

Historical developments linking economy, education, and language have been well covered elsewhere (e.g. Gopinathan 1997, 2007; Silver 2005; Chap. 2). Of importance for this discussion is that policies aimed at improving economy-education-language linkages are a significant contributing factor to long-standing, on-going curricular innovation in Singapore. Within the broader socio-political environment, the educational landscape is managed through a central governing body which sets system-wide goals and policies (e.g. language education policies) intended to integrate with larger national goals, as well as establishing standards for learning outcomes and high stakes assessments. However, the system is decentralised at the local level (schools, school departments) where responsibility for interpreting the goals and standards, preparing students for high stakes assessment, implementation and evaluation of learning outcomes resides (Tan and Ng 2007; Chap. 2). Curriculum development and innovation links national, school and classroom levels with different ideological and practical concerns influencing potential innovators at each level in Singapore (Towndrow et al. 2010) and elsewhere (see Honig 2006, for discussion). With that in mind, this chapter presents findings on English Language (EL) instruction at the lower primary level in the context of policies of curricular innovation at national, school and classroom levels. Our focus is on policies which connect national and school levels and on how they might be interpreted when implemented in multiple schools within Singapore's educational system.

Language Policy, Educational Innovation and Classroom Pedagogy

Singapore's achievements in economic development, educational attainment and bilingualism in the official languages are substantial and well-documented (see, e.g. Singapore Department of Statistics 2011; Chaps. 2 and 12). However, Singaporean policy makers, rather than resting on the country's laurels, prefer to continually push for further development and improvement. Hence the constant emphasis on curriculum innovation and renewal. This is evident in the Thinking Schools Learning Nation (TSLN) "vision" which sets its sights on enhanced capacity through innovation, enterprise and life-long learning. Specifically, the TSLN vision encourages upgrading as a nation, through continued economic development, job training throughout the career span, as well as continuous improvements in education in schools (Goh 1997; also see Chaps. 2 and 4). For school-based education, TSLN envisions a "global future" with schools which are more autonomous, teachers who are reflective and continuously involved in professional development and students who have a passion to learn (ibid).

Following up on the TSLN vision, Prime Minister Lee Hsien Loong called for ways for teachers to "teach less, so that our student can learn more" (MOE 2005: para. 2) leading to the Teach Less, Learn More (TLLM) initiative which emphasises the need "to improve the quality of interaction between teachers and learners" (para. 3) (also see Chap. 7) in order to encourage students to learn more actively and independently. Continuing the ideas introduced with TSLN but specific to schooling,

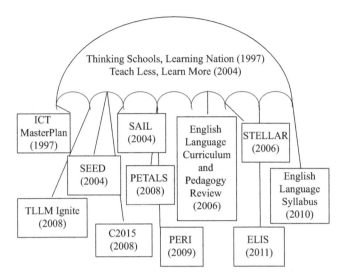

Fig. 9.1 Overview of TSLN policy enactment

TLLM acts as an umbrella under which a variety of educational reform efforts have been initiated (Fig. 9.1) – all in keeping with the idea that Singaporeans must be grounded in local values but educated for participation in a globalised society.

Among the initiatives associated with TSLN and TLLM is Curriculum 2015 (C2015) which focuses, in particular, on the anticipated skills and competencies a child born in 2014 might need by the time of graduation and entering the workforce, and the implications of those needs for educational reform today (see Chaps. 3 and 14). Other initiatives include SAIL (Strategies for Active and Independent Learning), SEED (Strategies for Engaged and Effective Development), and PETALS (Use of Pedagogies, Experiences of Learning, Tone of Environment, Assessment for Learning, and Learning Content) which are intended to influence education from primary grade 1 through primary grade 6 (P1–P6), across subjects. Still others, such as TLLM Ignite!, focus on professional development in light of TLLM (see Chap. 7).

In addition, some policy initiatives are targeted specifically at lower primary with the idea that initial stages of education are crucial for future educational achievement. Class size reduction for P1 and P2 (from 40 to 30 students) is one recent example. Other initiatives are subject specific. Recent EL reform efforts include a curriculum and pedagogy review, syllabus revision, the establishment of ELIS (English Language Institute of Singapore) for teacher professional development, and the introduction of the STELLAR (Strategies for English Language Learning and Reading) curriculum. Most recently the Primary Education Review and Implementation (PERI) review was completed. The PERI report (PERI Committee 2009) made three main recommendations: enhance infrastructure; invest in a quality teaching force; and balance knowledge with skills and values in a whole-school curriculum, all of which MOE is now acting on. This sample of reform initiatives (see Appendix for weblinks to each) indicates Singapore's constant attempts to push educational reform forward, always with an eye toward the anticipated needs of the twenty-first century workforce and a perspective of globalisation at the heart of those needs. As noted by Ng Eng Hen, Minister for Education,

> To an observer, MOE and our schools are constantly on the move. Even when we have attained high standards, we are still seeking to improve. There is a reason for this unabating activity. The many changes across decades, different ministers, different administrators, do have continuity in purpose and motivation. There is a melody that runs through and a motif that keeps on recurring. Very simply, we treasure our human resource as the most valuable asset in Singapore (2008: para 7).

Policy making tends to be heavily top-down in Singapore with a variety of policies initiated by the MOE. However, not all policies are intended to be implemented with uniformity across the nation. Instead, some policies are intended to be developed on a whole-school basis and some are intended to encourage initiative by teachers in individual classrooms. For example, the ICT Masterplan, now in its third iteration, has fostered nation-wide upgrading of ICT equipment including most recently the introduction of a wireless network that students can tap into while at school (Lim 2010). However, individual schools have a choice of how and in what ways to integrate ICT in learning. For example, a few schools have moved toward whole-school student laptop adoption while others maintain more traditional computer labs. In all schools, teachers and students have access to MOE sponsored websites for online learning which teachers can choose to assign as homework, suggest as supplementary work, or disregard in setting assignments. Thus different policies work at one or more layers of implementation: national, school, and classroom.

To examine the issue of how the education system nurtures its most valuable assets, children, we were interested not only in providing summary descriptions of classroom pedagogy, but also in presenting the voices of those educators engaged within and across the different layers of innovation in order to better understand the broadest range of perspectives possible. This led us to ask two key research questions:

1. How are these policies and innovations interpreted and implemented across layers (i.e. national, school, class)?
2. To what extent and in what ways, are they visible in classroom pedagogy?

Data Sources and Analyses

For this investigation, we adopted a multi-method approach including a case study of P2 instruction undertaken at two schools and individual lesson observations done at 10 schools in the same administrative "zone"[1] in Singapore. The combination of case study and individual lesson observations provided opportunities to address implementation processes horizontally and vertically across layers (e.g. national, school, classroom) and in multiple sites.

---

[1] There are four geographic zones in Singapore: North, South, East and West.

The case study component (CSC) followed two classes of students and their form teachers for two periods of five full days. It also included interviews with school leaders and classroom teachers, as well as focus group discussions with parents. In contrast to the intensive investigation in the CSC, the lesson observation component (LOC) emphasised examination of individual lessons at P1 and P2 in 10 schools, using a pre-determined coding scheme. A total of 19, 1-h, EL lessons were observed for the LOC. To gain some context for the individual lesson observations, we included brief pre-observation interviews with each teacher (e.g. "Is this a topic you have been teaching or is this the first lesson on this topic?"). Follow-up interviews with a sub-set of seven teachers were also undertaken to provide a glimpse into the teachers' perspectives and beliefs (c.f. Borg 2006). In these interviews, teachers watched a video recording of their own lessons with a researcher, and offered spoken reflections while viewing. Thus, the lesson observation component provided a basis for comparative analysis with the more detailed CSC. All data were collected from Terms 3 and 4 of the academic year (July–December) of 2009. Detailed descriptions of data collection instruments and protocols can be found in Stinson et al. (2010).

For the CSC, field notes from observed lessons along with transcribed interviews and parent focus group discussions were analysed using the framework of content analysis (Berg 2004). Emerging themes were identified by looking for ideas which surfaced repeatedly in the data and/or comments about known policy initiatives (e.g. alternative assessment, STELLAR, ICT). The data were coded by one trained Research Associate and one trained Research Assistant under the guidance of the Principal Investigators. Rather than coding independently and calculating inter-coder agreement as with frequency analyses, these data were initially coded collaboratively to surface emerging themes. Subsequently, when the team had agreed on important themes to be traced, the two RAs coded the lessons which they had observed. Then, the entire set of data and codes were re-checked through iterative readings. In this way, patterns in the analysis were confirmed, disconfirmed and finalised.

In contrast, analysis of LOC data was intended to facilitate comparison of the individual lessons, provide a normative overview of EL lessons at P1 and P2, and allow for the expression of individual teacher's perspectives via post-observation interviews with a subset of teachers. Coding was done within the context of a larger study which looked at core subjects (EL, maths, Mother Tongue) in P1 and P2. (See Silver et al. 2011, for details of the larger study.) Inter-coder agreement was verified using a sub-set of six English and four Math lessons (27 % of the total observations for those two subjects), checking for pair wise inter-coder agreement with a 'master coder' – a Research Associate who helped to develop the coding scheme (Silver et al. 2010). Agreement for English lessons was above 80 % overall which was deemed to be sufficient for our purposes. Subsequently, coding across lessons was collated to establish common classroom patterns. A total of seven EL teachers were interviewed from the LOC. These interviews were coded using the categories derived from the CSC. Specifically, the Research Associate who was involved in the analysis of CSC data subsequently coded the teacher interviews for the LOC, using the same themes where appropriate and noting new themes as needed.

Finally, data from both CSC and LOC were synthesised according to the three levels in which the policies are intended to operate in the Singapore system: *national policies* promulgated by the MOE, *school policies* instituted by the individual school, and *class policies* developed by the teacher. Overall findings were generated by moving recursively between CSC and LOC to synthesise pertinent themes at the three levels. Our findings are drawn from that synthesis.

Working Through the Layers

In this section we summarise our findings, referring to both CSC and LOC. We integrate information from the classroom observations and interviews to address issues of implementation and interpretation within and across layers: national, school and classroom.

National Policies

First, a number of *national policies* were familiar to school leaders and classroom teachers alike. Some of these same initiatives were also mentioned by parents in focus group discussions at the case study schools. However, other national policies seemed to be relevant only to school leadership and were not apparent in classroom lessons or teacher interviews. Two area of national policy were most evident in attempting to influence classroom pedagogy: (1) administrative reforms such as the implementation of 'single sessions' and related opportunities for changes in the classroom physical environment, and (2) introduction of a new English curriculum (STELLAR) coupled with school-based professional development.

Administrative Reforms

Cohen and Ball define innovations as "… a departure from current practice – deliberate or not, originating in or outside of practice, which is novel" (2007, p. 19). They discuss educational innovations in light of who innovates, types of innovations, and environments for innovation, noting that innovations need not directly target instruction. Administrative reforms are one type of innovation which can intentionally or unintentionally influence pedagogy. In Singapore, a few recent administrative reforms have been initiated as intentional efforts to encourage instructional change. One is the shift to single-session schools. 'Single sessions' refers to the way school facilities are scheduled for teaching. Previously, schools scheduled a 'morning session' and an 'afternoon session' at each school. Students attended one or the other, thus allowing for 'double sessions' in one school building and maximising the use of the facilities. The downside of this arrangement, as noted by the PERI report (PERI Committee 2009, pp. 47–49), was that it discouraged more holistic education as well as limiting opportunities for meaningful interaction between students and teachers. The educational system has been moving toward single sessions since 2004 and all schools are to convert to single sessions by 2016. This has already been implemented in many of the schools in the LOC as well as one of the case study schools.

In general, the move toward single-session was viewed positively by school leadership and teachers. One teacher who was still at a double-session school commented, "Personally, I'm looking forward to having a single session for our school." Parents were quite enthusiastic as well saying, "I like it!" and "I'm all for it" with only one parent demurring that school facilities might be too cramped if all of the children tried to fit into the school for single session. However, specific comments on the change to single sessions were related to changes in the physical environment rather than opportunities for holistic education, meaningful student-teacher interaction or classroom pedagogy. In our lesson observations and school visits, we found that teachers had taken advantage of the classroom ownership allowed by single sessions to decorate their P1/P2 classrooms with colorful literacy prints and displays of student work. Arrangements for group seating were also common in P1/P2 classrooms at these schools. In contrast, teachers in double-session schools had to compromise on classroom design due to sharing by different grade levels in the other session.

Teacher efforts to improve the physical environment were in accord with SEED and STELLAR philosophies on increasing student interest and engagement through physical changes. These were intended to enhance the socio-emotional environment of classrooms. However, there was no evidence that these physical changes influenced teacher pedagogy, student learning or interactions in daily lessons. For example, the literacy prints and student work were not referred to in any of the observed lessons; and, while students were seated together, they very rarely worked together. Instead, lessons were heavily whole-class, 'eyes on the front', teacher-led. Students appeared 'engaged' in the sense that they were largely on-task and compliant. There was little evidence of cognitive or affective engagement in student questions, comments or responses (Christiansen and Silver 2012; Silver et al. 2011), so the quality of engagement in the learning process is open to question. Our 2009 classroom data mirrored findings summarized by Deng and Gopinathan (1999):

> In most classrooms teachers tend to dominate most instructional discourse: teachers see their role primarily as transmitting knowledge and skills to students through didactic telling, explaining, and some limited doing, while students are expected to absorb knowledge and skills through passive listening, watching, drilling, and practising (p. 34).

Deng and Gopinathan follow this description with a suggestion for change in professional development, noting that, "reform in professional development must act together, not in isolation, with other innovations and developments" (p. 37). The reverse is self-evident – curriculum innovation must work together with reform in professional development.

Curriculum Reform Coupled with Professional Development

On-going efforts in professional development link national and school-based reform efforts. For example, several teachers mentioned that they had received formal training for the new STELLAR curriculum through MOE workshops. They also worked with a STELLAR mentor, an MOE staff member, in their own schools. In a few of the schools, individual teachers had not received formal STELLAR training but an in-school mentor provided guidance. Thus, curriculum reform and professional development were intended to work together, crossing national and school levels to encourage implementation in the classroom. To some extent, this was successful as our lesson observations showed substantial uniformity across all EL lessons at the different schools.

While this consistency speaks well for the uptake of STELLAR and the effectiveness of the professional development, it also suggests that school-based curriculum was simply subsumed under the more structured, MOE initiative. Specifically, most of the teachers in the observed lessons used a recommended STELLAR technique (Share Book Approach), with books and materials provided by MOE. They rigorously followed the detailed lesson plans that accompanied the materials, consistently using questions and prompts taken from the lesson plans. While a current concern is more differentiated learning, the structured approach to introducing STELLAR instead lead to an homogenised pedagogy. Uniformity is expected in a centralised system such as Singapore's, but rote replication of lesson plans is not ideal.

Based on the observational data, there is some concern that the implementation of STELLAR resulted in surface level changes (i.e. teachers prioritising the lesson plans) rather than a reflection of deeper understanding (i.e. teachers engaging with pedagogical principles of engagement such as enjoyment or on-task behaviour)[2] (Christiansen and Silver 2013) at least in these initial stages. For example, one teacher while watching her lesson video commented, "This is er one of the, the just following the STELLAR…like re-reading, then tuning in, then re-reading, and then lesson proper." Interestingly, while STELLAR guidelines stress the importance of re-reading to develop reading comprehension, for this teacher, that pedagogical strategy was superfluous to the real work, the "lesson proper" (i.e. the teacher-fronted content). Nevertheless, she followed through because she believed that following the steps of the lesson plan was equivalent to implementing the curriculum.

Rigid following of the lesson plan, in fact, contradicts the spirit of STELLAR, which was intended to encourage teachers "to adapt and innovate to original suit the needs of their students" (MOE 2008). A Senior Teacher mentioned that her school modified STELLAR by adding their own 'skill-based' worksheets, and one teacher stated categorically that "STELLAR is good but you must tailor it to the needs of the children in your class." Another teacher explained that

> The whole basis of this STELLAR is that we are given a very standard and specific set of guidelines to follow. So as far as possible, the teachers would have to follow strictly to the guidelines in order for that particular topic or unit to be completed on time. Because there

---

[2] See Silver et al. (2010) for discussion of coding for student engagement in observational studies.

will, I mean, there will be checking, and things like that so in a way I would say that 60 % of what the teachers in the level are doing are all the same because they are all following the guidelines but the other 40 % it would depend on the teacher like maybe they would supplement with their own worksheets, or they might just change a little bit of the language experience, like for example, let's say the current topic that I'm doing. I got my kids to make percussion instruments, er, and then just shakers, and I got them to do a dance but another class might do it differently. Like they will get them to do hmm percussion instruments or they might hold a mini competition to see like whose instrument is the most creative, things like that. (Sheila, P2 teacher)[3]

However, our lesson observations in the case study schools and across all 19 lessons of LOC showed higher than 60 % uniformity in lesson content and activity selection. We observed a consistent twin emphasis on the authority of the packaged lessons plan over teacher curricular expertise and on tight interactional control by teachers over the sort of dynamic classroom interaction and development of independent student learners espoused by TLLM, C2015 and PERI (Curdt-Christiansen and Silver 2011, 2012).

School Policies

School-level policies followed national reforms, acting as the mediating layer between national initiatives and classroom innovations. This was particularly evident in the crucial area of assessment and in the ways assessments were linked to student placement. National policy encourages 'streaming' or performance-based placement throughout the broader educational system. This is done through national examinations such as the Primary School Leaving Examination (PSLE) which all students are required to take in P6. Scores from the PSLE influence the selection of secondary school and several other choices in secondary education, such as whether the students will study 'sciences' or 'humanities'. Within the primary grades, current national policy recommends 'subject-based banding' so that students who excel in Mother Tongue but are weaker in English, for example, can be banded according to their strengths for each subject rather than taking all courses with the same classmates based on averaged scores. In our sample, most schools implemented subject-based banding at P2 but a few introduced it in P1.

Formal Examinations and "Alternative" Assessments

Examinations play an important part in determining a student's placement for the next year, despite continued efforts to introduce more alternative assessments (e.g. use of show-and-tell rather than a pencil-and-paper examination). All of the schools in our sample had formal examinations from P1 onwards and the results were a

---

[3] Teacher names, where used, are pseudonyms.

substantial part of banding decisions. However, there was variation from school to school in the way formal exams were implemented, when they were given and for which subjects. While some schools had a special end-of-term exam timetable, others had started to introduce exams following the regular class timetable. Also, some schools had moved toward reducing or doing away with formal examinations at the end of every term (4 per year) and instead opted for these sorts of exams only at the end of the mid-year and final semesters. All schools had introduced some 'alternative' assessments such as regularly scheduled class tests, scoring homework as part of the overall course marks, or use of classroom presentations scored with rubrics for a percentage of the total marks each term. Despite the introduction of these alternative assessments, there was an enduring belief in the importance of formal examinations. Even the way activities were managed in class was influenced by formal examination structure and requirements. Comments such as "Because this is in accordance to examinations" or "Because, say for example, reading alone, accounts for 20 marks [on the exam]" were common in teacher interviews. As one teacher emphasised "Because all will go back, in the end all will go back to sitting there, to take exams without complaining."

Yet, the PERI report encourages "schools to move away from an overly strong emphasis on examinations" and to begin exploring "the use of bite-sized forms of assessment which place more emphasis on learning rather than on grades alone" (p. 35). Some schools were moving toward this goal more quickly than others. In the case study schools, for example, one school had started to implement alternative forms of assessment rather than relying on formal examinations at P2, while the other school was still planning for the introduction of some form of alternative assessment. The fact that changes in assessment practices were open to dialogue showed that these were school-based decisions, influenced by national policy objectives, and gradually working their way into teachers' decisions about classroom implementation.

Classroom Policies

Teachers frequently referred to MOE initiatives which influenced their teaching. This linkage was particularly common when discussing assessments and the introduction of STELLAR. Teachers also commented on how school leadership had worked to implement these initiatives school-wide. Thus, a connection between national policy and classroom practice with mediation at the school level was evident.

Following Policy

Speaking specifically about STELLAR, Chris, a P2 teacher, said,

> So basically most of the time I follow, I refer to the guidelines to help me with the lesson. And it's quite helpful because er the fact that there's group work and um, there's

actually written work for them to do after the group work. It actually helps them put two and two together.

Viewing group work less positively but still 'exploring' its use because it was supported by the school and MOE, Nurliza, a P1 teacher said:

> So they, the principal, or the MOE, doesn't want us to sit in rows like this. Um. So we'll try our best to make them [students], move around. So one advantage of moving about is that they will like this very much. Then its disadvantage is, very noisy, bad classroom management. This is what I have always been exploring.

There seemed to be a certain trust between teachers, schools and those working at the national level which helped to strength the connections between national-school-classroom policies. One Head of Department (HOD) articulated this explicitly, "… with STELLAR, everything is systematic … And the fact that it's a direction from MOE, and thought has been gone through, has gone into it, we kind of knew that there must be substance in it." However, she went on to say "I first had to tell, sell them [teachers] STELLAR. And kind of went through it with them, er, what STELLAR is about, and like I said they were very excited about it. I guess to get anything moving there must be buy-in." For teachers, it is important to see innovation as relevant to their own concerns. For example, a number of teachers commented that fewer formal assessments in P1 and P2 were appropriate and 'going in the right direction' and so they were working to introduce the 'alternative' assessments described above, despite some continuing concerns about assessments in general.

Adapting Policy

Although there are many national reforms implemented in top-down fashion, with mediation at the school level, it would be incorrect to leave the impression that teachers were thoughtlessly following a path laid out by others. As in the quote from Nurliza above, although she was not always comfortable with the new physical arrangement, she was considering both pros and cons and exploring how to work with it. Use of group work was one area in which opinions differed and teachers often followed their own perceptions rather than external recommendations. Group work and social interaction are emphasised in the PERI report, suggested for some STELLAR activities, and recommended for some alternative assessments. In our data, a few teachers used group work throughout a lesson, but the majority used group work not at all. Teachers felt free to make modifications in types of activities, introduction of materials and tools (e.g. videos, puppets, songs, dances), and selective omission of some worksheets. One teacher explained:

> STELLAR is good but you must tailor it to the need of the children in your class. So, there must be freedom, for example, like Class A, the best class can do six books in one term. OK, fine, go ahead. But Class H is not as fast as them, you must tell them, OK no problem. As long as you read the book with them. But, you know, if the grammar item is covered already in the previous term … there is no point in it.

Teachers were most likely to make adaptations that they felt were important for specific groups of students, usually because of their 'ability level'. However, these were small-scale changes in classroom practices.

Leading Policy

Teachers appeared to be leading policy innovations in one area – the teaching of values and social skills. This was clearly apparent in classroom lessons and teacher interviews, yet it rarely came up in discussions with school leaders and was not a dominant theme in national policies at the time of data collection. A few teachers were quite explicit about what was appropriate and inappropriate during lessons; others broached the teaching of values through their use of instructions for activities to be undertaken or in their feedback on student behaviour and ideas (especially for social skills such as sharing or working together). The teaching of moral values was especially evident in the discussions of stories, with many teachers noting that they intentionally brought out the moral values implicit in the stories read during lessons. In addition, teachers were exceptionally reflective about their own efforts to bring the teaching of values into a lesson. For example, while viewing her own lesson, one teacher explained that she was teaching the students about the importance of sharing while reading the story *The Little Red Hen*. On reflection, she was not completely satisfied with her own treatment of the subject, recognizing that the performance of values might need to be more nuanced in daily life.

> But urm there was one area I feel I should improve on. It's that beside telling ya the children suggested that the urm the red hen could share but I must also bring across the fact that urm you have to urm earn your own, work for your own... You cannot let people take advantage of you at the same time...Which I didn't drive across. And then I went back and think about it ya I feel that I should have said something so so that the children will not be misled that every time you know people ask me I'm obliged to do it. (Shih Fen, P2 teacher)

In their integration of values into daily teaching, the teachers foreshadowed the latest wave of policy reform as introduced by the Minister of Education, Heng Swee Keat at the annual Workplan Seminar for Singaporean educators in 2011. Minister Heng focussed on moral values in education saying,

> We need moral values, such as respect, responsibility, care and appreciation towards others, to guide each of us to be a socially responsible person. In particular, for our multi-racial, multi-cultural society, a sense of shared values and respect allows us to appreciate and celebrate our diversity, so that we stay cohesive and harmonious. (2011: para 41)

We note that in these comments, Minister Heng echoes earlier, and consistently used, arguments for linking economic development, education and social cohesion.

Conclusion

Given the close links between national policy setters at MOE, school leadership and teachers, it is not surprising that national policies have influenced classroom teaching in ways that closely align with those initiatives. In their analysis of 'implementation' of National Curriculum policy in the UK, Ball and Bowe discuss the re-interpretations of policy at different levels of enactment, highlighting the multiple factors that can influence how policies are 'recreated' rather than 'implemented' (1992, pp. 113–114). For example, they point out the crucial role of HODs in making sense of change at a school and with colleagues. In our data, various school leaders (e.g. Principal, Senior Teacher) could and did provide the necessary leadership for implementation of new policies. However the new STELLAR curriculum was also supported by MOE staff who offered training and in-school mentoring. This is certainly one factor in the great uniformity of classroom lessons under STELLAR.

Ball and Bowe (1992) also point out conflicts around funding, staffing and assessment – only some of which were visible in our data. For example, they found problems in unequal resource distribution to their case study schools which had a carry-on effect in implementation. This was not an issue in the schools in our sample, all of which were well-funded. The schools in Singapore were also fully staffed, although there were concerns about new and inexperienced teachers trying to carry out new initiatives. As one HOD explained, in her school only the P1 teachers received MOE training and there was concern that lack of expertise would negatively influence the introduction of the curriculum. Therefore, they offered in-school training with a buddy system. These sorts of 'innovations' highlight the important mediating influence of the school in the implementation plan, as discussed above. Concerning assessments, national assessments were viewed negatively by teachers in Ball and Bowe's study, but these have always been the norm in Singapore. In fact, it seems that schools now have somewhat more autonomy in deciding assessment timing and type in these early years, though they are still concerned about and constrained by the national PSLE, as above.

On the other hand, adoptions and adaptations of policy innovations at the classroom level were somewhat superficial: they were more related to changes in educational facilities and procedures than in philosophies. We found, for example, that even though there was wide-scale adoption of STELLAR teaching materials and strategies, lessons were tightly structured with predominantly teacher-fronted interactions (Curdt-Christiansen and Silver 2011). These areas are more resistant to change because they are more closely linked to teacher beliefs and cultural values than to procedures and programmes.

It is also true that there was little evidence of *policy initiation* or *curriculum innovation* at the classroom level. Although school leaders and teachers felt it was important to let teachers adapt ways of presenting the curriculum, this is not the same as teacher-initiated school-based curriculum development to address specific school goals or student learning objectives. In addition, classroom instruction continued to prioritise examinable subjects over holistic education, and formal assessments over other measures of learning, even in the first 2 years of primary school. Finally, despite multiple initiatives to encourage the TSLN vision of students with a passion to learn as well as efforts to improve the quality of classroom interaction under the auspices of TLLM, we saw lessons which were well-planned and well-managed, but rarely encouraged passionate pursuit of knowledge, higher-order thinking or open-ended interaction. This leaves the door open for further reform efforts, and raises the question of whether the same types of reform efforts are the way forward.

Innovation, engagement and a futures orientation to teaching and learning are persistent themes in the many policy innovations introduced at the national level. To foster further innovation, Ng (2004) has suggested that schools adopt an organisational change model in order to reflect upon and evaluate their own innovation journey. In such a change model, leaders and teachers within each school would need to consider their own innovation objectives ("goals"), the programmes they wish to propose ("business"), the mindset and beliefs of people in the school ('culture'), the workflow to achieve the proposed programmes ('processes'), and the resources and tools that are needed ("enablers"). This makes sense in light of our view that the school acts as the mediating layer for national policies and classroom implementation. However, it does not fully take into account the way schools adopt national policies. National leaders, such as former Minister of Education Ng Eng Hen, might see the common melody and recurring motif of policy innovations, but schools and teachers often become more focused on dancing to the latest tune. An alternative view is that the next stage in educational innovation should not be based on asking, "How do we encourage teachers to innovate?" but "What sorts of innovations do teachers see as necessary and useful, within their schools, and for their students' future?"

Acknowledgements We gratefully acknowledge funding by the Office of Educational Research, National Institute of Education, Singapore. The views expressed in this paper are the authors' and do not necessarily represent the views of the Centre or the Institute. We would also like to acknowledge Peter Taylor for the training sessions on content analysis and focus group discussions and express our appreciation to our research team:

Cai Li
Wartik bte Hassan
Alamu Venkatachalam
Tan Ying Quan
Santhakumari d/o N. Krishnan

Finally, we offer our sincere thanks to the study participants – students, teachers, parents and school leaders – for their time and efforts on behalf of the project.

Appendix

MOE policy/ initiative	Abbreviation	Year	Subject	Further information
Thinking Schools, Learning Nation	TSLN	1997	All	http://www.moe.gov.sg/media/ speeches/1997/020697.htm
				http://www.moe.edu.sg/corporate/ mission_statement.htm
Teach Less Learn More	TLLM	2004	All	http://www3.moe.edu.sg/bluesky/ tllm.htm
				http://www.moe.gov.sg/about/ yearbooks/2005/teach.html
Strategies for Engaged and Effective Development	SEED	2004	All	http://www.moe.gov.sg/about/ yearbooks/2005/enrichment/ sowing_project_seed.html
				http://www3.moe.edu.sg/corporate/ contactonline/2006/issue08/ sub_BigPicture_Art02.htm
Strategies for Active and Independent Learning	SAIL	2004	All	http://www.moe.gov.sg/media/ press/2004/pr20040325.htm
				http://www.moe.gov.sg/media/ speeches/2004/sp20040325.htm
Strategies for English Language Learning and Reading	STELLAR	2006	EL	http://www.stellarliteracy.sg/
English Language Curriculum and Pedagogy Review	ELCPR	2006	EL	http://www.moe.gov.sg/media/ press/2006/pr20061005.htm
Use of Pedagogies, Experiences of Learning, Tone of Environment, Assessment for Learning, and Learning content	PETALS	2008	All	http://www.moe.gov.sg/media/ press/2008/01/more-support-for-schools-teach.php
				http://www.moe.gov.sg/media/ press/2008/01/more-support-for-schools-teach.php#annex-b
Curriculum 2015	C2015	2008	All	http://www.moe.gov.sg/media/ speeches/2008/09/25/ speech-by-dr-ng-eng-hen-at-the-moe-work-plan-semi-nar-2008.php
TLLM Ignite!	–	2008	All	http://www.moe.gov.sg/media/ press/2008/01/more-support-for-schools-teach.php

(continued)

(continued)

MOE policy/ initiative	Abbreviation	Year	Subject	Further information
Primary Education Review and Implementation	PERI	2009	All	http://www.moe.gov.sg/media/press/files/2009/04/peri-report.pdf
English Language Syllabus 2010		2010	EL	http://www.moe.gov.sg/education/syllabuses/languages-and-literature/files/english-primary-secondary-express-normal-academic.pdf
English Language Institute of Singapore	ELIS	2011	EL	http://www.moe.gov.sg/media/press/2011/09/english-language-institute-of-singapore-launch.php http://www.elis.edu.sg/

References

Ball, S., & Bowe, R. (1992). Subject departments and the 'implementation' of National Curriculum policy: An overview of the issues. *Journal of Curriculum Studies, 24*(2), 97–115. doi:10.1080/0022027920240201.

Berg, B. L. (2004). *Qualitative research methods for the social sciences* (5th ed.). Boston: Pearson.

Borg, S. (2006). *Teacher cognition and language education: Research and practice.* London: Continuum International Publishing Group.

Cohen, D. K., & Ball, D. L. (2007). Educational innovation and the problem of scale. In B. L. Schneider & S.-K. McDonald (Eds.), *Scale-up in education: Ideas in principle* (Vol. 1, pp. 19–36). Plymouth: Rowman & Littlefield.

Curdt-Christiansen, X.-L., & Silver, R.E. (2011). Learning environments: The enactment of educational policies in Singapore. In C. Ward (Ed.), *Language education: An essential for a global economy*, RELC Anthology, #52, (pp. 2–24). Singapore: SEAMEO, Regional English Language Centre.

Curdt-Christiansen, X.-L., & Silver, R.E. (2012). Educational reforms, cultural clashes and classroom practices. *Cambridge Journal of Education, 42*(2), 141–161.

Curdt-Christiansen, X.-L., & Silver, R. E. (2013). New wine into old skins: The enactment of literacy policy in Singapore. *Language and Education, 27*(3), 246–260. doi:10.1080/09500782.2012.704046.

Deng, Z., & Gopinathan, S. (1999). Integration of information technology into teaching: The complexity and challenges of implementation of curricular changes in Singapore. *Asia-Pacific Journal of Teacher Education and Development, 2*(1), 29–39.

Goh, C.T. (2 June 1997). Speech by Prime Minister Goh Chok Tong at the Opening of the 7th International Conference on Thinking. Singapore: Suntec City Convention Centre. http://www.moe.gov.sg/media/speeches/1997/020697.htm

Gopinathan, S. (1997). Education and development in Singapore. In J. Tan, S. Gopinathan, & Ho Wah Kam (Eds.), *Education in Singapore: A book of readings* (pp. 33–54). Singapore: Prentice Hall.

Gopinathan, S. (2007). Globalisation, the Singapore developmental state and education policy: a thesis revisited. *Globalisation, Societies and Education, 5*(1), 53–70. doi: 10.1080/14767720601133405.

Heng, S.K. (2011) Opening address by Mr. Heng Swee Keat, Minister for Education, at the Ministry of Education (MOE) Work Plan Seminar. Singapore: Ngee Ann Pollytechnic Convention Centre.

Honig, M. I. (2006). Complexity and policy implementation: Challenges and opportunities for the field. In M. I. Honig (Ed.), *New directions in education policy implementation: Confronting complexity* (pp. 1–23). Albany: State University of New York Press.

Lim, T.S. (2010). *Use of ICT in schools aimed at enhancing teaching and learning*. Forum Letter Replies. Ministry of Education, Singapore. Available at http://www.moe.gov.sg/media/forum/2010/06/use-of-ict-in-schools.php

MOE. (2005). Teach less, learn more. *Singapore Education Milestones 2004–2005*. Available at http://moe.edu.sg/about/yearbooks/2005/teach.html

MOE. (2008). Welcome to STELLAR/Feedback/Frequently Asked Questions. http://www.stellarliteracy.sg

Ng, P. T. (2004). Innovation and enterprise in Singapore schools. *Educational Research for Policy and Practice, 3*(3), 183–198.

Ng, E.H. (2008). Speech by Dr. Ng Eng Hen, Minister for Education and Second Minister for Defence, at the MOE Work Plan Seminar, 2008. Ngee Ann Polytechnic Centre, Singapore. Available at http://www.moe.gov.sg/media/speeches/2008/09/25/speech-by-dr-ng-eng-hen-at-the-moe-work-plan-seminar-2008.php

PERI Committee. (2009). *Report of the Primary Education Review and Implementation Committee*. Singapore: Ministry of Education. Available at http://www.moe.gov.sg/media/press/files/2009/04/peri-report.pdf

Silver, R. E. (2005). The discourse of linguistic capital. *Language Policy, 4*(1), 47–66.

Silver, R.E., Pak, S., & Kogut, G. (2010). *Curriculum Implementation in Early Primary Schooling (CIEPSS): Coding scheme manual*. Singapore: Centre for Research in Pedagogy and Practice, National Institute of Singapore. Available at http://repository.nie.edu.sg/jspui/handle/10497/2911

Silver, R.E., Wright, S.K., Amasha, S.A., Abduallah, R., Curdt-Christiansen, X.-L., Lakshmi, S., Yang, Y., Yeo, J.K.K., & Pak, S. (2011). *Curriculum implementation in early primary schools in Singapore (CIEPSS)*. Final Report. Singapore: National Institute of Education. Available at http://repository.nie.edu.sg/jspui/handle/10497/4453

Singapore Department of Statistics. (2011). *Census of Population 2010 Statistical Release 1: Demographic Characteristics, Education, Language and Religion*. Key Findings. Available at http://www.singstat.gov.sg/pubn/popn/c2010sr1/findings.pdf

Stinson, M., Silver, R.E., Amasha, S.A., Pak, S., & Wright, S. (2010). *CIEPSS handbook of research protocols: Volume 1*. Singapore: Centre for Research in Pedagogy and Practice, National Institute of Education. Available at http://hdl.handle.net/10497/3725

Tan, C., & Ng, P. T. (2007). Dynamics of change: decentralised centralism of education in Singapore. *Journal of Educational Change, 8*(2), 155–168.

Towndrow, P., Silver, R. E., & Albright, J. (2010). Setting expectations for education innovations. *Journal of Educational Change, 11*, 425–455.

Chapter 10
National and Global Citizenship Education: Case Studies from Two Singapore Social Studies Classrooms

Li-Ching Ho

Introduction

Despite the multitude of meanings, interpretations, theories, and ideological positions attributed to the term "globalization," few deny its impact on the nature of the relationship between the state and the citizen. One of the key challenges of globalization, therefore, is the need to redefine concepts such as nationhood, national identity, and community. In many countries, educational reform and policy play a significant role in mediating and managing this shifting relationship between individuals, state, and society. Schools are, consequently, important sites for nation-building as they are locations in which teachers and students negotiate the tensions between cultural, national, and global affiliations (Abu El-haj 2010).

Social studies and civic education in many countries share similar goals, including an emphasis on developing a common national identity, and generating affective attachment and a sense of shared commitment to a state (Davies and Issitt 2005; Morris and Cogan 2001). Yet, numerous tensions remain, most notably the competing demands of national, sub-national and supranational affiliations. In particular, schools, teachers, and students have to navigate the exclusive demands of a nation-state requiring allegiance and the forces of globalization indicating the increasing irrelevance of such national attachments (Feinberg and McDonough 2005).

In the past decade, the Singapore government has implemented numerous reforms to address these concerns, including the introduction of the Thinking Schools Learning Nation (TSLN) framework in 1997 and the twenty-first century Competencies framework (see Chaps. 2, 3, and 4). In 2001, the Singapore Ministry of Education introduced a relatively new interdisciplinary subject, social studies, to serve as a vehicle for the promulgation of civic knowledge, national identity, and state-determined national values (Ministry of Education 2007; also Chap. 5). The

L.-C. Ho (✉)
National Institute of Education, Nanyang Technological University, Singapore
e-mail: liching.ho@nie.edu.sg

Z. Deng et al. (eds.), *Globalization and the Singapore Curriculum: From Policy to Classroom*, Education Innovation Series, DOI 10.1007/978-981-4451-57-4_10, © Springer Science+Business Media Singapore 2013

current secondary Singapore social studies curriculum reflects some of the tensions faced by nation-states as a result of changing social realities caused by the forces of globalization. Most notably, teachers and students have to grapple with two very different goals articulated in the national curriculum – "Being Rooted" and "Living Global." Through the use of interviews and classroom observations, this qualitative study, therefore, seeks to investigate the ways in which the teachers and students articulate their understandings of the relationship between the individual citizen, the nation-state, and the world.

National and Global Affiliations

Education systems have traditionally been used to help promote and legitimize national identity, historical traditions, symbols, and values (Smith 1991; Hobsbawm 1994; Popkewitz 2003). A citizen's affiliation to the nation-state involves a process of differentiating the national collective and this consciousness can be raised through the use of historical narratives, public ceremonies, and symbols such as the national flag (Hobsbawm 1994). Even though nation-states are, according to Tomlinson (2003), "compromised by globalization in their capacity to maintain exclusivity of identity attachments" (p. 269), the nation-state remains the primary focus of citizenship education in most countries. For instance, Davies and Issitt (2005) reviewed citizenship education programs in Australia, Canada, and England and found that the textbooks in all three countries emphasized national priorities and avoided large conceptions of citizenship. Similarly, in the United States, the topic of globalization has not been an integral and substantive part of social studies curricula because of the schools' emphasis on "national history for patriotism" (Myers 2010, p. 111).

Several scholars, however, assert that education should not take national boundaries as fixed, immutable, and morally salient. Nussbaum (2002), for instance, argues that students should be taught to give their primary allegiance to "the moral community made up by the humanity of all human beings" (p. 7). Nation-states need not be defined in terms of a people sharing a similar culture within a bounded territory as studies have shown how citizens who live within the boundaries of other states maintain strong social, political, cultural, and economic ties to the nation-state of their forebears (Basch et al. 1994). Students, therefore, should be taught how to address issues of diversity beyond the boundaries of the nation-state (Gaudelli 2003). They should, in addition, recognize and challenge cross-border inequalities brought about by globalization (Buras and Motter 2006) and be taught about the interconnectedness of the shared experiences of humanity (Merryfield and Subedi 2001).

While the production of official curricular knowledge is important, the use of these curricula may vary greatly at the school and classroom level because teachers and students are engaged in a continuous attempt to make sense of, negotiate, and perhaps even resist the curricular scripts imposed on them by the state (Buras and Apple 2006). Likewise, Thornton (2004) argues that the implementation of curriculum change is "not necessarily change institutionalized" (p. 212) because the official curriculum is mediated at multiple levels by schools, teachers, and students. Epstein (1998, 2000) and Cornbleth (2002), for instance, observed that students' backgrounds had a significant impact on how they interpreted national history and their belief in the existence of a common national identity. Similarly, teachers in Singapore and elsewhere navigate a complicated and occasionally treacherous terrain comprising of educational policy, societal values and priorities, and personal beliefs. Hess (2009), for instance, discussed how teachers' personal experiences and perspectives shape their understanding of controversial public policy issues. Teachers' pedagogical decisions are also influenced by school and societal contexts such as testing and a climate of conservatism (Cornbleth 2001; Gaudelli 2003). Political constraints such as government and education policies also shape teachers' understanding of the curriculum and their practice (Alviar-Martin and Ho 2011). In addition, social studies teachers face tensions between teaching global perspectives within national educational systems that unambiguously promote nationalist ideals. For example, in his study of teachers in New Jersey, Gaudelli (2003), observed that teachers adopted different approaches to teaching social studies based on their beliefs about ethnic/cultural nationalism, civic democratic nationalism, cosmopolitan nationalism, and eclectic nationalism.

Social Studies Education in Singapore

Within the public school system, social studies is seen as the ideal subject for identity building and creating a sense of historical consciousness. One of the main instruments used by the Singapore government to ensure the diffusion of a national narrative known as "The Singapore Story" (Lee 1997) is the subject, social studies (also see Chaps. 4, 5, and 13). Unlike the U.S. where there is there is little or no consensus on the meaning of citizenship and its implications for curriculum and instruction (Thornton 2005; Evans 2004), the Singapore education system faces little overt contestation or opposition from the public as it is highly centralized and standardized. The Ministry of Education (MOE) controls schools and the education system in numerous ways, including the production of textbooks and curriculum materials, curriculum development, administration of national examinations, teacher employment, and school funding. Schools are also subject to the MOE's guidelines and rules, and curriculum officials are the primary arbiters of the value of curriculum content, knowledge, and skills. Teachers and students are, furthermore, constrained by the prescriptive national curricula and textbooks, high-stakes assessments, and nebulous political boundaries that determine whether or not particular topics are "out-of-bounds" (Ho 2010; also see Chap. 2).

Like many other countries (e.g. Malaysia and Japan), social studies education in Singapore has generally served a fairly conservative agenda as it is seen as a vehicle for the state to promote a state-approved version of national history, national values, and national identity. Nevertheless, the Singapore government has also recognized that there is a need to balance national identity formation with more cosmopolitan values and skills that will help Singapore remain economically competitive. The state enacted a range of strategies and reforms that not only served as a means of "retooling the productive capacity of the system" (Gopinathan 2007, p. 59; also see Chap. 2), but was also a way for the state define a unitary Singapore identity through the National Education citizenship education program. This national ideological framework, launched in 1997, emphasizes Singapore's geopolitical vulnerabilities and aims to "develop national cohesion, cultivate instincts for survival and instill confidence" in Singapore's future (see Chap. 5). Underscoring these goals are messages such as "Singapore is our homeland; this is where we belong" (Ministry of Education 2007, p. 1). More recently, the Singapore government introduced the twenty-first century Competencies framework for schools that highlighted desired competencies such as civic literacy, global awareness, and cross-cultural skills (see Chaps. 3 and 14). The press release issued by the MOE provided a particularly instrumental rationale for these competencies:

> Our society is becoming increasingly cosmopolitan and more Singaporeans live and work abroad. Our young will therefore need a broader worldview, and the ability to work with people from diverse cultural backgrounds, with different ideas and perspectives. At the same time, they should be informed about national issues, take pride in being Singaporean and contribute actively to the community. (Ministry of Education 2011)

All secondary school students in Singapore, regardless of academic track, are required to attend social studies classes (or its equivalent) for at least 2 years. The goals and content of the curriculum are differentiated according to academic track (Ho et al. 2011). Currently, students in the vocational Normal Technical track are taught social studies at the lower secondary level (Secondary One and Two), with the curriculum focusing primarily on domestic policy issues such as housing and education. The majority of the students in Singapore belong to the 4 and 5 year Express and Normal Academic tracks. They are required to complete the Singapore-Cambridge General Certificate in Education (GCE) "O" Level social studies course at the upper secondary level. Because this program culminates in a high stakes national examination that determines, among other things, school rankings and access to higher education, the GCE social studies course is accorded a relatively high status in schools compared to the low-stakes social studies program for vocational students (see Chap. 2).

The current national social studies curriculum, introduced in 2007, is designed to provide students with an understanding of Singapore's geopolitical situation, including its constraints and vulnerabilities. Closely linked to the educational reforms instituted by the MOE, this mandatory inter-disciplinary subject includes topics from the social sciences and the humanities such as history, economics, political science, and geography (Ho 2009). It is organized around the two core ideas – "Being Rooted" and "Living Global" and focuses on national, regional and international issues deemed central to the development of Singapore as a nation. The curriculum is divided into six thematic units: (1) Singapore as a nation in the world; (2) Understanding governance; (3) Conflict and harmony in multi-ethnic societies; (4) Managing international relations; (5) Sustaining economic development; (6) Facing challenges and change (Ministry of Education 2008). This curriculum, dominated by a narrative emphasizing Singapore's geopolitical vulnerabilities and the need to ensure economic survival (Sim and Ho 2010) clearly reflects the emphasis on the importance of adopting global perspectives, albeit with a distinctly nationalist, parochial and instrumental focus.

Method and Data Sources

Utilizing the case study methodology outlined by Creswell (1998) and Stake (1995), this study was conducted at two Secondary Three Express Social Studies classes in two academically differentiated government secondary schools identified by their pseudonyms, Pasir Secondary and Panjang Secondary. Considerations of representation, balance, variety, and accessibility, affected the selection of cases (Stake 1995). The sites were purposefully selected based on the national academic ranking of the schools, their racial composition, their gender distribution and access.

During the study, I conducted individual interviews of 17 Secondary Three (14 or 15 year old) students from two classes in the two schools. The interview protocol consisted of two parts. First, the 17 students from the two classes were asked to complete a photo elicitation task. Students were asked to select ten pictures from a list of 30 images representing important events in Singapore's history to form a narrative of Singapore's past and present. The students were then asked to answer questions relating to their understanding of citizenship, national and group culture, the Social Studies and National Education curricula, Singapore's geopolitical situation, and Singapore's history.

The second part of the study consisted of classroom observations conducted during the course of one full school term (10 weeks). During these observations, the teachers from both schools taught the chapter, *Conflict and Harmony in Multiethnic Societies*. In particular, I focused on how the teachers and students from the two social studies classes interpreted one international case study of ethnic conflict in Sri Lanka. Premised on the understanding that teachers and students jointly constructed and produced the curriculum through engagement in classroom tasks (Doyle 1992), the observations focused largely on elements related to citizenship development and the national narrative, such as the emphasis placed by the teacher on particular aspects of the syllabi, the pedagogical methods used, as well as student-teacher and student-student interaction. During observations, a systematic focus was kept on key categories, paying attention to background conditions that had the possibility of influencing subsequent analysis. These key issues/categories were adjusted as necessary during the course of the observations. Multiple observation visits were conducted to ensure that students and teachers became familiar with my presence. This method of data collection allowed me to capture, in a natural social setting, the main patterns of instruction and interaction in the Social Studies classrooms, and served to corroborate the findings from the other sources of data. The benefits of this strategy were, however, limited by the fact that there might have been an element of performance, on the part of both the students and teachers that would have affected the interactions within the classroom.

Social Studies Teaching in Pasir and Panjang Secondary Schools

Pasir Secondary School was one of the first English-medium government schools and it is located within a public housing estate in the southern part of Singapore. The buildings of the school are attractively painted in the school colors of purple and grey. Pasir Secondary typifies the average secondary school in Singapore, in terms of its academic and extracurricular achievements. It has consistently been ranked in the middle of the MOE's school ranking table, with a significant proportion of its students progressing to junior colleges and polytechnics. Pasir Secondary offers Chinese, Malay and Tamil language classes as its ethnic distribution closely mirrors that of Singapore's population.

Panjang Secondary School, another co-educational government school with a total enrollment of approximately 1,400 students, is located in the central part of the island and is surrounded by a mix of public and private housing. It was awarded autonomous status by the MOE and this allowed the school administration more flexibility in numerous areas, such as the implementation of educational programs and the recruitment of students. Panjang Secondary has consistently been positioned near the top of the school ranking tables as its students are among the best in their cohort. Approximately 95 % of the student population is categorized as Chinese, 3 % Malay, and 1 % Indian. Panjang Secondary also has a large population of foreign scholarship recipients, especially from China. These students were awarded scholarships to study in Singapore after a rigorous selection exercise.

In Pasir Secondary, the social studies teacher for Secondary 3B, Mr. Tan, chose to adopt one of the most common and conservative methods of teaching social studies in Singapore. Each teacher in his school was solely responsible for teaching the subject to 2–4 classes of approximately 40–45 students each. The lessons were conducted twice weekly in the students' regular classroom and focused on the teaching of subject content and preparing students for the essay and document-based questions that form part of the national examination. An energetic Chinese man in his mid-30s, Mr. Tan's routine seldom varied. Before the start of each lesson, he insisted that the students cleaned their classroom, reminding them that it was not only their moral duty to keep their classroom clean, but that it was also part of their responsibility to the larger community: "Please pick up the litter around you. We just need each person to do their part to make the world a better place." The Pasir Secondary social studies class consisted of 42 male and female students. Thirty students were Chinese, seven were Malay, while five were Indian. The relationship between the different students seemed cordial and there did not seem to be any visible animosity between them. The classroom was set up in a conventional manner typical of many Singapore classrooms. The students were paired up – males and female students were partnered – and their individual desks were lined up in neat rows.

In contrast, Panjang Secondary School used a lecture-tutorial system to teach social studies. Once a week for about 45 min, three classes attended content-based joint lectures in the school's air-conditioned auditorium. On another day, the different classes attended separate tutorial sessions during which their teachers focused on skills necessary for the examination such as document analysis and essay writing. Unlike Pasir Secondary, Panjang Secondary chose to clearly demarcate the division between the delivery of content and the teaching of historical and essay skills.

Two young and highly motivated female teachers identified by the pseudonyms, Ms. Ong and Ms. Ratnam, were in charge of the Social Studies program for the Secondary Three level. Ms. Ong was Chinese and Ms. Ratnam was of Indian extraction. They alternated lecturing but they were both present for all the lectures. Each teacher then took sole charge of four or five tutorial classes. The students were well-behaved and very attentive, both during the lecture and the class. The tutorial class, Secondary 3A, consisted of 45 male and female students, mostly from Singapore. Approximately five of the students were from China. The vast majority of the students were Chinese and there was only one Indian boy in the class.

During the study, teachers in both schools taught the unit titled *Conflict and harmony in multi-ethnic societies* framed by an overarching question: "Why is harmony in a multi-ethnic society important to the development and viability of a nation?" (Ministry of Education 2008, p. 11). According to the curriculum, Singapore needs to be "vigilant against the forces of divisiveness that cause conflict and disintegration of societies" (11) in order to ensure the survival of the nation-state. Notably, the social studies curriculum does not focus exclusively on historical episodes of domestic inter-ethnic or inter-religious conflict. Two international case studies of societies affected by long-term and intractable ethnic and religious conflict – Sri Lanka and Northern Ireland – help provide students with an introduction to similar ethnic or religious conflicts in other countries. Students explore the discrimination faced by various groups such as the Catholics and the Tamils, evaluate the historical causes of the conflict, and the political, social and economic repercussions of the conflict such as foreign intervention. These case studies, together with other themes in the social studies curriculum, remind students of the importance of the Singapore state's priorities including national survival, national interest, patriotism, sovereignty, and vigilance.

Findings

In Singapore, a key dilemma faced by educators includes balancing nationalist ideals and promoting a national identity with other more cosmopolitan values and skills that are deemed essential for Singapore survival in the global marketplace.

As described in the previous sections, these goals engendered, on one hand, a push for greater incorporation of global perspectives and issues in the Social Studies curriculum, and on the other, a greater emphasis on a more nationalistic and parochial focus on the nation-state. Based on the individual student interviews and classroom observations, this section examines two significant themes that emerged from the data: (1) the primacy of national survival; and (2) tensions between national and global citizenship.

The Primacy of National Survival

The themes of national vulnerability and survival, encapsulated in the 1997 National Education citizenship and social studies education programs, are key ideological constructs of the Singapore government. This is clearly expressed in the official historical narrative that focuses on Singapore's survival and geopolitical vulnerabilities (Loh 1998; Han 2007; Sim and Ho 2010). This survival narrative governs policy decision-making processes and provides much of the impetus for maintaining national vigilance against real and perceived threats from foreign countries.

During the interviews, many of the students described citizenship in terms of national duties and obligations. Clearly reflecting the national narrative of survival, the most popular responses included defending the country through national military service, being law-abiding, maintaining inter-racial harmony, being an economically productive citizen, and caring for other Singaporeans. For instance, the concept of a citizen soldier protecting Singapore's sovereignty and independence dominated much of the discussion on the responsibilities of a Singapore citizen. Two Panjang students, including Weijie, a Chinese boy, spoke of the need to defend the country by serving in the military: "Being a citizen, the responsibility of defending and of course improving the state of your country is in your hands." Similarly, the introduction of National Service proved to be a particularly significant historical event to Bashir, a Malay boy from Pasir Secondary. He explained that military service was important to ensure that "Singaporeans are disciplined and ready to attack if there is another war … to defend our country."

When asked whether National Service should be eliminated, all but one of the interviewees adamantly insisted that it should be retained, asserting that it was essential for Singapore's survival. Charles, a Chinese boy from Pasir Secondary bluntly stated, "(if there is) no defence, die lor [sic]. Everybody says one bomb Singapore gone already [sic], like that time America bombed Japan." The importance of the concept of self-reliance was also constantly reiterated by female students such as Constance, from Panjang Secondary who stated,

> If we do not protect ourselves and train people who can protect us, we are … going to like, make another error like we did in the past … Trusting others to protect us. I think it's better if we protect ourselves.

Constance's response explicitly reflected her lack of trust in other countries and she showed skepticism of the possibility of other countries coming to the aid of Singapore.

Within the social studies classrooms, both teachers drew on similarly nationalistic frameworks. Both implicitly assumed that students should be primarily committed to a nation-state with internationally recognized boundaries and echoed the dominant narrative of national vulnerability and survival promoted vigorously by the Singapore state. Both Mr. Tan and Ms. Ong constantly reiterated this theme throughout their lessons and regularly emphasized the impact of internal conflict on a country's ability to maintain its sovereignty and independence. Mr. Tan, for instance, described how the Indian government intervened in Sri Lanka:

(A consequence of this ethnic conflict is) foreign intervention … India tried to be a mediator in 1983 … In 1987, India tried to send aid to Jaffna. In July 1987, Sri Lanka signed a peace accord with India but the Tamil Tigers failed to surrender their arms to the Indian peacekeeping forces. As a result, Indian troops took control of them by force. … It's an irony that the peacekeeping forces are supposed to keep the peace but they are fighting.

Likewise, Ms. Ong spoke of "pressure from the Indian government on the Sri Lankan government" on the issue of citizenship rights for Tamil Indians.

On numerous occasions, both Mr. Tan and his students expressed what appeared to be a deeply ingrained nationalist belief in the need for a country to be independent and self-reliant. Concurrently, both the teacher and his students expressed skepticism of the effectiveness of international institutions, norms, and diplomatic ties in protecting Singapore's national interest. For instance, Mr. Tan decided to play the movie, Hotel Rwanda, to introduce the conflict in Sri Lanka. In his summary of the movie, he chose to highlight the ineffectiveness of the United Nations peacekeeping force in Rwanda:

(I'm going to show you) part of the movie, Hotel Rwanda. … Note what are the effects of an ethnic conflict in society (sic). What are the limitations of the UN? Witness the refugees moving into the hotel. The UN was supposed to protect them but was asked to move out.

Next, he played a 5 minute segment of the movie featuring Paul Rusesabagina, the hotel manager, calling the hotel's Belgium headquarters. At the end of the segment, he started asking leading questions about the role of international United Nations peacekeeping force in the country:

Mr. Tan	European countries are not going to get involved. Why do you think they don't want to get involved?
Student A	It's nothing to them
Student B and C	(It's) not their business
Student D	No gain
Mr. Tan	Yes, (they get) no benefits. This is one limitation of the UN. Paul had to call his friends in other countries to help them

Interestingly, in subsequent interviews, numerous students including Enling, a Chinese girl from Mr. Tan's class, echoed this perspective. Drawing on her own knowledge of the events in World War II, she observed that the British "left Singapore to suffer … when there's trouble they leave, because it doesn't belong to them."

Similarly, Ms. Ong, the social studies teacher from Panjang Secondary, appeared to agree with Mr. Tan's assumptions about the nation-state being the primary actor in international relations although she did not explicitly share Mr. Tan's cynicism about the effectiveness of international organizations such as the United Nations. In general, she paid more attention to the unique values and attributes ascribed to nation-states. The lectures were pitched at a much higher level compared to Pasir Secondary, indicating the academic ability of the Panjang students. As a result, Ms. Ong addressed complex issues that were not introduced in Pasir Secondary, such as national sovereignty, territorial integrity, and international jurisdiction. The example below illustrates Ms. Ong's position:

> For this next slide, you need to highlight the word 'sovereignty'. India's role in the conflict in 1987 ... (India) violated Sri Lanka's airspace and gave food and supplies to rebels fighting the Sri Lankan government. It was blatant interference in the internal affairs of the country. Blatant means "very obvious." Airspace is also not free for all, (and) countries are very touchy about it.

The use of the adjective "blatant" appeared to reflect her explicit disapproval of India's infringement of Sri Lanka's state sovereignty and it highlighted her implicit belief in the inviolability of a sovereign state's territory and the international norm of non-intervention in the internal affairs of other nation-states. Notably, Ms. Ong did not address the legitimacy of political or military intervention by the United Nations or other countries for humanitarian purposes.

Tensions Between National and Global Citizenship

Within social studies, educators need to address the nation-state's relative loss of hegemony over its ability to define its population's sense of identity vis-a-vis other forms of identity positions and affiliations. Educators also have to grapple with the scope and definition of citizenship education and the extent to which it should focus on cosmopolitan values (Gaudelli 2003). During the interviews, most of the student participants demonstrated an awareness and understanding of perennial social issues such as ethnic conflict and many drew parallels to similar issues in Singapore. Students specifically compared Singapore to other countries, such as Northern Ireland and Sri Lanka. For example, Constance, a Chinese girl from Panjang Secondary, explicitly linked the racial riots in Singapore to the conflict in Sri Lanka and Northern Ireland: "This racial tension between Chinese and Malays led to racial riots ... these two groups are something like what we learnt in Social Studies. It's like Tamil Tigers and the people in Northern Ireland." Her classmate, Junhui, also stated that this case study "serves as a reminder to Singaporeans not to be separated, or else we will be like these two countries."

While it was apparent that most students did not lack knowledge of international issues, particularly the issues contained in the secondary Social Studies curriculum, few students felt connected to, or demonstrated empathy towards, others outside of their immediate circle of friends, family and fellow citizens. A few students spoke of their responsibility to help people in foreign countries such as the people affected by the Sichuan earthquake and the Thai and Indonesian tsunami victims. In general, however, feelings of loyalty and responsibility were largely limited to the nation-state. Many students expressed a clear lack of trust in the motives of other nation-states and were keenly aware of Singapore's geopolitical limitations. Half of the students, reflecting the national historical narrative presented in their textbooks, agreed that Singapore's primary vulnerabilities included its small size, large population, and the lack of natural resources. The students also felt that Singapore was in danger of being "bullied" by other countries. This quote from Constance, a Chinese student from Panjang Secondary, was typical of the realist views held by the students.

> Singapore is quite a small country and it's somehow reliant on other countries. For example if Indonesia and Malaysia don't want to sell us water then quite… because most of the water source comes from Malaysia, if they raise the price I think… or if they like, don't sell to us, I think it'll affect the economy.

Her classmate, Weijie, was even more pessimistic: "Weaknesses? It's too small. So if like, other country [sic] wants to bully us or stop us from anything, we cannot do very much things … so we're like, in the clutches of other countries." Similarly, Haowei, a Chinese boy from Panjang Secondary gloomily noted that Singapore could not really do much to defend itself in the event of a war. Students from both schools did not have trust in Singapore's ASEAN neighbors and were extremely wary of their motives. For example, Bertha, a Chinese student from Panjang Secondary, highlighted measures such as the use of desalination plants to increase water supply. Enling, a Chinese girl from Pasir, raised the issue of the recent disagreements that Singapore had with Thailand and Indonesia, "Singapore is a small country. Many countries bully us. We every time [sic] treat them so well, like the tsunami, but they do not appreciate. Never give us sand or water, Singtel, not our fault. Thaksin, they also blame Singapore." Overall, a higher proportion of the more academically inclined Panjang Secondary students showed greater awareness of these issues and they were able to accurately describe the geopolitical problems faced by Singapore. However, they also appeared less positive about Singapore's international position compared to students from Pasir Secondary.

Within the social studies classroom, the two teachers diverged in their belief in the type of civic and nationalist values that should be taught to students. In spite of their shared understandings outlined in the previous section, there were also significant differences in how the two teachers introduced cosmopolitan ideals to their students. Despite expressing his belief in the primacy of the nation-state as the container for citizens' loyalties, Mr. Tan also explicitly referred to broader cosmopolitan ideals as defined by Nussbaum (2002) and other scholars in his lessons. Ms. Ong, on the other hand, mostly drew on personal narratives and her students' experiences to make the curriculum more relevant.

Notwithstanding his nation-centric focus, Mr. Tan occasionally made reference to cosmopolitan ideals such as the need for students to care for the larger global community. In one of his lessons, he played the song, *Gimme Hope Joanna*, in order to introduce his students to the concept of apartheid. At the conclusion of the song,

Mr. Tan utilized the example of Martin Luther King to remind his students of the positive impact that they, as Singapore citizens, could have on the world:

> If everyone does their part, it will make the world a nicer place. One person who made a difference was Martin Luther King. Many people idolize the US and think it is a great country. I took history and I realized that no country is perfect, there was discrimination against the Blacks ... the proper term is African Americans. The African Americans were treated badly throughout history by the whites ... A lot of people in African American history stood up and tried to make a difference, e.g. MLK who made speeches against discrimination ... Even as an individual, you can still stand up and make a difference.

Mr. Tan concluded the lesson by playing a recording of Martin Luther King's inspirational speech, "I have a dream." The teacher's statements and examples reflect Nodding's (2005) call for citizenship education to be closely tied to developing global citizens who "value the lives of all people, not just those of ... (their) nation" (17).

On the other hand, Ms. Ong frequently drew parallels to her students' immediate experiences and did not speak of larger humanitarian ideals. For instance, in an attempt to find volunteers for an activity, she explicitly linked volunteering to the moral character of the students:

> I don't want to force you, I expect people to volunteer, especially for your class, I expect more from your class. Why I am asking you to volunteer is because even though you don't have anything to gain from it, it speaks well of your character because the 2 merit points mean nothing to you.

In another class, Ms. Ong used an example of a teacher noticing and reprimanding a student for his untidy appearance to illustrate the point of the Indian government's intervention in Sri Lanka.

While Ms. Ong made frequent references to the need for students to prepare for the national examinations, she did make an attempt to draw a parallel between the ethnic conflicts in Sri Lanka to her students' personal character traits. For instance, she attempted to impress upon her students a moral lesson derived from the Sri Lankan case study. Focusing on the use of violence by the rebel Tamil Tigers, she told the class:

> Why did the Tamils have to fight? We have been trying to teach you that even if you are upset and unhappy, you don't fight. The Tamils initially made peaceful demands. When these were not met, they took up arms. Please do not go away with the idea that all Tamils support the LTTE. Generalizations don't work with humans like what we discussed before because bombs also hurt the innocent. Some Tamils prefer to work or negotiate with the government.

Unlike Mr. Tan, however, references to values appeared almost incidental to her lessons which were dominated by frequent allusions to exam preparation.

Discussion

Young people have been progressively, and perhaps inexorably, pulled into multiple allegiances that increasingly challenge the hold of the nation-state. While policy-makers in countries like Singapore are concerned about fostering nationalist values and identities in increasingly transnational contexts, they are also cognizant of the need to develop globally-oriented economically cosmopolitan citizens. The Singapore national secondary social studies curriculum clearly reflects this dilemma. It revolves around two apparently incompatible themes – being rooted and living globally. Students, according to the curriculum, have to be responsible citizens with "a deep sense of shared destiny and national identity" *and* have a global perspective (Ministry of Education 2008, p. 1).

The findings from the study suggest that the students strongly identify with the national priorities outlined by the Singapore state but are less committed to the cosmopolitan values espoused by Nussbaum (2002) and others. Students felt that one of their key responsibilities as citizens was to protect and defend their vulnerable country against numerous immediate external threats. This was accompanied by a corresponding level of distrust in the ability of foreign countries or international organizations to defend Singapore's sovereignty. Notably, the students' positions closely mirrored the two teachers' positioning of the role and limitations of international organizations such as the U.N. Mr. Tan, for instance, selected the case study of Rwanda to illustrate how the U.N. peacekeeping forces failed in their attempt to protect the Rwandan civilians.

While national security is a recurring theme in many history textbooks in countries such as the U.S. (Hess et al. 2008), the Singapore social studies and history curricula, however, accord far greater emphasis to this issue. This theme is clearly reflected in two of the National Education messages: "No one owes Singapore a living: We must find our own way to survive and prosper," and "We must ourselves defend Singapore: No one else is responsible for our security and well-being" (Ministry of Education 2007). These National Education messages guide the selection of content for the official national curriculum, particularly for social studies and history. Within the social studies curriculum document, for instance, students are reminded about Singapore's turbulent past and are told: "New nations face political, social and economic challenges to survive and progress in the international community" (Ministry of Education 2008, p. 9).

Mirroring this focus on national security, many students referred to the example of the British surrender and the Japanese Occupation of Singapore to illustrate the need to be self-reliant as a nation. History textbooks use the Japanese invasion of Singapore a negative consequence of relying on an external country for protection. Echoing this perspective, Charles, a Chinese boy from Pasir Secondary, felt that the British surrender indicated that the "British didn't treat us as their own." Consequently, he argued that this experience "taught us not to depend on others." Claudine, a Chinese girl from Panjang Secondary, also endorsed this view: "(This episode) tells us that we cannot like believe others to protect us … and then, if we rely on others too much, when they give up on us, it will be the end of us."

Despite the emphasis accorded to the development of loyal national citizens who are also economic cosmopolitans, a discourse of standards and accountability has also greatly impacted the teaching of social studies in Singapore. Classroom observations suggest that the teachers from both Pasir and Panjang Secondary schools had very little freedom to deviate significantly from the national curriculum and they relied almost exclusively on the textbooks, workbooks, and national assessments produced by the Ministry of Education. Both Ms. Ong and Mr. Tan spent a significant amount of time preparing students for the national examinations. During the observations, Mr. Tan and his class appeared to be very concerned about the skills required to interpret primary and secondary sources. Mr. Tan made constant reference to the "skills" that the students needed for the examinations. Likewise, Ms. Ong was very practical and pragmatic in her approach to social studies education. She focused most of her attention on what was absolutely necessary given the grading expectations and the time allocated for the exams. In another lesson, Ms. Ong appeared to dismiss her students' concerns about giving in-depth and logical answers to questions and focused exclusively on what was required for the examination.

Notwithstanding these structural and institutional constraints, teachers also have the ability to be curricular instructional gatekeepers (Thornton 2005). The case of Mr. Tan from Pasir Secondary illustrates this potential, albeit in a limited way. During one of the classroom observations, Mr. Tan decided to deviate from the prescribed national curriculum and create an additional authentic assignment that required students to reflect on the perspectives of the Sri Lankan people who were affected by the war:

> Imagine that you are Sri Lankan and have witnessed the conflict in your country. Express the causes and consequences of conflict and your thoughts or feelings through one of the following ways, write a letter to a pen pal (I know many of you use email so you can pretend that you are writing an email but please use proper English). For those who are more artistic, write a poem, (or) a song and I can allow you to perform … during the school assembly … You are not confined to these 4 medium, you can sculpt too.

He then explained to the students that it was important for them to do this assignment even though it was not immediately relevant to their examinations:

> You have to complete this little individual assignment because when you study the humanities, (you need) more than intellectual knowledge. We are concerned with values. When you study conflict, you must feel and care.

Notably, while he was very conscious of the need to prepare his students for the high-stakes national examinations, he also demonstrated an emerging awareness of the importance developing in his students what Hanvey (1982) termed, perspective consciousness. Anecdotal evidence, however, suggests that Ms. Ong's exclusive focus on preparing students for the national examinations appears to be more typical, mirroring the findings of other studies that show how high stakes testing impact teachers' ability to select curricular content to address students' needs and concerns (Mathison et al. 2006).

Conclusion

In general, nation-states remain committed to the preservation and maintenance of a nationalist identity through the formation of nation-centric allegiances and values (Davies and Issitt 2005). At the same time, policy-makers in Singapore are also preoccupied with the challenge of producing and managing globally-minded cosmopolitans who are motivated more by goals of global competitiveness and the need to excel in the global marketplace.

The cases remind us of the crucial role of political and institutional contexts in shaping teachers' enactment of the social studies curriculum. Teachers and students are also involved in dynamic authoring of curriculum events as they jointly produce and transform curriculum (Doyle 1992). Classrooms are spaces of tension and negotiation, and these two case studies underscore the significant impact of high-stakes national examinations on modes of instruction and teachers' pedagogical choices. Due to the emphasis on high stakes examinations, teachers in Singapore tend to accord less priority to caring *for* and caring *about* others (Noddings 2005). Focusing on the importance of relational ethics in teaching, Noddings (1988) makes a case for caring as a moral orientation. She writes:

> There is … more than intellectual growth at stake in the teaching enterprise. Teachers, like mothers, want to produce acceptable persons — persons who will support worthy institutions, live compassionately, work productively but not obsessively, care for older and younger generations, be admired, trusted, and respected. (p. 221)

Gaudelli (2010), in addition, critiqued the "self-serving ethos" (p. 151) present in schools, where students are seen as customers, teachers as providers, and knowledge as commodity. These perspectives are particularly relevant to the individualistic and competitive educational environments in Singapore that are engendered by the constant reiteration of the principle of meritocracy and a narrow definition of success and achievement (see Chap. 2). As a result, potentially rich subjects such as social studies are seen merely as another academic hurdle to be overcome in order to gain access to the next level of education.

Finally, this study illustrates some of the national and global discourses present in two social studies classrooms against a backdrop of the numerous curricular and policy reforms instituted by the Singapore state in response to the forces of globalization. In both schools, students and teachers appeared to explicitly support the dominant national narrative of survival and vulnerability (see Chap. 5 for this narrative) while paying far less attention to larger cosmopolitan ideals such as concern for economic, social and political justice, as well as for the well-being of the physical environment. In an increasingly globalized and interdependent world, however, social studies should not be tethered primarily to nationalistic goals. The subject should focus more on the "soulful dimensions of curriculum" (Gaudelli 2010, p. 145) and should motivate and inspire students to look beyond the confines of national boundaries. Children, according to Walzer (1983), should "learn to be citizens first – workers, managers, merchants, and professionals only afterward" (p. 203). In sum, as future global citizens, students should be empowered to reflect and act on global concerns and issues in order to promote ethical and equitable outcomes for all.

References

Abu El-Haj, T. R. (2010). "The Beauty of America": Nationalism, education, and the war on terror. *Harvard Educational Review, 80*(2), 242–274.

Alviar-Martin, T., & Ho, L. C. (2011). "So, where do they fit in?" teachers' perspectives of multi-cultural education and diversity in Singapore. *Teaching and Teacher Education, 27*(1), 127–135.

Basch, L., Schiller, N. G., & Blanc, C. S. (1994). *Nations unbound: Transnational projects, postcolonial predicaments and deterritorialized nation-states*. Basel: Gordon and Breach.

Buras, K. L., & Apple, M. (2006). Introduction. In M. W. Apple & K. L. Buras (Eds.), *The subaltern speak: Curriculum, power and educational struggle* (pp. 1–39). New York: Routledge.

Buras, K. L., & Motter, P. (2006). Toward a subaltern cosmopolitan multiculturalism. In M. W. Apple & K. L. Buras (Eds.), *The subaltern speak: Curriculum, power and educational struggles* (pp. 243–270). New York: Routledge.

Cornbleth, C. (2001). Climates of constraint/restraint of teachers and teaching. In W. B. Stanley (Ed.), *Critical issues in social studies research for the 21st century* (pp. 73–96). Greenwich: Information Age Publishing.

Cornbleth, C. (2002). Images of America: What youth do know about the United States. *American Educational Research Journal, 39*(2), 519–552.

Creswell, J. W. (1998). *Qualitative inquiry and research design: Choosing among five traditions*. Thousand Oaks: Sage.

Davies, I., & Issitt, J. (2005). Reflections on citizenship education in Australia, Canada and England. *Comparative Education, 41*(4), 389–410.

Doyle, W. (1992). Curriculum and pedagogy. In P. W. Jackson (Ed.), *Handbook of research on curriculum* (pp. 486–516). New York: Macmillan.

Epstein, T. (1998). Deconstructing differences in African-American and European-American adolescents' perspectives on U.S. history. *Curriculum Inquiry, 28*(4), 397–423.

Epstein, T. (2000). Adolescents' perspectives on racial diversity in U.S. history: Case studies from an urban classroom. *American Educational Research Journal, 37*(1), 185–214.

Evans, R. W. (2004). *The social studies wars: What should we teach the children?* New York/London: Teachers College Press.

Feinberg, W., & McDonough, K. (2005). Liberalism and the dilemma of public education in multicultural societies. In K. McDonough & W. Feinberg (Eds.), *Citizenship and education in liberal-democratic societies: Teaching for cosmopolitan values and collective identities* (pp. 1–22). New York: Oxford University Press.

Gaudelli, W. (2003). *World class: Teaching and learning in global times*. Mahwah: Lawrence Erlbaum Associates.

Gaudelli, W. (2010). Seeking a curricular soul: Moving global education into space/place, with intimacy and toward aesthetic experience. In B. Subedi (Ed.), *Critical global perspectives: Rethinking knowledge about global societies* (pp. 143–160). Greenwich: Information Age Publishing.

Gopinathan, S. (2007). Globalisation, the Singapore developmental state and education policy: A thesis revisited. *Globalisation, Societies and Education, 5*(1), 53–70.

Han, C. (2007). History education and 'Asian' values for an 'Asian' democracy: The case of Singapore. *Compare, 37*(3), 383–398.

Hanvey, R. (1982). An attainable global perspective. *Theory into Practice, 21*(3), 162–167.

Hess, D. (2009). *Controversy in the classroom: The democratic power of discussion*. New York: Routledge.

Hess, D., Stoddard, J., & Murto, S. (2008). Examining the treatment of 9/11 and terrorism in high school textbooks. In J. Bixby & J. L. Pace (Eds.), *Educating democratic citizens in troubled times: Qualitative studies of current efforts* (pp. 192–226). Albany/New York: State University of New York Press.

Ho, L. C. (2009). Global multicultural citizenship education: A Singapore experience. *The Social Studies, 100*(6), 285–293.

Ho, L. C. (2010). Don't worry, I'm not going to report you: Education for citizenship in Singapore. *Theory and Research in Social Education, 38*(2), 217–247.

Ho, L. C., Alviar-Martin, T., Sim, J. B.-Y., & Yap, P. S. (2011). Civic disparities: Exploring students' perceptions of citizenship within Singapore's academic tracks. *Theory and Research in Social Education, 39*(1), 298–316.

Hobsbawm, E. (1994). The nation as an invented tradition. In J. Hutchinson & A. D. Smith (Eds.), *Nationalism* (pp. 76–82). Oxford: Oxford University Press.

Lee, H.L. (1997). A speech by BG Lee Hsien Loong, deputy prime minister at the launch of national education. http://www.moe.gov.sg/media/speeches/1997/170597.htm. Accessed 26 Dec 2009.

Loh, K. S. (1998). Within the Singapore story: The use and narrative of history in Singapore. Crossroads: An interdisciplinary. *Journal of Southeast Asian Studies, 12*(2), 1–21.

Mathison, S., Ross, E. W., & Vinson, K. D. (2006). Defining the social studies curriculum: Influence of and resistance to curriculum standards and testing in social studies. In E. W. Ross (Ed.), *The social studies curriculum: Purposes, problems and possibilities* (3rd ed., pp. 99–114). Albany: State University of New York Press.

Merryfield, M. M., & Subedi, B. (2001). Decolonizing the mind for world-centered global education. In E. W. Ross (Ed.), *The social studies curriculum: Purposes, problems, and possibilities* (Revth ed., pp. 277–290). Albany: State University of New York Press.

Ministry of Education. (2007). *Report of the committee on national education*. Singapore: Ministry of Education.

Ministry of Education. (2008). Combined humanities ordinary level social studies syllabus (Syllabus 2192). http://www.seab.gov.sg/SEAB/oLevel/syllabus/2008_GCE_O_Level_Syllabuses/2192_2008.pdf

Ministry of Education. (2011). Press release: MOE to enhance learning of 21st century competencies and strengthen art, music and physical education. http://www.moe.gov.sg/media/press/2010/03/moe-to-enhance-learning-of-21s.php. Accessed 18 Oct 2011.

Morris, P., & Cogan, J. (2001). A comparative overview: Civic education across six societies. *International Journal of Educational Research, 35*(1), 109–123.

Myers, J. P. (2010). The curriculum of globalization: Considerations for international and global education in the 21st century. In B. Subedi (Ed.), *Critical global perspectives: Rethinking knowledge about global societies* (pp. 103–120). Greenwich: Information Age Publishing.

Noddings, N. (1988). An ethic of caring and its implications for instructional arrangements. *American Journal of Education, 96*(2), 215–230.

Noddings, N. (2005). Global citizenship: Promises and problems. In N. Noddings (Ed.), *Educating citizens for global awareness* (pp. 1–21). New York: Teachers College Press.

Nussbaum, M. C. (2002). *For love of country?* Boston: Beacon.

Popkewitz, T. S. (2003). National imaginaries, the indigenous foreigner, and power: Comparative educational research. In J. Schriewer (Ed.), *Discourse formation in comparative education* (Vol. 2nd, pp. 261–294). Frankfurt am Main: Peter-Lang.

Sim, J. B.-Y., & Ho, L. C. (2010). Transmitting social and national values through education in Singapore: Tensions in a globalized era. In T. Lovat, R. Toomey, & N. Clement (Eds.), *International research handbook on values education and student wellbeing* (pp. 897–917). Dordrecht: Springer.

Smith, A. D. (1991). *National identity*. Reno: University of Nevada.

Stake, R. E. (1995). *The art of case study research*. Thousand Oaks: Sage.

Thornton, S. J. (2004). Citizenship education and social studies curriculum change after 9/11. In C. Woyshner, J. Watras, & M. S. Crocco (Eds.), *Social education in the twentieth century: Curriculum and context for citizenship* (pp. 210–220). New York: Peter Lang.

Thornton, S. J. (2005). *Teaching social studies that matters: Curriculum for active learning*. New York: Teachers College Press.

Tomlinson, J. (2003). Globalization and cultural identity. In D. Held & A. McGrew (Eds.), *The global transformations reader: An introduction to the globalization debate* (2nd ed., pp. 269–277). Cambridge: Polity Press.

Walzer, M. (1983). *Spheres of justice: A defense of pluralism and equality*. New York: Basic Books.

Chapter 11
Enacting Teach Less, Learn More in Mathematics Classrooms: The Case of Productive Failure

Manu Kapur and Huey Woon Lee

Introduction

With globalization, countries around the world are facing a rising competition. For a resource-scarce nation like Singapore, the prime source of competitive advantage lies in its workforce (Tan and Gopinathan 2000). So, it is crucial that Singapore's workforce be equipped with critical thinking skills and the ability to be creative and flexible to meet the challenges of the twenty-first century (Ng 2008; also see Chaps. 2 and 6).

To address this need, the Ministry of Education (MOE) set Thinking Schools, Learning Nation (TSLN) as its vision in 1997 (see Chaps. 2 and 4). TSLN has two components: "Thinking Schools" and "Learning Nation." The "Thinking Schools" component refers to the transformation of Singapore's education landscape into one that fosters students into active learners with critical thinking skills, an innovative and enterprising spirit and a national identity (Tan and Gopinathan 2000). The "Learning Nation" component aims to build a culture of learning at all levels of the society. To embark on and pursue this ambitious vision, many initiatives were introduced, such as the introduction of ability-driven education, interdisciplinary project work, innovation and enterprise and a replacement of schools ranking system with a new banding system instead (Deng 2012; Ng 2005; also Chap. 2).

Despite such initiatives, researchers observe that there are still not enough opportunities for students to develop their higher-order skills, such as creativity, critical thinking, and conceptual and complex understanding (Deng 2012; Hogan and Gopinathan 2008; Kapur 2009; also Chaps. 8 and 9). In many cases, teachers are more concerned with knowledge transmission rather than with engaging students in knowledge construction despite the latter's effectiveness in developing students' higher-order skills (Deng 2012; Hogan and Gopinathan 2008; also Chaps. 8 and 9).

M. Kapur (✉) • H.W. Lee
National Institute of Education, Nanyang Technological University, Singapore
e-mail: manu.kapur@nie.edu.sg

Z. Deng et al. (eds.), *Globalization and the Singapore Curriculum: From Policy to Classroom*, Education Innovation Series, DOI 10.1007/978-981-4451-57-4_11,
© Springer Science+Business Media Singapore 2013

Thus, the Teach Less, Learn More (TLLM) initiative was introduced to help transform the classroom environment into one that allows for the cultivation of the higher-order skills. TLLM aims to change the focus of education from quantity to quality, with quality referring to an increase in "classroom interaction, opportunities for expression, the learning of life-long skills and the building of character through innovative and effective teaching approaches and strategies" (MOE 2009). Like TSLN, TLLM consists of two aspects. The first is engaged learning, which calls for students to be proactive in their learning. The second is teachers' sustained engagement with or constant reflection on the three basic questions – the "why," "what," and "how" of teaching (Deng 2012; also Chap. 7).

This chapter focuses on the second aspect of TLLM. We contextualize the examination of the "why," "what" and "how" in our program of research on Productive Failure (Kapur 2008; Kapur 2009, 2011a; 2012; 2013) in Singapore schools. We start with a brief examination of the three questions in mathematics teaching and learning followed by a description of the design principles of Productive Failure. We then report findings from two sets of quasi-experimental studies with mathematics students in Singapore. We end by discussing our findings, and deriving implications for initiatives such as TLLM.

The "Why," "What" and "How" of Teaching Mathematics

Mathematical education is largely dominated by pedagogical concerns: What is the nature of children's mathematical understandings? How can we teach mathematical concepts better? What kinds of problems, activities, and tools are best suited for understanding mathematical concepts? What curricular design principles are more effective than others, and so on? Such questions and their answers are vital in helping teachers teach more effectively. But, all too often, teachers are perhaps driven so much by the pedagogy, or the "how", that they neglect the epistemological concerns, or the "why" and the "what."

Here, we would like to stress that it is by perhaps not a coincidence that the policy makers have put the "why" and "what" before the "how." By putting the "how" last, policy makers may be signaling a shift from the pedagogical concerns to epistemological concerns (Bielaczyc and Kapur 2010). To be clear, we are not saying that the pedagogy is of no concern. What we are saying is that pedagogy should be in alignment with epistemological concerns, and that only after we have answered the "why" and the "what" questions can we proceed to address the "how" in teaching mathematics. In this section, we will examine the questions "why," "what" and "how" in sequence and demonstrate that by answering the "why" and "what" of mathematical education, we can derive principles for the "how."

First, let us consider the "why," or the goal, of mathematics education. From the focus of research and practice, it would appear that the goal of a mathematics education is to develop students' mathematical content knowledge and problem solving skills (Dillon 1982; Kapur 2009; Ramirez 2002; Silver et al. 2005). In other words, the goal is to get students to learn *about* mathematics. Undoubtedly, learning about mathematics is a key part of learning mathematics. But that is only the first part. There is a second part of learning mathematics that needs to be attended to. This other part of learning mathematics, and arguably the more important one perhaps, is to engage in the practice of mathematics akin to that of mathematicians. It involves learning *to be like* a member of the mathematical community (Brown et al. 1989; Thomas and Brown 2007), to learn and do what mathematicians do. It involves a "mathematical" way looking at the world, understanding the constructed nature of mathematical knowledge, and persisting in participating in the construction and refinement of mathematical knowledge.

So, if learning mathematics comprises both learning about mathematics and learning to be like mathematicians, then the goal of a mathematical education should also address both types of learning. In our view, there should be two goals. First, teachers need to develop students' mathematical content knowledge and problem solving skills, that is, to ensure that students learn about mathematics. Second, teachers need to develop students' mathematical way of thinking, that is, to ensure students learn to be like mathematicians. We of course do not advocate that we must design learning to produce mathematicians. What we do advocate instead is that by designing learning opportunities for students to engage in mathematical practice akin to those of mathematicians, we are more likely to target both kinds of learning so that the students can truly develop the dispositions necessary to compete in the twenty-first century.

Knowing the goals of mathematical education is the first step. We also need to know "what" to teach the students. This brings us to the content of mathematical education. In order to teach, we need to know what exactly comprise mathematical content knowledge and problem solving skills. Similarly, we need to know what comprises a mathematical way of thinking.

Researchers and practitioners alike would agree that when we refer to mathematical content knowledge and problem solving skills, we are talking about the ability to understand mathematical concepts, strategies, and procedures, and apply them to solve a diverse set of problems, simple or complex, routine or non-standard. Students who acquire these skills have deep mathematical understanding and are able to apply their knowledge flexibly. A mathematical way of thinking is related to but distinct from content knowledge and problem solving skills. Thinking mathematically consists of inventing representational forms, developing domain-general and specific methods, flexibly adapting and refining or inventing new representations and methods when others do not work, critiquing, elaborating, explaining to each other, and persisting in solving problems (diSessa and Sherin 2000). Students who acquire a mathematical way of thinking will be able to exercise and develop these epistemic resources of mathematical practice. In sum, a student, at the end of his mathematical education, should not only be able to apply mathematical concepts, strategies, and procedures, but also know how to collaborate with his peers and persist in developing solutions to problems.

So far, we have discussed the "why" and "what" of mathematical education. If developing students' mathematical content knowledge and problem solving skills as well as a way of thinking mathematically are the goals of a mathematical education, then how should we design learning environments such that we can achieve these goals?

The answer from the policy perspective seems simple: teachers are to develop students' mathematical content knowledge and problem solving skills by "teaching less"; they should focus on key conceptual understanding instead of trying to convey all aspects of mathematical content. In doing so, students "learn more" because they are not bogged down by irrelevant aspects of mathematical content. While this answer is good, it needs to be further expanded. It is easy to say that we want to teach for conceptual understanding. But what does this mean exactly? In our view, to fully understand a concept, students need to know what the concept is and what it is not; that is, they need to know how the targeted concept is similar to or different from the concepts that they already know. This can only come about with the activation of students' prior knowledge structures. When these structures are activated, it will prepare the ground for teachers to build on students' prior knowledge.

Once teachers know what students' prior knowledge structures are, the burden is on the teacher to structure their teaching such that there is a deliberate attempt to integrate students' ideas with the canonical solution. It is only when teachers actively connect students' prior knowledge structures and the targeted concepts that the students will be able to develop deep conceptual understanding of the targeted concept. We contrast this with a teacher who tries to convey key conceptual features of the content but fails to address students' priors. Although the teacher is teaching less, students may also be learning less because the teachers are not building on their prior knowledge. Thus, for effective learning of mathematical content knowledge and problem solving skills, we need to design a learning environment such that students' prior knowledge structures are activated, and following that, teachers must build on these knowledge structures.

At this point, the reader may say, "To understand students' prior knowledge, we can simply design and administer a pretest." This may be the case if we were building only on *formal* prior knowledge but we take a more expansive view of prior knowledge. While students may not have formally learnt a concept, they may have some intuitive and informal knowledge which a well-structured pretest may not be able to pick up. Therefore, there is a need to develop activities such that teachers will be able to elicit not only the formal but also the informal prior knowledge structures.

That only addresses the first part of the "how" of teaching mathematics. As mentioned earlier, there is a second part to learning mathematics that must be addressed. If one of the goals of a mathematical education is also to develop students' mathematical thinking, then we also need to design opportunities for students to be able to engage in invent and refine representational forms and methods, collaborate and critique one another and persist in solving problems (Brown et al. 1989; diSessa and Sherin 2000; Thomas and Brown 2007).

In summary, we need to design a learning environment that will:

1. Activate students' prior knowledge structures,
2. Afford students opportunities to engage in activities that mirror actual mathematical practice, and

3. Afford students opportunities to build upon their prior knowledge structures, often under the guidance of an expert such as a teacher.

Having derived the three principles of a learning environment that will help us achieve the goals of mathematics education, we now show how the teaching method that is most common and prevalent in practice, Direct Instruction (DI), is inadequate.

DI involves the explicit instruction of a concept followed by problem-solving practice and feedback (Schwartz and Martin 2004; Sweller 2010). In such environment, firstly, teachers do not make a deliberate attempt to understand students' prior knowledge. As such, students often do not have the necessary prior knowledge differentiation to be able to discern and understand the affordances of the domain-specific representations and methods underpinning the targeted concepts given during direct instruction (e.g., Even 1998; Schwartz and Martin 2004; for a similar argument applied to perceptual learning, see Garner 1974; Gibson and Gibson 1955). Secondly, in DI, the mode of teaching is usually lecture and then solitary practice. In such a case, students are often only exposed to one part of mathematical work; mainly, mathematical content knowledge and problem solving, which as we mentioned is important but inadequate for a mathematical education. Thirdly, in DI, concepts are presented in a well-assembled, structured manner such that students may not understand why those concepts, together with their representations, and methods, are assembled or structured in the way that they are (Schwartz and Bransford 1998; diSessa et al. 1991; Anderson 2000; Chi et al. 1988). There is no conscious attempt to integrate students' prior knowledge structures with the canonical solutions. All in all, DI is problematic when it comes to meeting the goals of mathematical education. Therefore, we need alternative pedagogies that can address all three principles.

One research program that has sought to do so is Productive Failure (PF). In the following section, we will describe PF, the design principles, the mechanisms they embody, and how these address the three aspects.

Designing for Productive Failure

PF is a learning design that provides students with the opportunities to take the first steps towards developing context-dependent, epistemic resources (Hammer et al. 2005) that we mentioned earlier. It entails the design of conditions for learners to persist in generating and exploring representations and solution methods (RSMs) for solving complex, novel problems. Though such a process may initially lead to failure to generate canonical RSMs, it has a hidden efficacy that is germane for learning provided an appropriate form of instructional intervention follows that can consolidate and assemble student-generated RSMs into canonical RSMs.

PF is designed such that it focuses on engaging students' critical cognitive processes which prepare students for subsequent direct instruction. These processes, or core mechanisms, are: (a) activation and differentiation of prior knowledge, (b) attention to critical features, (c) explanation and elaboration of these features, and

(d) organization and assembly into canonical RSMs. From these core mechanisms, we derived three design principles, which guide the design of PF:

1. Create problem-solving contexts that involve working on complex problems that challenge but do not frustrate, rely on prior mathematical resources, and admit multiple RSMs (mechanisms a and b);
2. Provide opportunities for explanation and elaboration (mechanisms b and c); and
3. Provide opportunities to compare and contrast the affordances and constraints of failed or suboptimal RSMs and the assembly of canonical RSMs (mechanisms b–d).

Next we elaborate upon the principles and how they relate to the two PF phases – a generation and exploration phase followed by a consolidation phase. Readers may wish to note that each of the principles correspond to the three principles of designing learning environment that we mentioned in the previous section.

1. Principle 1: In the generation and exploration phase, the focus is on affording students the opportunity to leverage their formal as well as intuitive prior knowledge and resources to generate a diversity of solutions for a complex problem; a problem that targets concepts that they have not yet learnt. A growing body of research has demonstrated that children have intuitive yet sophisticated set of rich constructive resources to generate representations and methods to solve problems without any direct or formal instruction (diSessa et al. 1991; Hesketh 1997; Kapur 2008, 2011b; Kapur and Kinzer 2007, 2009; Kapur and Rummel 2009; Schwartz and Martin 2004). For example, diSessa et al. (1991) found that when sixth graders were asked to invent static representations of motion, students generated and critiqued numerous representations, and in the process, demonstrated not only design and conceptual competence but also meta-representational competence. Here, in PF, the expectation for the generation and exploration phase is not for students to be able to solve the problem successfully. Instead, it is to generate and explore the affordances and constraints of a diversity of solutions for solving the problem (Kapur, Voiklis and Kinzer, 2005; Kapur, Voiklis, Kinzer and Black, 2005). This process both activates and differentiates prior knowledge (mechanism a).
2. Principle 2: Students work in groups to solve the complex problem and the very acts of representing problems, developing domain-general and specific methods, flexibly adapting or inventing new representations and methods when others do not work, critiquing, elaborating, explaining to each other, and ultimately not giving up but persisting in solving complex problems are epistemic resources that mathematicians commonly demonstrate and leverage in their practice (Bielaczyc and Kapur 2010). Student can expand their repertoire of epistemic resources situated within the context of classroom-based problem solving activity structures (Hammer et al. 2005). The more such opportunities for elaboration and explanation are designed for students, the better they will develop such epistemic resources.
3. Principle 3: Research has suggested that one cannot expect students, who are novices to the target content, to somehow generate or discover the canonical representations and domain-specific methods for solving the problem (Kirschner

et al. 2006). So, simply uncovering children's constructive resources is not sufficient. We need to design learning (environment, tasks, activity structures, etc.) so as to be able to build upon their generative structures, compare and contrast them with each other and with the canonical structures. This is where the second phase of PF – the consolidation phase – comes in. The central focus is to work with the teacher to engender a whole-class discussion focused on understanding the affordances and constraints of the various RSMs as well as to compare and contrast student-generated RSMs with canonical ones. This activity affords students the opportunity to attend to and understand the critical conceptual features of the targeted concepts as well as the assembly of these features into the canonical RSMs (Kapur and Bielaczyc 2012; Kapur and Rummel 2012).

Taken as a whole, this two-phase design allows for the process of generating and exploring the RSMs to engender sufficient knowledge differentiation and attention to critical features that in turn will prepare students to better discern and understand those very concepts and RSMs when presented in a well-assembled form during the consolidation phase (diSessa et al. 1991; Schwartz and Bransford 1998; Spiro et al. 1992). In other words, the generation and exploration phase provides the necessary foundation for developing deeper understanding of the canonical concept during the consolidation phase (Kapur 2010, 2011a, 2012; Schwartz and Martin 2004).

In the following section, we will show how a classroom-based research program based on the PF achieves the goals of mathematical education. The program was implemented in public schools in Singapore for two major topics: average speed and variance. For purposes of this chapter, we will summarize the results of our studies on the concept of average speed. We will then describe an extension study that targeted the concept of variance, provide just enough details of methods and results to allow for interpretation, and discuss the implications for mathematics teaching and learning. Fuller reports of the two studies can be found elsewhere (Kapur 2012; Kapur and Bielaczyc 2012).

Productive Failure in Singapore Mathematics Classrooms on the Concept of Average Speed

In our initial studies on the concept of average speed in three Singaporean schools of significantly different PSLE profiles, we compared the PF design with a DI design and found three significant results (for a fuller report, see Kapur and Bielaczyc 2012):

1. PF engendered deeper conceptual understanding than DI without compromising performance on basic procedural fluency. In other words, PF students were not only able to do basic textbook and exam-type questions just as well as DI students but also demonstrated significantly better conceptual understanding than DI students.

2. RSM diversity was high for student groups in the PF condition, across the different PSLE profiles. On average, student groups produced around 5–6 RSMs. Although we found a significant difference among schools in terms of their students' ability to generate RSMs for solving the novel, complex problems, this difference among the schools had a notably smaller effect size ($\eta^2 = 0.04$) than preexisting differences in general ability ($\eta^2 = 0.85$) and mathematical ability ($\eta^2 = 0.44$) as measured by the PSLE. In other words, differences in the ability of students to generate RSMs to novel, complex problems are not as large as one would expect given the differences in general and mathematical abilities.
3. RSM diversity was correlated with learning outcomes; that is, the greater the RSM diversity, the better the learning outcomes on average. Furthermore, the effect of RSM diversity on learning outcomes far exceeded the effect of school or preexisting differences in prior knowledge; the effect of RSM diversity was about 9 times stronger than the effect of pretest and 13 times stronger than that of the school.

As hypothesized, the PF design invoked learning processes that not only activated but also differentiated students' prior knowledge (as evidenced by the diversity of student-generated solutions). PF students worked with the solutions that they generated and the canonical solutions (that they received during direct instruction), but DI students worked with only the canonical ones. Hence, DI students worked with a smaller diversity of solutions, and consequently, their prior knowledge was arguably not as differentiated as their PF counterparts. Proponents of DI have repeatedly questioned the utility of getting students to solve novel problems on their own. Instead, they argue that students should be given the canonical solutions (either through worked examples or direct instruction) before getting them to apply these to solve problems on their own (Sweller 2010). This series of studies suggest that there is in fact a utility in having students solve novel problems first. What prior knowledge differentiation affords in part is a comparison and contrast between the various solutions – among the student-generated solutions as well as between the student-generated and canonical solutions. Specifically, these contrasts afford opportunities to attend to the critical features of the targeted concept that are necessary to develop a deep understanding of the concept, which achieves the goal of developing students' mathematical content knowledge and problem solving skills.

The second finding, high RSM diversity for students in PF condition, demonstrates that students were able to come up with not only one solution but were able to persist in adapting or inventing new RSMs when others do not work. This underscores that students in the PF condition, despite being of different PSLE profiles, were able to develop a mathematical way of thinking when given opportunity to do so.

The third result shows that there is an interaction between the "what" of mathematics education. Students who were more engaged in mathematical activity (as evidenced by their higher number of RSMs) had larger learning gains. Essentially, this means that students who developed a mathematical way of thinking also developed better mathematical content knowledge and problem solving skills. Taken together, we can see that a learning environment that activates students' prior knowledge structures, allows students to engage in activities that mirror actual mathematical practice and allows teachers to build on students' prior knowledge structures helps us achieve the goals of a mathematical education.

The average speed studies however raise an important question. If exposure to both student-generated and canonical solutions is what is essential, then instead of getting students to generate solutions, why not simply let students study the student-generated solutions first (e.g., in the form of well-designed worked examples) and then give them the canonical solutions through direct instruction? In other words, is it necessary for students to engage in mathematical activities for prior knowledge activation and differentiation? Can evaluating the products of mathematical activity suffice? In common parlance, can students learn from others' failures or is learning from their own failure more efficacious? We designed the following study to answer this question.

Productive Failure in Singapore Mathematics Classrooms on the Concept of Variance

The purpose of this study was to extend the findings of the studies on average speed. In the studies on average speed, we compared PF with DI to show that PF engenders better prior knowledge differentiation (as evidenced in student-generated RSMs), and affords opportunities for students to attend to critical features of the targeted concept. In this study, we compare PF with a new condition, Evaluation (EV) to examine the difference between: (a) having students generate solutions to solve a novel problem, and (b) having them study and evaluate student-generated solutions.

Participants and Design

Participants were 54, ninth-grade mathematics students (14–15-year-olds) from two intact classes in an all-boys public school in Singapore. One class ($n=31$) was assigned to the PF condition, and the other class ($n=23$) to the EV condition. Both classes were taught by the same teacher. First, all students took a five-item paper and pencil pretest on the concept of variance. Next, all classes participated in four, 55-min periods of instruction on the concept as appropriate to their assigned condition.

In the PF condition, students spent two periods working face-to-face in triads to solve a data analysis problem on their own. The data analysis problem presented a distribution of goals scored each year by three soccer players over a 20-year period. Students were asked to design a quantitative index to determine the most consistent player. During this generation phase, no instructional support or scaffolds were provided. Following this, two periods were spent on direct instruction where the teacher first consolidated by comparing and contrasting student-generated RSMs with each other, and then explained the canonical solution, which is square of the standard deviation $\left(SD^2 = \sum_{1}^{n} \left(x_i - \bar{x} \right)^2 / n \right)$.

The EV condition differed from the PF condition in one important aspect: The generation phase was replaced with an evaluation phase; the subsequent direct instruction phase was the same as in the PF condition. Whereas PF students had to collaboratively generate solutions to solve the complex problem during the first two periods, EV students took the same two periods to collaboratively study and evaluate the peer-generated solutions (available from the PF condition). To ensure that students were motivated to understand the given solutions, students were asked to evaluate and rank order the solutions so that they would indirectly be forced to compare and contrast the solutions. Each solution was presented on an A4 sheet of paper with the prompt: "Evaluate whether this solution is a good measure of consistency. Explain and give reasons to support your evaluation."

The number of solutions given was pegged to the average number of solutions produced by the PF groups, that is, seven. The most frequently-generated solutions by the PF students were chosen for EV condition, and none of the chosen solutions contained misconceptions. The seven solutions included one on central tendencies, two on qualitative methods (dot diagram and line graph), two on frequency methods (frequency of the mean and frequency of the mean relative to away from the mean), and two on deviation methods (sum of year-on-year deviation with signs, and average year-on-year deviations without signs). Because student-generated solutions sometimes lack conceptual clarity in their presentation that may make it difficult for other students to understand and evaluate them, they were converted into well-designed worked examples. EV students received these solutions in the form of worked examples one-by-one (counterbalanced for order), and were given approximately 10–12 min for each. The remaining time (approximately 30 min) was spent on rank ordering the solutions.

All students took a six-item, paper and pencil posttest comprising:

1. One item on procedural fluency (calculating SD for a given dataset),
2. Two items on data analysis (comparing means and SDs of two samples; these items were isomorphic with the data analysis problems covered during instruction), and
3. Two items on conceptual insight (requiring students to evaluate sub-optimal solutions; one item dealing with sensitivity to ordering of data points, and another with outliers)
4. One item on near transfer (requiring students to add data points to a given dataset without changing its mean and SD)

Maximum score for each of the three types of items was 10.

Results

On the pretest, no student demonstrated canonical knowledge of SD, and there was no significant difference between the conditions, $F(1, 63) = 1.16$, $p = 0.285$. On the posttest, performance on the four types of items formed the four dependent variables. Controlling for the effect of prior knowledge as measured by the pretest,

Table 11.1 Experiment 2 posttest performance by item type

Experiment 2	PF M (SD)	EV M (SD)	p/η^2
Procedural fluency	9.60 (0.98)	9.43 (1.73)	ns
Data analysis	9.83 (0.90)	9.34 (2.28)	ns
Conceptual insight	4.77 (1.02)	3.44 (1.67)	0.001*/0.19
Near transfer	7.50 (3.35)	5.08 (4.73)	0.039*/0.08

ns: not significant
*: significant effect

$F(4, 48) = 1.04$, $p = 0.398$, a MANCOVA revealed a significant multivariate effect of condition, $F(4, 48) = 3.34$, $p = 0.017$, partial $\eta^2 = 0.22$ (Table 11.1).

PF students significantly outperformed their EV counterparts on conceptual insight and near transfer problems without compromising on procedural fluency and data analysis. Consistent with Roll (2009), exposing students to and having them evaluate student-generated solutions does not seem to be as efficacious as having them generate those solutions before direct instruction. In other words, for better learning outcomes, teachers must engage students in mathematical activity itself instead of simply having them evaluate the products of mathematical activity.

General Discussion

In this chapter, we argued that teachers are perhaps so much driven by the "how," or pedagogy, that they pay minimal attention to the "why" and the "what," answers to which can be found in the epistemology of mathematics. To demonstrate how the epistemology can drive the pedagogy, we first examined the "why" and "what" and then derived three principles of designing learning environment to inform the "how." We then presented a research program on PF that embodies the three principles. Our findings show that the PF design develops both students' mathematical content knowledge and problem solving skills as well as their mathematical way of thinking, thereby developing the higher-order skills targeted by TSLN.

We presented two sets of studies targeting at different concepts: one on average speed and the other on variance. In the studies on average speed, we found that students in the PF conditions perform significantly better on conceptual understanding than students in the DI condition while not compromising on procedural fluency. This suggests that PF enhances students' learning about the targeted mathematical concept. More importantly, we also found that PF allows students to exercise and develop epistemic resources. Students in the PF condition produced a diverse set of RSMs suggesting that in working to solve the complex problem during the first phase of PF, students generate and revise RSMs, collaborate with and critique one another, and persevere in their problem solving efforts. Granted that students were exposed to PF for only a short 2 weeks but we believe that if students were exposed to a range of different mathematical topics taught the PF way over the course of their educational career, there will be a greater likelihood that they may internalize the practice of mathematics, and begin to demonstrate the dispositions necessary to compete in today's globalized society.

Findings also suggest that there is an interaction between students' mathematical problem solving skills and their mathematical way of thinking. When students develop their mathematical way of thinking by engaging in activity that mirror practitioners' work, they also develop better learning outcomes. Finally, we tested whether it was necessary for students to generate solutions themselves (to engender prior knowledge differentiation), or can these solutions be simply given to the students to study and evaluate. Findings showed that PF students performed significantly better on conceptual insight and near transfer without compromising on procedural fluency and data analysis, suggesting that students should be given the opportunity to engage in mathematical activity instead of just evaluating products of mathematical activities.

In sum, therefore, our studies in Singapore schools suggest that there is indeed an efficacy in having learners generate and explore representations and methods for solving problems on their own even if they do not formally know the underlying concepts needed to solve the problems, and even if such unsupported problem solving leads to failure initially. Our findings underscore the importance of designing opportunities for students to participate in the processes of inventing and refining representational forms and methods, collaborating and critiquing each other, persisting in solving problems, and a way of working with mathematical knowledge; processes that mirror the practice of mathematics (diSessa and Sherin 2000; Thomas and Brown 2007); processes that are germane for the development of twenty-first century skills and dispositions for creating and working with knowledge and ideas.

LMTL: A Twist to TLLM

Since PF seems to achieve the aims that MOE intended to achieve with TLLM (i.e. higher-order skills such as critical thinking and conceptual understanding), one can argue that PF embodies TLLM and is an example of how teachers might translate policy intent into classroom practice in a principled manner. However, in our work with schools and teachers, a common interpretation of TLLM is one where the teachers teach less content and the students learn more as a result of self-directed learning. This conception foregrounds teaching less, not *differently*. Furthermore, it transfers the burden of designing for learning on the student; after all, all the teacher has to do is teach less. This conception, in our view, is not only problematic but also inconsistent with the policy intent of TLLM.

PF offers a twist in how we can interpret TLLM. In PF, the focus is on the teachers; teachers learn more and teachers teach less, and in that order. In short, we advocate teachers to LMTL, or Learn More, Teach Less. Readers may find it strange that we extend 'learning more' to teachers and even stranger that we choose to invert TLLM. We explain why we advocate LMTL.

As we mentioned before, the goal of education is to develop students' mathematical content knowledge and problem solving skills as well as their mathematical thinking.

To achieve these aims, we need to build upon learners' prior knowledge. However, one cannot build upon prior knowledge if one does not know what this prior knowledge is in the first place. It follows that at the very least the burden on the designer (e.g., teacher, researcher) is to first understand the nature of learners' prior knowledge structures. This accomplishes a dual objective: teachers learn more about students' priors, and students participate in activities that mirror authentic mathematical practice. Only after this understanding of students' prior knowledge structures can the teacher build upon them, and because such teaching is more focused and organized around students' priors, teachers can potentially teach less by focusing on key conceptual features and help students assemble better knowledge structures. A further benefit of developing such deeper conceptual understanding is that time that may otherwise be spent re-teaching and remediating may also be saved, again contributing to teaching less on the part of the teacher should the teacher be prepared to invest in learning more about students' priors.

Designing for PF presents one way of doing so, wherein students first generate and explore representations and methods, and in the process externalize their prior knowledge structures, before consolidation. Due to learners using their prior knowledge to try to solve the problem, the schemata relevant to the new concept will have been triggered. If teachers recognize and capitalize on this by building on students' prior conceptions to introduce the new concept, learning will be enhanced (Dochy 1994; Yuen and Hau 2006). This is exactly what happens in PF. Students' RSMs allow teachers to get a clear picture of their prior knowledge regarding the concept. The subsequent instruction is structured based on what teachers have learned about their students so that students will achieve deeper conceptual understanding. When teachers "learn more" about what students' prior knowledge is, they may be better able to target their teaching such that they "teach less" but more effectively.

Whether it is TLLM or LMTL, there are still many challenges ahead for policy makers who want to restructure the education. In the final section, we provide three broad reasons for resistance to education restructuring.

Challenges for TLLM

Despite TLLM having been introduced for close to a decade, students and teachers persist in using old learning methods and pedagogies to meet the new learning requirements. This suggests that providing new programs and structures may not necessarily transform the education landscape (Ng 2008). We have identified three broad reasons for this.

The first reason is that the teachers' perception of teaching has remained unchanged. Under TLLM, teachers have to reevaluate their approach to the "why", "what" and "how" of education. The problem is that the current group of teachers has been educated and trained in a system with a very strong focus on pedagogical concerns. Because teachers' pedagogies are highly influenced by their experiences as learners (Grant 1996), they may not be able to change their teaching methods as quickly as expected (Ng 2008). So, teachers may be resistant to new pedagogies because they challenge their prevailing beliefs system. This is one of the major stumbling blocks in convincing teachers to try new pedagogies.

However, it does not mean that all teachers are averse to using new methods to teach students. In our work, we have a core group of teachers who are very enthusiastic about teaching in the PF way. Although their enthusiasm is commendable, having enthusiasm alone may not lead to effective teaching. This brings us to our second reason. For effective teaching, especially in instructional designs that allow students to engage in activities that mirror practitioners' work, teachers need to be equipped with the necessary knowledge and skills to understand students' preconceptions and focus on students' growing understanding when teaching a concept (Krainer 2004). Teachers not only need to know what the students' preconceptions, they need to also understand students' misconceptions, anticipate students' difficulties and be able to address them (Ball et al. 2008). This may be overwhelming for some teachers as pre-service courses do not target such skills and so, some teachers may be deterred from using new pedagogies. This problem can be mitigated with professional development sessions that build up teachers' capacity in terms of mathematical and pedagogical content knowledge. At project level, this is how we help our teachers so that they are able to execute the kinds of designs that not only engender learning about mathematics but also provide opportunities to students to learn to be like mathematicians. We hope that TLLM (or LMTL) advocates will do the same as this may help lighten the burden on the teachers.

The third reason is a perennial issue–the national high-stakes assessment. TLLM is a process-oriented initiative. However, this is at odds with the teachers' concerns about high-stakes examinations. When assessment is used as a way to sort students for school admission, the costs of making fundamental changes are high, making it harder for teachers to try a non-established method of teaching (see Chap. 2). In a country like Singapore with high-stakes examinations, our experience suggests that teachers would rather keep to the established methods that have yielded results on high-stakes examinations.

This focus on performance is endemic not only teachers but also other stakeholders, such as school leaders and parents. School leaders provide support in the school environment for teachers to try innovative pedagogical approaches. However, they face strong pressure from parents, who too, have a performance-oriented psyche and may be resistant to schools using alternative pedagogies to teach their children. In fact, we are detecting the beginnings of a trend in our work. It appears that although students' academic performance does not suffer and in fact may improve as a result of PF, the schools that are committed to long-term collaboration with us are average ability schools. Schools with higher academic ability students rarely continue working with us after one or two studies. We can only speculate that these schools may be locked into the high-performance regime that have produced the desired results for them, and are unable to break free from conventional modes of teaching that focus largely on learning about a subject without adequately focusing on and developing the dispositions necessary to compete in today's globalized society.

References

Anderson, J. R. (2000). *Cognitive psychology and its implications*. New York: Worth Publishers.

Ball, D. L., Thames, M. H., & Phelps, G. (2008). Content knowledge for teaching: What makes it special? *Journal of Teacher Education, 59*(3), 389–407.

Bielaczyc, K., & Kapur, M. (2010). Playing epistemic games in science and mathematics classrooms. *Educational Technology, 50*(5), 19–25.

Brown, J. S., Collins, A., & Duguid, P. (1989). Situated cognition and the culture of learning. *Educational Researcher, 18*(1), 33–42.

Chi, M. T. H., Glaser, R., & Farr, M. J. (1988). *The nature of expertise*. Hillsdale: Erlbaum.

Deng, Z. (2012). Teach less, learn more: Reclaiming a curricular idea. In J. Tan (Ed.), *Education in Singapore: Taking stock, looking forward* (pp. 17–31). Singapore: Pearson.

Dillon, J. T. (1982). Problem finding and solving. *Journal of Creative Behavior, 16*, 97–111.

diSessa, A. A., & Sherin, B. L. (2000). Meta-representation: An introduction. *The Journal of Mathematical Behavior, 19*, 385–398.

diSessa, A. A., Hammer, D., Sherin, B. L., & Kolpakowski, T. (1991). Inventing graphing: Meta-representational expertise in children. *The Journal of Mathematical Behavior, 10*, 117–160.

Dochy, F. (1994). Prior knowledge and learning. In T. Husen & T. N. Postlethwaite (Eds.), *International encyclopedia of education* (2nd ed., pp. 4698–4702). Oxford/New York: Pergamon Press.

Even, R. (1998). Factors involved in linking representations of functions. *The Journal of Mathematical Behavior, 17*, 105–121.

Garner, W. R. (1974). *The processing of information and structure*. Potomac: Erlbaum.

Gibson, J. J., & Gibson, E. J. (1955). Perceptual learning: Differentiation or enrichment? *Psychological Review, 62*, 32–41.

Grant, S. G. (1996). Locating authority over content and pedagogy: Cross-current influences on teachers' thinking and practice. *Theory and Research in Social Education, 24*(3), 237–272.

Hammer, D., Elby, A., Scherr, R. E., & Redish, E. F. (2005). Resources, framing, and transfer. In J. P. Mestre (Ed.), *Transfer of learning from a modern multidisciplinary perspective* (pp. 89–120). Greenwich: Information Age.

Hesketh, B. (1997). Dilemmas in training for transfer and retention. *Applied Psychology: An International Review, 46*, 317–386.

Hogan, D., & Gopinathan, S. (2008). Knowledge management, sustainable innovation, and pre-service teacher education in Singapore. *Teachers and Teaching: Theory and Practice, 14*, 369–384.

Kapur, M. (2008). Productive failure. *Cognition and Instruction, 26*, 379–424.

Kapur, M. (2009). Moving beyond the pedagogy of mathematics: Foregrounding epistemological concerns. In B. Kaur, B. H. Yeap, & M. Kapur (Eds.), *Mathematical problem solving* (pp. 265–271). Singapore: World Scientific.

Kapur, M. (2010). Productive failure in mathematical problem solving. *Instructional Science, 38*, 523–550.

Kapur, M. (2011a). A further study of productive failure in mathematical problem solving: Unpacking the design components. *Instructional Science, 39*, 561–579.

Kapur, M. (2011b). Temporality matters: Advancing a method for analyzing problem-solving processes in a computer-supported collaborative environment. *International Journal of Computer-Supported Collaborative Learning (ijCSCL), 6*(1), 39–56.

Kapur, M. (2012). Productive failure in learning the concept of variance. *Instructional Science, 40*, 651–672.

Kapur, M. (2013). Comparing learning from productive failure and vicarious failure. *The Journal of the Learning Sciences*. doi:10.1080/10508406.2013.819000.

Kapur, M., & Bielaczyc, K. (2012). Designing for productive failure. *The Journal of the Learning Sciences, 21*, 45–83.

Kapur, M., & Kinzer, C. (2007). The effect of problem type on interactional activity, inequity, and group performance in a synchronous computer-supported collaborative environment. *Educational Technology Research and Development, 55*, 439–459.

Kapur, M., & Kinzer, C. (2009). Productive failure in CSCL groups. *International Journal of Computer-Supported Collaborative Learning (ijCSCL), 4*(1), 21–46.

Kapur, M., & Rummel, N. (2009). The assistance dilemma in CSCL. In A. Dimitracopoulou, C. O'Malley, D. Suthers, & P. Reimann (Eds.), *Computer Supported Collaborative Learning Practices- CSCL2009 community events proceedings,* (Vol. 2, pp. 37–42). International Society of the Learning Sciences

Kapur, M., & Rummel, N. (2012). Productive failure in learning and problem solving. *Instructional Science, 40*, 645–650.

Kapur, M., Voiklis, J., & Kinzer, C. (2005). Problem solving as a complex, evolutionary activity: A methodological framework for analyzing problem-solving processes in a computer-supported collaborative environment. In *Proceedings the computer supported collaborative learning (CSCL) conference* (pp. 252–261). Mahwah: Erlbaum.

Kapur, M., Voiklis, J., & Kinzer, C. (2005). Problem solving seen through the lens of complex evolutionary activity: A novel theoretical and analytical framework for analyzing problem-solving processes. In B. G. Bara, L. Barsalou, & M. Bucciarelli (Eds.), *Proceedings of the cognitive science conference* (pp. 1096–1101). Mahwah: Erlbaum.

Kirschner, P. A., Sweller, J., & Clark, R. E. (2006). Why minimal guidance during instruction does not work. *Educational Psychologist, 41*(2), 75–86.

Krainer, K. (2004). Editorial. *Journal of Mathematics Teacher Education, 7*(2), 87–90.

Ministry of Education (2009). Teach less learn more.

Ng, P. T. (Ed.). (2005). *Shaping Singapore's future: Thinking schools, learning nation*. Singapore: Prentice Hall.

Ng, P. T. (2008). Education reform in Singapore: From quantity to quality. *Educational Research for Policy and Practice, 7*(1), 5–15.

Ramirez, V. E. (2002). Finding the right problem. *Asia Pacific Education Review, 3*, 18–23.

Roll, I. (2009). *Structured invention activities to prepare students for future learning: Means, mechanisms, and cognitive processes*. Doctoral dissertation, Retrieved from Dissertations and Theses database. (UMI No. 3394002).

Schwartz, D. L., & Bransford, J. D. (1998). A time for telling. *Cognition and Instruction, 16*, 475–522.

Schwartz, D. L., & Martin, T. (2004). Inventing to prepare for future learning: The hidden efficacy of encouraging original student production in statistics instruction. *Cognition and Instruction, 22*, 129–184.

Silver, E. A., Ghousseini, H., Gosen, D., Charalabous, C., & Strawhun, B. (2005). Moving from rhetoric to praxis: Issues faced by teachers in having students consider multiple solutions for problems in the mathematics classroom. *Journal of Mathematical Behavior, 24*, 287–301.

Spiro, R. J., Feltovich, R. P., Jacobson, M. J., & Coulson, R. L. (1992). Cognitive flexibility, constructivism, and hypertext. In T. M. Duffy & D. H. Jonassen (Eds.), *Constructivism and the technology of instruction: A conversation* (pp. 57–76). Hillsdale: Erlbaum.

Sweller, J. (2010). What human cognitive architecture tells us about constructivism. In S. Tobias & T. M. Duffy (Eds.), *Constructivist instruction: Success or failure* (pp. 127–143). New York: Routledge.

Tan, J., & Gopinathan, S. (2000). Education reform in Singapore: Towards greater creativity and innovation? *National Institute for Research Advancement (NIRA) Review, 7*(3), 5–10.

Thomas, D., & Brown, J. S. (2007). The play of imagination: Extending the literary mind. *Games and Culture, 2*(2), 149–172.

Yuen, K. M., & Hau, K. T. (2006). Constructivist teaching and teacher-centred teaching: A comparison of students' learning in a university course. *Innovations in Education & Teaching International, 43*(3), 279–290.

Part V
International, Comparative and Future Perspectives

Chapter 12
Singapore's School Curriculum for the Future Beyond: National Development?

Kerry J. Kennedy

In this chapter my purpose is to provide an international perspective on Singapore's curriculum. It is essentially the perspective of an "outsider" – of someone who has not been involved in Singapore or its curriculum development. It is a daunting task except for the fact that the school curriculum is a common feature of most societies and its importance has been heightened over the past decade. In what follows, therefore, I provide what is more of a comparative perspective drawing on trends and issues that are common across societies while also seeking to identify the unique features within Singapore. In undertaking this task I am reminded of Schwab's (1969) "curriculum commonplaces"- commonalities across time, location and even purpose. In what follows I shall seek to identify such "commonplaces" in current curriculum discourse within Asia. In this globalized world, as I shall show, students and their learning maintain their status as the key issues in curriculum deliberation.

There is not a jurisdiction in Asia and the Pacific that has not recognized the significance of the school curriculum to both social and economic development (Kennedy and Lee 2010). At times it may seem that the economic impetus is emphasized over the social. Yet as the twenty-first century has progressed it has become increasingly clear that the social outcomes of schooling are at least as significant as the economic. Stable and tolerant societies are more able to promote economic growth than those that are not. Engaged citizens are more likely to contribute productively and creatively to the economic life of a nation than those who are not. The so called "Arab Spring" has shown how discontent related to political institutions, corruption and unequal sharing of resources can lead to upheavals on such a scale that economies can be ground to a halt. The fact for example, that Libya was one of the world's leading oil producing nations did not prevent social and political upheaval – this has been an important lesson for politicians and policy makers everywhere.

K.J. Kennedy (✉)
Hong Kong Institute of Education, Hong Kong, China
e-mail: kerryk@ied.edu.hk

Z. Deng et al. (eds.), *Globalization and the Singapore Curriculum: From Policy to Classroom*, Education Innovation Series, DOI 10.1007/978-981-4451-57-4_12,
© Springer Science+Business Media Singapore 2013

The macro context for Singapore in no way resembles the upheavals of the "Arab Spring." Yet it will be challenging in its own way. The Asian Development Bank (2011, pp. 4–5) has recently released a report that paints scenarios for Asia's development: "the Asian century" scenario in which by 2050 "Asia would have incomes similar to Europe's today"; and "the middle income trap scenario" in which Asian economies are unable to make the transition "to productivity driven growth" thereby missing significant economic "take off". In these scenarios Singapore, along with other developed economies in the region, has a special role to play (Asian Development Bank 2011, p. 7):

> This group of seven economies (i.e. high-income developed economies), especially Japan, Republic of Korea, and Singapore – should lead the rest of Asia in two areas: making the scientific and technological breakthroughs that are crucial to Asia; and moving beyond high economic growth toward promoting broader social well-being.

Thus Singapore has special roles in the region – both in terms of economic and social development. Its responsibilities are not just for national development – the traditional focus of Singapore's trajectory in post-colonial times – but for regional development as well. It is future citizens who will have responsibility for these roles and therefore the extent to which the school curriculum will prepare them is of crucial importance. The remainder of this chapter will focus on making an assessment of Singapore's readiness for this new regional role in terms of the school curriculum as the key tool in the preparation of future citizens. In particular it will highlight:

- Globalization issues, the response of nation states and implications for the school curriculum
- Singapore's curriculum response to globalization – post colonial curriculum reform
- Singapore's curriculum response to new challenges – curriculum reform for the future
- Assessing Singapore's readiness for regional leadership

Globalization Issues, the Response of Nation States and Implications for the School Curriculum

The school curriculum is clearly a micro element in broader social, political, economic and cultural macros contexts. Its key role is to provide opportunities for nurturing future citizens who themselves will influence those contexts in different ways. The nature of the curriculum – its form, its content, its delivery and its assessment- is therefore of fundamental importance in preparing young people for their future roles in society as well as supporting them personally as they grow into adulthood. Yet it exerts its influence alongside other agents of socialization such as parents, peers, the media and community groups. For governments, however, the school curriculum is the centre piece of public policy designed to benefit future economic growth and social development. Traditionally, it has been viewed very much as an instrument of national development. Yet by the end of the twentieth century national development, that had driven growth for most of the century, was challenged by globalization. This new focus highlighted economic integration across borders driven by technological innovation that effortlessly traversed territorial boundaries. How important has this globalization push been, especially in relation to programmes of national development?

Despite the prediction of globalization forecasters concerning the end of the nation state (Ohmae 1995), there is little evidence in this new century that the nations have withered away. Rather, Kennedy (2010) has argued that there is now a powerful neo-statism that has resurrected the power of the state in the light of globalized financial crises that could only be combated by the governments of individual nation states. In addition, enhanced border security now seeks to protect nation states in an age where non state actors are seen as a continual threat to borders so the so called 'borderless' world has simply not become a reality. Finally, the plethora of wars that have characterized the twenty-first century remind us of the military might of individual nation states that have been in no way averse to using such might either in direct attacks on other such nations (e.g. in Iraq and Afghanistan) or to support domestic uprisings (e.g. in Libya). As the second decade of the century develops the power of nation states is intact and very visible across different types of social, political and economic actions.

This is not to say globalization is a spent force – it certainly is not. But there is now a much more obvious tension between the forces of globalization such as free trade, technological innovation and multinational businesses on the one hand and the need for nation states to ensure that these forces do not overwhelm local development. While this tension is often played out in business and political contexts, it also enters the realm of values. This means that hyper capitalism and its advocates often run into local values that are more concerned with explicit virtues, personal relationships and obligations to the community. The challenge of this tension is that while globalization may have much to offer nation states, it is not unconditional: preserving local values and priorities remains important at the local level. There is thus nothing inevitable or deterministic about globalization and it is important to understand how local resistance manifests itself in different aspects of the lives of citizens in nation states.

The development of resistance is particularly important to understand when it comes to education since the development of a nation's young people is fundamental to the future of nation states. In this context it is the school curriculum that is an essential tool by which governments seek to influence future generations. Singapore's current Minster for Education, Heng Swee Keat (2011a), highlighted this point very clearly in a recent speech when he referred to the purposes of citizenship education:

> Firstly, our pupils should grow up to be loyal citizens, with a strong sense of belonging to Singapore and a strong sense of national identity, committed to the well-being, defence and security of our nation. Secondly, they should show care and concern for others, and be willing to contribute actively to improve the lives of others. Thirdly, in our multi-racial society, our pupils need to be socio-culturally sensitive and do their part to promote social cohesion and harmony. Finally, our pupils must have the ability to reflect on and respond to community, national and global issues, and to make informed and responsible decisions.

The Singapore curriculum, therefore, is as much related to national development as it is to the needs of a globalized economy. It is as much a political construction as it is an educational tool to advance student learning. In articulating the local needs of Singapore as he does above, Heng Swee Keat, must also be aware of the economic needs of the small nation state in a competitive global economy, the priority that must be placed on human capital development to produce the necessary skill sets and the need for technological innovation that can influence global success. How does a government balance these competing priorities that inevitably influence the shape and priorities of the school curriculum?

It is not too much to say that the twenty-first century has been an age of reform and improvement when it comes to the school curriculum, not just in Singapore but throughout Asia (Kennedy and Lee 2010). The characteristic of these processes has been the balancing of the global and the local – national development in a globalized context. In the following section, Singapore's response to the demands of both the local and the global will be reviewed in the context of seeking post-colonial solutions to the reform of the school curriculum.

Singapore's Curriculum Response to Globalization: Post Colonial Curriculum Reform

It is instructive to recall that while Singapore's long history can be dated to the eleventh century, its most recent post-colonial history dates from just 1963. This means that the most significant recent influence on education development in Singapore was British colonialism. When it came to education, British colonialism produced remarkable uniformity across its colonies in Asia. Whether it was Singapore, Malaysia, Hong Kong or even Australia, schools, especially secondary schools and most particularly universities, were for the elite and this lasted for much of the twentieth century. The model was the English grammar school and in different places such as Hong Kong and Singapore this model often competed with local vernacular schooling. The English model reflected the academic emphasis of the grammar school so that technical education was for the less able and students for academic study were selected from amongst the rich or meritocratically from the intelligent within the under classes. This model had served Britain well in the nineteenth century and it dominated education thinking in colonies such as Singapore (but also Australia, Hong Kong, and Malaysia) throughout most of the twentieth century. Yet under the threat of globalization it could not be the curriculum for the twenty-first century.

A real turning point in Singapore's educational development away from a colonial curriculum to a more indigenous curriculum came in 1997, although this was not the first attempt at local curriculum reform. It was the then Prime Minister, Goh Chok Tong (1997) who argued that "we cannot assume that what has worked in the past will work for the future. The old formulae for success are unlikely to prepare young people for the new problems and circumstances they will face." Importantly, just before making this statement he also acknowledged that "we will learn and adapt from foreign experiments where useful, but we must chart our own future." He then asserted the new education vision:

> Singapore's vision for meeting this challenge for the future is encapsulated in four words: THINKING SCHOOLS, LEARNING NATION. It is a vision for a total learning environment, including students, teachers, parents, workers, companies, community organization and government.

This vision involved radical change – one whereby "THINKING SCHOOLS must be the crucible for questioning and searching, within and outside the classroom, to forge this passion for learning among our young." Yet it was not only schools that needed to be transformed – but society as a whole. Learning was seen to be a lifelong process, innovation was seen as the driver of change within companies, within the communities and within families and deep learning was seen as the way in which Singapore could develop its competitive advantage and stay ahead in the global village. Thus this new vision inextricably linked learning and the economy – a reflection of what was popularly called the "knowledge economy."

As a result of this vision, Gopinathan (2007, pp. 60–61) noted that there have been curriculum changes in Singapore related to "the teaching of thinking skills, through infusion and direct teaching (and) the introduction of interdisciplinary project work". Ng (2008, p. 6) has also provided a description of reform initiatives under the "Thinking Schools, Learning Nation" banner:

> Syllabi, examinations and university admission criteria were changed to encourage thinking out of the box and risk-taking. Some students are now more engaged in project work and higher order thinking questions to encourage creativity independent and inter-dependent learning. Singapore's Masterplan for IT in Education, launched in 1997, lays out a comprehensive strategy for creating an IT-based teaching and learning environment in every school so that every student becomes literate in IT skills by the time they leave school.

Ng also referred to new initiatives such as "'Innovation and Enterprise' (that) aims to develop intellectual curiosity among the students and a spirit of collective initiative" and "Teach Less, Learn More" that "is about transforming learning from quantity to quality". From this it seems clear that there were concerted efforts to reorient the curriculum in the direction of the reform – away from an overly academic curriculum of the grammar school type to one more suited to the times.

Yet the new Singapore vision was not just about a new focus on learning, critical thinking and innovation. Prime Minister Goh (1997) referred explicitly to a new emphasis on "National Education, through formal lessons as well as outside the classroom, so as to develop stronger bonds between pupils and a desire to contribute to something larger than themselves." As Gopinathan (2007, p. 61) has pointed out national education was simply a continuation of citizenship development that had characterized Singapore from the earliest post-colonial times. Yet this is an important point since it indicates that even in the face of globalization there was the desire to anchor young Singaporeans in local values and ideas – especially the promotion of Singapore itself as a place of which to be proud and which was worth protecting.

Just 1 month before Prime Minister Goh's 'Thinking Schools, Learning Nation' 'statement, his Deputy, Lee Hsien Loong (1997), had officiated at the public launch of National Education outlining its main features:

> National Education aims to develop national cohesion, the instinct for survival and confidence in our future. We cannot offer our next generation any fixed formula for success, or even any set goals in life. They will face new circumstances and problems. They will need to think through and work out their own solutions. But we must equip them with the basic attitudes, values and instincts which make them Singaporeans. This is the common culture that will give them a shared perception of life, and draw them closer together as one people when confronted with serious problems. This will give them a well-founded faith in the country's future. This is the DNA to be passed from one generation to the next.

This is the "national" side of Singapore's curriculum reform. Although perhaps it is more accurate to see it is a continued focus on national development, especially in light of the pressures posed by globalization. Globalized workers remain national citizens in Singapore's vision for the future. The school curriculum may be redesigned to stress innovation, creativity and problem solving, but when it comes to basic values and loyalties, these remain local. This is how nation states such as Singapore resist globalization and it is a key part of their reform agenda (also see Chaps. 2, 4, and 5). Yet it is important to understand that Singapore was not alone in this curriculum reorientation, but rather fitted into a pattern of curriculum reform across the region.

Elsewhere I have shown how a specific jurisdiction such as Hong Kong responded to the need for curriculum reform (Kennedy 2005) and how such reforms permeated the region (Kennedy and Lee 2010). I have also shown that the reform agenda was not implemented in the same way across the region (Kennedy 2007). Developed economies such as Singapore, Hong Kong, Korea, Taiwan, and Japan moved almost immediately into redeveloping curriculum to meet the needs of their emerging "knowledge economies" while the growing economies of Malaysia, Indonesia and Thailand also adopted the "knowledge economy" motif in their reform agendas. Yet countries such as Nepal, Pakistan, Bhutan had other problems to overcome such as low participation rates, lack of qualified teachers, poor educational facilities etc. that meant their resources were more focused on building infrastructure in order to provide the foundations for more relevant and meaningful curriculum in the future. Asia is too diverse to be regarded as on entity – level of development determines goals and priorities. Yet Singapore, as a highly developed economy, moved with other such economies to grasp new opportunities presented by a new century. It was Singapore's first step in a genuine post-colonial curriculum. Yet perhaps the result is better conceptualized as a 'globalized' curriculum. By this I mean a curriculum for a 'globalized' world: a curriculum that was both national and global, individualistic and collective, liberal and conservative, innovative and traditional. It was a neo-progressive curriculum (Kennedy 2005) blending different strains of progressivism into a new post-modern curriculum designed to serve the needs of a globalized economy but also national and social development. But did it go far enough?

Gopinathan (2007) noted that structural rigidities still existed in the Singapore system, especially the streaming practices in secondary schools and the continued use of "O" and "A" level examinations to sift and sought students into different post-secondary tracks (see Chap. 2). The dominance of examination cultures in Asia's school systems is well known and it seems that despite the government's expressed wish to reengineer its schools, this did not include high stakes examinations. The co-existence of approaches to curriculum that seek more creative and problem solving skills and a dominant examination system is beyond the scope of this chapter to evaluate but it remains an important issue for Singapore's future. Yet it is a feature not only of Singapore but of the region as well. Examinations serve a very special role across Asia – not only in the so called Confucian heritage societies (Kennedy and Lee 2010). Brown et al. (2011) have recently shown that the examination culture is deeply embedded in teachers' conceptions of assessment both in Hong Kong and in Mainland China. Thus amidst significant curriculum change high stakes examinations remain in place. The issue for the future is whether exam preparation and creativity will go together especially given the social role of examinations in societies that remain basically meritocratic despite extensive curriculum reform.

Singapore's Curriculum Response to New Challenges: Curriculum Reform for the Future

While the early years of the twenty-first century witnessed widespread curriculum change and improvement agenda's across Asia, there has been no let up on reform in the second decade of the century. China has issued *the National Plan for Medium and Long-Term Education Reform and Development (2010–2020)* (Ministry of Education 2010), Thailand has announced the *Second Education Reform 2010–2018* (Royal Thai Embassy 2010) and Korea has adopted a strategy that "will concentrate more on ensuring that the existing policies take firm root rather than developing new policies" (Ministry of Education, Science and Technology 2008). Singapore has also continued its efforts with *Curriculum 2015* – a blueprint for the continuation of change and reform of the school curriculum. Thus there is a second decade of curriculum reform underway in Asia – deepening, extending and refining the earlier decade's work and seeking outcomes that will further enhance economic and social development.

Deng (2010, pp. 95–96) has commented on C2015 (as it is known locally):

Curriculum 2015 (C2015) …is a response to the current rapidly changing context caused by globalization, changing demographics, and technological advancement. Foregrounding the importance of preparing students for life and work in the 21st century, policymakers have enumerated a set of broad C2015 learning outcomes centred upon generic skills (such as critical thinking, communication, collaboration and management skills) and capacities (in terms of civic, information and media, technological and multicultural literacy). The creation of C2015, Hogan (2009) argues, signals a transition that the Singapore curriculum needs to undertake—a transition from the transmission of academic knowledge and skills to the development of 21st century skills and capacities.

This statement could as well have applied to the initiatives carried out under "Thinking Schools, Learning Nation"– or indeed to any of the regional curriculum reform agendas described in the previous section. So what is the difference – how does C2015 advance Singapore's reform agenda?

It does so in a number of ways. First, C2015 adopted a vision of "Strong Fundamentals, Future Learning" signalling that the basics, especially Mathematics, Science, Languages and Humanities, had a role to play in the future curriculum. Second, it recognized the fundamental importance of a high quality teacher work-force committing to an "all graduate" teaching profession. Third, it highlighted the importance of school leadership, collegiality and team work. Fourth it recognized the need for a degree of school autonomy in curriculum decision making but without relinquishing national direction and values. In an important sense, C2015 appears to be a more integrated approach to reform – less political in its overtone and more educational seeking to work at the system level to bring about change. Despite the new foci outlined above, C2015 is broadly consistent with "Thinking Schools, Learning Nation" extending it and deepening it. In the area of values education, however, C2015 goes further seeking greater emphasis on developing not just national values, but personal values as well. It is conceptualized by joining together "character" and "citizenship" to form a new "citizenship and character education" for Singapore's schools (also see Chap. 14).

Dr. Ng Eng Hen (2010), then Minister for Education, highlighted the importance of citizenship and character education for the future, "only right values can shape positive character and committed citizenship in 'moulding the future of our nation'". This view has also been highlighted by Mr. Heng Swee Keat (2011b), the current Minister for Education:

> If values provide the philosophical underpinning, character development makes these values come alive. Character development is about developing social emotional compe-tencies, and the habits and inner disposition based on sound values to act in a consistent way. Personal values such as grit, determination and resilience enable the individual to realise his or her potential, and develop 'performance character'. Moral values enable the individuals to develop 'moral character'.

This may seem a long way from the "National Education" focus of "Thinking Schools, Learning Nation." It is more personal, more individualistic more overtly moralistic. Yet such an approach will resonate across the region where citizenship education has always been more aligned with moral education than Western notions of civic education. Ironically "character education," despite its connections to both Eastern and Western philosophical traditions, has been related in its more recent manifestations to socially conservative movements in the United States and the United Kingdom. Its importation to Singapore at this time is not inconsistent with strong local traditions that have always highlighted moral education. Yet it is not clear exactly why it was felt to be necessary to import "character education" into a society that is itself rich in moral traditions, including religious and philosophical traditions that provide a much stronger basis for moral action than modern character education (also see Chap. 14).

It is interesting to note that later in his speech, Minister Heng Kwee Keat went on to link creativity, innovation and values – a significant value chain. In noting how

Apple had out-valued Exxon as a corporate entity, Heng alluded to the importance of values in the economic realm. Thus while C2015 is geared to the needs of economic development it also recognizes that such development is not an end in itself. This is an important recognition compared to how the reform agenda in the early part of the century may be seen. Economic development at all costs seemed to characterize the thinking of many governments and business leaders as the new century got underway. Yet the financial crisis of 2008 and its aftermath has undoubtedly sent strong signals about the absence of values in many parts of the financial sector, the capacity of citizens to make financial and economic decisions and the responsibility of governments when markets go badly wrong. Perhaps values education, embedded as it was in national education, was too implicit in the earlier reforms. In C2015, however, values education is taking centre stage. The rationale may well have been the moral vacuum demonstrated by the financial crisis as well as the spectre of international terrorism that has dominated the twenty-first century. At the same time, there is another pervasive reason for highlighting values, and it cannot have escaped the attention of Singapore's policy makers.

Since the end of 2005 there have been immigrant youth riots in Paris, school shootings in Finland, widespread youth riots in London and other English cities, a major catastrophe in Norway involving a young gunmen and, of course, the "Arab Spring" that has been fuelled by young people unable to tolerate any longer the social and economic oppression of corrupt regimes. I do not wish to trivialize these significant international phenomena or suggest there are simple solutions. Each example above has its own etiology embedded in distinctive cultural, social and political contexts. Yet in at least one context schools were seen as part of the solution to youth radicalism. In the England the former Department of Schools, Families and Children (Bonnell et al. 2010, p. 1) had commissioned research into the topic of youth extremism prior to the English 2011 riots. Schools were highlighted as a bulwark against extremism so that "the primary aim of the research was to provide a strong evidence base for schools and other education providers to help them adopt and commission the appropriate interventions to build resilience to extremism." The results of the English study, summarized below, could well apply to Singapore's renewed emphasis on citizenship and character education:

> This research suggests that a well-designed, well-facilitated intervention will go a long way to building resilience. To be more confident of **longer-term, sustainable resilience**, however, an additional focus is needed, over and above good design and facilitation, on building 'harder' skills, knowledge, understanding and awareness, including practical tools and techniques for personal resilience.

Schools cannot be the whole answer to youth radicalism, since many youth issues are deeply embedded in the social, political, cultural and economic structures of societies. Yet the issue cannot be ignored, because it seems clear that youth themselves can no longer be ignored. If this is the case, then Singapore's citizenship and character education has a very significant role to play in the future – not simply as a new component of the school curriculum but as a very real means to build a tolerant, fair and just society that will obviate the need for radicalism and extremism.

It is too early to evaluate C2015 but its importance cannot be overestimated. Yet it not just the importance of the initiative for Singapore, although that is of great significance. As mentioned at the beginning of this chapter, the Asian Development Bank has placed Singapore in a regional leadership role as this new century progresses. The rationale, of course, is economic given that Singapore is one of the leading regional economies. Yet economies are fuelled by the human resources available in a nation and human resources are developed through education, starting with schools. How well equipped, then, is Singapore for this new regional leadership role? This issue will be addressed in the final section of this chapter.

Assessing Singapore's Readiness for Regional Leadership

In this final section of the chapter I want to outline what I think are the challenges for Singapore's curriculum in the future. In particular, I want to focus on the Asian Development Banks's (2011) scenario leading up to 2050 where Singapore is seen as a regional leader. My reason for doing so is that I believe the future is very much about the region of which Singapore is a part – the most populous region of the world where economic growth is likely to outstrip the rest of the world and where solutions found to problems may well have generalizability beyond the region. I want to focus on three main issues:

* Does Singapore have the curriculum basics in place?
* Can we develop a better understanding of international benchmarking?
* How might a better future be constructed?

Does Singapore Have the Curriculum Basics in Place?

International reviews of Singapore's education system are overwhelmingly positive – whether it is Singapore students' performance in large scale international assessments, rankings in the Global Competitiveness Report (Porter et al. 2008), judgments made by McKinsey Consulting (Mourshed et al. 2011) or reports from the Organization for Economic Cooperation and Development (2011). This international recognition is important but it needs to be viewed in the context of the specific requirements of Singapore and the region in the future. I shall return to this point at the end of this section. The Asian Development Bank (2011), for example, has identified two key priorities that impact on Singapore's regional role – its potential as a technology hub and its commitment to the well-being of all citizens. Thus these are more relevant proximal benchmarks for judging Singapore's future capacity. As Singapore moves forward in the second decade of the century these are the two areas that will characterize its potential for regional leadership. How well equipped does Singapore appear to be for this role and how might the school curriculum contribute?

It may seem unusual to link such a macro issue such as capacity for regional leadership to the school curriculum. It might seem equally unusual to link the creation of a technology hub and the social well-being of society to the curriculum. Yet the point I want to make is that schools do have a responsibility for providing what might be seen as foundation knowledge and skills for later life. Schools may not be the vehicle for directly creating engineers, technicians, nurses or doctors but they should contribute to understandings and skills formation that make these eventual employment destinations possible. Of course, schools can do more than this – they can also contribute to the development of an intelligent and active citizenry that is creative and tolerant, caring and innovative, critical and productive. At the same time schools must also be concerned with the personal well-being of their students. Thus a great deal is asked of the school curriculum and the question is how will Singapore be placed in the future?

C2015 with its focus on the "fundamentals" appears to be a good vehicle to provide the kind of foundational skills and knowledge that will support Singapore's future development. The focus is on Mathematics, Science, Humanities and Technology but these school subjects are not the whole curriculum. In addition there is also an emphasis on what have come to be called "twenty-first century skills" – critical thinking, multicultural and technological literacies, communication and collaboration There is also an explicit outcomes focus to the curriculum that is designed to produce "confident people," "self-directed learners," "concerned citizens," and "active contributors." This approach to curriculum development can best be described as a "mixed model" that seeks the best from different ways of selecting content. It is a move away from the traditional academic curriculum by incorporating more generic learning outcomes and more socially-oriented outcomes. Yet the academic orientation remains important – it is simply not the only orientation.

If it can be assumed that the kind of curriculum described above will be the curriculum for all students, it could well be argued that all students will be well prepared for the future. If the creation of a technology hub is an important goal then it seems that schools will be in a position to provide foundational skills that can contribute to that goal. At the same time multicultural literacies and active and engaged citizenship skills may well provide for the well-being of Singapore's future citizens. Yet much will depend on the implementation of C2015 objectives and how far these can be extended beyond an elite to all students. Can C2015 produce outcomes that benefit not just an elite but all students? Can the social well-being of all become a key objective for C2015 alongside the production of a technologically oriented and committed workforce? These questions will be addressed in the following section.

Can We Develop a Better Understanding of International Benchmarking?

Large scale international assessments such as PISA, PIRLS, TIMSS, and ICSS have become popular tools for policy makers seeking to benchmark student achievement internationally. Yet there is a growing literature that should act as a caution for policy makers keen to exploit the results of these international tests (Hopmann 2008; Ringarp and Rothland 2010; Rutkowski and Engel 2010; Bulle 2011). It is not so much that there is anything inherently wrong with the tests themselves. Rather, it is the emphasis that is placed on the results as "league tables" and the fundamental lack of understanding that surrounds the results. Singapore is a good case in point.

When the Ministry of Education (2010) announced the results of PISA 2009 Singapore students were rightly praised for their performance in Mathematics, Science and Reading – the curriculum basics. The importance of these results should not be underestimated but it is not the whole story for PISA 2009 as a recent OECD (2011, p. 167) report noted:

> Singapore has very high mean achievement scores in mathematics and science but there is also a very long tail to the achievement distribution. On other measures, too, socio economic status has a significant impact on achievement.

That is to say, not all Singapore students do well on PISA – there are winners and losers. This can also be seen in the distribution of students across proficiency levels for the combined literacy scale. 30.6 % of Singapore students fall into the lowest levels (Below 1b to Level 2) compared to 17.3 % in Shanghai, 23.1. % for Hong Kong and 24.8 % for Finland (National Centre for Educational Statistics 2011, pp. 24–29). The big challenge for Singapore's curriculum, therefore, is to reduce these numbers and move all students to higher levels of proficiency. It is by no means an easy challenge and there are several reasons for this.

First, there are technical reasons. The tendency of large scale assessments to report achievement in terms of a single scale score reduces the complexity of student learning. Chow and Kennedy (2011) have shown how alternative analytical techniques applied to data from large scale assessments can yield more nuanced results capable of reflecting underlying complexities in the data. These kinds of analyses are often left to secondary data analysis but the tools are available to the teams undertaking the original international analyses. If these teams were more intent on producing useful data for system improvement rather than international league tables it would be possible for education systems to gain better insights not just into the top performers in their systems but to the full range of student performance. This is not to say that the results for top performers are unimportant but if policymakers are to cater for all students in a system like Singapore's they need more and better information from large scale assessments. In particular, policy makers need information that can lead to systems improvements rather than data, such as single scale scores, that are primarily used for the creation of international league tables. The importance of this issue has already been recognized in Singapore, but it requires a new mind-set for test development agencies.

Second, there are the underlying causes for poor performance and in this regard the OECD report referred to above highlight the effect of socioeconomic status on the achievement of Singapore's students. A report focused on explaining social background and learning opportunities (OECD 2010, p. 55) indicated that for PISA 2009 a unit increase in the PISA index of economic and social status was associated with a 47 score point difference in reading achievement for Singapore students. This compares with a 17 score point difference for Hong Kong students, 27 points for

Shanghai students and 31 points for students in Finland. That is, economic and social status weighs more on learning in Singapore than education systems with which it likes to compare itself. Singapore's score point difference is also above the OECD average at 38 points. Yet only 15.3 % of the variance in student achievement in reading can be accounted for by economic and social status which is not significantly different from the OECD average of 14 % but above the average of 10 % for Hong Kong, Shanghai and Finland. That is, disadvantaged students do have a chance to succeed in Singapore but not to the extent of similar students in like-systems. Thus in Singapore 12 % of disadvantaged students has been classified as "resilient" (i.e. disadvantaged students who score in the top one quarter of the sample) compared to an average of 15 % for Hong Kong, Shanghai and Finland. Understanding how disadvantaged students become "resilient" should be a key policy priority for Singapore in the future.

The above analysis has focused on socioeconomic status because this has been PISA's focus so attention has not been paid to other equity areas such as gender or ethnicity that might provide additional perspectives. Nevertheless, the results have shown that beneath the surface of Singapore's top PISA performers is a group of under performers who are in need of the education system's attention. This is an important social justice issue in itself but is also important in terms of Singapore' role as a regional leader. In terms of the ADB scenario, not only is Singapore seen as a regional hub providing technological innovation for the region but also as an exemplar of catering for the well-being of its citizens. This means that while the system can be well proud of its top achievers, it must also find ways to extend that kind of learning to all students. How it might be able to do this will be addressed in the final section of this chapter.

How Might a Better Future Be Constructed for All of Singaporean Students?

In this section I would like to focus on three broad issues that have the potential to enable Singapore's education system to focus its resources on the kind of curriculum that can support all students while at the same time maintaining its status as a world class system. I shall highlight three particular issues:

- Research with a focus on learning
- School Based Curriculum Development (SBCD) and curriculum differentiation
- Professionalizing assessment

Research with a Focus on Learning

Singapore's education system is well known for its support of research – perhaps more so than most other governments in the region. Yet the key question for the future is what kind of research. C2015 talks about supporting "a wider variety of pedagogies" and Hogan (2010) outlined models for partnerships that would enhance pedagogies in Singapore's schools. Pedagogy, of course, is an important adjunct to the school curriculum – the daily operation of the curriculum in the lives of students. Yet a sole focus on searching for new pedagogies may miss the point, especially in light of the successes attributed to the current system. Bulle (2011), in a secondary analysis of PISA data, has identified the relationship between type of education system and student achievement. This kind of classification is important to understand in pursuit of more equitable education outcomes.

Having identified ideal types of educational systems, of which the "East Asian" type (classified as a "mixed" system (as opposed to "differentiated" or "undifferentiated" systems) with 'academic" (as opposed to 'progressive') objectives, Bulle (2011) shows that in terms of students' achievement the "East Asian type" of education system consistently produces better student performance. Even when it comes to tests of creativity and problem solving, students from East Asian type systems perform very well (Bulle 2011, p. 511). Thus Bulle's (2011, p. 512) conclusion is:

> The comparison shows the clear advantage presented by those systems which propose a form of study course diversification based on the students' achievements and aspirations, and where teaching is academically oriented. Hence, the overall results of the Northern model tend to be diametrically opposed to those of the East-Asian model. The fact that the students' actual successful attainment in the taught subjects is directly linked to the academic orientation of the educational systems is a general and coherent result which does not prejudge the pedagogical adaptation of teaching but concerns the aims of the school programmes.

An exception to this general conclusion is Finland that generally fits into the "Northern system type" – undifferentiated and progressive -but whose students perform very well, often better than students from East Asia. Bulle's (2011) explanation of this is that student learning is closely monitored in Finnish schools and support is provided to ensure that students do not fall behind. In this sense she sees Finland as closer to a "mixed model type" than a totally undifferentiated model. To this is added an important teacher variable whereby Finnish teachers appear to have maintained a somewhat conservative attitude towards teaching rather than be swept along by the raft of progressivist reforms. The contrary case is that of France that has taken up such reforms with consequent declines in student performance (Bulle 2011, p. 514).

All of this should not be taken as an unreserved support for the "East Asian type" of education system. On the contrary Bulle (2011) has reservations despite the apparent success. Nevertheless, there does appear to be some important lessons that can be learnt for the future. Pedagogies in and of themselves are probably not the solution to the issue of providing support for low achieving students. Rather, the focus should be on identifying ways in which the learning of such students can be enhanced – what kind of support, in what contexts, over what period of time. This may result in the identification of both traditional as well as innovative pedagogies depending on student needs and preferences. That is, there is not a single pedagogy for all students but multiple pedagogies that can cater for ethnicity, gender, socioeconomic background or any other variable that might influence the way and what students learn. The case of Finland is instructive here because classrooms contain multiple levels of support for students – not just the teacher at the front of the classroom. Paying close attention to individual learning needs may be the best way to support the learning of all students with the assumption being that students learn in different ways and classrooms should cater for the diversity of learning needs.

This calls for a very special kind of research agenda and it is one linked closely to teachers. What happens in classrooms is fundamentally the concern of teachers – and under C2015 their allied helpers. Teachers need to have both the skills and the mind-sets to be active researchers in finding those ways of learning that characterize the different students in their classrooms. They may well be helped in this by in-service training or links to universities – but in the end it is the day by day use of different pedagogies with different students that will produce the best outcomes for those students. This takes a highly skilled teacher workforce – another objective of C2015 – and it takes resources since smaller classes and more attention to low achieving students will cost the system more than simply focusing on the top performers. Yet the latter will not be neglected – finding new ways to engage top performers should also be an important part of this research agenda.

What needs to be avoided in this research agenda is the top down imposition of particular pedagogies as though a single pedagogy will provide the answer for low achieving students. A focus on learning means understanding what will facilitate learning for different students in different contexts. It needs to be accepted that within a single classroom multiple pedagogies may need to operate at the same time – small groups, direct instruction, research processes and cooperative learning. All of this needs to be well managed by teachers (and their assistants) and it also needs to be documented. Classrooms will not look the same from school site to school site as teachers experiment to find what works for particular students. This is a challenging agenda for schools and teachers as well as for the system but if the outcome is improved learning for low achieving students it will have been worthwhile.

School Based Curriculum Development (SBCD) and Curriculum Differentiation

The kind of research agenda outlined above can only be achieved in an education system where schools have the freedom to adapt the curriculum to the needs of their students. SBCD – another C2015 objective – is one way to achieve this flexibility. It is not an easy process and it has been tried in many jurisdictions as Law and Nieveen (2011) have recently shown. Often the results have been counter intuitive where teachers opt for the use of readymade curriculum packages rather than respond to the specific needs of students in their schools. Nevertheless, SBCD can be a powerful tool for recognizing the diversity of learning within a school and teachers can work together to create adaptations that are tailored specifically to meet the needs of low achieving students. An outcomes focus in the curriculum is helpful in this context because it means that relevant content can be used rather than predefined content that does not recognize special needs for specific groups of students.

SBCD in the context of Bulle (2011) referred to above is the means of catering for the diverse needs of learners in the context of a "mixed" system. It does not mean that common elements in the curriculum disappear or that the "fundamentals" of C2015 can be ignored. These fundamentals will remain important for all students but there will be adaptations where they will better help students to learn. This requires once again a highly professional teacher workforce equipped not just to implement a centrally directed curriculum but to make judgments about the ways a centrally devised curriculum can be adapted to meet the special needs of specific groups of students. This is the kind of curriculum translation referred to by Deng (2010) where teachers have the role of ensuring that learning can be made meaningful and relevant for all students. This is not done by the implementation of a 'one size fits all' curriculum but by judicious selection of content, pedagogy and assessment according to the specific needs of students in specific locations.

But the skills and leadership needed for successful SBCD should not be under-estimated. Curriculum development is a professional activity and in a system like Singapore's where central rather than local direction has been the main form of delivery the challenge to localize even part of the curriculum is a very significant one. There are implications for initial and ongoing teacher education as well as for school leadership. New teacher recruits need to be ready to embrace their curriculum roles and leaders need to distribute leadership in such a way that there are levels of responsibility throughout the school and not just in the Principal's office. Parents also need to be involved so that they understand how the balance between central and local directions is being maintained and how they themselves have a significant role to play in enhancing the learning of their children. With SBCD, it will not be 'business as usual' in Singapore's schools but it will business designed to support all students and their learning.

Professionalizing Assessment

In 'East Asian type' education systems high stakes assessment plays a significant role – more so than in most other systems. While there have been extensive reforms in Korea, Taiwan, Hong Kong and even Mainland China examination systems have remained in place. C2015 indicates that it will be the same in Singapore. What is more research has shown that examinations and tests are very much part of Chinese teachers' conceptions of classroom assessment (Brown et al. 2011). Assessment, therefore, is a very special issue for Singapore's policy makers seeking to enhance the learning of low achieving students (also see Chap. 2).

The backwash of high stakes assessment on the curriculum is well known, especially in Asian contexts (Watkins and Biggs 1996). Yet assessment in these contexts is not just for assessment's sake. It serves an important social purpose being seen very much as an important social elevator that can lift students into good high schools, universities and careers. In all likelihood this is why teachers in Chinese contexts are so committed to examinations because they understand the importance of their social purpose (Brown et al. 2011). This situation is not likely to change in the future. Yet the need to ameliorate the backwash on the curriculum remains important otherwise low achieving students will continue to feel the effects of a curriculum designed for top performers on pathways to elite universities.

One approach to this situation is to provide more emphasis on differentiated assessment and the scaffolding of learning tasks so that students are moved at different rates towards the desired learning outcomes. That is to say, rather than one test for all students, consideration should be given to assessments that will move students forward in their learning irrespective of the starting point. This is a natural complementary to SBCD and a research focus on learning. Start where the students are and develop strategies – pedagogies, tasks, assessments – that move them forward. Let all students experience success but be held to high standards and expectations. Teachers would need to know the desired outcome (the learning destination) and then the map the way for each student to get there. Assessment serves the important purpose of providing feedback on the progress students are making in their learning – it is assessment for learning rather than assessment of learning (although this distinction, that is often made in the literature, should not be held too rigidly since these modes of assessment are not necessarily mutually exclusive).

Such an emphasis on differentiated assessment does not obviate the need for system wide monitoring of student achievement or examinations the purpose of which is to select for university entrance. Yet it does mean that teachers need to be much better prepared for their assessment roles. They cannot just rely on externally developed tests – they themselves need to become test makers and developers monitoring student learning within schools. School based assessment, therefore, should become an important adjunct of SBCD. As such, it can contribute to system wide examinations just as it does in all Australian States/Territories. Teachers' assessment judgments are known to be very reliable and moderation processes are a natural way to ensure that both within and across schools there can be consistency of judgment about student performance on specific tasks. System wide monitoring itself can act as a moderator of teacher judgments so that differentiated assessment can work alongside whole of system testing in the interests of ensuring fair and equitable assessments for all students.

Assessment will be the biggest challenge facing Singapore in the future if new forms of assessment are to be used to nurture the learning of low achieving students (also see Chap. 2). Teachers will need to focus on individuals and groups of students whose learning progress may not be uniform and thus will need to be monitored in different ways. Moving all students along the learning continuum rather than just getting top students into elite universities may need to become a new objective for schools and the system as a whole. It is a new way of looking at assessment and it is designed to benefit all students rather than just a few.

Conclusion

Singapore's future is a very positive one although there are also significant challenges. Developing a school curriculum that will benefit all students rather than a select few should be a key priority. It is only by doing this that Singapore can demonstrate its concern for the well-being of all students. As Singapore's policy makers, school leaders and teachers reflect on the considerable success of their education system, the real issue for the future is to make it a success for all students. It is a great challenge for public policy, for leadership and for classroom practice.

At the same time, Singapore's concerns can move beyond national development, where there have been great achievements since the 1960s. Its gaze can now be on to the region where two of the world's economic giants reside but where economic development remains uneven, where poverty is rampant, where security continues to be an issue, where values are given a high priority and where there are regime types ranging from dictatorships to liberal democracies with many shades in between. The school curriculum's role is to provide the foundational skills and understandings for all students. In turn they can support the broader goals Singapore must have to support regional development. It is a new role for the city state and one that could change the lives of many providing a safer, more productive, and more stable environment not just for Singapore but for the region as a whole.

References

Asian Development Bank. (2011). *Asia 2050 – realizing the Asian century*. Manila: Asian Development Bank.

Bonnell, J., Copestake, P., Kerr, D., Passy, R., Reed, C., Salter, R., Sarwar, S., Sheikh, S. (2010). *Teaching approaches that help to build resilience to extremism among young people*. https://www.education.gov.uk/publications/eOrderingDownload/DFE-RR119.pdf. Accessed 28 Dec 2011.

Brown, G., Hui, S. F. K., Yu, F. W. M., & Kennedy, K. (2011). Teachers' conceptions of assessment in Chinese contexts: A tripartite model of accountability, improvement, and irrelevance. *International Journal of Educational Research, 50*, 307–320.

Bulle, N. (2011). Comparing OECD educational models through the prism of PISA. *Comparative Education, 47*(4), 503–521.

Chow, J.K.F., & Kennedy, K. (2011). Citizenship and governance in the Asian region: Insights from the International Civic And Citizenship Education Study. In International conference on 'Governance and Citizenship in Asia: Paradigms and Practices', Hong Kong, 18–19 Mar 2011.

Deng, Z. (2010). Curriculum transformation in the era of reform initiatives: The need to rethink and re-conceptualize content. *Journal of Textbook Research, 3*(2), 93–113.

Goh, C. (1997). *Speech*. http://www.moe.gov.sg/media/speeches/1997/020697.htm. Accessed 20 Dec 2011.

Gopinathan, S. (2007). Globalisation, the Singapore developmental state and education policy: A thesis revisited. *Globalisation, Societies and Education, 5*(1), 53–70.

Heng, S.K. (September 22, 2011a). *Opening Address by Minister for Education, at the Ministry of Education (MOE) Work plan seminar at Ngee Ann polytechnic convention centre*. http://www.moe.gov.sg/media/speeches/2011/09/22/work-plan-seminar-2011.php. Accessed 27 Dec 2011.

Heng, S.K. (November 8, 2011b). *Speeches*. http://www.moe.gov.sg/media/speeches/2011/11/08/opening-address-by-mr-heng-swee-keat-at-1st-nie-moe-cce-conference.php. Accessed 6 Dec 2011.

Hogan, D. (2009). *Toward a 21st century pedagogy for Singapore*. A presentation to the Principals Curriculum Forum on Assessment-Pedagogy Nexus, Ministry of Education, Singapore. Quoted in Deng (2010).

Hogan, D. (November 2, 2010). *Current and future pedagogies in Singapore – Synopsis of presentation at the TE21 Seminar*. http://www.nie.edu.sg/files/Current_and_Future_Pedagogies_in_Singapore-final.pdf. Accessed 4 Jan 2012.

Hopmann, S. (2008). No child, no school, no state left behind: Schooling in the age of accountability. *Journal of Curriculum Studies, 40*, 417–456.

Kennedy, K. (2005). *Changing schools for changing times- New directions for the school curriculum in Hong Kong*. Hong Kong: Chinese University Press.

Kennedy, K. (2007). Curriculum reforms and instructional improvement in Asia. In T. Townsend (Ed.), *International handbook on school effectiveness and improvement* (pp. 807–824). Dordrecht: Springer.

Kennedy, K. (2010). Neo-statism and post-globalization as contexts for new times. In A. Reid, J. Gill, & A. Sears (Eds.), *Globalisation, the Nation-State and the Citizen: Dilemmas and directions for civics and citizenship education* (pp. 223–229). London: Routledge.

Kennedy, K., & Lee, J. (2010). *Changing schools in Asia – Schools for the knowledge society*. New York: Routledge.

Law, E. H. F., & Nieveen, N. (Eds.). (2011). *Schools as curriculum agencies – Asian and European perspectives on school-based curriculum development*. Rotterdam: Sense Publishers.

Lee, H.L. (May 17, 1997). *Speech by Lee Hsien Loong, Deputy Prime Minister at The Launch of National Education on Saturday 17 May 1997 at Tcs Tv Theatre at 9.30 am*. http://www.moe.gov.sg/media/speeches/1997/170597.htm. Accessed 20 Dec 2011.

Ministry of Education, Science and Technology. (2008). *Message*. http://english.mest.go.kr/web/1673/site/contents/en/en_0194.jsp. Accessed 27 Dec 2011.

Ministry of Education. (2010). *International OECD Study affirms the high quality of Singapore's education system*. http://www.moe.gov.sg/media/press/2010/12/programme-for-international-student-assessment-2009.php. Accessed 3 Jan 2012.

Mourshed, M., Chinezi, C., & Barber, M. (2011). *How the world's most improved school systems keep getting better*. http://mckinseyonsociety.com/downloads/reports/Education/How-the-Worlds-Most-Improved-School-Systems-Keep-Getting-Better_Download-version_Final.pdf. Accessed 5 Jan 2012.

National Centre for Educational Statistics. (2011). *PISA 2009 – Data, tables, figures, exhibits*. http://nces.ed.gov/pubs2011/2011004_1.pdf. Accessed 3 Jan 2011.

Ng, P. (2008). Educational reform in Singapore: From quantity to quality. *Educational Research, Policy and Practice, 7*(1), 5–15.

Ng, E.H. (September 23, 2010). *Speech by Dr. Ng Eng Hen, Minister for Education and Second Minister for Defence, at the MOE work plan seminar at the Ngee Ann polytechnic convention centre*. http://www.moe.gov.sg/media/speeches/2010/09/23/work-plan-seminar-2010.php. Accessed 27 Dec 2011.

OECD. (2010). *PISA 2009 results: Overcoming social background – Equity in learning opportunities and outcomes* (Vol. 2). Paris: OECD.

OECD. (2011). *Strong performers and successful reformers in education: Lessons from PISA for the United States*. Paris: OECD.

Ohmae, K. (1995). *The end of the nation state*. London: HarperCollins.

Porter, M., Schwab, K., & Sala-I-Martin, Z. (2008). *The global competitiveness report 2007–2008*. Geneva: World Economic Forum.

Ringarp, J., & Rothland, M. (2010). Is the grass always greener? The effect of the PISA results on education debates in Sweden and Germany. *European Educational Research Journal, 9*(3), 422–430.

Royal Thai Embassy. (2010). *Second decade of education reform to focus on vocational and skills development*. Retrieved Dec 2011, from, http://media.thaigov.go.th/pageconfig/viewcontent/viewcontent1e.asp?pageid=472&directory=1944&contents=52023. Accessed 3 May 2012.

Rutkowsi, D., & Engel, L. (2010). Soft power and hard measures: Large-scale assessment, citizenship and the European Union. *European Educational Research Journal, 9*(3), 381–395.

Schwab, J. (1969). *College curricula and student protest*. Chicago: University of Chicago Press.

Watkins, D., & Biggs, J. (1996). *The Chinese learner: Cultural, psychological and contextual influences*. Hong Kong/Melbourne: Comparative Education Research Centre/Australian Council for Education Research.

Chapter 13
Reforming Curriculum in Singapore and Hong Kong

S. Gopinathan and Michael H. Lee

Introduction

Globalization, which generally refers to the compression of time and space as a result of transportation, communication and technological innovations, enhances economic integration (Giddens 1991). Economic globalization is the consequence of the intensification of increased trade flows and the development of global markets which are beyond the control of individual nation-states (Dale 2000; Daun 2002). The "big market, small government" logic of governance has put pressure on the welfare state because the promotion of innovation and enterprise, and to allow market requires a smaller state freer reign (Cerny 1990; Dale 2000). Under these circumstances, according to Bottery (2000), a number of educational convergences are noticeable, including increased post-compulsory education participation and a greater emphasis upon lifelong learning. In Singapore and Hong Kong, education policymaking has been influenced by the assumption that choice and market forces are crucial for improving the quality of education (Kennedy 2005; Chubb and Moe 1990).

The economic value of education has been similarly emphasized; policy is directed towards improving the quality of human capital and enhancing labour productivity via a greater emphasis on languages, mathematics, science and technology, and more learning-oriented pedagogies to cater for the needs of boosting knowledge and skill levels (Gopinathan 1999; Green 1997). Globalization offered not only new opportunities but also more risks and uncertainties (Beck 1992), and it is more difficult for individual nation-states to keep tight control over their own economies and societies in face of uncontrollable external influences (Giddens 1999).

S. Gopinathan (✉)
National Institute of Education, Nanyang Technological University, Singapore
e-mail: s_gopinathan@ymail.com

M.H. Lee
The Chinese University of Hong Kong, Hong Kong, China

Z. Deng et al. (eds.), *Globalization and the Singapore Curriculum: From Policy to Classroom*, Education Innovation Series, DOI 10.1007/978-981-4451-57-4_13,
© Springer Science+Business Media Singapore 2013

Nevertheless, globalization does not prevent both city-states' governments from influencing the making of public and social policies, including education which is increasingly seen as a tool of economic policy (Rizvi and Lingard 2010). Curriculum remains an important policy instrument controlled by the state to shape the development of education and human capital. Therefore, an analysis of curriculum from a comparative perspective will reveal how convergently and divergently Singapore and Hong Kong are responding (Kennedy 2005).

The focus of the curriculum reforms in Singapore and Hong Kong is not confined to the transmission of disciplinary content and twenty-first century skills, but also the inculcation of citizenship values, national identity, and political allegiance among the young populace. On the one hand, policies for reforming the curriculum are aimed at coping with the economic challenges of the global knowledge-based economy. On the other hand, curriculum reform is a means of alleviating the impact of globalization's problems and challenges through the reinforcement of political and national consciousness among the citizens for social solidarity (Gopinathan and Sharpe 2004). In Singapore and Hong Kong, the state remains significant in reforming the curriculum, even though the ways the reforms are approached differ between the two city-states; a crucial factor in explaining the differences is the strength of the state.

This chapter compares how the curriculum reforms in Singapore and Hong Kong are similar and different from each other, and also discusses how the state factor affects the formation and implementation of policy and reform initiatives. There are four sections in this chapter. The first section reviews and compares the policy context of the curriculum policies and reforms in Singapore and Hong Kong. The second reviews and compares major curriculum policies and reforms in Singapore and Hong Kong. The third section provides an account on the latest development of Character and Citizenship Education (CCE) and Moral and National Education (MNE) in Singapore and Hong Kong respectively to illustrate the importance of local factors in shaping the curriculum development under the profound influence of globalization. The final section summarizes the discussion.

Contexts

As schooling systems are embedded socio-cultural constructions, any analysis of the place, nature and changes in curriculum in Singapore and Hong Kong must attend to the local contexts in both city-states although their socio-economic developments are similarly not immune from the profound influence of globalization.

Similarities

Similarities can be identified between Singapore and Hong Kong. Historically, both Singapore and Hong Kong were British colonies and key nodes in Britain's maritime empire for more than one and a half centuries. It is therefore not surprising that the education systems in both city-states have long been shaped by the British model and tradition. Economically, both city-states are major entrepots and financial hubs where the presence of a large pool of high quality, well-educated and bilingual manpower is widely considered necessary for enhancing their comparative advantages. Socio-culturally, Singapore and Hong Kong are Chinese-dominant societies embedded with values and beliefs which strongly emphasize the importance of education as an instrument of social mobility, and one in which individual and family effort is important.

Moreover, from the educational perspective, Singapore and Hong Kong's education systems operate on a "flattened playing field" (Friedman 2005) in which competition takes place through a series of international competitions. High rankings in such comparative studies as the Trends in International Mathematics and Science Study (TIMSS), the International Association for the Evaluation of Educational Achievement (IEA), the Programme for International Student Assessment (PISA), and the Progress in International Reading and Literacy Study (PIRLS), together with the high-profile media coverage, put pressure on policymakers to ensure that the label "world class" sticks to their systems, and to adopt cutting-edge international practices in order to maintain top rankings in these international comparisons (Morris and Adamson 2010). In spite of these similarities, Singapore and Hong Kong differ significantly in terms of political status, state power, and policymaking approaches leading to divergences in the curriculum developments and reforms in both city-states.

Differences

Politically, although both city-states were once under British colonial rule, their divergent pathways of political development resulted in different political status. While Singapore has been an independent nation in 1965, Hong Kong has been a special administrative region in the People's Republic of China (China, hereafter) since 1997.

Since the People's Action Party (PAP) won the general elections in 1959, the PAP-led government has attained a high level of political legitimacy in making policies to solve critical socio-economic issues like employment, public housing, and education. Since Singapore gained independence in 1965, the Singapore government has adopted "a politics of survival" mode of governance, seeking to overcome resource scarcity through corruption-free and efficient government, and emphasizing meritocracy and social cohesion (Chan 1971; Quah 1991). Moreover, the PAP-led government made the conscription policy to recruit male adults to serve in the army in line with the principle of self-reliance in national defence (Turnbull 2005).

In a phrase coined by its first and longest serving prime minister Lee Kuan Yew, Singapore was able to develop from 'third world to first world' in three decades (Lee 2000). Apart from tackling social, economic and security problems, education policy came in for special attention for human capital was declared the only resource for sustaining socio-economic development. With an emphasis on strong and credible governance, which is largely built on the basis of strong political legitimacy, policies are often made swiftly without much public consultation. For education, the policy goal is to build a modern, efficient, high quality education system. English instead of mother tongues is used as the major medium of instruction thus not privileging any particular ethnic group. With the streaming policy since the late 1970s (Ministry of Education 1979), the curriculum comprises both academic and technical or vocational subjects to cater to the needs of students with different academic abilities. In addition, the state designates university education for the most academically able students but simultaneously invests heavily in the polytechnic and technical education sectors to provide sufficient high quality manpower for the economy (Goh and Gopinathan 2008; also Chaps. 2, 5, and 14).

In contrast, Hong Kong is governed as a special administrative region in China according to the "one country, two systems" model proposed by paramount leader Deng Xiaoping in the early 1980s (Vogel 2012). Hong Kong is entitled a high degree of autonomy in all local governance areas except national defence and foreign affairs. Unlike Singapore, where the British parliamentary system is adopted though with modifications, the head and cabinet of the government in Hong Kong are not voted through universal suffrage. For the government lacking democratic credentials without much public participation in governance, it has limited capacity in garnering popular support for implementing policies, such as new 334 (3-year junior secondary, 3-year senior secondary, and 4-year undergraduate education) academic structure (Education and Manpower Bureau 2005) and MNE. The weaker power of the state in Hong Kong can be revealed in the sluggish and inefficient process of policymaking for a considerable amount of time has to be spent on public consultation, which is seen as a means to legitimize the government's decisions and policies. Nevertheless, it should be noted that there is a greater degree of the freedom of press, speech and assembly in Hong Kong as compared with Singapore where mainstream media is heavily influenced by the state. This contributes to more vocal criticisms in Hong Kong against controversial policies for the government's performance is scrutinized by mass media and stakeholders including political parties, teachers' unions, and pressure groups.

These contextual similarities and differences should be taken into account in comparing curriculum developments and reforms in Singapore and Hong Kong. In the following section, the similarities and differences of the curriculum policies and reforms in Singapore and Hong Kong are compared.

Policies

Since the 1990s, education reforms in both Singapore and Hong Kong have aimed at equipping students with competencies to cope with global societal and economic changes. Considering information and knowledge as the driving forces for the global economy and future socio-economic developments, both curriculum and pedagogic reforms have been deemed critical. One of the most important tasks of curriculum reform is to get rid of the culture of rote-learning, which used to prevail in Asian schooling systems, including Singapore and Hong Kong, and stifled the cultivation of creative and critical thinking skills that are considered the key to success in the global knowledge economy. Comprehensive reviews were carried out to look for solutions to weaknesses of the education systems, resulting in numerous reform initiatives proposed by both the Singapore and Hong Kong governments at the turn of the new millennium.

Moving Towards Ability-Driven Curriculum

In 1998, the Singapore government set up the Singapore 21 Committee to map out the directions of development for the city-state in the twenty-first century. The committee's report affirmed that the education system should provide new opportunities for people to pursue learning on a lifelong basis and students should be inculcated with a spirit of curiosity and continual learning (Singapore 21 Committee 1999). This echoed proposals in a seminal speech by then Prime Minister Goh Chok Tong in 1997 about the need to produce and use knowledge to transform schools as model learning organizations and to teach students critical and innovative thinking and problem-solving skills under the notion of "Thinking Schools, Learning Nation" (TSLN) (1997). Similarly in Hong Kong, the education reforms were launched shortly after 1997 "to create more room for schools, teachers and students, to offer all-round and balanced learning opportunities, and to lay the foundation for lifelong learning" (Education Commission 2000, p. 1). The reforms were aimed at developing Hong Kong into a society that values lifelong learning with the notion of "Learning for Life, Learning through Life" (Education Commission 2000). The promotion of the lifelong learning idea is in line with the transformation towards the knowledge-based society which requires manpower to be equipped with up-to-date knowledge and skills for maintaining global economic competitiveness.

In Singapore, a curriculum review in 1998 pointed out that the existing curriculum was overcrowded and content should be reduced to make room for more interaction-based teaching and learning strategies, such as project work and extra-curricular activities, so as to meet the needs and interests of students and also to cultivate an enthusiasm for lifelong learning (Ministry of Education 1998). This curriculum review was followed by the reform of the junior college system, aimed at providing students a broader and flexible curriculum. This was resulted in the launch of the Integrated Programme (IP), which allows high achieving secondary school students to proceed to junior colleges without taking the O-Level Examination (Ministry of Education 2002). In 2005, the Teach Less, Learn More (TLLM) initiatives were introduced by the Ministry of Education to put more emphasis on the quality but not quantity of the curriculum contents in order to nurture critical thinking, creativity, and a spirit of innovation and enterprise, and develop a core set of life skills and attitudes among students, teachers and school leaders. TLLM, which refers to reducing the amount of content in the curriculum, is aimed to shift the focus from "quantity" to "quality" in education. The old practices of rote-learning and repetitive tests should be replaced by more classroom interaction, opportunities for expression, the learning of lifelong skills and the building of character through innovative and effective pedagogical approaches and strategies (Shanmugaratnam 2005).

The latest development in the curriculum reform in Singapore is marked by the formation of the Curriculum 2015 (C2015) Committee with a stress on the development of thinking, communication, collaboration and management skills, which are referred as "21st century skills," and also the building up of students as confident students, self-directed learners, concern citizens and active contributors to the Singapore society (Ministry of Education 2008). C2015 focuses on the imparting of new skill sets and character traits of students (Ng 2008). This prompted reviews on primary and secondary education. The Primary Education Review and Implementation Committee recommended that greater emphasis be placed on the cultivation of soft-skills and a stepping back from formal examination in the local grades. Schools are encouraged to put more emphasis on building students' confidence and desire to learn. Teachers are required to provide more feedback on students' development in academic and non-academic areas and not to focus on grades alone (Ministry of Education 2009). In 2010, the Secondary Education Review and Implementation (SERI) Committee recommended that secondary education should give students a wider range of experiences and opportunities to develop the skills and values they need for a productive life. The committee also recommended the strengthening of character and citizenship education in the secondary school curriculum in order to inculcate values, competencies and skills among students to develop as useful citizens. Although more attention would be placed on the non-academic performance of students, the SERI Committee stressed that English Language and Mathematics teaching remained fundamental to the curriculum and would be strengthened (Ministry of Education 2010; also see Chap. 2).

In Hong Kong, the curriculum reforms are aimed at building a lifelong learning society, improving the overall academic performance of students, allowing more diversity in the schooling system, including modes of educational finance and curriculum focus, creating an inspiring learning environment, acknowledging the importance of moral education, and developing an education system which is rich in tradition but cosmopolitan and culturally diverse (Education Commission 2000). In fact, much more attention has been placed on the senior secondary school curriculum reforms because of the policy of the 334 academic structure and the revamping of the public examination system since the mid-2000s (Education and Manpower Bureau 2005). A new Hong Kong Diploma of Secondary Education (HKDSE), which takes over the Hong Kong Certificate of Education Examination and the Hong Kong Advanced Level of Examination, would be made the public examination for Secondary six leavers in Hong Kong from 2012 onwards.

Under the new academic structure, all students would be able to receive 6 years of secondary school education. The new senior secondary curriculum framework comprises three components. First, students are required to take four core subjects, including Chinese Language, English Language, Mathematics, and Liberal Studies. Second, they are required to take two to three elective subjects. Third, senior secondary students need to acquire non-academic experiences for personal development with a wide coverage of moral and civic education, community service, work-related experiences, and aesthetic and physical or sporting activities. Among these changes as mentioned above, the most significant change in the senior secondary curriculum is the introduction of the new subject, Liberal Studies as a core requirement for all students, who are expected to be able to grasp a better understanding about Hong Kong society, modern China, and globalization and have developed a range of lifelong learning skills, including critical thinking skills, creativity, and problem-solving skills (Curriculum Development Council and Hong Kong Examinations and Assessment Authority 2007).

Emphasizing National Education

Apart from stressing the importance of innovation, critical thinking and problem-solving skills in order to prepare globalized citizens in the age of globalization, the curriculum reforms in Singapore and Hong Kong are also commonly concerned about issues related to the needs of national and social development such as the transmission of social norms and basic values, and the cultivation of a sense of national belonging and loyalties.

In response to challenges from the rise of individualism and materialism as a global trend, the Singapore government has also sought to strengthen younger Singaporeans' sense of national belonging and thus develop national cohesion through the National Education (NE) programme since 1997 (Lee 1997). The NE programme aims to foster Singaporean identity, pride and self-respect, to teach about Singapore's nation-building successes against the odds, to understand Singapore's unique developmental challenges, constraints and vulnerabilities, and to instill core values such as meritocracy and multiracialism in order to protect the long-term interests of all Singaporeans (Tan 2008). The Social Studies curriculum also covers issues related to Singapore's governance principles and the roles of key institutions such as the Singapore Armed Forces, Housing Development Board, and Central Provident Fund (Lee 1997). More recently, the NE programme has been integrated with co-curricular activities and the Civic and Moral Education curriculum into a new CCE curriculum. Under the new CCE curriculum framework, schools will explore the ways to better infuse values education in such subjects as the Mother Tongue Languages and literature lessons in order to better achieve the objectives of the NE programme. The importance of curriculum development in preserving racial harmony, social stability and national unity is vividly reflected in the implementation of the NE programme in 1997 and the introduction of the CCE curriculum in 2011 (Heng 2011; also see Chaps. 2, 5, and 14).

In Hong Kong, curriculum development is similarly characterized by a growing emphasis on moral and civic education to develop students' character and interpersonal skills and cultivate a sense of social responsibility and commitment. For moral and civic education, the focus is placed on the promotion of Chinese history and culture as a means for the construction of a national identity and civic commitment among students (Curriculum Development Council 2000). In 2011, the government proposed the introduction of a MNE curriculum, which aims to provide citizenship and moral education with sufficient coverage of developments in China since 1949. The objective of national education is to instill in students positive values to facilitate identity building and thus develop affection for the country (Curriculum Development Council 2011, 2012). Nevertheless, some critics contend that the proposed MNE curriculum does not offer a fair representation of events and views of different stakeholders on socio-political developments in Hong Kong and the Chinese Mainland.

From the above, the curriculum policies and reforms in Singapore and Hong Kong are not only aimed at catering for the needs of global knowledge economy, but also serving local or national interests as revealed from the latest policies on consolidating the national education programmes. In this sense, both global and local issues simultaneously affect the design and implementation of the curriculum in the two city-states.

Balancing Centre-Based and School-Based Curriculum Development

Moreover, what is common in both Singapore and Hong Kong is that the functions of the school curriculum are now seen in a more expansive manner (Heng 2011). This is due to the much stronger societal expectations, due in part to the emergence of more fluid societal dynamics and the risk society we alluded to earlier, concerning how the school curriculum can contribute to societal development and to the needs of all individuals and stakeholders. The conceptions of the school curriculum, as Kennedy (2005) suggests, are now multifaceted and should be viewed from non-educational perspectives as well. The school curriculum has a cultural function to ensure the transmission of valuable cultural norms to the next generation. At the personal level, individuals are expected to benefit from the school curriculum for it provides them for their intrinsic needs. The vocational function of the school curriculum is to enable students to participate actively in the world of work. For its social function, the school curriculum should ensure students are equipped with the knowledge, skills and values to contribute to social harmony. From the economic perspective, the school curriculum is expected to enable students to attain productive capacity for improving their economic chances (Kennedy 2005, p. 41). While the school curriculum serves multiple ends and purposes as viewed from educational and non-educational perspectives, the developmental directions and orientations of the school curriculum are inevitably influenced by different stakeholders whose concerns and interests may appear to be divergent. There is, however, a common belief that the school curriculum should support young people in preparing themselves for an uncertain future in tandem with growing risks in the era of globalization.

Apart from striking a balance between different stakeholders' interests in planning and reforming the school curriculum, there have been growing concerns about how the needs and varied learning abilities of individual students can be more adequately catered for with the practice of school-based curriculum development (Kennedy 2005, p. 95). Schools and teachers are increasingly being allowed more autonomy to "articulate their own visions and goals of teaching, develop their own curriculum materials in the light of their visions and goals, and put the materials into practice with students" but they need to adhere to curriculum goals and instructional guidelines developed at the national or state level (Deng 2010, p. 385). Besides the trend of customizing curriculum, pedagogy, and assessment according to students' profiles, interests, abilities and talents from bottom-up, there has been a strong emphasis on national, citizenship, moral and value education with the ongoing reviews and reforms of the existing school curriculum from top-down in Singapore and Hong Kong (Heng 2011; Lee 1997; Ministry of Education 2008; Curriculum Development Council 2011, 2012). Thus, school curriculum developments in Singapore and Hong Kong have been simultaneously decentralized and centralized in seeking a balance between different stakeholders' interests.

Citizenship/Value Education Policies in Context

While there are many language-in-education policies and curriculum aspects that would provide a focus for comparison, citizenship/value education is chosen as our focus for analysis. State character, degree of legitimacy and strength would have a bearing on how state-citizen relations are constructed and schools used as sites for identity construction. Singapore, a fully sovereign state, is much more multi-ethnic and linguistically diverse than Hong Kong and this too could be expected to have an impact on how language, citizenship and values curricula are positioned and developed.

Singapore

Singapore's education legacy from the colonial period was a segmented school system, with unsettled issues over the place of language and culture; an immigrant mentality pervaded and the bulk of the population was alienated from the English-speaking elite. A short-lived merger heightened ethnic consciousness and Indonesian hostility to merger increased feelings of vulnerability and insecurity. Clearly, apart from having the schools help in building a skilled labour force, schools had to be used as sites for identity formation and building social cohesion (Gopinathan 1974).

Though Singapore's leading political party, the PAP, struggled for dominance with other left-leaning parties at the beginning, by the end of the 1960s, it had become the dominant party. A clear vision for Singapore's future – a united, equal society, an industrial economy, meritocratic, efficient government, and a capacity to grow the economy and vastly improve infrastructure, among others, helped cement its legitimacy and power. The *Report of the All-Party Committee of the Singapore Legislative Assembly on Chinese Education* in 1956 led the efforts to address issues of multilingualism, cultural identity and the role of English. Its principles of "equality of treatment" and bilingualism with English as a neutral link language and economically important language and the mother tongues as heritage languages rooting future citizens in ancestral traditions, values and norms went a long way in meeting majority aspirations. From 1965 onwards there were determined efforts to faithfully implement the equality of treatment principle. English's economic value was quickly and readily grasped. It was proved harder to maintain enthusiasm for mother tongue learning as Singapore becomes more cosmopolitan. While the politics has been taken out of language-in-education issues, curriculum and pedagogy remain contentious. Nevertheless, a major socio-linguistic shift has occurred over the past three decades, as indicated by a majority of households now reporting that English is a major medium of communication; dialect use has declined considerably (also see Chaps. 2 and 14).

It is useful for analytical purposes to separate values education from citizenship education. Early values education curricula, for example, Education for Living and later Being and Becoming were non-controversial, emphasizing as they did the importance of nation-building, responsibilities and duties, valuing cultural traditions and respecting difference (see Gopinathan 2012). Policymakers were always aware of the potential of ethnic diversity to divide as well as the energizing potential of being inheritors of long enduring cultural traditions. In an effort to place values education on a more solid foundation, the government introduced a Religious Knowledge curriculum in 1982. The development of the curriculum, teacher preparation, and pedagogy were all difficult and against a background of increased religious activity, nationally and internationally, the programme was withdrawn in 1989 (Gopinathan 1995; Tan 1997). More recently, there has been an emphasis on character education (see Chap. 14).

The curriculum development for citizenship education has been more contested, not surprising given political contestation over merger with Malaysia and differing conceptions of the future Singapore state. By the mid-1970s the PAP were firmly in power and able to develop unchallenged a meta-narrative of Singapore's birth, vulnerabilities and principles to ensure survival. The PAP's ability to deliver a steady rise in living standards and social mobility gave it unchallenged and hegemonic power – it also led to a compliant citizenry, the loss of voice and agency and disinterest in politics, and the nation's history. The curriculum response to this was National Education launched in 1997 and supplemented by revisions to Social Studies and History curricula. Though intended, in line with the TSLN vision to assist in the development of a thinking, questioning but Singapore-committed citizenry, it is not yet clear how successful this has been. Research studies have indicated uncritical acceptance of the PAP's version of history (Ho 2010), a passive citizenship orientation (Sim and Print 2009), and lack of subjective nationhood (Hogan 2011). Yet in the 2011 General Election, young Singaporeans were active participants, and involved in the political process as never before. Since then, there has been a trend of re-politicization in the Singapore society especially for well-educated and post-65ers, who were born after 1965, have become more politically conscious so as to serve as a proper check and balance to the power and authority enjoyed by the PAP as the ruling party (Da Cunha 2011). There is also now a growing literature on alternative conceptions of Singapore's historical journey (Hong and Huang 2008). Additionally, concerns over growing income inequality and reduced social mobility, and the PAP's admission of policy mistakes are likely to create conditions for a revision of the purpose and character of citizenship education (also see Chap. 2).

Hong Kong

Similar to Singapore, Hong Kong was a British colony and an important node in Britain's maritime empire. It is nowadays one of Asia's financial hubs and economic powerhouses, a major financial centre and to some extent mirrors Singapore's economic role in Southeast Asia with its proximity to the Chinese mainland. As mentioned earlier, the most fundamental difference between Singapore and Hong Kong is that the latter is not a sovereign state but part of China and it is far less diverse ethnically. The political agreement between China and the UK in 1984 led to Hong Kong's integration with China on 1 July 1997 with its legal status defined in the Sino-British Joint Declaration, which allows Hong Kong as a Special Administrative Region (SAR) in China to maintain this status for 50 years with substantial degrees of political activism, rights, and rule of law in accordance with the "one country, two systems" principle. As stipulated in the Basic Law, Hong Kong's mini constitution, the Hong Kong SAR Government is free to formulate policies regarding education, curriculum, and public examinations as appropriate for Hong Kong conditions without any interference from the central government in Beijing.

Given Hong Kong more homogeneous makeup, there has been less emphasis on social cohesion issues as the fault lines of race and religion are not so impactful in Hong Kong. As with Singapore, in an earlier period there has been contestation over language-in-education policies. Cantonese is an important marker of Hong Kong's cultural identity, English proficiency is desired for the occupational and social mobility it brings while Mandarin is the national language of China. It is therefore not surprising that there has been widespread concerns over the declaration of Cantonese as the medium of instruction in a majority of secondary schools in Hong Kong in 1998, while only slightly over a 100 out of around 500 secondary schools were allowed to use English as the medium of instruction (Tsui 2004). The differentiation between Cantonese-medium and English-medium secondary schools strengthened the general perception that English-medium schools had better academic standards and were considered more selective and elitist than a majority of Cantonese-medium ones. This situation caused the government to fine-tune the medium of instruction policy in 2011 to allow secondary schools more autonomy to offer both Cantonese-medium and English-medium classes in response to students' needs. At the same time, there has been more emphasis on the use of Mandarin as the teaching and learning language of subjects like Chinese language in line with the growing importance and popularity of the language in the global, regional and local economy.

It is in the area of citizenship/national education that there is most disagreement. The objective of national education is to instill schoolchildren positive values to facilitate identity building and thus develop affection for the country. The coverage is generally positive and sensitive political events like the June Fourth Incident in 1989 are glossed over. Liberal Studies of the HKDSE curriculum is already considered a major tool for cultivating a sense of national identity and belonging, in addition to deepening their understanding about the developments in Hong Kong. The proposed introduction of a separate subject, MNE, on top of Liberal Studies at the senior secondary level has aroused widespread concerns, particularly among school teachers and principals over whether the two subjects overlap with each other and it is worthy for teachers and students to spend extra time and efforts on studying the non-examinable MNE subject.

In addition, some critics contend that the proposed MNE curriculum does not offer a fair representation of events and views of different stakeholders on socio-political developments in Hong Kong and the mainland. For Hong Kong citizens used to open and robust political debate with considerable space for political activism, the fear is that the curriculum would not lead to the development of an informed citizenry, capable of looking at the evidence and making up their minds; rather, there will be an exorable trend towards "mainlandization," "mainlandism," and mainland style patriotic education, eventually leading to a diminution of rights in Hong Kong. Surveys conducted by the two major teachers' trade unions in Hong Kong, namely the Professional Teachers' Union and the Federation of Education Workers, demonstrate strong reluctance among teachers to work on the proposed MNE curriculum which is widely deemed not well-prepared and without sufficient training and support for teachers to spend teach the new subject. The Catholic Diocese of Hong Kong has also opposed the MNE proposal. Cardinal Joseph Zen sees the proposed curriculum as an effort to "brainwash students … into mainland style patriotic education" (Chong 2011).

Others see an implied criticism that Hong Kong citizens and youngsters are not patriotic enough and thus MNE is an attempt "to develop positive values and attitudes so as to facilitate identity building through developing "affection for the country." Though the subject will not be formally examined in schools or public examinations, one suggested technique is peer evaluating each other to see if they have demonstrated the desirable qualities of a national citizen. Because of strong opposition from schools and teachers, the formal launch of the proposed MNE curriculum would be delayed until the 2015–2016 academic year (Chong 2012). In April 2012, after the public consultation process, the guidelines of the MNE curriculum were finalized by the Curriculum Development Council and recommended to the Education Bureau for implementation. According to the guidelines, apart from making students to be more patriotic towards China, teachers can teach students global values as democracy, equality, freedom and justice and also guide students to have discussion rationally about challenges and problems in the politico-socio-economic developments in China (Curriculum Development Council 2012).

In Hong Kong, according to Morris and Adamson (2010), some education policies like civic and moral education should be considered as examples of symbolic policies, which refer to the confined role of the government to promote changes at the policy level while the implementation of those policies would be left to individual schools. While the government would provide guidelines on how the topics and themes to be incorporated and approached within the existing curriculum, it is individual schools which are responsible to decide how to implement the policies and changes proposed by the government. For civic and moral education is not part of the examined curriculum, it is more likely for schools to ignore the guidelines and the responsibility of implementation is eventually passed to nobody as teachers would consider this is merely an extra workload imposed from top-down without the entitlement of additional financial and manpower assistance. It is suspected that the proposed MNE curriculum may induce even more resistance from teachers, who tend to think that it is because of the political pressure induced from Beijing to "brainwash" students with patriotism without critical thinking skills. In addition to other cases showing the ineffectiveness of the government to implement education policies like the medium of instruction policy and its failure to regulate the prices of school textbooks, it is not surprising that stakeholders tend to resist whatever the government, which does not have strong political mandate, decides even though there are strong rationales behind those policies.

In fact, this situation pinpoints a major difference between the effectiveness of the formulation and implementation of policies concerning citizenship/value education between Singapore and Hong Kong. In Singapore, because of the political status as an independent nation which has long been influenced by the state's call for crisis mentality and self-reliance and the ruling party is elected through popular votes, this provides a stronger foundation for the state in Singapore to make public policies without facing much resistance provided the policymakers are entrusted by the people to take care of the national interests. On the contrary, in Hong Kong, the government is not popularly elected and it can enjoy a very limited degree of political legitimacy which occasionally hampers the confidence of the general public about the effectiveness of policies proposed by the government. Even public consultation as a means for the government to collect opinions from the general public, they are more likely deemed to be a ritual which has very limited effect on enhancing the public acceptance of policies. The weak state power in Hong Kong is not only a result of the lack of political legitimacy and mandate to govern, but also because it needs to cater for political needs of the central government in Beijing even though the government is supposed to run on the "one country, two systems" principle. What is more important is effective policy implementation needs an efficient and effective government which can waste no time in dealing with conflicts and controversies in society.

Conclusion

Our analysis has shown that curriculum developments in Singapore and Hong Kong are shaped by globalization and by local political and economic factors. The curriculum remains a main agent of socialization in both societies. Traditional values remain important for both societies in Singapore and Hong Kong in the face of globalization challenges revealed in the rise of individualism and materialism. While global trends such as twenty-first century skills prevail in both city-states, policymaking and implementation of the school curriculum continues to be responsive to local contexts and needs. In both societies, curriculum reform has been incremental in nature, building on strong foundations and high academic achievement. In both societies, while there is now a greater role for teachers and less central prescription, the state remains the principal curriculum actor. As we indicated in our case study of value and citizenship education, the legitimacy and strength of the state vis-à-vis stakeholders will have an impact on how well curriculum implementation proceeds at the school and classroom level. While implementation has been smooth in Singapore, the frequency of revisions and constant emphasis on the importance of CCE/NE perhaps indicates some unease about effectiveness. In Hong Kong's case, the reform itself is being challenged and the motives for introducing it are suspect with some key stakeholders, including school management, teachers, parents and pressure groups like teachers' trade unions. This is likely to make school-level implementation more difficult and outcomes less satisfactory.

Last but not least, an important lesson which can be learnt from the comparison of the curriculum policies and reforms in Singapore and Hong Kong is that the notion of "thinking global, staying local" applies in both city-states. There was not a retreat of the state in the field of educational governance, which covers the design, formulation and implementation of curriculum, but strong will upheld by the governments in both city-states to revitalize and reinforce the needs of national, civic, moral and value education. This ensures the younger generation to make sacrifices for the sake of local or national interests in favour of economic growth, politico-social progress and stability, and racial harmony as shown in the case of Singapore, where one of the aims of education is to integrate students into society and make them Singaporeans (Gopinathan 1988). The notion of striking a balance between global and local reflects that local interests would never been forsaken entirely by global trends. Moreover, the latest state intervention in the free global market amidst the global economic crisis in the late 2000s makes it clear that the state remains crucial in dealing with risks and instability induced from economic globalization, which in turn affects the fate of individual countries or economies.

References

Beck, U. (1992). *Risk society: Towards a new modernity*. Thousand Oaks: Sage.
Bottery, M. (2000). *Education, policy and ethics*. London: Continuum.
Cerny, P. (1990). *The changing architecture of politics: Structure, agency, and the future of the state*. Thousand Oaks: Sage.

Chan, H. (1971). *Singapore: The politics of survival 1965–1967*. Singapore: Oxford University Press.

Chong, D. (2012). National education subject to be delayed. *South China Morning Post*, 26 January.

Chong, T. (2011). Zen criticizes agenda. *South China Morning Post*, 27 September.

Chubb, J., & Moe, T. (1990). *Politics, markets & America's schools*. Washington, DC: The Brookings Institution.

Curriculum Development Council. (2000). *Learning to learn: The way forward in curriculum development – Consultation document*. Hong Kong: The Government Printer.

Curriculum Development Council. (2011). *Moral and national education: Curriculum guide (Primary 1 to Secondary 6) – Consultation draft*. Hong Kong: Curriculum Development Council.

Curriculum Development Council. (2012). *Moral and national education: Curriculum guide (Primary 1 to Secondary 6)*. Hong Kong: Curriculum Development Council.

Curriculum Development Council and Hong Kong Examinations and Assessment Authority. (2007). *Liberal studies curriculum and assessment guide (Secondary 4–6)*. Hong Kong: Education and Manpower Bureau.

Da Cunha, D. (2011). *Breakthrough: Roadmap for Singapore's political future*. Singapore: Straits Times Press.

Dale, R. (2000). Globalization: A new world for comparative education? In J. Schriewer (Ed.), *Discourse formation in comparative education* (pp. 87–109). Berlin: Peter Lang.

Daun, H. (2002). Globalization and national education systems. In H. Daun (Ed.), *Educational restructuring in the context of globalization and national policy* (pp. 1–31). New York: Routledge Falmer.

Deng, Z. (2010). Curriculum planning and systems change. In P. Peterson, E. Baker, & B. McGraw (Eds.), *International encyclopedia of education* (Vol. 1, pp. 384–389). Oxford: Elsevier.

Education and Manpower Bureau. (2005). *The new academic structure for senior secondary education and higher education: Action plan for investing in the future of Hong Kong*. Hong Kong: Education and Manpower Bureau.

Education Commission. (2000). *Learning for life, learning through life: Reform proposals for the education system in Hong Kong*. Hong Kong: The Government Printer.

Friedman, T. (2005). *The world is flat: A brief history of the globalized world in the 21st century*. New York: Penguin.

Giddens, A. (1991). *The consequences of modernity*. Cambridge: Polity Press.

Giddens, A. (1999). *Runaway world: How globalization is reshaping our lives*. London: Profile Books.

Goh. C. (1997). Speech by Prime Minister Goh Chok Tong at the opening of the 7th International Conference on Thinking on 2 June: Shaping our future – Thinking schools, learning nation. Singapore: Ministry of Education.

Goh, C., & Gopinathan, S. (2008). The development of education in Singapore since 1965. In S. Lee, C. Goh, B. Fredriksen, & J. Tan (Eds.), *Toward a better future: Education and training for economic development in Singapore since 1965* (pp. 12–38). Washington, DC/Singapore: The World Bank/National Institute of Education, Nanyang Technological University.

Gopinathan, S. (1974). *Towards a national education system in Singapore 1945–1973*. Singapore: Oxford University Press.

Gopinathan, S. (1988). Being and becoming: Education for values in Singapore. In W. Cummings, S. Gopinathan, & Y. Tomada (Eds.), *The revival of values education in Asia and the West* (pp. 131–145). Oxford: Pergamon.

Gopinathan, S. (1995). Religious education in a secular state: The Singapore experience. *Asian Journal of Political Science, 3*(2), 15–27.

Gopinathan, S. (1999). Preparing for the next rung: Economic restructuring and educational reform in Singapore. *Journal of Education and Work, 12*(3), 295–308.

Gopinathan, S. (2012). *Are we all global citizens now? Reflections on citizenship and citizenship education in a globalising world (with special reference to Singapore)*. Hong Kong: Centre for Governance and Citizenship, The Hong Kong Institute of Education.

Gopinathan, S., & Sharpe, L. (2004). New bearings for citizenship education in Singapore. In W. Lee, D. Grossman, K. Kennedy, & G. Fairbrother (Eds.), *Citizenship education in Asia and the Pacific: Concepts and issues* (pp. 119–131). Hong Kong/Norwell: Comparative Education Research Centre, The University of Hong Kong/Kluwer Academic.

Green, A. (1997). *Education, globalization and the nation state*. Basingstoke: Macmillan.

Heng, S. (2011). Opening address by Mr. Heng Swee Keat, Minister for Education, at the Ministry of Education work plan seminar, on 22 September. Singapore: Ministry of Education.

Ho, L. (2010). Don't worry, I'm not going to report you: Education for citizenship in Singapore. *Theory and Research in Social Education, 38*(2), 298–316.

Hogan, D. (2011). *Interim report on instructional practices in Singapore in secondary 3 Mathematics and English*. Singapore: Unpublished manuscript, National Institute of Education

Hong, L., & Huang, J. (2008). *The scripting of a national history: Singapore and its pasts*. Hong Kong: Hong Kong University Press.

Kennedy, K. (2005). *Changing schools for changing times: New directions for the school curriculum in Hong Kong*. Hong Kong: The Chinese University Press.

Lee, H. (1997). *Speech by BG Lee Hsien Loong, Deputy Prime Minister at the launch of national education on 17 May: National education*. Singapore: Ministry of Education.

Lee, K. (2000). *From third world to first: The Singapore story, 1965–2000*. New York: HarperCollins.

Ministry of Education. (1979). *Report of the Ministry of Education (1978)*. Singapore: Ministry of Education.

Ministry of Education. (1998). *Learning, creating, communicating: A curriculum review*. Singapore: Ministry of Education.

Ministry of Education. (2002). *Report of the junior college/upper secondary education review committee*. Singapore: Ministry of Education.

Ministry of Education. (2008). *Recent developments in Singapore's education system: Gearing up for 2015*. Paper presented at International Education Leaders' Dialogue: Third conference. Singapore: Ministry of Education.

Ministry of Education. (2009). *Report of the primary education review and implementation committee*. Singapore: Ministry of Education.

Ministry of Education. (2010). *Report of the secondary education review and implementation committee*. Singapore: Ministry of Education.

Morris, P., & Adamson, B. (2010). *Curriculum, schooling and society in Hong Kong*. Hong Kong: Hong Kong University Press.

Ng, E.H. (2008). Speech by Dr. Ng Eng Hen, Minister for Education and Second Minister for Defence, at the Ministry of Education work plan seminar 2008, on 25 September. Singapore: Ministry of Education.

Quah, J. (1991). *In search of Singapore's national values*. Singapore: Times Academic Press.

Rizvi, F., & Lingard, B. (2010). *Globalizing education policy*. London: Routledge.

Shanmugaratnam, T. (2005). Speech by Mr. Tharman Shanmugaratnam, Minister for Education, at the Ministry of Education work plan seminar 2005. 22 September. Singapore: Ministry of Education.

Sim, J., & Print, M. (2009). The State, teachers and citizenship education in Singapore Schools. *British Journal of Educational Studies, 57*(4), 380–399.

Singapore 21 Committee. (1999). *Singapore 21: Together, we make the difference*. Singapore: Singapore 21 Committee, Prime Minister Office, The Government of Singapore.

Tan, J. (1997). The rise and fall of religious knowledge in Singapore secondary schools. *Journal of Curriculum Studies, 29*(5), 603–624.

Tan, J. (2008). Whither national education? In J. Tan & P. Ng (Eds.), *Thinking schools, learning nation: Contemporary issues and challenges* (pp. 72–86). Singapore: Prentice Hall.

Tsui, A. (2004). Medium of instruction in Hong Kong: One country, two systems, whose language? In J. Tollefson & A. Tsui (Eds.), *Medium of instruction policies: Which agenda? Whose agenda?* (pp. 97–116). Mahwah: Lawrence Erlbaum Associates.

Turnbull, C. (2005). *A history of modern Singapore, 1819–2005*. Singapore: NUS Press.

Vogel, E. (2012). *Deng Xiaoping and the transformation of China*. Cambridge: Belknap Press of Harvard University Press.

Chapter 14
The Development of a Future-Oriented Citizenship Curriculum in Singapore: Convergence of Character and Citizenship Education and Curriculum 2015

Wing On Lee

Introduction

Curriculum is a broad concept, and there are varied approaches in examining its features. First, curriculum is in general and often referred to as an organisation of study, defined in terms of planned teaching and learning experiences for students, prepared as a set of subjects, a set of materials, a sequence of courses, a course of study, and/or a set of performance objectives. At times it is referred to as syllabus, content outline, textbooks, and sometimes even teaching materials (Oliva 1992; Marsh 1997; Posner 1998). Second, curriculum can be perceived as a learning orientation. From this perspective, Eisner and Vallance (1974) point out that there are five types of curriculum orientations: cognitive process orientation, self-actualization orientation, technological orientation, academic-rationalist orientation and social reconstructionist orientation. Longstreet and Shane (1993) identify four types of curriculum orientations, namely society-oriented curriculum, student-oriented curriculum, knowledge-oriented curriculum and eclectic curriculum. The latter looks at curriculum from the broadest possible perspective that involves various compromises related to the purpose and process of teaching and learning. Third, curriculum can be understood in terms of school operation. From this perspective, Esiner (1994) alleges that there are three types of curriculum: official curriculum (or formal curriculum), operational curriculum (implemented curriculum), and hidden curriculum. The hidden curriculum, one that transmits implicit social norms and political expectations in an implicit way as a part of school life, is well known for its close relationship to citizenship education, particularly in respect to political socialization (MacDonald 1977).

These different definitions show that rather than being simply an organisation of study, the nature and function of curriculum has been understood broadly and

W.O. Lee (✉)
National Institute of Education, Nanyang Technological University, Singapore
e-mail: wingon.lee@nie.edu.sg

Z. Deng et al. (eds.), *Globalization and the Singapore Curriculum: From Policy to Classroom*, Education Innovation Series, DOI 10.1007/978-981-4451-57-4_14,
© Springer Science+Business Media Singapore 2013

variably, often in terms of its contextual function, and the social and political contexts in particular. These broader perspectives are expressed sometimes in terms of the stakeholders (such as students) involved in the education system; sometimes in terms of the knowledge to be learned and how it is to be learned (such as seeing school subjects as disciplines but also valuing the technological aspect of learning); and sometimes in terms of the context of learning (such as the school, the society, and the political system within which the curriculum operates). When curriculum is discussed in contextual terms, its linkage to citizenship education becomes more salient, especially in its social reconstructionist functions. Further, curriculum is generally perceived as explicit, tangible and content specific in the course of learning, but it can also be invisible and intangible, subsumed in the school life and even the society's political atmosphere that both the teachers and students experience every day.

According to Williams (1976), the school curriculum is never ad hoc, but a kind of selectivity, being coined as a selective tradition, or as selection from the larger culture (Giroux 1981). The selectivity is an intentional activity, representing the way in which from a whole possible area of past and present, certain meanings and practices are chosen for emphasis, and certain other meanings and practices are neglected and excluded. In this way, school also becomes an agent of cultural incorporation, initiating the younger generation into selected cultural traditions. Giroux (1981) concedes that school is reproductive in the cultural sense, functioning to distribute and legitimate forms of knowledge, values, languages, and modes of style that constitute the dominant culture and its interests. Freier (1974) further points out that education is a means of cultural action and schooling functions as a system of communicating a particular cultural message.

This broader perspective towards curriculum is described as "the institutional or policy curriculum" by Doyle (1992a, b). The institutional curriculum, or the policy curriculum, defines the connection between schooling and society, embodying a conception of what schooling should be with respect to the society and culture. Since social and cultural contexts often change rapidly, school systems always use the institutional curriculum as convenient instrument to communicate responsiveness to the outside communities.

The purpose of this chapter is to discuss how the broader social, political and economic situations may impact the curriculum in the making and how the larger environment will affect the discourse of the citizenship curriculum as reflected in the curriculum changes over time in Singapore. It also aims to identify the direction the citizenship curriculum is currently moving, and the conception and forms that it takes with reference to the development towards Curriculum 2015 (commonly known as "C2015"), a major curriculum reform initiative in Singapore.

The approach towards the analysis is adapted from the author's previous attempts of analysing citizenship curriculum development in China and Hong Kong. For example, based on Franklin (1989) framework on discourse shifts, Lee (2002) has analysed the shifts in moral education policies in the various periods of ideological debates (namely 1979–1989; 1980–1982; 1983–1984; 1985–1987; 1988–1989). Lee and Ho (2005, 2008) have identified further periods of analysis, (namely 1989–1991;

1992–1995; 1996–1999, and 2000 onward). In the main, these analyses captured the pendulum between liberalisation and conservatism, how further liberalisation progressed out of this pendulum, and how moral education policies changed that would reflect those changes in ideological debates in China. Likewise, the author has captured the debates during the political transition in Hong Kong in the years around 1997, when Hong Kong was returned to the Chinese sovereignty, and how the citizenship curriculum changed that would reflect the changing political circumstances of Hong Kong (Lee and Sweeting 2001; Lee 2008).

The Social, Political and Economic Context of Singapore

Some contextual features of Singapore are important to capture in order to understand the development of Singapore's citizenship education curriculum and the broader curriculum. The smallness of the city-state of 710 sq. km. with limited resources underlie many of the education policy decisions, particularly in its emphasis on talent as the most valuable resource, i.e. human resources, of the country. With a population of 5.08 million and a population density of 7,526 per km^2, Singapore is one of the most densely populated cities in the world, lower than Seoul and Tokyo but higher than Hong Kong. With a diversity of ethnicities (74.1 % Chinese, 13.4 % Malay, 9.2 % Indian and 3.3 % others), religions (e.g. Buddhism, Christianity, Islam, Taoism and Hinduism) and languages (such as Chinese, Malay and Tamil) being crammed together in this densely populated city-state, the social cohesion in diversity was naturally seen as an a priori citizenship education agenda of the country.

Being a small island adjacent to a large Malayan peninsula (or mainland), with a dense population and without natural resources, the nation from its start had to think of survival strategies, and how to create best talents from within and attract more from outside to make Singapore successful, beyond survival, as a world class city-state. And all these efforts of the nation have been very successful, as demonstrated by the various international studies such as TIMSS and PISA. Economically, Singapore is growing to become the "Capital of the World", with exponential and disproportional influence in the world economy as a country that is being seen as important far beyond its physical size, not in terms of land and population, but in terms of human capacity.

There are different interpretations of Singapore's development phases in education. A commonly cited framework as acknowledged by the Ministry of Education is: Survival-driven phase (1959–1978); efficiency-driven phase (1979–1996); and ability-driven, aspiration-driven phase (1997 to present) (MOE 2008; Mourshed et al. 2010; OECD 2010). Kwong et al. (1990) offer another classification: Conflict resolution and quantitative expansion (1946–1965); qualitative consolidation (1965–1978); refinements and new strides (1979–1984); and towards excellence in education (1985–1990). Although the period classifications are quite different, the development of Singapore from quantity to quality dimensions is quite clear, and that the system was refined and attuned to the needs of the times as well. This chapter will adopt the former framework for analysis as it is so commonly cited that it has almost become an official framing to understand Singapore's education development (see Tan 2005; Goh and Gopinathan 2006; OECD 2010).

The survival-driven phase (1957–1978) is characterised by the creation of a public national education system. The main thrust of educational provision in this phase was to produce trained workers in the early years of Singapore's independence and industrialisation. The expansion of education system was notably fast with the achievement of universal primary schooling in 1965 and lower secondary schooling in the early 1970s. The extension of education for every child was necessary both for nation building and for developing the industrial base of an export-oriented economy that would attract foreign manufacturers and would provide jobs for the people, also developing expertise for a manufacturing economy. The founding of the nation had to cope with an ethnically diverse population, and a bilingual policy was introduced so that children would learn English as a common language, but they would also learn their own languages to respect and inherit their own cultures (also see Chaps. 2, 5, and 13). However, the quantum of expansion was too fast for the whole population to cope with, with high dropout rates and low teacher morale. That led to the education reforms in the next phase (OECD 2010).

Educational development in the efficiency-driven phase (1979–1996) was mainly to fine tune the system to produce skilled workers for the economy in the most efficient way. At the same time the government projected manpower needs and trained people to fit into the jobs. The efficiency-driven phase was marked off by the 1978 Goh Report (1979a), which pointed out many issues in the education system. Particularly, the one-size-fits-all schooling should be modified towards multiple pathways to improve the quality of learning for all and students with diverse learning abilities, in order to reduce drop-out rates and produce more technically-skilled labour force to achieve new economic goals. In the main, the Curriculum Development Institute of Singapore (CDIS) was established in 1980 to produce high quality textbooks, a streaming system was introduced to enable differential learning, and the Institute of Technical Education (ITE) was established in 1992 to introduce technical and vocational education for the students who are less academically inclined but would become a more productive labour force for the industries (OECD 2010).

The ability-based, aspiration-driven phase began in 1997, a year with many implications for Singapore. The Asian financial crisis took place in 1997, and Singapore realised that the country had to move towards a global knowledge economy in order to be competitive in the world economy. In the same year, the government launched the "Thinking School, Learning Nation" agenda, which has become a fundamental change concept in Singapore's education reforms in the years that followed. In the same year, the Singapore 21 Committee was set up to explore Singapore's development agenda towards the twenty-first century, and the *Singapore 21 Report* was published in 1999, that shaped the development agenda towards globalization in Singapore. This phase was mainly characterized by the government's attempts to equip and prepare students to meet the challenges in the knowledge economy by taking into consideration of individual abilities and talents. The concept of intellectual capital emerged, and there was more provision of flexibility in the education system, such as introducing the integrated programme that would allow some students to move onto junior college education without going through "O" Level examinations, and the establishment of specialised schools in arts, physical education and technologies respectively to cater for students with diverse learning orientations (also see Chap. 2).

Kanagaratnam (2011) suggests that Year 2000 onwards could become another phase in Singapore to be characterized by the advent of the information age. With further development of ICT in the larger society and the school environment, the society has become more transparent, schools enjoy more autonomy in the school-based development agenda, teacher-led reforms are facilitated with the establishment of professional learning communities, and student-centric pedagogies emerge, with citizenship education to be balanced by character education that would focus on the individual (in respect to social emotional learning) and national education that would focus on citizenship.

Changes in the Citizenship Education Curriculum

The above sketch of the development phase would provide a framework for understanding changes in Singapore's citizenship education curriculum and the emergence of Curriculum 2015 that seems to converge with citizenship education goals for the future. Using a juxtaposition method for macro analysis (cf. Bereday 1969), it is telling just by listing out the citizenship education curriculums being introduced since 1959.

Figure 14.1 shows a list of the 12 citizenship education curriculums being introduced from 1959 to 2010, and the frequency of change in terms of time frame. It is

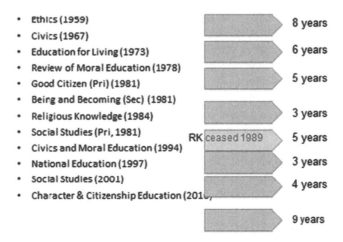

Fig. 14.1 Frequency of change in the citizenship education curriculum

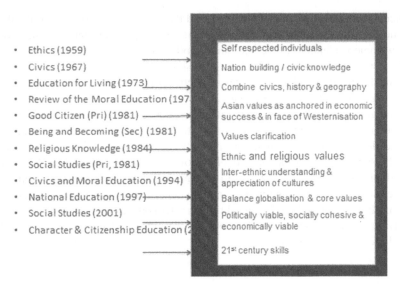

- Ethics (1959)   Self respected individuals
- Civics (1967)   Nation building / civic knowledge
- Education for Living (1973)   Combine civics, history & geography
- Review of the Moral Education (197   Asian values as anchored in economic
- Good Citizen (Pri) (1981)   success & in face of Westernisation
- Being and Becoming (Sec) (1981)   Values clarification
- Religious Knowledge (1984)   Ethnic and religious values
- Social Studies (Pri, 1981)   Inter-ethnic understanding &
- Civics and Moral Education (1994)   appreciation of cultures
- National Education (1997)   Balance globalisation & core values
- Social Studies (2001)   Politically viable, socially cohesive &
- Character & Citizenship Education (2   economically viable

                                                       21ˢᵗ century skills

Fig. 14.2 Change of values emphases in the citizenship education curriculum

easily observable that lots of changes have taken place in citizenship education, particularly with a new curriculum being introduced at an interval between 3 and 5 years during the efficiency-driven phase. A change of curriculum in an interval of 3 years is quite swift, as this almost means that as soon as one curriculum is introduced the planning for another one would start. It is therefore important to ask what the reasons for such swift changes are. It can only be understood from the changing social, economic and political conditions that have triggered such need for changes in the curriculum.

Figure 14.2 provides some insight to address the above question by identifying the changing values propositions and emphases in the course of curriculum change in citizenship education. As the figure shows, there are pendulum attempts in values emphases, moving between developing the individuals and the national citizens, between global values and national values, between combined/shared values and sub- ethnic or cultural values; and the latest change is towards character and citizenship education catering for the knowledge economy and for developing twenty-first century skills in order to prepare Singapore to face globalisation.

Figure 14.3 looks at the changing discourse in each education phase. Broadly speaking, the citizenship education curriculum can be characterized as firstly focusing on the good citizen (in the survival phase), secondly on respecting personal and ethnic and religious values but at the same time be mindful of the national values (in the efficiency phase), and thirdly towards character and citizenship education that focuses on social-emotional learning for the individuals, to be balanced by national concerns, in preparing the students to become critical and independent citizens for the knowledge economy.

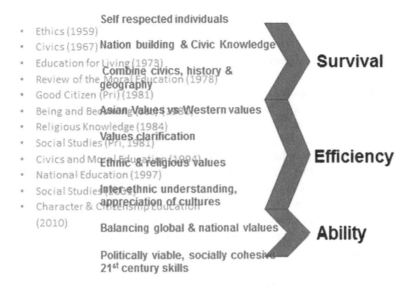

Fig. 14.3 Changing discourse in the citizenship education curriculum

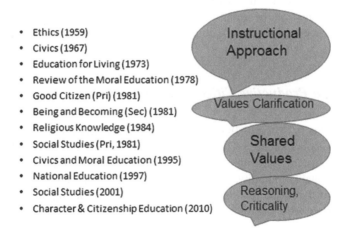

Fig. 14.4 Changing pedagogical approaches in the citizenship education curriculum

Figure 14.4 shows the changing emphases of pedagogical approaches in the course of curriculum change in citizenship education. The course of change in the citizenship education curriculum has impacted, or been reflected in, the different pursuance of citizenship pedagogies, from instructional approaches (e.g. Ethics and Civics), to values clarification (e.g. Being and Becoming), to emphasizing shared values (e.g. Civics and Moral Education and National Education), and recently, to be in accord with the agenda of the Thinking Schools and Learning Nation and for developing twenty-first century skills, towards reasoning and criticality (e.g. Social Studies and Character and Citizenship Education).

Becoming a Good Citizen for the New Nation

All these citizenship programmes were launched in view of the perceived societal needs of the time, and also as a response to some of the major issues of debate in the society. In 1959, Singapore gained full self-government, and *Ethics* was introduced to lay a good foundation for the newly built nation, by nurturing students to become 'self-respected individuals', 'good citizens', with 'good habits', 'right conduct', and the ability to uphold justice and to respect law and order (Sim 2005; Kanagaratnam 2011). In 1965, Singapore became an independent nation, and *Civics* was introduced in 1967 to replace *Ethics*, introducing such topics as the constitution, legislation and international relations, and such values as patriotism, loyalty and civic conscious-ness. It aimed to foster a sense of social and civic responsibility and a love for their country and its people, and was a response to the existing racial tensions as a factor of political instability for a new nation (Sim 2005; Kanagaratnam 2011). Moreover, *Civics* was taught as a part of the history and geography curriculum (Berlach 1996). In 1973, *Education for Living* was introduced to the primary schools. It was an attempt of proactive planning in face of the impending economic changes, and a means to bind people together, and to continue to ensure the country's survival and success. It also reflected the government's concern to develop in children a sense of national identity in the initial years of Singapore's independence. It was taught through an integrated subject, combining civics, history and geography.

Becoming a Productive Citizen for the Economy

Singapore in the 1970s and 1980s experienced rapid industrialisation and modernisation. Heightened economic and social interaction with Western economies also created heightened concern to position the Singapore values system in its interaction with the international community, and the discourse on Asian values emerged in this process. Two significant reports were published and both had significant impact on the development of citizenship education in Singapore, namely the Goh Keng Swee *Report on the Ministry of Education* (1979b) and Ong Teng Cheong *Report on Moral Education* (1979), which was published after a major review of moral education in 1978 (Chew 1998; Teo 2010; also see Chap. 2). The Goh and Ong Reports responded to the need of the times by emphasising the need to teach values that were responsible for economic success, that would bind people together, which was perceived as necessary to ensure the country's survival and success. The Reports identified a host of values regarded as important for these purposes, including habit formation (e.g. diligence, courtesy and thrift), character development (e.g. integrity, honour, inquiry, obedience, self-discipline, filial piety, respect for others and tolerance), sense of belonging (e.g. civic consciousness, respect for others, respect for law and order, and group spirit), respect for cultural heritage (e.g. understanding and appreciation of one's cultural heritage and beliefs), love of the country (sense of national identity, upholding democracy, patriotism, justice and equality), and nation-building (e.g. appreciation of the country's pioneers in nation building, and understanding of internal and external threats of the country) (consolidated by Berlach 1996).

As a result, two new programmes were introduced in 1981 to replace the old ones, namely *Good Citizens* (for primary) and *Being and Becoming* (for secondary). *Good Citizens* was designed for primary school, and adopted a rather didactic approach to teaching values, whereas *Being and Becoming* was designed for secondary school, and it adopted a values clarification approach. Sim (2005) described it as a deliberative approach which encourages pupils to deliberate and reflect on values issues, then debate and arrive at their own judgment. This was also a soft approach to syncretise the values of the various ethnic and religious groups within the country. Further recognition of ethnic and religious values of the population was made when *Religious Knowledge* (RK) was introduced to replace Civics at the upper secondary levels as a compulsory subject. Biblical Knowledge, Buddhist Studies, Hindu Studies, Islam Studies, Sikh Studies and Confucian Ethics were options available under Religious knowledge. However, in the process of implementation, it was found that the teaching of religious values heightened religious fervour and it was difficult for schools to achieve a 'neutralizing influence' on religion. Instead of achieving religious harmony, there was a tendency of segregating ethnic and religious groups in the teaching of Religious Knowledge. As a result, the programme ceased to be compulsory in 1989 (Kanagaratnam 2011; Sim 2005).

Developing Citizenship with Shared Values for Social Cohesion and Global Perspectives

Civics and Moral Education (CME) was introduced at the secondary levels in 1994, with a specific aim to enable students from diverse ethnic and cultural groups to interact with each other and to foster inter-ethnic understanding and appreciation of each other's cultures and practices. The moral education syllabus at the primary levels was also revised and replaced by CME in the same year.

The 1990s was a decade of complexities in terms of finding a pathway that would address various issues that emerged with Singapore's further success in its economy, Asia's economic crisis, and increased diversities coming along with the growing internationalisation of Singapore's economy. Economically, Singapore experienced further successes and has grown into "a prosperous financial, trading and internationally oriented manufacturing centre of sophisticated products and services" (Han et al. 2001). At the same time, Singapore has become more globally engaged and active, and Singapore's internationalisation has intensified. This brings about the issue of balancing globalisation with localisation, and the pursuit for such balance was manifested in the citizenship education agenda in the 1990s as well.

To acknowledge diversity, yet to enhance efforts towards localisation, a White Paper, entitled *Shared Values* was published in 1991, specifying several values that the government expected the populace to uphold in order to sustain a nation with social solidarity, namely 'nation before community and society above self', 'family as the basic unit of society', 'community support and respect for the individuals', 'consensus, not conflict', and 'racial and religious harmony' (White Paper 1991). The White Paper on Shared Values is regarded as a search for national values and Asian values in the process of globalisation (Tan 2001; Suryadinata 2000).

In accord with these concerns to pursue national values in globalisation, *National Education* was introduced to schools in 1997, in order to shape positive knowledge, values and attitudes of Singapore's young citizenry, and to develop national cohesion, the instinct for survival and confidence in the future of Singapore. In particular the programme was designed to (1) foster a sense of identity, pride and self respect among young Singaporeans, (2) relate the Singaporean story about how Singapore succeeded in becoming a nation, (3) understand Singapore's unique challenges, and (4) teach the core values of the society (Sim 2005; also Chap. 5).

To further pursue the national values agenda in the midst of globalisation, a Singapore 21 Committee was set up in 1997, and a report entitled *Singapore 21 Report* (1999) was published in 1999. 'Singapore 21' was described as a vision for a new era. This document was an outcome of consultations of 6,000 Singaporeans from all walks of life, reflecting many people's wishes and a diversity of viewpoints (http://marklsl.tripod.com/Writings/singapore21.htm). It espouses five key ideas: (1) every Singaporean matters, (2) strong families: our foundation and our future, (3) opportunities for all, (4) The 'Singapore Heartbeat': feeling passionately about Singapore, and (5) active citizens: making the difference.

Singapore 21 represents efforts to sustain national values, and it was also a furtherance of 'shared values' in terms of inclusivity for cultural diversity. *Singapore 21* positions the country in the twenty-first century as a global and cosmopolitan city, and calls for the need to prepare Singaporeans to become global citizens, rooted locally and nationally. The document depicts the citizen of the twenty-first century as a cosmopolitan Singaporean with a culture of internationalisation. It further emphasized that this direction is not a choice, but a necessity (*Singapore 21* 1999).

As much as *Singapore 21* has provided a balance for *Shared Values* in terms of nationalisation and internationalisation, in respect to the citizenship education, National Education was balanced by the new *Social Studies* programme launched in 2001 as a compulsory subject offered at upper secondary levels. Social Studies is a vehicle for socialisation, but it is also a vehicle for higher order thinking and criticality. According to Barr et al. (1977), social studies can serve three functions: citizenship transmission, learning the discipline, and learning reflective inquiry and thinking. The *Social Studies* programme introduced in Singapore also serves the three functions. In addition to developing a deep sense of shared destiny and national identity among the students, the new Social Studies programme also aims to enable the students to understand the issues that affect the socio-economic development, the governance and the future of Singapore, and to learn from the experiences of other countries to build and sustain a politically viable, socially cohesive and economically vibrant Singapore, and develop citizens who have empathy towards others and who will participate responsibly and sensibly in a multi-ethnic and multi-cultural and multi-religious society. More importantly, *Social Studies* was meant to prepare the students to adopt a more participative role in shaping Singapore's future in the twenty-first century (MOE 2010). In line with the spirit of *Singapore 21*, the *Social Studies* motto is: "Being rooted, Living global" (http://www.scribd.com/doc/41183103/Social-Studies-Syllabus).

Citizenship Education for the Twenty-First Century: Future-Oriented Citizenship

The above review attempts to explain why Singapore was 'busy' with curriculum change in citizenship education. The frequency of change reflects the intensity of review and critique, and the search for new solutions for new problems arising at times, to the degree that while one solution was perceived to be responsive, by the time the new curriculum was introduced, it was no longer sufficient to accommodate the new challenges emerging over the curriculum development period. Such a frequency and pattern of change is noteworthy for curriculum developers, particularly in terms of curriculum adjustment in rapidly changing societies, and the above analysis shows that Singapore is a worthwhile case for further study in this respect.

The *Singapore 21* project was conducted hand-in-hand with the *Thinking Schools, Learning Nations* agenda launched in 1997. In June 1997, Prime Minister Goh Chok Tong delivered a hallmarking speech at the seventh International Conference on Thinking, entitled "Shaping our future: thinking schools, learning nation." The opening remark of the speech pinpointed the urgency and significance of preparing the nation for the future (twenty-first century): there will be increased international competitions across countries in the global age, there will be increasingly rapid changes and the change will be unpredictable; people's knowledge, innovation and capacity to learn is crucial for the future competitiveness of the country (http://www.moe.gov.sg/media/speeches/1997/020697.htm). This development direction laid the ground for the emphasis on reflective inquiry, thinking and criticality in the new *Social Studies* programmes launched since 2001. It marked off Singapore's journey of preparing the nation for the twenty-first century, and this became the national development agenda that formed a significant grounding for the emergence of the current *Character and Citizenship Education* programme in Singapore.

Twenty-First Century Skills and Citizenship

Globalization and the knowledge economy have opened up worldwide agendas for national development, and facilitated the flow of information and knowledge. Most immediately, the driving force for the new global knowledge economy is the intellectual capital of citizens. The urgency in building the capacity of students as future

Table 14.1 Multidimensional citizenship

Personal	A personal capacity for and commitment to a civic ethic characterised by responsible habits of mind, heart, and action
Social	Capacity to live and work together for civic purposes
Spatial	Capacity to see oneself as a member of several overlapping communities – local, regional, national, and multinational
Temporal	Capacity to locate present challenges in the context of both past and future in order to focus on long-term solutions to the difficult challenges we face

Source: Cogan and Derricott (1998)

workers is readily apparent in many countries, as many educational systems make parallel changes to prepare their students for the new world beyond the classroom. Indeed, the last 20 years have witnessed two decades of education reforms. Kennedy (2008) notes that almost all Asian countries have embarked on curricular reforms of sorts related to developing what is known as 'twenty-first century skills' which broadly cover critical, creative and inventive thinking; information, interactive and communication skills; civic literacy, global awareness and cross-cultural skills.

In general, it is observed that a key aspect of twenty-first century skills bears similarity to Putnam (1995) social capital, otherwise known as 'soft skills' that broadly includes trust, teamwork, social cohesion, and social networks. These 'soft skills', scholars have argued, are critical for economic advancement in the new global environment (Heffron 1997; see also http://www.bettersoftskills.com/research.htm; Heckman 2010). Notably, the twenty-first century skills are also closely related to the skills and values pertinent for active citizenship in the global and interdependent society. For example, Merryfield and Duty (2008) describe four skills necessary for active global citizenship. They include (1) skills in perspective to understand points of views of people different from themselves; (2) intercultural competence to participate effectively in today's multicultural societies; (3) critical thinking skills, especially the ability to evaluate conflicting information; and (4) habits of mind compatible with civic responsibilities in a global age, such as to approach judgments and decisions with open-mindedness, anticipation of complexity, resistance to stereotyping, and develop the habit of asking – is this the common good. Similarly, Cogan and Derricott's (1998) multidimensional citizenship model requires citizens to address a series of interconnected dimensions of thought, belief and action expressed in terms of the personal, social, spatial and temporal dimensions, as briefly summarized in Table 14.1.

Singapore's Curriculum 2015

In Singapore, the Curriculum 2015 (C2015) and the development of the twenty-first century citizenship competencies has to be seen in the context of developing the intellectual capital of its young citizens in order that Singapore would thrive in the new environment. Similar to the value foci of the above-mentioned education reforms in other countries, the twenty-first century citizenship competencies

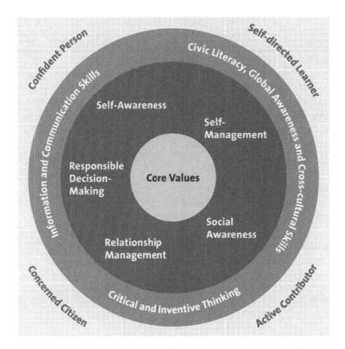

Fig. 14.5 Twenty-first century competencies and desired student outcomes (Source: MOE 2010)

framework in Singapore is underpinned by values. The first statement of the framework reads: "Knowledge and skills must be underpinned by values. Values define a person's character. They shape the beliefs, attitudes and actions of a person, and therefore form the core of the framework of twenty-first century competencies" (MOE 2010; also Chap. 3). These values include respect, responsibility, integrity, care, resilience and harmony. The twenty-first century competencies, when effectively developed, will result in the desired outcomes of education and citizenship attributes as embodied in the "confident person", "self-directed learner", "active contributor" and "concerned citizen" of the C2015, as shown in Fig. 14.5.

There is a host of other soft skills attached to the four major attributes, such as interpersonal skills, leadership skills, self-management skills, problem-solving skills, cross-cultural skills, civic skills, and etc. The skills espoused in the C2015 can also be found in the citizenship education literature, and are described as citizenship skills as well (see Table 14.2).

Future-Oriented Citizenship

The notion of preparing citizenship for the future departs from the traditional concepts of citizenship which are by and large socialising the younger citizens into

Table 14.2 Future-oriented citizenship education articulated in curriculum 2015, Singapore

C2015 student outcomes	Associated C2015 skills & mindsets
Confident person	
Thinks independently/Communicates effectively/ Has good inter-personals skills	Thinking skills/Communication skills/ Collaborative skills/Interpersonal skills/Leadership skills
Self-directed learner	
Takes responsibility for own learning/Questions, reflects, perseveres/Uses technology adeptly	Self-management skills
	Problem-solving skills
	Information and media literacies
	Technological literacy and skills
Concerned citizen	
To be informed about the world and local affairs/ Empathizes with and respect others/Participates actively	Multicultural literacy
	Cross-cultural skills
	Civic literacy
Active contributor	
Exercises initiative and takes risks/Is adaptable, innovative, resilient/Aims for high standards	Planning skills
	Management and organizational skills
	Innovative skills

the mainstay of the current social, economic and political entity. Lee and Fouts (2005) have studied and traced the development of citizenship concepts, as follows:

- Classical citizenship: citizens were a privileged class, as distinctive from slaves;
- Liberal citizenship: people were liberated to have a right to be citizens;
- Social citizenship: people's citizenship rights were extended towards entitlement to social welfare;
- National citizenship: the citizenship concept was closely linked to the concept of nation-state, and citizenry was defined in legal terms by the state;
- Post-national citizenship: the citizenship concept was extended beyond the state with increased migrations and globalisation;
- Global citizenship: the citizenship concept generated from the idea of a global village, reminding people of the global responsibility on top of their responsibilities at national levels, and that one's behaviour in a corner of the world may have global impacts, especially environmental implications; and
- Multiple citizenship: the citizenship concept was further extended with people identifying themselves with more than one nation, also as a result of globalisation.

The conceptual change of citizenship reflects the changing social-political conditions of the time, and people's concept towards human rights. However, all the above concepts can be regarded as a reflection of the contexts where the citizenship concepts stem from, and they also reflect 'the here-and-now' nature of citizenship and citizenship education. Across nations, as mentioned in the hidden curriculum agenda outlined at the beginning of this chapter, a common approach to citizenship education is through socialisation, and because of this, there are controversies about how much the state should socialise the citizens, and how much the socialisation process allows for individual inputs, including room for them to counter-socialise or make inquiry to be critically enculturated. Nevertheless, the discourse, however controversial and dispute-engendering it may be, reflects what is deemed to be right for here-and-now.

Citizenship education for the future is a different matter – it is a bold step forward, and a leap of faith. As distinctive from the here-and-now, future oriented citizenship acknowledges the reality and necessity of change, it looks beyond the present and accepts uncertainty. It moves from being to becoming. It requires an open mind towards what is emerging, and ability in sense making about what is emerging. It needs significant confidence of the state about the future, and trust in the people that they will shape the future positively and constructively. Once a nation adopts a future-oriented approach to citizenship, the state of play for citizenship education will be changing from state-led to collective construction or co-construction of the future. To achieve this, it requires not only invitation from the state, but also active engagement and participation from the citizens.

Based upon this, we can perceive that the C2015 is not only a new curriculum for the twenty-first century, but it is a citizenship education curriculum for the future per se. The four attributes stipulated as the desired outcomes of C2015 are actually citizenship attributes (see Table 14.1). These learning outcomes significantly depart from the academic learning outcomes of traditional curriculums – they are all soft skills – soft outcomes, such as self-directed, confident, critical, inventive, communicative, managing relationship, etc. So far, we are not yet too sure how to measure these outcomes, and not yet sure how these outcomes work to make a person more successful or achieving, whether for further studies or for career. However, given that the knowledge economy does differ from the manufacturing economies as it requires knowledge competencies to create new economic opportunities, and the speed of change in job nature is so fast that only the most flexible, innovative and creative lifelong learners can survive, the necessity of these soft skills is convincing. Moreover, since the UNESCO Delors' Report, learning to know, learning to do, learning to be and learning to live together (as a team player) have become recognised worldwide as the attributes of the new learners in the twenty-first century, these learning attributes are also a convincing target of learning for the new age.

What this new learning, especially learning for future need, opens up is to develop an awareness of learning for future, and learning for the uncertainty. To some extent, this is the nature of learning, as according to Jerome Bruner's learning theory (1960, 1966), learning is by itself a paradoxical process of moving from the state of unknown to known. In the process of learning, the learner actually does not know what he/she is going to learn, as by definition it is when one learns something one doesn't know, then one can describe this process as 'learning'. Learning is thus a process of learning something unknown, and yet to be known, and the learner would have the confidence that by the time he/she knows, there is something out there to know, and worth knowing, but there is no absolute guarantee what really is to be known, and how much is to be known, and how useful that known-to-be for the learner, after learning *it*.

A future-oriented approach to citizenship education best describes Singapore's twenty-first century learning agenda. In terms of the twenty-first century skills, it prepares the nation for the future, and in terms of citizenship education that coincides of the C2015, it prepares the citizens for the future. The government sets the agenda, and because it is an agenda that requires a collective exploration and continuous adjustment, it has become a process of co-construction – the government sets the agenda, and the public defines it. As inspired by Bruner, this learning process of a process of shifting between known and unknown, and a sandwich interaction about 'known-unknown-known' and 'unknown-known-unknown' (Easterbrooks and Estes 2007).

Future-oriented citizenship expects and requires the citizens to be an active agent in the society – active with a sense of belonging, active in the sense of being concerned about the society, and active in participating in the co-constructing of a better society together with the state. *Singapore 21* has made it clear that the expectation for the future citizen should be one of an active citizen, concerned about the future of Singapore, and committed to building a better society and making the society more competitive and more successful in the international arena. Because of its requirement for having active individuals, and the attributes of the twenty-first century competence are mostly psychological attributes, such as being confident, self-directed, active, concerned, creative, adaptive and collaborative, the individual citizens must be in very good psychological health to acquire and exercise these attributes so that they will become constructive contributors to the society. In this context, having good social-emotional learning for character building is important as this directly addresses the personal quality of the individual citizens. A citizen with good character and social-emotional health, is the foundation of good citizenship. The attention to individual-oriented citizenship education is as important as state-oriented citizenship education, thus *Character and Citizenship Education*, the latest citizenship programme to be introduced to Singapore schools is going to be a very important one that will address both individual and state concerns, and provide a good balance for both perspectives.

Total Curriculum: Whole School and Whole-of-the-Society Approach

The Curriculum 2015 under planning is to adopt a total curriculum approach. This should apply to the implementation of *Character and Citizenship Education* as well. Internationally, how citizenship education should be implemented is always under debate and so far there is no consensus. In the two international citizenship education studies conducted by the International Association of the Assessment of Educational Achievements (IEA) in 1995 and 2009, it was discovered that there is a 50–50 split among the countries involved between teaching citizenship education (and/or moral education, values education) as an independent subject and teaching citizenship education across the curriculum. There are strengths and weaknesses in both approaches. One problem of teaching citizenship as a separate subject is to make moral discussion compulsory in the classroom, and it is not always productive to require pupils to engage in moral talks deliberately. Oftentimes, the moral discussion can only be meaningful when a certain issue arises in the society and/or out of life experience. Enforcing a talk on a moral or civic topic when people are not ready to talk may generate unproductive effects such as avoidance. Thus, it is commonly pointed out in the literature that the civic curriculum will turn into teaching facts rather than values, attitudes and beliefs. Another problem is that many teachers do not want to conduct these discussions, as teachers also have different value beliefs themselves, and they are not necessarily the expert or role model for particular moral issues. Further, when the responsibility of teaching citizenship is assigned to a few teachers, other teachers may not feel a responsibility for it; but then the assigned teachers may become overly burdened to take charge of the civic morale of the whole school. On the other hand, it is important to note that education is not value-free, but value-laden; and there are values across the curriculum (Tomlinson and Quinton 1986). The values inherent in the curriculum are taught, whether we are aware of it or not. The total curriculum approach is therefore important in making explicit the tacit values inherent in the curriculum, and in this sense, citizenship education is not only limited to the teachers being specifically assigned as civic teachers, but all teachers bear some responsibility, and the whole school becomes a community enhancing civic virtues. It is established in the field of values education that the whole-school approach is needed for effective values education, as it requires values commitment by the whole school community for sustainability in values education. The values that the school upholds should be reflected in the school's vision and mission, and the values espoused by the school should be reflected in school ethos and policies for students to understand the significance of those values (Tudball 2007).

Conclusion

The above analysis shows the evolvement of the citizenship education curriculum in Singapore. The changing curriculum reflects the changing social, economic and political situations of the time, the needs of the country in different periods, and how citizenship education is to be adjusted for the future directions of the country. The changing curriculum also shows the struggles of values to be taught in order to balance diverse and sometimes opposing demands of the society, particularly between individual needs and collective needs. There are pendulum shifts, and these shifts illustrate that these struggles are not easy to resolve. However, a macro review of the changes shows a gradual shift in pedagogical approaches from more instructional and didactic approaches towards values clarification, shared values and a balance of socio-emotional learning at a personal level and the national citizenship at a societal level. Interestingly, the agenda of development towards globalization has become a yardstick that allows the general curriculum (i.e. C2015) to merge with the citizenship education goals, and a future-oriented citizenship education agenda penetrates the two curriculums.

This development direction has led to the realisation that for general curriculum and the citizenship education curriculum to be integrated, a whole curriculum and school system is to be required. In addition to adopting a future-oriented approach to citizenship education, integrating citizenship education with the total curriculum will be another major initiative in the experimentation with citizenship education, that would provide a significant reference for contemplating an integrated education system that builds citizenship outcomes into the overall learning outcomes of the broader curriculum, and vice versa. Indeed, this concurs with the concept that "education is by nature citizenship education", a view held by many educators (e.g. Crick and Porter 1978; White 1996). According to this view, literacy is the basic requirement for a citizen to perform citizenry function, and sufficient literacy, being described as political literacy, is required for a citizen to understand state policies and respond to them (which is an obligation for active citizenry). Moreover, it also requires the citizens to understand state policies in order for the state to be accountable to them. Education is thus the foundation for effective citizenship and active citizenship. Kelly (2009) alleges that we need to see curriculum as 'total curriculum', seeing it beyond a subject and as a totality including content, product, knowledge and process. As mentioned at the beginning of this chapter, curriculum means much more than an organisation of study. It is referred to learning orientations, school operation, and the larger context of learning. The target of learning changes in time in response to the particular social, economic and political needs. As far as value is concerned, these changes are more reflected in citizenship education, as it is more directly related to values, but unless the whole-school is involved in the delivery of values teaching, citizenship education will become compartmentalized and marginalized (Lee 2008). On this the 'total curriculum', an 'integrated approach' and the 'whole-school perspectives' that Singapore employs in launching C2015 is a significant recognition that it requires the whole system to work together to make citizenship education work.

References

Barr, R. D., Barth, J. L., & Shermis, S. S. (1977). *Defining the social studies* (Bulletin, Vol. 51). Virginia: National Council for the Social Studies.

Bereday, G. Z. F. (1969). Reflections on comparative methodology in education. In M. A. Eckstein & H. J. Noah (Eds.), *Scientific investigations in comparative education* (pp. 3–23). London: Collier-Macmillan.

Berlach, R. (1996). Citizenship education: Australian and Singapore perspectives. *Australian Journal of Teacher Education, 21*(2), 1–15.

Bruner, J. (1960). *The process of education*. Cambridge: Harvard University Press.

Bruner, J. (1966). *Toward a theory of instruction*. Cambridge: Harvard University Press.

Chew, J. O. A. (1998). Civics and moral education in Singapore: Lessons for citizenship? *Journal of Moral Education, 27*(4), 505–524.

Cogan, J. L., & Dericott, R. (1998). *Citizenship for the 21st century: An international perspective on education*. London: Cogan Page.

Crick, B., & Porter, A. (1978). *Political education and political literacy*. London: Longman.

Doyle, W. (1992a). Curriculum and pedagogy. In P. W. Jackson (Ed.), *Handbook of research on curriculum* (pp. 486–516). New York: Macmillan.

Doyle, W. (1992b). Constructing curriculum in the classroom. In F. K. Oser & J. Patry (Eds.), *Effective and responsible teaching: The new syntheses* (pp. 66–79). San Francisco: Jossey-Bass.

Easterbrooks, S. R., & Esters, E. L. (2007). *Helping deaf and hard of hearing students to use spoken language*. London: Sage.

Eisner, E. W. (1994). *The educational imagination* (3rd ed.). New York: Macmillan.

Eisner, E., & Vallance, C. (Eds.). (1974). *Conflicting conceptions of curriculum*. Berkeley: McCutchan.

Franklin, R. (1989). Intellectuals and the CCP in the post-Mao period: A study in perceptual role conflict. *Journal of Developing Societies, 5*(2), 203–217.

Freire, P. (1974). Education: Domestication or liberation? In I. Lister (Ed.), *Deschooling* (pp. 18–21). Cambridge: Cambridge University Press.

Giroux, H. (1981). *Ideology, culture, and the process of schooling*. London: Falmer Press.

Goh, K. S. (1979a). *Report on the ministry of education 1978*. Singapore: Singapore National Printers.

Goh, K. S. (1979b). *Report on the ministry of education*. Singapore: Ministry of Education.

Goh, C.B., & Gopinathan, S. (2006). *The development of education in Singapore since 1965*. Background paper prepared for the Asia Education Study Tour for African Policy Makers, 18–30 June. Available at http://siteresources.worldbank.org/EDUCATION/Resources/278200-1121703274255/1439264-11 53425508901/Development_Edu_Singapore_draft.pdf. Retrieved 24 Jan 2013.

Han, C., Chew, J., & Tan, J. (2001). Singapore: Values education for a knowledge-based economy. In W. K. Cummings, M. T. Tatto, & J. Hawkins (Eds.), *Values education for dynamic societies: Individualism or collectivism*. Hong Kong: University of Hong Kong.

Heckman, J. (2010). *What's the rate of return on social skills?* Available at: http://sciencestage.com/v/33162/what-s-the-rate-of-return-on-social-skills?-james-heckman.html. Accessed 31 Aug 2013.

Heffron, J. M. (1997). Defining values. In J. D. Montgomery (Ed.), *Values in education: Social capital formation in Asia and the Pacific* (pp. 3–27). Hollis: Hollis Publishing.

Kanagaratnam, T. (2011). Unpublished Ph.D. working drafts. Singapore, National Institute of Education, NTU.

Kelly, A. V. (2009). *Curriculum: Theory and practice*. London: Sage.

Kennedy, K. J. (2008). Globalized economies and liberalized curriculum: New challenges for national citizenship education. In D. Grossman, W. O. Lee, & K. Kennedy (Eds.), *Citizenship curriculum in Asia and the Pacific* (pp. 13–26). Hong Kong: Springer/Comparative Education Research Centre, University of Hong Kong.

Kwong, J. Y. S., Peck, E. S., & Chin, J. Y. Y. (1990). 25 years of educational reform. In J. Y. S. Kwong & W. K. Sim (Eds.), *Evolution of educational excellence: 25 years of education in the republic of Singapore* (pp. 31–58). Singapore: Longman.

Lee, W. O. (2002). Moral education policy in China: The struggle between liberal and traditional approaches. *Perspectives in Education, 18*(1), 5–22.

Lee, W. O. (2008). The development of citizenship education curriculum in Hong Kong: Tensions between national identity and global citizenship. In D. L. Grossman, K. J. Kennedy, & W. O. Lee (Eds.), *Citizenship curriculum in Asia and the Pacific* (pp. 29–42). Hong Kong/New York: Comparative Education Research Centre/Springer.

Lee, W. O., & Fouts, J. T. (2005). *Education for social citizenship: Perceptions of teachers in the USA, Australia, England, Russia and China*. Hong Kong: Hong Kong University Press.

Lee, W. O., & Ho, C. H. (2005). Ideological shifts and changes in moral education policy in China. *Journal of Moral Education, 34*(4), 413–431.

Lee, W. O., & Ho, C. H. (2008). Citizenship education in China: Changing concepts, approaches and policies in the changing political, economic and social context. In J. Arthur, I. Davies, & C. Hahn (Eds.), *The SAGE handbook of education for citizenship and democracy* (pp. 139–157). London: Sage.

Lee, W. O., & Sweeting, A. (2001). Controversies in Hong Kong's political transition: Nationalism versus liberalism. In M. Bray & W. O. Lee (Eds.), *Education and political transition: Themes and experiences in East Asia* (pp. 101–121). Hong Kong: University of Hong Kong Comparative Education Research Centre.

Longstreet, W. S., & Shane, H. G. (1993). *Curriculum for a new millennium*. Boston: Allyn and Bacon.

MacDonald, M. (1977). *The curriculum and cultural reproduction*. London: The Open University Press.

Marsh, C. J. (1997). *Key concepts for understanding curriculum* (Vol. 1). London: Falmer Press.

Merryfield, M., & Duty, L. (2008). Globalization. In J. Arthur, I. Davies, & C. Hahn (Eds.), *Handbook for citizenship and democracy* (pp. 80–91). London: Sage.

Ministry of Education (MOE). (2008). *Keynote speech by Mr. Masagos Zulkifli BMM, senior parliamentary secretary, ministry of education, at the association of Muslim professionals' community in review seminar on Saturday, 26 January 2008 at Holiday Inn Parkview Hotel at 10.00 am*. Available at: http://www.moe.gov.sg/media/speeches/2008/01/26/keynote-speech-by-mr-masagos-z.php. Accessed 19 June 2012.

Ministry of Education (MOE). (2010). *MOE to enhance learning of 21st century competencies and strengthen art, music and physical education*. Available at: http://www.moe.gov.sg/media/press/2010/03/moe-to-enhance-learning-of-21s.php. Accessed 26 June 2012.

Mourshed, M., Chijioke, C., & Barber, M. (2010). *How the world's most improved school systems keep getting better*. London: Mckinsey & Company.

OECD. (2010). *Strong performers and successful reformers in education: Lessons from PISA for the United States*. Paris: OECD.

Oliva, P. F. (1992). *Developing the curriculum* (3rd ed.). New York: Harper Collins.

Ong, T. C. (1979). *Report on moral education*. Singapore: Ministry of Education.

Posner, G. J. (1998). Models of curriculum planning. In L. E. Beyer & M. W. Apple (Eds.), *The curriculum: Problems, politics and possibilities* (2nd ed., pp. 79–100). Albany: State University of New York Press.

Putnam, R. D. (1995). Bowling alone: America's declining social capital. *The Journal of Democracy, 6*(1), 65–78.

Sim, J. B.-Y. (2005). Citizenship education and social studies in Singapore: A national agenda. *International Journal of Citizenship and Teacher Education, 1*(1), 59–73.

Singapore 21 Committee. (1999). *Singapore 21: Together we make the difference*. Singapore: Singapore 21 Committee.

Suryadinata, L. (2000). *Nationalism and globalisation: East and West*. Singapore: Institute of Southeast Asian Studies.

Tan, E. (2001). Singapore shared values. *Singapore Infopedia*. Available at: http://infopedia.nl.sg/articles/SIP_542_2004-12-18.html. Accessed 31 Aug 2013.

Tan, C. (2005). The potential of Singapore's ability driven education to prepare students for a knowledge economy. *International Education Journal, 6*(4), 446–453.

Teo, W. (2010). *The effectiveness in measuring character development outcomes in Singapore schools through the Character Development Award*. Doctoral thesis, University of Durham. http://etheses.dur.ac.uk/704. Accessed 31 Aug 2013.

Tomlinson, P., & Quinton, M. (Eds.). (1986). *Values across the curriculum*. Sussex: Falmer Press.

Tudball, L. (2007). Whole-school approaches to values education: Models of practice in Australian schools. In D. Aspin & J. Chapman (Eds.), *Values education and lifelong learning: Principles, policies, programmes* (pp. 395–405). Dordrecht: Springer.

White, P. (1996). *Civic virtues and public schooling: Educating citizens for a democratic society*. New York: Teachers College Press.

White Paper. (1991). *On shared values*. Singapore: National Printers.

Williams, R. (1976). Base and superstructure in Marxist cultural theory. In R. Dale et al. (Eds.), *Schooling and capitalism: A sociological reader*. London: Routledge & Kegan Paul.

Part VI
Conclusion

Chapter 15
The Singapore Curriculum: Convergence, Divergence, Issues and Challenges

Zongyi Deng, S. Gopinathan, and Christine Kim-Eng Lee

The aim of this book is to provide a multifaceted and critical analysis of the Singapore curriculum within the context of national educational and curriculum reform as a response to the economic, social, and cultural challenges of globalization. Curriculum is framed in terms of the *policy curriculum* (reform visions, discourses and initiatives), *programmatic curriculum* (curriculum structures, programmes and operational frameworks that translate reform visions and initiatives), and *classroom curriculum* (instructional activities and events that reflect how teachers enact reform initiatives). Contributors to this volume analyse how the government has responded in the policy arena to the challenges of globalization (Chaps. 2, 3, and 4), how curriculum reform initiatives have been translated into programmes, school subjects, and operational frameworks (Chaps. 5, 6, and 7), and enacted in classrooms (Chaps. 8, 9, 10, and 11). Finally, curriculum reform in Singapore is also examined from international, comparative, and future perspectives (Chaps. 12, 13, and 14).

In this concluding chapter we discuss how policy, programmatic and classroom curricula reflect, on the one hand, global features and tendencies, and on the other, distinct national traditions and practices. In other words, we examine issues of convergence (due to pressures and influences created by globalization) and of divergence (due to distinct national culture, traditions and practices) (see Anderson-Levitt 2008) with respect to the three curriculum domains (Chap. 1). Through this examination, we relate what has been happening in Singapore to what has been happening in the world in terms of curriculum reform and globalization, and make clear how curriculum reform policy, curriculum development, and classroom enactment in Singapore have responded to globalization in *distinctive* ways. We conclude by identifying a set of issues, problems, and challenges that not only concern policymakers and reformers in Singapore but (which we believe) would be generally useful for policymakers, educators, and researchers in other countries.

Z. Deng (✉) • S. Gopinathan • C.K.-E. Lee
National Institute of Education, Nanyang Technological University, Singapore
e-mail: zongyi.deng@nie.edu.sg

Z. Deng et al. (eds.), *Globalization and the Singapore Curriculum: From Policy to Classroom*, Education Innovation Series, DOI 10.1007/978-981-4451-57-4_15, © Springer Science+Business Media Singapore 2013

Convergence and Divergence

Reform Vision, Discourses and Initiatives

A high degree of convergence can be seen in the policy arena. As in many countries, both developed and developing, reform discourses in Singapore are also largely *economic* in orientation, driven by the imperative of the state to advance in a competitive, globalized world (Chaps. 2 and 3). The TSLN reform is primarily "a way of retooling the productive capacity of the system" in response to the human and intellectual capital requirements of global markets and economies (Gopinathan 2007, p. 59; also see Chap. 2). Policymakers recognize that in such a world, knowledge and innovation are absolutely essential if countries want to keep up, and therefore, education and training become fundamentally important (Chaps. 3, 4, and 13). Reform initiatives have therefore been introduced with a central focus on the development of ICT competencies, problem solving skills, and critical thinking, and the cultivation of creativity, innovation, entrepreneurial flair or risk taking among students. They are underpinned by related innovations like structural flexibility and responsiveness, content reduction in the national curriculum, the introduction of project work, experiential learning, and changes in the examination systems, among others (Chap. 2). The underlying argument is global in nature: that "the prosperity of post-industrial information and knowledge driven societies would depend [inescapably] on the optimal development [and exploitation] of the human capital of all its citizens" (Buchberger 2000, p. 3).

The aims of schooling also take on a globally recognizable form, with a central focus on the formation of competent citizens (cf. Rosenmund 2006). As indicated in the Desired Outcomes of Education (issued in 1998), the central purpose of schooling is stated to be the formation of the "whole person" who is equipped with the "skills, values and instincts Singaporeans must have to survive and succeed in a bracing future" in the twenty-first century (Ministry of Education (MOE) 1998, para 3; also see Chap. 3). In Curriculum 2015 (C2015), the central purpose of schooling is defined as the formation of "a confident person," "a self-directed learner," "an active contributor," and "a concerned citizen," with an emphasis on the mastery of a set of twenty-first century competencies deemed essential for life and work in a globalised world (Chaps. 3 and 14). This resonates well with the current global discourse on curriculum policy, implementation, and assessment that foregrounds the importance of helping students develop twenty-first century competencies (Voogt and Roblin 2012; also see Dede 2010a, b).

These signs of convergence can be explained as a response to common global pressures and the internationalization of education. As in other countries, curriculum reform in Singapore is a response to common external pressures on the curriculum which "have been largely economic and have focused on how to prepare students to be employable in an increasingly competitive economic environment" (Yates and Young 2010, p. 4). As in many other countries, education policymakers in Singapore have been actively engaged in the process of "policy borrowing" (cf. Phillips 2005).

The development of the TSLN vision, discourses and reform initiatives was based upon the government's global reassessment of other education systems, particularly those of the US, the UK, and East Asian economies (Chaps. 3 and 4). The Desired Outcomes of Education, for instance, was "a product of intensive studies into trends emerging in Singapore, the region and the world today" (MOE 1998, also see Chap. 3). The twenty-first century competencies rhetoric, Tan observes, "is remarkably similar to policy initiatives in other countries like the UK and Australia as various governments borrow ideas internationally in a seemingly endless quest for that one magical formula for reforming education" (Chap. 3, p. 42). Nevertheless, policy borrowing is not a simple, straightforward process; what is borrowed has to undergo a process of modification, adaptation, and transformation in a particular socio-cultural context (See Phillips 2005; also Deng 2011).

As in many other countries (e.g. China, Finland, and Germany), there is a strong effort in Singapore to maintain national values and traditions. National Education, for instance, represents the government's attempt to maintain national traditions in the current globalized age. It attempts to strengthen the identification of Singaporeans with the nation through helping them understand and appreciate national history and traditions (see Chaps. 2, 4, 5, 10, 13, and 14). So even in this globalization age, Kennedy observes, "there was the desire to anchor young Singaporeans in local values and ideas" (Chap. 12, p. 219). This seems to contradict the assertion made by some scholars, e.g., Meyer (2006), that with the increased homogenization of curriculum across the globe, national history and traditions tend to be marginalized in the school curriculum of a particular country.

Overall, the instituting of TSLN reform initiatives shows that the government has actively engaged with the opportunities and challenges of globalization in the educational arena, with no signs of retreating under the onslaught of globalization. This is in contrast to the popular claim about the diminishing role of the nation state in the age of globalization in the literature (cf. Ohmae 1995). In Singapore, while the state is under some pressure, there is no evidence of a weakened state (Chaps. 2 and 13). Apart from addressing the economic challenges created by globalization, the government well recognizes that meeting these pressures of globalization necessarily involves responding to distinct local exigencies – the concerns for Singapore's survival, ethnic pluralism, geopolitical vulnerabilities, etc. (Chaps. 2, 4, 5, 10, and 13). The TSLN reform thus aims to produce citizens "who have the 'right' skills to go 'global' yet with their hearts rooted to 'local'/'national' identity, traditions and values" (Chap. 4, p. 54; also see Chap. 10).

Programmes, School Subjects and Operational Frameworks

There are signs of convergence too in programmatic curriculum making. The ways of translating reform initiatives into the programmatic curriculum reflect a global trend in curriculum development – a move toward delineating learning outcomes uniformly across various school subjects which serve as an essential frame of reference for planning, implementing and evaluating curriculum reform (Yates and Young 2010). The Desired Outcomes of Education systematically delineate specific developmental outcomes at different stages of the education cycle, and are meant to "drive our policies and programmes, and allow us to determine how well our education system is doing" (MOE 2010; also see Chap. 3). The critical thinking initiative entails the specification of a set of learning outcomes – in terms of thinking skills, processes and attributes – that serve to guide and evaluate teaching and learning activities across different subject areas (Chap. 6). C2015 consists of a set of learning outcomes centred on twenty-first century competencies, which are to be "infused" into all school subjects as well as informal learning experiences, and provide an important direction for curriculum planning, implementation, and assessment (Chaps. 3, 13, and 14).

Another sign of convergence is indicated in the attempt to diversify the programmatic curriculum, through decentralization, creating flexibility and choice in school types, programmes, and structures. The creation of independent schools since 1987 with greater autonomy over budget, staffing, and curriculum was the first step in loosening up the system. Different school types like the "Singapore Sports School," "School of the Arts," and "NUS High School of Science and Mathematics" are intended to provide relevant and a wider range of schooling opportunities for students with talents in specific areas. Integrated programmes (IP) have been introduced, which allow students to skip their "O" level examinations and move directly to the junior college curriculum, thus weakening a little the dominance of the "O" level examinations for academically high performing students (Gopinathan 2007; also Chap. 2). The streaming system "has been altered by wider curricular options and by more and flexible pathways" (Chap. 2, p. 24). Such an effort is believed to be essential for preparing diverse talents for an innovation-driven growth, and frequent and unpredictable change in economic and social environment (Chap. 2). The attempt to diversify the curriculum in these ways is congruent with the international trend toward greater flexibility in curriculum, considered as being able to prepare school leavers for twenty-first century challenges (Yates and Young 2010).

Convergence is also reflected in the Ministry's support of school-based curriculum development (SBCD) and innovation. Within the "Ignite!" framework teachers are provided with opportunities for "designing, implementing and studying new or improved teaching and learning approaches, and…in curriculum design, pedagogy and assessment" (MOE 2007, p. 1; also see Chap. 7). The MOE is committed to providing "top-down support for bottom-up" school-based curriculum innovations. Teachers are provided with more time to prepare, reflect on and share ideas to make teaching more responsive to student needs, and more space and opportunities for professional development (Chap. 7; also Leong et al. 2011). This, to a certain extent, reflects the global movement toward decentralization in curriculum decision making, teacher professionalism and autonomy (Anderson-Levitt 2008).

However, there is also clear evidence of divergence from international trends and tendencies. Unlike the outcomes-based model adopted by many countries in implementing curriculum reform which tends to undermine the importance of academic content (see Yates and Collins 2010), the approach to curriculum making used in

Singapore has retained academic content as the "fundamental" in teaching and learning (Chap. 2). For instance, while adopting a sort of outcomes-based approach to curriculum making, the critical thinking and National Education initiatives are intended to strengthen, not supplant, the academic content of the school curriculum; the learning outcomes of both critical thinking and National Education are *infused* into the formal and informal curricula (Chaps. 5 and 6). C2015 adopts a vision of "Strong Fundamentals, Future Learning," signaling that academic subjects like languages, mathematics, science, and humanities continue to play an important part in the new curriculum (see Chaps. 3, 12, and 14). This can be accounted for by the recognition of the government that "academic excellence" for a majority of students is a strength. Therefore, curriculum reform in the Singapore context builds upon existing strengths while seeking to accommodate a wider definition of talent and ensuring that weaker students can access a relevant and meaningful curriculum within the system.

With regards to school-based curriculum development (SBCD), a process that started in 1987 when the first independent school was established, teachers in Singapore mostly participate in what Gopinathan and Deng (2006) call *school-based curriculum enactment*, which consists largely of adapting, modifying, and translating curriculum materials and resources developed or mandated by the Ministry in view of their specific school contexts and situations. SBCD is mostly a strategy employed by the Ministry to delegate a certain degree of autonomy to teachers, so as to promote school-based curriculum innovations within the existing policy and curriculum framework (cf. Westbury 1994; also see Chap. 7). Teachers have to work in a "contradictory context of top-down versus bottom-up educational reform" (Leong et al. 2011, p. 51). In Singapore, SBCD is best characterized by "decentralized centralism," which gives rise to "the paradoxical situation of decentralizing curriculum powers to the school level to promote innovation but pre-empting the risk of declining standards in the absence of central quality control" (p. 59).

Enacting Reform Initiatives in Classrooms

As we have noted, there have been sustained efforts at curriculum and pedagogy reform since 1987. Overall, while there has been some progress and a "hybrid pedagogy" is emergent, this is limited, not system wide, and falls short of the goals of the TSLN and TLLM vision (Hogan 2011, also see Chaps. 2 and 8).

In classrooms, we see little evidence of convergence with international "norms" of effective practice promulgated in the literature and with the TSLN reform vision. Hogan and colleagues find that pedagogical practices in Singapore classrooms are far from consistent with contemporary understanding of "good" pedagogy in the international literature represented, say, by Hattie's framework of "visible learning" (Chap. 8). In schools and classrooms, the enacted curriculum markedly diverges from the intent of TSLN reform initiatives. For instance, the enactment of reform initiatives in language education in classrooms, according to Silver et al, is "somewhat superficial," with "little evidence of policy initiation or curriculum innovation" (Chap. 9, p. 163). Classroom teaching "continued to prioritise examinable subjects over holistic education, and formal assessments over other measures of learning." Lessons "were well-planned and well-managed, but rarely encouraged passionate pursuit of knowledge, higher-order thinking or open-ended interaction" (Chap. 9). Hogan (Chap. 8) also finds that the impact of TLLM on the enacted curriculum is very limited.

The lack of reform impact on the classroom curriculum is further revealed by the empirical findings generated by the Centre for Research in Pedagogy and Practice (CRPP), based on the classroom coding and observation of 920 primary and secondary lessons from 56 schools in key curriculum areas over a 2-year period (2004–2005).[1] Notwithstanding multiple reform initiatives to encourage the TSLN vision, teachers in Singapore still tend to a large degree to rely on whole class forms of lesson organization, with whole class lectures and question and answer sequences (IRE) as the dominant methods. Classroom pedagogy is still largely focused on the transmission and assessment ("reproduction") of subject based curriculum knowledge (Hogan 2009). As we noted above, a mixed, distinctive "hybrid pedagogy" with a strong focus on direct instruction and traditional pedagogical practices and a much weaker focus on constructivist learning principles has emerged. There is limited formative assessment and feedback to students and high stakes summative examinations (like the PSLE [Primary School Leaving Examination], "O" and "A" levels) limit teacher efforts in pedagogical innovations (cf. Chap. 2). Paradoxically, this seems to explain in part Singapore students' success in TIMSS and PISA – which leads many policy makers in the US, UK, and Australia to seek answers to their problems in the Singapore model.

The lack of reform impact on the enacted curriculum, according to Hogan et al., can be accounted for by several factors, including "neglect of the tight coupling of the national assessment system and classroom instruction," "a pervasive folk culture of teaching and learning across the system," "an implementation strategy unable to support substantial and sustainable pedagogical improvement", and "the weak professional authority of teachers" (Chap. 8, p. 121; also see Chaps. 9 and 10).

Overall, our analysis confirms Anderson-Levitt (2008) observation that curriculum is converging or "globalizing" at the policy level as reformers and policy-makers around the world are promoting a common set of curriculum reforms, and yet enacted curricula continue to diverge in classrooms, shaped by the distinct national and local cultures, traditions and pedagogical practices. The findings on the lack of reform impact on pedagogical practice in classrooms are consistent with what has been shown in the international literature about implementing educational and curriculum reforms (e.g., Cohen and Ball 1990; Fullan 2008; Tyack and Cuban 1995).

---

[1] See Luke et al. (2005) for a detailed description of the study.

Issues, Problems and Challenges

What are the issues, problems, and challenges surrounding policy, programmatic and classroom curricula in Singapore? How can we make sense of the lack of impact of reform initiatives on what schools teach and what teachers do? How can we come to terms with the limitations of "curriculum making" at the policy level? What is entailed in translating reform initiatives into programmes, school subjects, and operational frameworks? We now address these questions in terms of policy, programmatic and classroom curricula.

The policy curriculum of TSLN – characterized by the reform vision, initiatives, and discourses – typifies what school is for in Singapore and what should be valued and sought after by Singaporeans in the era of globalization (Chaps. 2 and 4). It embodies an idealized vision of schooling in relation to society and culture, or an "educational imagining," which serves to pave the way for educational and curricular change (Chap. 4). The instituting of TSLN reform entails what we call *vision-instigated curriculum making* in the social and policy arena. Through creating the TSLN vision and related discourses, the government has drawn attention to new educational ideals and expectations (embodied in the concept of TSLN and the Desired Outcomes of Education) and put forth new curriculum policies and reform initiatives to be implemented in schools and classrooms (see Chaps. 2, 3, and 4).

However, this way of reforming curriculum is not without its problems. The TSLN vision and discourses are inevitably selective, foregrounding certain economic and social challenges and issues facing the nation – challenges and issues that have to do primarily with the rapid development and application of technologies, intense economic competition, unstable global economic environments, and socio-political vulnerabilities and constraints of Singapore (see Chaps. 2 and 4). Other equally important socio-political and economic issues seem to be overlooked or silenced in the TSLN's vision and discourses – issues pertaining to income inequality, ethnicity and underachievement, the effect of socioeconomic status on students' academic achievement, the growth of civil society, the need to promote and strengthen inclusiveness, etc. (Chap. 2). Furthermore, the issues and problems facing schools as public institutions in Singapore (e.g., the pressure of high-stakes examination, high parental expectations, the prevalence of private tutoring, the "long tail" of underachievement, and heavy teachers' workload) also do not seem to have received sufficient attention (see Chap. 2). Vision-instigated curriculum making, often undertaken by elite elements in society, entails sketching an ideal curriculum at the policy arena, which is supposed to become "a template that schools should mirror and against which they can be evaluated" (Westbury 2005, pp. 97–98). Yet the complexities of schooling as a public institution, especially in a time of uncertainty and complexity, "are swept away in the name of a single vision" of what schooling ought to be (Westbury 2008, p. 49). This way of curriculum making almost always loses connections with school and classroom realities, and might account for why reform fails to create a lasting impact on classroom practice (Simola 1998).

Other kinds of issues confront programmatic curriculum making that *translates* the TSLN vision and initiatives into school programmes, subjects and operational frameworks that provide the "ultimate basis" for schools in implementing TSLN reform. Such a translation is a socio-political process involving a selection and recontextualization of socio-political ideologies that have to do with issues of distribution of power relations, ideological control, and inequality (Chaps. 3, 5, and 6). Concerning translating the Desired Outcomes of Education into different programmes, Tan questions "whether the outcomes are really meant to be attained by every student, whether the various stakeholders in education truly desire these outcomes, and whether the various stakeholders are in fact equally well-placed to attain these outcomes" (Chap. 3, p. 33). The translation of the critical thinking initiative into the Thinking Programme, Lim argues, is aligned to the "discourse of economic imperatives," where alternative discourses like liberal democracy and critical pedagogy are silent (Chap. 6). The making of the National Education curriculum, Sim argues, is driven by the government's "ideology of survival," "sense of vulnerability," and the perceived threat of globalization to nation building (Chap. 5, p. 69) This is different from current international discourses that foregrounds cosmopolitican and global citizenship education in a globalized age (Chap. 10; also see Satio 2010).

Ideological and political issues aside, translating a TSLN initiative (e.g., critical thinking and National Education) into programmes, school subjects, and operational frameworks entails a sophisticated endeavor of curriculum making which has to do with issues of content selection, transformation and framing in view of *both* the intent of the initiative *and* the activities of teaching and learning in classrooms (Deng 2009, 2010; also see Chaps. 6 and 7). However, this complex task of curriculum making tends to be bypassed in favor of simple procedural solutions. The National Education curriculum is made through prescribing "core events" and "learning journeys" according to the predetermined learning outcomes (Chap. 5). Similarly, the Thinking Programme was made through prescribing a body of learning outcomes in terms of thinking skills, processes and attributes, together with pedagogical approaches to teaching thinking (Chap. 6). How subject matter content can be (re) organized, transformed, and framed in a way that renders opportunities for critical and innovative thinking has not been taken into consideration (see Deng 2001, 2010). In both cases the task of curriculum making is "simplified and stripped of its complexities to facilitate the prescribed solution" (Chap. 5, p. 75).

The classroom curriculum, or the enacted curriculum, is the arena where most TSLN reform initiatives seek to have an impact. In classrooms, we cannot disentangle what is taught from how it is taught, or indeed, assessed. Teaching takes the form of instructional events which are fundamentally *curricular* because they reflect how a teacher interprets and enacts syllabuses and curriculum materials – embodiments of the TSLN vision, expectations and initiatives – for students of a particular age and backgrounds. The interpretation and enactment are shaped by multiple factors – students' interests and experience, instructional strategies, curriculum resources, teacher's pedagogical beliefs, practice and expertise, parental expectations, school organization, community and culture, high-stakes examinations, curriculum policies, and so forth (see Chaps. 8, 9, 10, and 11). Therefore, transforming how and what classroom teachers actually teach is a highly sophisticated endeavour, which cannot be achieved by just tweaking one or two factors in isolation (see Chap. 8). This can explain the lack of impact of TSLN reform initiatives on classroom practice as well.

In our view, classroom practice is nested in the socio-cultural, institutional, and instructional contexts of schooling and is, in a variety of ways, influenced by the policy, programmatic and classroom curricula. Three types of challenges pertaining to changing classroom practices can be identified based on the above discussion.

The first type of challenge concerns the need to develop curriculum policies and initiatives that are not only animated by reform visions but are grounded in a more realistic and complex understanding of schooling in relation to society and culture in the present and future. Apart from addressing questions like "What social and economic challenges are the nation facing?" and "What sorts of knowledge and competencies would Singaporeans need to have or develop?", policymakers need to address *specific* issues or problems surrounding the institutions and practices of schooling in the country. Some of these issues are, for example, what are the public understandings of, and expectations for, schooling as a public institution? What are the socio-demographic, community, cultural and linguistic, and institutional factors contributing to students' academic achievement? What are the specific issues and challenges facing principals and classroom teachers within specific schools and classrooms? What constitutes the experience of schooling for the vast majority of Singaporean students? What features characterize Singaporean students at different levels, their views of the future, their aspirations? What account should we take of gender, ethnicity, and social class as we view curriculum at the three levels? These issues cannot be addressed only through surveys and/or focus group discussions, which are useful for ascertaining the strengths and concerns of the school system as a whole. They call for sophisticated empirical studies like CRPP's Core Project consisting of multilevel analyses of Singaporean schooling, pedagogy, youth and educational outcomes (Luke et al. 2005), and a willingness to listen to and act upon the data. More sophisticated research projects of this kind are needed if policymakers and reformers are to gain a more realistic, sophisticated, and contextual understanding of the work and function of Singapore schooling at the present stage of its development. Such an understanding is crucial for developing curriculum policies and initiatives that would have a sustained and meaningful impact on classroom practice (Westbury 2002).

The second type of challenge has to deal with the complex endeavour of translating a curriculum initiative into programmes, school subjects, or operational frameworks that are responsive to the present realities. This involves sophisticated "curriculum making" tasks that entail the reconceptualising, reorganising, reframing, and transforming of curriculum content in view of both the aims or expectations of the initiative and teaching and learning activities in classrooms (Deng 2009, 2010). These tasks take on greater significance in the light of the current emerging new curriculum landscape in Singapore. The creation of C2015, according to Hogan (2009), signals a transition that the Singapore curriculum needs to undertake – a transition from the transmission of academic knowledge and skills to the development of twenty-first century competencies. How might the C2015 learning outcomes be translated into various school subjects in the school curriculum? How might school subjects be formulated or reformulated in a way that supports the cultivation of twenty-first century competencies? To what extent should strong subject boundaries be maintained? How might the content of a school subject be (re) organized, framed, and transformed in view of C2015 learning outcomes, their relevance for future workplace environments, and prevalent classroom practice? Simple procedural solutions – which ignore complex conceptual issues of content reorganization, framing and transformation for the development of twenty-first century competencies – will not work. The success of the above transition, Hogan (2009) argues, depends on how well Singaporean policymakers and curriculum developers are able to "re-conceptualize the relationship between knowledge, teaching and learning–indeed, school subjects" in ways that support the cultivation of 21st competencies.

The third type of challenge has to do with the complexity of changing classroom practice or the enacted curriculum. There is a need for reform initiatives centred on classrooms that challenge the "pervasive folk culture of teaching and learning" and enhance "transparency and visibility" of teaching and learning in classrooms (Chap. 8). These reform initiatives need to acknowledge, on the one hand, the key role of classroom teachers as curricular and pedagogical change agents (see Fullan 1993) and, on the other hand, the need for well-developed curriculum materials, frameworks or models in guiding, supporting, and enabling curricular change at the classroom level (see Ball and Cohen 1996; Davis and Krajcik 2005). Three conditions are critical. First, there needs to be coherence among new reform visions, intended outcomes, curriculum frameworks and materials, assessments and examinations, and teacher professional development. The greater the degree of misalignment, the greater the chance of different and divergent interpretations of curricular change, and thus outcomes. The current high-stakes examinations (like PSLE, the "O" and "A" levels) must be reformed and teacher professional autonomy enhanced (cf. Chap. 2). Second, curriculum frameworks and materials need to be developed in a way that supports teachers' classroom enactment in view of reform visions (Cohen and Hill 2001). Curriculum frameworks and materials can be effective agents that enable classroom teachers to plan for significant change in a particular classroom context, if they were designed to "place teachers in the centre of curriculum construction and make teachers' learning central to efforts to improve instruction" (Ball and Cohen 1996, p. 7). Third, teachers need to have substantial opportunities for professional learning that are grounded in practice and in specific curricular changes (Cohen and Hill 2001; Fang and et al. 2009). The newly established Academy of Singapore Teachers could be a stimulus for the further professionalization of the teaching force through developing professional learning communities (PLCs) in schools and the promotion of Lesson Study as an important platform for teacher learning and development. More schools in Singapore are currently embarking on Lesson Study and providing opportunities for their teachers to collaborate and re-examine curriculum and classroom practices (Lim et al. 2011).

We have sought to provide a multi-faceted and critical analysis of the Singapore curriculum within the current context of curriculum reform as a response to globalization. The issues and challenges we have identified are, of course, not unique to Singapore only; we believe they are generally useful for other countries when embarking on curriculum reform. What makes the context unique is that the Singapore system is already perceived as a successful system as shown in its performance in TIMSS and PISA (OECD 2010; also Chap. 12). The various chapters of the book, we hope, will provide readers with a well-informed interpretive view of the Singapore curriculum. The conceptual framework – the three domains of curriculum together with the themes of convergence and divergence – (we believe) would be informative and useful for researchers and scholars across the globe to analyse complex issues and problems in their own countries of curriculum reform in relation to globalization. We hope as well that Singapore's achievements and challenges will be of interest to policy makers, researchers, and practitioners in other systems.

References

Anderson-Levitt, K. M. (2008). Globalization and curriculum. In F. M. Connelly, M. F. He, & J. Phillion (Eds.), *The Sage handbook of curriculum and instruction* (pp. 349–368). Thousand Oaks: Sage.

Ball, D., & Cohen, D. K. (1996). Reform by the book: What is – Or might be – The role of curriculum materials in teacher learning and instructional reform? *Educational Researcher, 25*(6–8), 14.

Buchberger, F. (2000). *Searching for a missing link – Towards a science of/for the teaching profession*. Paper presented at the annual meeting of American Educational Research Association, New Orleans.

Cohen, D. K., & Ball, B. L. (1990). Policy and practice: A commentary. *Educational Evaluation and Policy Analysis, 12*, 331–338.

Cohen, D. K., & Hill, H. C. (2001). *Learning policy: When state education reform works*. New Haven: Yale University Press.

Davis, E. A., & Krajcik, J. S. (2005). Designing educative curriculum materials to promote teacher learning. *Educational Researcher, 34*(3), 3–14.

Dede, C. (2010a). Technological supports for acquiring 21st century skills. In E. Baker, B. McGaw, & P. Peterson (Eds.), *International encyclopaedia of education* (3rd edn.). Oxford: Elsevier. Available online at: http://learningcenter.nsta.org/products/symposia_seminars/iste/files/Technological_Support_for_21stCentury_Encyclo_dede.pdf. Accessed 30 July 2012.

Dede, C. (2010b). Comparing frameworks for 21st century skills. In J. Bellanca & R. Brandt (Eds.), *21st century skills* (pp. 51–76). Bloomington: Solution Tree Press.

Deng, Z. (2001). The centrality of subject matter in teaching thinking: John Dewey's idea of psychologising the subject matter revisited. *Educational Research Journal, 16*(2), 193–212.

Deng, Z. (2009). The formation of a school subject and the nature of curriculum content: An analysis of liberal studies in Hong Kong. *Journal of Curriculum Studies, 41*(5), 585–604.

Deng, Z. (2010). Curriculum policies and syllabus translation in the era of educational initiatives: Rethinking and re-conceptualizing curriculum content. *Journal of Textbook Research, 3*(2), 93–113.

Deng, Z. (2011). Confucianism, modernization and Chinese pedagogy: An introduction. *Journal of Curriculum Studies, 43*(5), 561–568.

Fang, Y. P., Lee, K. E. C., & Haron, S. T. (2009). Lesson study in mathematics: Three cases from Singapore. In K. Y. Wong, P. Y. Lee, B. Kaur, P. Y. Foong, & S. F. Ng (Eds.), *Mathematics education – The Singapore journey* (pp. 104–129). Singapore: World Scientific.

Fullan, M. G. (1993). Why teachers must become change agents. *Educational Leadership, 50*(6), 12–17.

Fullan, M. G. (2008). Curriculum implementation and sustainability. In F. M. Connelly, M. F. He, & J. Phillion (Eds.), *The Sage handbook of curriculum and instruction* (pp. 113–122). Thousand Oaks: Sage.

Gopinathan, S. (2007). Globalization, the Singapore developmental state & education policy: A thesis revisited. *Globalization, Societies & Education, 5*(1), 53–70.

Gopinathan, S., & Deng, Z. (2006). Fostering school-based curriculum development in the context of new educational initiatives in Singapore. *Planning and Changing: An Educational Leadership and Policy Journal, 37*(1&2), 93–110.

Hogan, D. (2009). *Toward a 21st century pedagogy for Singapore.* A presentation to the Principals' Curriculum Forum on Assessment-Pedagogy Nexus, Ministry of Education, Singapore.

Hogan, D. (2011). *Culture and pedagogy in Singapore: An institutionalist account of the fate of the teach less, learn more policy initiative.* Paper presented at the 4th Redesigning Pedagogy: Transforming Teaching, Inspiring Learning International Conference, National Institute of Education, Nanyang Technological University, Singapore.

Leong, K.-L., Sim, J. B.-Y., & Chua, S.-H. (2011). School-based curriculum development in Singapore: Bottom-up perspective of a top-down policy. *Curriculum Perspectives, 31*(1), 51–61.

Lim, C., Lee, K. E. C., Saito, E., & Thalha-Haron, S. (2011). Taking stock of lesson study as a platform for teacher development in Singapore. *Asia-Pacific Journal of Teacher Education, 39*(4), 353–365.

Luke, A., Freebody, P., Lau, S., & Gopinathan, S. (2005). Towards research-based innovation and reform: Singapore schooling in transition. *Asia Pacific Journal of Education, 25*(1), 5–28.

Meyer, J. W. (2006). World models, national curricula, and the centrality of the individual. In A. Benavot & C. Braslavsky (Eds.), *School knowledge in comparative and historical perspective: Changing curricula in primary and secondary education* (CERC studies in comparative education, Vol. 19, pp. 259–271). Hong Kong: University of Hong Kong, Comparative Education Research Centre.

Ministry of Education. (1998). *Perspective: The desired outcomes of education.* Retrieved 29 June 2011, from http://www1.moe.edu.sg/contact/vol14/web/pers.htm

Ministry of Education. (2007). *The PETALS™ Primer.* Singapore: Author and Association for Supervision and Curriculum Development (Singapore).

Ministry of Education. (2010). *Building a national education system for the 21st century: The Singapore experience.* http://www.edu.gov.on.ca/bb4e/Singapore_CaseStudy2010.pdf. Accessed 29 June 2011.

OECD. (2010). *Singapore: Rapid improvement followed by strong performance in strong performers and successful reformers in education: Lessons from PISA for the United States.* Retrieved 30 July 2012, from http://www.oecd.org/dataoecd/34/41/46581101.pdf

Ohmae, K. (1995). *The end of the nation state.* London: HarperCollins.

Phillips, D. (2005). Policy borrowing in education: Frameworks for analysis. In J. Zajda (Ed.), *International handbook on globalization, education and policy research, part 1* (pp. 23–34). Dordrecht: Springer.

Rosenmund, M. (2006). The current discourse on curriculum change: A comparative analysis of national reports on education. In A. Benavot & C. Braslavsky (Eds.), *School knowledge in comparative and historical perspective: Changing curricula in primary and secondary education* (CERC studies in comparative education, Vol. 19, pp. 173–194). Hong Kong: University of Hong Kong, Comparative Education Research Centre.

Satio, H. (2010). Actor-network theory of cosmopolitan education. *Journal of Curriculum Studies, 42*(3), 333–351.

Simola, H. (1998). Constructing a school-free pedagogy: Decontextualization of Finnish state educational discourse. *Journal of Curriculum Studies, 30*(3), 339–356.

Tyack, D., & Cuban, L. (1995). *Tinkering toward utopia: Reflections on a century of public school reform.* Cambridge: Harvard University Press.

Voogt, J., & Roblin, N. P. (2012). A comparative analysis of international frameworks for 21st century competences: Implications for national curriculum policies. *Journal of Curriculum Studies, 44*(3), 299–321.

Westbury, I. (1994). Deliberation and the improvement of schooling. In J. T. Dillon (Ed.), *Deliberation in education and society* (pp. 35–65). Norwood: Ablex.

Westbury, I. (2002). "The educational situation as concerns the elementary school": Implication for our time. *Journal of Curriculum and Supervision, 17*(2), 120–129.

Westbury, I. (2005). Reconsidering Schwab's "Practicals": A response to Peter Hlebowitsh's "generational ideas in curriculum: A historical triangulation". *Curriculum Inquiry, 35*(1), 89–101.

Westbury, I. (2008). The making of formal curricula: Why do states make curricula, and how? In F. M. Connelly, M. F. He, & J. Phillion (Eds.), *The Sage handbook of curriculum and instruction* (pp. 45–65). Thousand Oaks: Sage.

Yates, L., & Collins, C. (2010). The absence of knowledge in Australian curriculum reforms. *European Journal of Education, 45*(1), 89–102.

Yates, L., & Young, M. (2010). Globalisation, knowledge and the curriculum. *European Journal of Education, 45*(1), 4–10.

Index

CPSIA information can be obtained at www.ICGtesting.com
Printed in the USA
LVOW01*1409180315

431069LV00007B/11/P